NEW TESTAMENT LETTERS FOR LIVING

NEW TESTAMENT LETTERS FOR LIVING

Daily Prayers, Wisdom, and Guidance

Mark Lanier

1845 BOOKS

Waco, Texas 76798

Book Design by Baylor University Press

Cover Design by *the*BookDesigners
Cover image: Shutterstock/ArtMari

Book Typeset by Scribe Inc.

Hardcover ISBN: 978-1-4813-2249-2
Paperback ISBN: 978-1-4813-2250-8

The Library of Congress has cataloged this book under ISBN 978-1-4813-2249-2.

Library of Congress Control Number: 2024025217

ACKNOWLEDGMENTS

Special thanks and a shout-out to those who dot the pages of this book, some by name, others anonymously, including the following:

My family—Mom, Dad, Becky, our children and their spouses (Will and Nora, Gracie and JT, Rachel and Lee, Rebecca and Daniel, Sarah and Jack), our grandchildren (Chloe, Mia, Ebba, Violet, John Henry, Francis, Lydia, Abigail, Caleb, and Zoe), and my sisters and brothers-in-law (Kathryn and Randy, Hollie and Kevin).

My friends, influences, and inspirations—Adam Wright, Alister McGrath, Dr. Bernie Morrey, Bob Conrad, Carl Cope, Carlus Gupton, Charles Mickey, Chip Herd, Cynthia Randall, Damon Shook, David Egilman, David Fleming, Dinah Gleason, Don Finto, Don Hunt, Drew Davis, Eddie Bell, Ernest Cannon, Fred Gray, Coach Gerald Myers, Dr. Harvey Floyd, Jan Manning, Jarrett Stephens, JD Hancock, Jenine Jordan, Joe Barnett, John King, John Michael Talbot, Joseph Skibell, Ken Dye, Kevin Parker, Larry Burgess, Larry Lipton, Lisa Blue Baron, Lorraine Hibbert, Louis Miori, Mary Adams, Melody Green, Mike Card, Mike Moriarity, Patrick Mahomes, Pete Weinberger, Rena Noack, Rhonda Lowry, Rick Reynolds, Skip McBride, Steve Naeher, Steve Robinson, Tim Wilson, Timm Reid, and Udo Middleman.

Thanks also to those who proofread for style and content (I own the typos and poor grammar!), especially Harvey Brown, Skip McBride, Leonard Allen, and Todd Still. A belated thanks to Melissa Rendsburg.

A special shout-out to Baylor University and its incredible staff (Cade Jarrell, David Aycock, David Nelson, Ely Encarnación, Jenny Hunt, and Michelle McCaig) for enabling and encouraging the five teaching devotional books that compose this series.

A final thanks to my friends and others responsible for the English Standard Version, which I have used in this and the other books in this series. Where the translation differs from the ESV, I have used my own translation.

INTRODUCTION

This book brings to completion a five-volume dream to produce on various sections of the Bible a collection of daily readings aimed at several objectives. I have sought to provide a faithful scholastic approach to Scripture that teaches, inspires, gives ideas for devotional living, and gives glory to God. Each day targets the parallel goals of producing a teaching moment as well as a devotional one.

The books that comprise the New Testament Epistles are subject to millennia of study by some of humanity's brightest minds. I have tried to glean from many of those sources and, at times, offer competing ideas of what a passage may mean or what its import might be. Most often, however, I have limited my expositions to those ideas that, for better or worse, make the most sense to me. As readers of various disciplines approach these pages, I ask for mercy, understanding, and perhaps even an open mind to the way I read the passages. Certainly some of my readings are not traditional for various other Christians reading in good faith.

I have ordered these studies in what I think is one possible order in which the Epistles were written. There is certainly room for debate—for example, I might transpose my placement of Jude and Peter.

A last note—the book of Hebrews seems to be more an ancient sermon than an ancient letter, but I have included it anyway as, if nothing more, a letter containing a sermon! The letters to the seven churches in Revelation are *not* included in this book, since they are part of a larger corpus of material.

May God be blessed, Christ be exalted, and the Holy Spirit given room to move in these pages, as I thank him for the chance to put ink to paper.

Mark Lanier
December 2024

JANUARY 1

James, a servant of God and of the Lord Jesus Christ, to the twelve tribes in the Dispersion: Greetings. (James 1:1)

I have two siblings, my sisters Kathryn and Hollie. Both love the Lord, and both love me. I've known Kathryn, the eldest, all my life. I've known the youngest, Hollie, all her life. They know me for who I am, and I have no shot at convincing them that I am anyone other than their brother.

This personal truth always stuns me as I read these opening words of James. Penned by James, the brother of Jesus, his claim to be the "servant of God and of the Lord Jesus Christ" should not be glossed over. A "servant of God" was a strong Jewish phrase found repeatedly in the Old Testament, but James uses it with a twist; the phrase ordinarily used the "name" of God, not God's title. For example, Moses is called the "servant of the LORD," with the capital letters in "LORD" indicating God's name, not the general word for "Lord" (Dt. 34:5).

James boldly states that he is the servant of God and adds the title "Lord" to Jesus the Messiah. Thus, he only uses Lord—God's ordinary name—for Jesus. ("Messiah" is the equivalent title in Hebrew of the Greek title "Christ.") James' confident claim of Jesus as Lord and Messiah is significant because James didn't always believe in Jesus' claims. Until the resurrection, James joined his brothers in ridiculing Jesus. This makes James' post-resurrection declaration stand out. To be God's servant was pious, noble, and righteous. But then to add that same status to the Lord Jesus Messiah in a letter, likely written around a decade after the resurrection, merits my personal consideration.

Who is Jesus to me? Is he an invented character who oddly appears on a historical scene with truly world-changing impact so soon after his death? That seems hard to believe. Certainly, his brother should know better! Is Jesus a good moral teacher who happened to die prematurely, tricking his brother into believing that he was worthy of the devotion properly given only to the Lord? Is Jesus a fraudster who gave up a good life for three years of itinerant ministry, followed by a Roman crucifixion because he wouldn't accede to the requests of the power structure?

I believe Jesus is the Lord Jesus Messiah. That means that I have the high calling and blessed opportunity to serve him today and every day.

Lord Jesus, Messiah and Savior, I live to be your devoted servant. Amen.

JANUARY 2

Count it all joy, my brothers, when you meet trials of various kinds, for you know that the testing of your faith produces steadfastness. And let steadfastness have its full effect, that you may be perfect and complete, lacking in nothing. (James 1:2–4)

Patience may be a virtue, but for much of my life, impatience has been my calling card. I don't like waiting. If I can't have something right now, then I want it yesterday! This isn't new to me. When I was a young teenager, my little sister (eight years my junior) would get on my nerves incessantly. I was thinking about my impatience with her when I came across this verse in James. It occurred to me that if I wanted to grow in patience (or "steadfastness," as it's translated in this verse), then I "just" needed to walk through various trials. But trials and tribulations don't sound like fun ways to find patience, so I don't readily seek them out!

Importantly, however, God doesn't turn a blind eye toward his children and their needs. God knew my need for patience, and he was set to develop it. So as I grew up physically, he saw to my spiritual growth, which, at times, has been processed by trials of all sorts.

Trials are battlegrounds. I have been tried on the fronts of struggling with sin and being stressed with relationships, frazzled over economics, distraught over deaths of loved ones, shaken with health crises, bewildered over life purpose, persecuted by cynics seeking to wreck my faith—the list goes on and on. Yet none of these struggles were simply "events." Each was used by God in his work in my life.

God has brought me through trials, giving me strength and solace as he set my course before me. Most of my trials were not overnight affairs. Unlike a TV drama, my struggles never resolved in an hour. But each moment spent involved in the struggle was a moment where God was working to his good ends. He produced in me "steadfastness" so I would grow up before him, better fitted to do that which he called me to do.

My concern is that I am still in need of more patience. I guess I better buckle my seat belt! But I do so knowing he will work in whatever comes my way.

Lord, grow me to serve you better. May my faith reflect your goodness. In Jesus' name, amen.

JANUARY 3

If any of you lacks wisdom, let him ask God, who gives generously to all without reproach, and it will be given him. But let him ask in faith, with no doubting, for the one who doubts is like a wave of the sea that is driven and tossed by the wind. (James 1:5–6)

My buddy Adam Wright is a busy soul. He is the president of a university, and the demands on his time are huge. He's also a family man with a wife and children. A man of faith, he spends daily time in the Scriptures and looks to live a life that exemplifies his love for the Lord. Recently I picked him up at the airport, and we headed to lunch. We were talking about life's challenges. Our conversation turned to the business of life.

Adam asked me how I decide what I do each day, knowing there are twenty-four hours of available options. After I mumbled through a reply, I asked the same question of him. Adam told me, "I basically pray James 1:5 every morning." Adam asks God for wisdom in how to use his day.

Adam's answer registered deep in my heart as brilliant on many levels. First, consider that we are often given more opportunities than we have the time or resources to take advantage of. Frequently in my job, I will be asked to take a deposition or give a speech on the same day in cities that are on opposite sides of the country. I must choose. Another example might be when people seek your financial support for worthy projects, and yet you are already completely committed to other worthy projects. You must choose. How are those choices made? Adam asks God for wisdom.

A second layer of brilliance underlies the biblical idea of wisdom. In the world's language, wisdom might be human insight and understanding. But godly wisdom is something more. The biblical idea of godly wisdom means to "see the world the way God sees it." That includes insight and understanding but elevates them to God's level. With God's wisdom, I see the world through his eyes. I see my options each day with a vision of what God wants me to accomplish, what God is leading me to do, how God wants me to serve him best.

Don't get me wrong, I think God often gives us choices with the promise to bless us however we choose. But I also know I won't make the best choices each day without seeing the world as he does!

Lord, please give me wisdom today. Let me choose wisely. In your name, amen.

JANUARY 4

Do not be deceived, my beloved brothers. Every good gift and every perfect gift is from above, coming down from the Father of lights, with whom there is no variation or shadow due to change. (James 1:16–17)

Do you know the platitude about an attitude of gratitude? If you'll allow me some latitude, I'll use my aptitude to . . . well, enough with those rhymes. The magnitude of the rhymes overwhelms me (last one, I promise!). But regardless of the words, the concept is front and center in today's verses. These verses challenge our gratitude response to the good things in life.

James is stating a simple yet profound truth. God is the source of all the good gifts in my life—from the food I eat to the job I enjoy, from the health I have to the work I can do, and from my beloved family to my dear friends. All these gifts are from the Lord above.

This truth challenges me to see whether I acknowledge God as the recipient of the blessings in my life and express genuine gratitude. Not just a thank-you when I am about to eat or even as I write this devotional. Do I thank him in the midst of the nitty-gritty of daily life? As the wheel of time turns, do I see each breath as a gift from God? Do I understand that every encounter is from his guiding hand?

I want to do better. These verses should change me on many levels. They should stir up constant expressions of "Thank you, God" for life's blessings. I have a friend whose life is very comfortable and who often says to me, "How did we get so lucky?" I don't want to see the good parts of life as luck. They are gifts from my Father God. Heaven forbid I say, "How lucky!" I need to say simply, "Thank you, God!"

Another level of challenge is that this passage forces me to see God's hand in—and to be grateful for—life's difficulties. James has already said several verses earlier that trials in life will grow you in faith, making you more patient and "perfect" or "mature" (the root meaning of the Greek word *teleios*—τέλειος). That means even the things in life that are trying and difficult can be things that make me better for living. In these things, too, I need an attitude of gratitude!

Today I resolve to be different. I am going to thank God for each and every gift.

Lord, thank you for this time and perspective. I give you glory. In your name, amen.

JANUARY 5

Know this, my beloved brothers: let every person be quick to hear, slow to speak, slow to anger; for the anger of man does not produce the righteousness of God. . . . If anyone thinks he is religious and does not bridle his tongue but deceives his heart, this person's religion is worthless. (James 1:19–20, 26)

A certain YouTube video series always makes me chuckle. A fellow who is a world-class weight lifter dresses in coveralls that disguise his cut build and make him look disheveled, ordinary in build, and a bit dorky. The fellow finds a personal trainer and tells the trainer, "I want to be a competitive weight lifter." He then asks to hire the trainer, adding, "I have signed up for a big competition—in two weeks." The trainers all act polite as they explain, "It takes years of lifting to be a competitive lifter." The disguised champion then says, "I am a fast learner!" After several lifting efforts that barely make it through a small weight, the fellow then proclaims himself ready for the competition. Over the trainer's discouragement, the fellow puts massive weights on the bar and then, to the trainer's utter dismay, lifts it like it was nothing.

The reality is that the fellow had spent hours a day for years on end lifting weights and developing into a powerlifter. It cannot happen overnight. I take solace from that as I look at today's passage: "Be quick to listen, slow to speak." That isn't an easy one! Nor, for many, is the added injunction to be slow to anger.

Like weight lifting, today's passage from James isn't a simple "learn it, do it, and move on to another verse." The problem with today's passage isn't the learning; it is the doing. Yet the passage starts with the command "Know this . . ." The command to "know" (*oida*—οἶδα) implies more than simply having cognitive knowledge; it means being intimately acquainted and familiar with the information. To return to our weight lifting story, it means one needs to not just know the principles but gain knowledge of them through repeated practice, gradually getting better and better.

This brings me to today. I want to grow and live in the truth of James' instruction. I want to be able to bridle my tongue. To accomplish this, however, I will need God's help and daily practice. I might not be ready for a competition, but I can start training on this immediately!

Lord, give me strength to control my tongue today. Let my words bring you glory. In Jesus, amen.

JANUARY 6

My brothers, show no partiality as you hold the faith in our Lord Jesus Christ, the Lord of glory. For if a man wearing a gold ring and fine clothing comes into your assembly, and a poor man in shabby clothing also comes in, and if you pay attention to the one who wears the fine clothing and say, "You sit here in a good place," while you say to the poor man, "You stand over there," or, "Sit down at my feet," have you not then made distinctions among yourselves and become judges with evil thoughts? (James 2:1–4)

In 1968, the *Journal of Social Psychology* published a study that asked whether people subconsciously treated people differently based on perceived wealth. In the study, people were given a scenario of being behind a car at a red light. The light turns green. The leading car doesn't move. The question asked was, "Would you honk at the car?" People consistently answered, "Yes." A follow-up question was asked: "Would it make a difference if it was a nice new car or a worn-out old car?" People overwhelmingly said, "No!"

Then the field experiment began with a nice car and a worn-out car at an intersection. The driver was the same in both cars. The same intersection was used. Huddled unseen in the back seat was a student with a clipboard and a stopwatch, keeping time and records on whether the car behind honked as the light turned green but the driver stayed still. The results were that 70 percent sounded their horns, but while 84 percent honked at the old, worn-out car, less than 50 percent honked at the nice new car. Furthermore, the honking at the old car happened much more rapidly. In other words, despite our best intentions, we have a tendency at a subconscious, unrecognized level to treat others differently based on perceived status.

James tells us this is wrong. We are not to treat those less fortunate or less economically successful differently than those who seem more well-off. God teaches us to see value in everyone. Some have a better lot in life; some make more money; some are smarter, faster, stronger, or more attractive. But everyone has the full love of God, and everyone should be treated with that same love.

I may say, "But I don't treat people differently!" Yet if the study is right, my tendency to do so is deeper than my conscious mind. I am going to make a real effort to learn and do better.

Dear God, please give me your love and heart for all. In Jesus, amen.

JANUARY 7

If you really fulfill the royal law according to the Scripture, "You shall love your neighbor as yourself," you are doing well. But if you show partiality, you are committing sin and are convicted by the law as transgressors. For whoever keeps the whole law but fails in one point has become guilty of all of it. . . . For judgment is without mercy to one who has shown no mercy. Mercy triumphs over judgment. (James 2:8–10, 13)

Most post offices in America maintain a list of the FBI's ten most wanted criminals hanging on the wall somewhere. Somebody has actually prioritized those fugitives. It has always struck me as odd. After all, what is the difference between number four and number five? I am certain you wouldn't want either one to babysit your child! But people tend to categorize or prioritize one thing above another.

We do the same with sin, and this sets up the concerns James expresses in today's verses. James explains that one really can't categorize one sin as worse than another, in the sense that we are all sinners in need of God's grace. We might say that murder is a first-class sin, while greed is a much lesser one, but that doesn't make greed OK. Adultery is a huge sin compared to gluttony, but both are sins that bring judgment and need God's grace.

James points out the fine line between the commands to love one's neighbor as oneself (a command found in Lev. 19:18 and described by Jesus in Mk. 12:30–31 as core to the entire law) and to be impartial between a rich person and a poor person. A violation of both violates the law. While we might see one law as more important than the other, neither violation is excusable.

This is key to understanding God's commandments. In a sense, we can fairly categorize them. After all, Jesus indicated that loving one's neighbor as oneself joined loving God with all one's heart as the "greatest" of the commandments. But they aren't the greatest because other commandments are lesser. They are the greatest because they subsume the other commandments.

In the end, all the purity of God is found in his commandments. We are to pursue his purity. Yet in that pursuit, we all fall short. We all need his mercy. But getting his mercy doesn't stop us from pursuing his holiness. It should drive us there!

Lord, give me mercy, and may I give mercy to others in your name! Amen.

JANUARY 8

What good is it, my brothers, if someone says he has faith but does not have works? Can that faith save him? If a brother or sister is poorly clothed and lacking in daily food, and one of you says to them, "Go in peace, be warmed and filled," without giving them the things needed for the body, what good is that? So also faith by itself, if it does not have works, is dead. (James 2:14–17)

Since the days of Martin Luther, the church has struggled with the issue of faith versus works. The focus has narrowed in responding to the question, "What brings you into a right relationship with God?" Is it something you do? Or is it putting your faith and trust in God and the forgiveness found in the cross of Christ? Luther stood for the Reformation principle that one is justified by faith alone.

Paul is often cited in support of Luther. For example, Paul said, "For by grace you have been saved through faith. And this is not your own doing; it is the gift of God, not a result of works, so that no one may boast" (Eph. 2:8–9). For many, this seems a direct rejection of the idea James sets forth in today's passage.

Yet these passages aren't in conflict. Part of the problem lies in the translation of the verb "save" (*sozo*—σῴζω in the Greek). The verb has a wide range of meanings, and therefore its meaning differs in different passages. Context is critically important to understanding the verb.

Consider the verbs in these passages: When the woman with a years-long illness touched Jesus' cloak, she thought to herself, "If only I touch his cloak, I will be *made well* [*sozo*]" (Mt. 9:21). Or when Jairus, the synagogue leader, sought Jesus' help with his dying daughter, we read of him imploring Jesus, "Come and lay your hands on her, so that she may be *made well* [*sozo*] and live" (Mk. 5:23).

The idea conveyed in the Greek word is preserving or rescuing someone from danger. It may mean an eternal salvation, as in rescuing one from the dangers of future judgment from sin. Or it may mean rescuing someone from a present danger, including sickness and disease—like how James uses it in 5:15, where he says that the prayer of faith will *save* (*sozo*) the sick. James isn't speaking into the Reformation debate in today's passage. James speaks to how to aid (save) a neighbor in need. Faith by itself does nothing. We need to put our faith into action! We rescue others with our deeds!

Lord, put me to work today. Let me live your compassion in your name! Amen.

JANUARY 9

Do you want to be shown, you foolish person, that faith apart from works is useless? Was not Abraham our father justified by works when he offered up his son Isaac on the altar? You see that faith was active along with his works, and faith was completed by his works; and the Scripture was fulfilled that says, "Abraham believed God, and it was counted to him as righteousness"—and he was called a friend of God. You see that a person is justified by works and not by faith alone. And in the same way was not also Rahab the prostitute justified by works when she received the messengers and sent them out by another way? For as the body apart from the spirit is dead, so also faith apart from works is dead. (James 2:20–26)

Martin Luther had doubts about whether James should be part of the Bible based on yesterday's and today's verses. To Luther, James seemed to directly contradict Paul. My concerns over these verses deviate from Luther's, in part, because Luther seemed to think the verses spoke of eternal justification, while I think the verses tend in a broader direction.

James says Abraham was "justified by works." The idea of "justification" includes being declared just before God in an absolute salvation sense. But the words also convey the simple Jewish idea of piety or righteous living. The lawyer Paul normally uses "justified" (Greek *dikaioo*—δικαιόω) in its more legal sense of "declared not guilty," or legally vindicated. But James wasn't a lawyer. He uses the term here in its Old Testament sense, even citing the Old Testament in his context. We see James' meaning in passages like Genesis 38:26, where Judah uses the same word in the Greek version of the Old Testament when he notes that Tamar is "more righteous [*dikaioo*] than [he]" in her actions.

Abraham had faith, but not one devoid of works. When Abraham "believed God, and it was counted to him as righteousness," the Old Testament repeatedly shows that Abraham's faith resulted in action. So a faith that is a righteous faith, whether for eternal salvation or righteousness on earth, is not the kind of faith that is a simple acknowledgment of one fact or another about God or Jesus. Even demons have that kind of faith. The faith of righteousness is one that motivates to action.

I can best show you my confidence in God by how I live, not by what I say. We don't just tell people we have faith; we must show them our faith. This kind of faith gives us full righteousness, now and eternally.

Lord, may my faith be genuine, evident in all I do for you. In your name, amen.

JANUARY 10

If we put bits into the mouths of horses so that they obey us, we guide their whole bodies as well. Look at the ships also: though they are so large and are driven by strong winds, they are guided by a very small rudder wherever the will of the pilot directs. So also the tongue is a small member, yet it boasts of great things. How great a forest is set ablaze by such a small fire! . . . For every kind of beast and bird, of reptile and sea creature, can be tamed and has been tamed by mankind, but no human being can tame the tongue. It is a restless evil, full of deadly poison. With it we bless our Lord and Father, and with it we curse people who are made in the likeness of God . . . My brothers, these things ought not to be so. (James 3:3–10)

I make a living with words. A wordsmith, I sculpt phrases and choose words with care to nuance meaning, motivate, educate, and report. My job depends on saying the right thing, the right way, at the right time. Yet far too often, I have found myself with my mouth open, with words coming out, all while my brain shouts, "*Nooooooooo!!!!*" These might be words said in haste to my children or wife, words spoken to coworkers or friends, or even those exchanged with complete strangers. (And yes, I am including what I type in texts, emails, and social media posts.)

Yet I can also affirm that my words have been used to praise God, edify his church, teach about and point others to him, and do other good things. How can this be?

We humans too often get caught up in the moment. We react rather than act deliberately. We speak without carefully thinking. We get things a bit out of order, akin to "*Ready, fire, aim*!" rather than "Ready, aim, fire!"

What is the solution? First, we must acknowledge the problem! James points it out for a reason. We need to mentally confess to God, "I am out of control!" Then we need to seek God's help. It will never do for any of us to say, "That's just the way I am!" No! That's the way we are without God!

With God, we can apologize when our tongue gets the worst of us. We can seek to rectify the damage we've incurred, and we can work to build up what we have torn apart. But we also need to think of practical ways God can change us. We must learn patience. We must grow in carefulness and compassion. Then we can see God taking over our tongues and guarding our words.

Lord, I confess my sinful words. From gossip to anger, I have used my words wrongly. Grow me. Mature me. Help me. I pray in Jesus' name, amen.

JANUARY 11

Who is wise and understanding among you? By his good conduct let him show his works in the meekness of wisdom. But if you have bitter jealousy and selfish ambition in your hearts, do not boast and be false to the truth. This is not the wisdom that comes down from above, but is earthly, unspiritual, demonic. For where jealousy and selfish ambition exist, there will be disorder and every vile practice. But the wisdom from above is first pure, then peaceable, gentle, open to reason, full of mercy and good fruits, impartial and sincere. And a harvest of righteousness is sown in peace by those who make peace. (James 3:13–18)

What kindergarten class didn't have show-and-tell? One day, our daughter Rebecca took her little sister Sarah for show-and-tell. Rebecca had been telling everyone she had a little sister, but one day, she got to show them.

We have show-and-tell every day, whether we realize it or not. We can tell people about what is important to us. We can tell others about our great wisdom and understanding. But how we live conveys a deeper truth. Our lives show whether our claims to wisdom ring true.

In today's passage, James lays this truth before his readers in meticulous ways. If people claim to be wise and understanding, then their actions should show it. That begins with "meekness of wisdom"—in other words, humility. In contrast, any wisdom that is accompanied by jealousy, ambition, or boasting is demonic, not godly. Godly wisdom isn't simply spoken; it is lived.

One finds the "show" part of godly wisdom in a life lived purely, experiencing the peace of God in day-to-day matters. Those with godly wisdom are at once gentle, merciful, and sincere. They are open to reason and strive to treat others impartially. This grows into a tree of righteousness in one's life.

I want to be wise before God. I want to grow in his wisdom and understanding. I want this to be something beyond "telling"; I want it to be shown in my life. I can progress in growing in this wisdom through my behavior. More mercy, less judgment; more peace, less strife; more caring, less jealousy; more sincerity, less fakery. As I grow in these ways, I will cultivate the righteous tree that accompanies godly wisdom.

Lord, grow your wisdom in me. Rid me of jealousy, spite, and selfishness. Create in me a heart of humility and peace as I spread your love in Jesus. Amen.

JANUARY 12

What causes quarrels and what causes fights among you? Is it not this, that your passions are at war within you? You desire and do not have, so you murder. You covet and cannot obtain, so you fight and quarrel. You do not have, because you do not ask. You ask and do not receive, because you ask wrongly, to spend it on your passions. (James 4:1–3)

As a new lawyer practicing in a Houston, Texas, courthouse, I would get into the elevator at the ground floor and announce my destination floor to the elevator operator, typically an older person seated on a stool. That person had a lever that would close the door and move the elevator up. I haven't seen such an antiquated elevator or an elevator operator in many decades. That job is rare, if not gone.

The job of being a peacemaker, however, will never go away. The need is too great. One might think that among the world of Christians, the fruits of God's Spirit—love, joy, peace, patience, kindness, gentleness, and self-control—would eliminate the need for peacemakers within churches. But as my friend Louis tells me, "People are people, and the church is full of them!"

The behavior of James' intended recipients toward one another was so appalling that James uses war metaphors to address the problem. Fighting, quarreling, and warring are the descriptors of a community that should be marked by peace, kindness, and self-control. What had gone amok?

The people were living worldly lives. They coveted things of the world. Their desires for the world's niceties had overridden their higher calling. These desires had become so strong that they affected their prayer lives. They were asking God for things of the world; they weren't praying for God's will and his kingdom.

Reading today's passage makes me pause. What do I value? What do I want to accomplish to make this a good day? Am I seeking to feed my own selfishness, or am I living today for God and his kingdom? Is my faith a convenience, or does it give me direction toward God's higher calling?

I want and need to do better!

Lord, please purify my heart and desires for you. Give me strength to turn from the world's pleasures and find pleasure in following your plans. In Jesus, amen.

JANUARY 13

Do not speak evil against one another, brothers. The one who speaks against a brother or judges his brother, speaks evil against the law and judges the law. But if you judge the law, you are not a doer of the law but a judge. There is only one lawgiver and judge, he who is able to save and to destroy. But who are you to judge your neighbor? (James 4:11–12)

I know a few people in my life who have appointed themselves as my watchdogs. They come to me to warn me about one person or another. They have told me about the nefarious motives of others more than once. The watchdogs determine motives typically based on their intuition. One time, I had to hear a haranguing that an individual was maliciously acting contrary to my interests! I then told this self-appointed watchdog that the individual in question was doing exactly what I had told him to do. The accusations of the other's ill motives were totally false.

What is it in us that makes us assume we can judge the hearts and minds of others? I'm sure different things are at work in us. For some, it might elevate their own importance to point out alleged evil in another. For some, it might be a disguise for gossip. Still others might find some satisfaction in seeing others pulled down a notch. Some might simply believe themselves to be the moral and social police.

I do believe that there are times when evil needs to be reported. If someone is abusing another, it demands immediate attention. But in my own life, I would say 95 percent of the time I speak—or see someone else speak—to someone's inadequacies, it isn't because of a godly need to bring darkness into light. Rather, the truer, darker reasons behind these words hide under the masquerade of good motives.

If you've ever seen those boxes that have a kajillion locks on them, you have a good picture of how I have decided to live my life. I don't want to speak evil of another unless each lock is opened. Before my mouth is used to trash another, accuse another, speak ill of another, or spoil another's name, I will test my words multiple times and ways to see if they are godly speech. After all, I am *not* the judge. I am *not* the perfect one. I live in a glass house and shouldn't be throwing stones at others.

Lord, I confess that I don't live purely in speech or motives. I want to do better. Set a guard on my tongue. Teach and help me find joy in positive speech, not in reviling another. In Jesus' name, amen.

JANUARY 14

Come now, you who say, "Today or tomorrow we will go into such and such a town and spend a year there and trade and make a profit"—yet you do not know what tomorrow will bring. What is your life? For you are a mist that appears for a little time and then vanishes. Instead you ought to say, "If the Lord wills, we will live and do this or that." As it is, you boast in your arrogance. All such boasting is evil. (James 4:13–16)

In the process of preparing some "Video Thoughts for the Day" on YouTube, I decided to speak for a week on trite Christian phrases that aren't biblically based. Phrases like "God helps those who help themselves" have dangerous messages if not applied correctly. In preparation, I conducted an internet search to find typical trite but biblically flawed phrases. I discovered that believers will often announce their plans and then add the phrase "God willing" or "The Lord willing and the creek don't rise."

That experience was further confirmation: don't believe everything on the internet! Today's passage exposes the internet's error. It's not biblically flawed to say, "God willing." In fact, James instructs his readers *to say*, "If the Lord wills." To do anything less is at best ignorance and more likely arrogance.

Neither you nor I know what life will bring tomorrow, today, or even in the next hour. We might assume what will come based on statistics, but statistics give odds, not truth. James gives counsel that is faith wrapped in common sense. Common sense has long taught that we "don't count our chickens before they hatch." (That expression goes back to Aesop's fables over one thousand years ago!) We "don't spend the money before it's in the bank." Similar proverbs and aphorisms are legion.

Yet we can anticipate what is coming. It is inherent in human nature to anticipate possible future events—plus good planning often requires it. The key is to wrap the common sense in faith. I do plan to do certain things today, and I will do them, *if God wills*. But if God has another plan for me, then that plan will supplant my expectations for the future.

James is telling his audience that we are not masters of our own destinies. There is a God who is over all, and we should recognize God in all we plan, think, or do.

Lord, I seek you as my God and Lord today in all my plans. Give me direction, strength, and success in your will today. In Jesus, amen.

JANUARY 15

Come now, you rich, weep and howl for the miseries that are coming upon you. Your riches have rotted and your garments are moth-eaten. Your gold and silver have corroded, and their corrosion will be evidence against you and will eat your flesh like fire. You have laid up treasure in the last days. Behold, the wages of the laborers who mowed your fields, which you kept back by fraud, are crying out against you, and the cries of the harvesters have reached the ears of the Lord of hosts. You have lived on the earth in luxury and in self-indulgence. You have fattened your hearts in a day of slaughter. (James 5:1–5)

God asked Solomon for his wish list. Solomon didn't seek fame or fortune. He wanted wisdom. God gave Solomon wisdom but piled on fame and fortune as well, noting Solomon hadn't asked for it. Fame and fortune were God's rewards to Solomon. Abraham was blessed with great livestock, a large workforce, and a transgenerational promise of land. The Israelites were pulled from slavery in Egypt to a promised land flowing with milk and honey. God prospers many.

Then James writes this passage, which at first blush might seem to impugn those with wealth. It's reminiscent of Jesus' admonition that it is harder for a camel to go through a needle's eye than for a rich person to enter the kingdom of heaven. What does a well-off person do with this, especially since most people in the West and East are rich compared to starving children in less-developed countries?

James is addressing the wrongful acquisition of wealth, including abusing people unfairly to get more in the bank. These folks aren't paying fair wages to their workers. They are interested only in getting more wealth, without regard to their responsibilities before God. Luxury and comfort have become their god, and the true God has noticed.

This should cause everyone to focus on the purpose of life. Do we live to accumulate things? Is our goal comfort and ease? What are we willing to do to get it? James speaks loudly that every believer should treat others fairly, especially when it comes to economics. Money is never the goal in life. Money is God's tool to bless others and build his kingdom. How we make money matters. So does what we do with it. God brings judgment in this arena, and the believer should live righteously.

Lord, be God in my life over everything I have or want. May serving you be my goal. In Jesus, amen.

JANUARY 16

Be patient, therefore, brothers, until the coming of the Lord. See how the farmer waits for the precious fruit of the earth, being patient about it, until it receives the early and the late rains. You also, be patient. Establish your hearts, for the coming of the Lord is at hand. Do not grumble against one another, brothers, so that you may not be judged; behold, the Judge is standing at the door. . . . You have seen the purpose of the Lord, how the Lord is compassionate and merciful. (James 5:7–11)

For some reason, my adolescence was spent around people who often spoke in short little statements that have survived in my mind many decades later. Several of them echo as I read today's passage. I can remember being in a hurry once in high school when a friend smiled and told me as she walked by, "Patience is a virtue, virtue's a grace, and grace is from God." Then poof—she was gone! I mused over the saying as I wanted to reply with my own pithy statement, "Easier said than done."

"Patience" and "endurance" are valuable traits that everyone should want. James points out their value and here gives the simple (but often difficult) instruction to "be patient." How can one be patient when the kids are running crazy and ignoring all instructions and calls to obedience, when pressures are mounting at work or school, when health wanes, when money is short, or when everything seems to go wrong all at once? The instruction "be patient" might seem useless. At those points in life, actions are on remote control. People are struggling just to get through the moment.

I liken it to someone flailing and thrashing in the water as they drown. Lifeguards must be strategic about rescuing thrashers because the drowning person can take down the rescuer. People often don't think clearly or exercise control in times of panic or stress.

Importantly, James doesn't leave this subject with the simple instruction. He gives practical and valuable advice. We shouldn't be grumbling. We should establish our hearts. We should work to see God's hand. We should remember that God has brought us through many difficulties in days gone by. Remembering these things will train us in patience. We will grow in patience and holiness. If we work on the things we can, we will see God producing great fruit in our lives. So don't grumble; remember God reigns, and let God take care of what is bothering you!

Lord, give me patient endurance as I focus on your mercy and love. In Jesus, amen.

JANUARY 17

But above all, my brothers, do not swear, either by heaven or by earth or by any other oath, but let your "yes" be yes and your "no" be no, so that you may not fall under condemnation. (James 5:12)

In 1975, Frankie Valli and the Four Seasons released the gentle-on-the-ears song "Swearin' to God." Frankie sings his loving lyrics, "Swearin' to God, I dedicate my life to loving you; Oh, I'm swearin' to God, I'd cross my heart and hope to die, I do. Just call me your one woman lover, I can't even look at another. Girl, I'm swearin' to God, so glad I'm livin'; I'm swearin' to God, for all he's given me. Swearin' to God, so glad he's given me you." Do you see a pattern in these lyrics? The sappy love song sounds admirable, and the love might seem deep, but saying "swearin' to God" over and over starts to lose its punch. I don't think the songwriters read this James passage!

I am always a bit perplexed by people who begin telling me something with the comment "Honestly" or "To tell you the truth . . ." All I can think of at that point is, "Does this mean when you tell me other things that you might be lying?"

In courtrooms, before a witness was allowed to testify, they used to take an oath along the lines of "Do you swear to tell the truth, the whole truth, and nothing but the truth?" But now courts typically ask, "Do you swear *or affirm* to tell the truth?" The reason for the change is that some individuals refuse to swear an oath based on this passage in James and a similar one by Jesus in the Sermon on the Mount: "Do not take an oath by your head, for you cannot make one hair white or black. Let what you say be simply 'Yes' or 'No'; anything more than this comes from evil" (Mt. 5:36–37).

Today's passage speaks directly to the heart of integrity. Honesty is to be a hallmark of the believer. No one should ever doubt the integrity and truth of what a believer says. A follower of Jesus should never say one thing and do another. Falsehood should never walk alongside a Christian. After all, Jesus noted he was the "truth," but Satan is the father of lies (Jn. 14:6; 8:44). One who speaks only truth will stand out in this world. That is a good thing.

Lord, I want to be honest before the world. Give me a burning heart for truth, and let my honesty be a light that shines and points people to you. I pray in the name of Jesus, the true one, amen.

JANUARY 18

Is anyone among you suffering? Let him pray. Is anyone cheerful? Let him sing praise. Is anyone among you sick? Let him call for the elders of the church, and let them pray over him, anointing him with oil in the name of the Lord. And the prayer of faith will save the one who is sick, and the Lord will raise him up. (James 5:13–15)

Over time, people figured out that if they took a needle and magnetized it, the needle would naturally align itself with the magnetized earth, pointing to the magnetic north and south of our planet. This is why the compass became a historically reliable navigation tool. The adventurer could be confident the needle pointed north and from that could derive other directions.

The believer has a spiritual compass to guide them through life. That compass is prayer. James taught not only the importance of prayer but also its power. Today's passage should give encouragement and direction to all who walk with the Lord. We should pray for our own circumstances and on behalf of others.

James begins by calling the suffering to prayer. When life's difficulties mount, we should set our issues before God, seek his wisdom, trust in his deliverance, and be confident that he is hearing our prayers. Now, sometimes life is going great. We have days when we are happy, and joy fills our hearts. These are the days we wish would last forever. James tells us in those days to express gratitude and praise to God. James says to sing it! (Many of our songs are prayers of praise to God.)

Then James addresses those who are sick. They are to call the church leaders in to pray. This admonishes not only us to pray in times of sickness but also leaders among God's people to pray for others. Often called "intercessory prayer," it is important for all God's people to pray for those in need. James notes that a prayer offered in faith will save the sick. We mustn't think this means that when healing doesn't come, we are faith deficient. Rather, the "prayer of faith" is a prayer offered under God's sovereign design. We can trust God with the consequence, whether it is earthly healing in this age or permanent healing in the age to come.

Prayer is our compass. It always points us to God.

Lord, lift me up and be praised. Bless those in need, in Jesus' name, amen.

JANUARY 19

Paul, an apostle—not from men nor through man, but through Jesus Christ and God the Father, who raised him from the dead—and all the brothers who are with me, To the churches of Galatia. (Gal. 1:1–2)

Everyone who goes to law school becomes familiar with a power of attorney. It is a legal document where you authorize someone to act on your behalf. Many people sign medical powers of attorney, authorizing another to act on their behalf for medical care and decisions when they are unable to make those decisions themselves.

If you cross a power of attorney with a FedEx delivery driver, you begin to get to the role of an "apostle"—Paul's title given to himself in this letter to the Galatians. Our English word comes directly from the Greek word, pronounced *apostolos* (ἀπόστολος). It references one who is sent on another's behalf and carries their authority. It isn't a claim Paul makes lightly. Jesus Christ and God the Father empowered and sent Paul. His message should be heeded carefully.

I am not an apostle. God has not empowered me to speak directly on his behalf, nor are my words equivalent to Scripture. But God doesn't authorize and empower only apostles. Paul himself taught that God chooses from a buffet of gifts to empower and entrust each follower of Jesus with a mission and purpose. All these gifts are important in God's eyes, and we all have a purpose in his plans.

As a later devotional will explore, Paul used the human body as an analogy to show that God makes some to be a hand and others an eye, ear, or nose. The challenge for each believer is to find where God has empowered them and how they might serve the larger kingdom of God and the Lord.

The use of God's gifts is my devotional focus this morning and my mission for today. How has God gifted me, and how can I use those gifts to edify others? Some might readily know the answers to those questions. Others may need to prayerfully mull them over. All of us, however, should pray about it and seek to fulfill our calling.

Paul used his role as an apostle to instruct and edify those in Galatia almost two thousand years ago. His work still edifies us today. I should be excited about how God will use me in this life, knowing it can make a difference for eternity.

Lord, show me your calling, and use me today for your kingdom. In Jesus, amen.

JANUARY 20

Grace to you and peace from God our Father and the Lord Jesus Christ, who gave himself for our sins to deliver us from the present evil age, according to the will of our God and Father, to whom be the glory forever and ever. Amen. (Gal. 1:3–5)

Medical professionals and scientists frequently read published papers to keep abreast of the latest advances. While a lot of ordinary people get their information from websites or books, there is a wealth of scientific articles that don't get published without first being "peer reviewed." This means that others who are experts in the applicable field have reviewed the paper to determine whether it is good science, well researched, and worthy of publication. Then once published, these articles follow a basic format. After listing the author(s), they contain an abstract or summary, which is basically a synopsis of what the article has to say. Many experts will read the synopsis first and then decide whether the article is worth reading.

In like manner, Paul gives an abstract of sorts for his letter to the Galatians. Paul fits it into the greeting that normally occurs at the beginning of a letter like this. Paul's greeting was that the grace and peace of God and Jesus would rest upon the Galatians (or audience). But Paul can't mention God's grace and peace without adding what becomes a theme in his letter. Bursting forth from Paul's pen is the proclamation that the Lord Jesus Christ gave himself for our sins to deliver us from the present age. Jesus' incarnation and death weren't some spur-of-the-moment decision. They were the will of the Father, the eternal one.

This abstract (of sorts) makes me want to read the whole letter and read it carefully. Paul didn't just bring this message to the people. Paul experienced the message. Notice Paul says that Jesus died for "our" sins to deliver "us." This was Paul's experience shared by his readers.

I know sin. Sin is sticky stuff that amasses in my life and is hard to run from. Yet I am going to be reading in this letter something profound. I will read how Christ died for those sticky sins. What is more, I will read that this delivers me from the present evil age. Just as I know sin, I know how this age is evil. I have seen evil people and even good people do evil things. I have seen disease and illness. I know the devastation of natural disasters. I want deliverance from this present age.

Lord, tune my mind and heart to hear your message in the coming days. Keep me studying your word and understanding your greatness in my life and in Jesus, amen.

JANUARY 21

I am astonished that you are so quickly deserting him who called you in the grace of Christ and are turning to a different gospel—not that there is another one, but there are some who trouble you and want to distort the gospel of Christ. But even if we or an angel from heaven should preach to you a gospel contrary to the one we preached to you, let him be accursed. (Gal. 1:6–8)

I prepared to cross-examine an expert on PPARs (peroxisome proliferator-activated receptors). These unseen parts of human cells were not in my knowledge bank. My degrees are in biblical languages and law. As I read the scientific papers on PPARs, I quickly discovered that I needed help. I sort of understood the vocabulary, but there were some terms of art that the articles assumed the reader understood. I had to learn those terms to better understand the science.

Sometimes knowing the vocabulary is especially important. That is true for today's verses. Three times in rapid succession, Paul uses the word *gospel.* Paul speaks of his readers turning from the true "gospel" to a different "gospel," which isn't really a "gospel"! What is Paul's "gospel"?

The word for "gospel" is *euangelion* (εὐαγγέλιον), a compound word in the Greek. It combines *eu,* which means "good" (we use it in words like *euphemism*), with *angelion,* or "message" (from which we get our word *angel*). If we were somehow able to put Paul's writing into straight English, we might see Paul speaking of the Galatians turning from the true good news to what they wrongly thought was good news.

Paul's good news, however, was the best news. He explained it in another letter. His good news was that Christ died for our sins, was buried, and was resurrected (1 Cor. 15:1–4). This truly is great news. The problem is that most of us want the news to be slightly different.

The true gospel strips you and me of any merit we might have based on our own performance. We don't enter God's kingdom because we try hard, meet certain standards, or are worthy by our own merit. No one has any ground to boast. We can have an eternal relationship with God for one reason only: we believe Jesus Christ paid the penalty for all our impure thoughts, selfish deeds, unholy words, and sinful acts. We stand before God only by his mercy and justice in Christ.

Lord, teach me humility in your gospel as I hold to Christ alone. In him, amen.

JANUARY 22

For am I now seeking the approval of man, or of God? Or am I trying to please man? If I were still trying to please man, I would not be a servant of Christ. (Gal. 1:10)

Confession: I am an affirmation junkie. I crave affirmation, and I'm sure I'm not alone. All five of our children and all our ten (as of now) grandchildren openly seek approval. They will come running up for a chance to show us what they are able to do. From cooking to dancing, from climbing to somersaulting, they want us to see and admire their accomplishments.

Seeking approval seems innate in most if not all of us. This drive comes into focus in today's verse. Paul doesn't dismiss the need for approval, but he clearly directs it. Paul wants his readers to know that he is living to receive God's approval, not the approval of his contemporaries. We would do well to use Paul as a model here.

Living for the admiration of others is fraught with problems. In the teenage years, peer pressure seduces many into deeds that they shouldn't do. In adulthood, peer pressure remains, although often cloaked and disguised. Additionally, approval-seeking conduct can cause people to live false lives, trying to appear to be something they aren't. This can sow distrust, discord, and disharmony in relationships as the truth is revealed over time.

Furthermore, as people live for others' approval, when they receive that approval, it often leads to pride, arrogance, and an unhealthy kind of self-esteem. Approval can be its own addictive drug. It has become more prominent than ever through the almost toxic levels of social media in use today. Many find "likes" and "friends" on social media accounts intoxicating.

Paul gives the believer a different focus. Seeking approval isn't to be stopped, for it is innate in us all. But Paul redirects it. Paul says we should be seeking God's approval. If we live to serve God, then the other matters take care of themselves. Boasting is gone, for we live to lift up the Father. Arrogance is nothing, for we know we exist through Jesus' righteousness alone. We aren't looking to be the center of our universe; we seek to make God the center of all things. I want to live for the approval of God!

Lord, may I live to serve you, seeking your approval in Christ, in whom I pray, amen.

JANUARY 23

When James and Cephas and John, who seemed to be pillars, perceived the grace that was given to me, they gave the right hand of fellowship to Barnabas and me, that we should go to the Gentiles and they to the circumcised. Only, they asked us to remember the poor, the very thing I was eager to do. (Gal. 2:9–10)

Please allow me to brag about my mom. A community leader in Lubbock, Texas, Mom started one of the nation's first (and soon largest) food banks in 1983. In 1993, she developed and opened Breedlove Dehydrated Foods, a processing plant that took in unwanted produce, dehydrated it, and sent the compact, lightweight product to groups serving starving people around the globe, including thirty-three million servings to North Korea's starving residents in 1997. It won Mom a coveted spot on ABC's *World News Tonight* as the "Person of the Week" on Thanksgiving Day.

Mom quickly comes to mind as I read today's passage. Paul has been taking the Jewish-originated faith out from its Jerusalem-based environment, led by its Jewish pillars of faith and Jesus-appointed Jewish apostles, and bringing it into the Gentile environment. Paul did this without requiring that the Gentiles first convert to Judaism to become Christians. This rocked the world of the early Jewish church.

Yet when Paul went back to Jerusalem and set this revolutionary message before the Jewish church leaders, the response was simply for Paul "to remember the poor"—a seemingly off-topic response! Yet it shows the significance of God's concern for those with to help those without. This isn't an afterthought to God; it's as important as any theological construct. It is the core of God's love being expressed.

Importantly, the Greek verbs here indicate a bit that is lost in English. Paul's use of a present-tense verb ("remember") indicates that Paul was already doing that very thing. One might fairly translate it as "Please go on remembering the poor," which Paul adds he was "eager to do."

Theology is important. It provides guardrails to keep us on the right road in life. But when theology meets its proper ends, it becomes expressed in good deeds before God. Those deeds include tending to the needy in this world. Mom did well. Let us go and do likewise!

Lord, give me an eye for those hurting around me. As I walk in your blessings, help me aid those in need. May I do so in Jesus' name, amen.

JANUARY 24

We know that a person is not justified by works of the law but through faith in Jesus Christ, so we also have believed in Christ Jesus, in order to be justified by faith in Christ and not by works of the law, because by works of the law no one will be justified. (Gal. 2:16)

Having tried lawsuits for almost forty years, the tensest moment in every case is the reading of the jury's verdict. The judge gets the jury's answers to certain questions, opens it, and in front of the entire courtroom, reads aloud the answers. Only then does everyone learn the answers. In criminal cases where one is accused of violating the law, the answers are either "guilty" or "not guilty."

In Israel's history, God gave the people a legal code for their community and religious lives. Knowing disputes would arise, God instructed them, "If there is a dispute between men and they come into court and the judges decide between them, acquitting the innocent and condemning the guilty," then certain punishments were meted out to the guilty (Dt. 25:1).

Paul was trained in the law. In a real sense, he was a Jewish lawyer. He knew the language and practice of the above verse in Deuteronomy. Paul takes the language from the Greek translation of that passage and others in the Old Testament in writing today's verses. The words "acquitting" and "innocent" used in Deuteronomy are roots of the words Paul uses in Galatians 2.

Paul notes that one's innocence before God is not established by one's own performance of God's law. No one is that good. No one is that pure. Even the best human deed is tainted by at least a smidgeon of selfishness, which makes it totally inadequate before the perfectly pure God.

Paul sees another model for the right relationship between God and his people. That model is based on trusting and believing in Jesus as Christ, the Greek word for "Messiah." Paul notes this is true for every human. No one stands right before God by how well one lives.

This encourages me. I know my own sins and inadequacies all too well. I walk in defeated guilt but for the grace of God expressed in Christ. Thank you, God!

Lord, I do thank you for the innocence you give me despite my true moral guilt. I entrust myself to forgiveness in Christ, through whom I pray, amen.

JANUARY 25

I have been crucified with Christ. It is no longer I who live, but Christ who lives in me. And the life I now live in the flesh I live by faith in the Son of God, who loved me and gave himself for me. I do not nullify the grace of God, for if righteousness were through the law, then Christ died for no purpose. (Gal. 2:20–21)

I've known Becky Smith since she was fourteen. She was this cute young lady who most everyone adored. She was a class favorite among the students as well as the teacher. Most likely to succeed, head cheerleader, homecoming court, "I Dare You" award winner—you name it, she won it. As she grew into adulthood, the men chasing her were legion. She was funny and a joy to be around. She had a heart for the hurting and always wanted to help those in need. She was my friend, but one day our relationship took a new turn. She agreed to move from the line of being my friend to going on a date. We eventually married. When I think that she gave her heart to me, I am still amazed.

My history with Becky comes to mind in reading today's passage. Paul personalizes the passage with repeated emphasis on himself. Paul doesn't write, "*We* have been crucified with Christ," even though it is true for all Christians. Paul doesn't add, "It is no longer *we* who live," although that is also true. Over and over, Paul punctuates this passage with the personal "*I*." "*I* have been crucified with Christ. It is no longer *I* who live. . . . Christ lives in *me*. . . . The life *I* live in the flesh, *I* live by faith in the Son of God who loved *me* and gave himself for *me*."

Paul was still stunned, well over a decade after receiving God's revelation of grace in Jesus, that Jesus did what he did for Paul, in a real personal sense. We should be stunned as well.

God's concern for you and me is personal. God didn't incarnate in Jesus and suffer the humiliation and death at Calvary for the holy with you and me coming along for the ride. Christ died for you and me. It is personal. It is rightfully stunning. The God of the universe, the unchanging, almighty one, knowing your name and mine, chose to come into space and time and die so we might live eternally.

We can be stunned by human love, but divine love is on another level altogether. I need to dwell on God's sacrificial love and personalize it as Paul did.

Lord, your love is stunning. It scares me in wonderment as I live in Jesus, amen.

JANUARY 26

O foolish Galatians! Who has bewitched you? It was before your eyes that Jesus Christ was publicly portrayed as crucified. Let me ask you only this: Did you receive the Spirit by works of the law or by hearing with faith? Are you so foolish? Having begun by the Spirit, are you now being perfected by the flesh? (Gal. 3:1–3)

Dr. Harvey Floyd was a masterful teacher of Greek—and so much more. Although I sat in his classes over forty years before writing this book, I still remember many of his illustrations. When teaching today's passage, Dr. Floyd didn't simply want us to translate it well; he wanted us to understand it.

Dr. Floyd gave us a hypothetical illustration. He said, "If I give you an exam, and if it is in a multiple-choice format but you only have two choices for an answer—if you must choose between A and B, you know that anyone writing C will be wrong. If only two answers are options, the answer *must* be one of those two."

He then explained that Paul asks a question here at the start of Galatians. Paul wants to know whether receiving the Spirit of God, a key gift God gives to those who become Christians, came about by (A) hearing of Christ's crucifixion and resurrection with faith or (B) working to earn it. It's one or the other. The answer is simple: our Christian walk begins by trusting (or having faith) in the death of Christ for our sins.

Knowing that to be true, Paul then follows up asking why the Galatians thought they had to maintain their relationship with God through works rather than faith.

Paul puts his finger on an almost overwhelming drive for believers in Jesus. Too often, we tend to think that we must please God to be loved by God. We think that the more we do for God, the more likely he will embrace and love us. We think that we need to earn God's love. We couldn't be more off base.

God loves us out of his choice, not our merit. No one is good enough for God. No one earns salvation because of their own merit or goodness. Salvation is a gift from God. End of story. This means I can't boast of my merit. It also means I shouldn't sulk in guilt. The answer to Paul's quiz can't be (C), "all of the above." It can't be faith *plus* works. It is faith alone by which we stand before God.

Lord, thank you for the gift of your love. It stirs me to do good deeds. In Jesus' name, amen.

JANUARY 27

Now before faith came, we were held captive under the law, imprisoned until the coming faith would be revealed. So then, the law was our guardian until Christ came, in order that we might be justified by faith. But now that faith has come, we are no longer under a guardian, for in Christ Jesus you are all sons of God, through faith. (Gal. 3:23–26)

One of a translator's biggest struggles is taking an ancient word, tied to the culture of its day, and translating it into modern English, where the word has no equivalent. That struggle takes place in today's passage. The word is *paidagōgos* (παιδαγωγὸς). It is a compound word made of the Greek word for a child typically under the age of puberty (*paidion*—παιδίον) and the word for "lead"/"bring" (*agō*—ἄγω). The word referred to a specific job of an adult who would "lead" a child in Greek family and community life.

Because the *paidagōgos* was something the Greeks had that has no English equivalent, the translations are a bit all over the map. The ESV translation I quote uses the word "guardian," but others use "trainer," "schoolmaster," "tutor," "guide," "disciplinarian," or "teacher." What to do? How did the "law" function?

Reading ancient Greek literature gives a good understanding of the role of the *paidagōgos*, even if we don't have an English equivalent. The *paidagōgos* was typically a slave attendant who took charge of a child once the child outgrew his nursemaid. The *paidagōgos* went with the child everywhere, keeping him safe on the streets and taking him to and from school. The *paidagōgos* also was responsible for teaching the child manners (even disciplining the child with a switch!). Once the child arrived home from school, the *paidagōgos* made sure the child did homework and would make the child recite lessons to reinforce memory, although the *paidagōgos* was not a teacher in the modern sense.

This was the role of the law (known as the "Torah" in Jewish tradition), the instructions of the "Old Testament." Paul saw the law as teaching manners and leading one to Christ. The law was never the goal; the law was a means to an end. Faith in Christ is the end.

This is where we often mess up. We think our obedience to God's commands is what life is about. But life is about trusting God in Christ. The rest are instructions on godly living, helping us find Christ.

Lord, bring me to Jesus today. Let me walk in him as I pray in him, amen.

JANUARY 28

There is neither Jew nor Greek, there is neither slave nor free, there is no male and female, for you are all one in Christ Jesus. (Gal. 3:28)

Yesterday, I awoke early, boarded a plane, and headed to Tuskegee, Alabama, for lunch with an icon. I ate lunch with ninety-two-year-old Fred David Gray, an extraordinary lawyer who still practices daily. Before lunch, I met with his sons and daughters. I had met Fred before, and I was eager to spend more time with him. Fred was the lawyer for Rosa Parks, who exploded onto the national scene when she wouldn't give up her seat on the bus for a white person. Fred was also the lawyer for Martin Luther King Jr., who Fred refers to simply as "Martin" in his conversations. Fred won monumental civil rights cases for black people in Alabama, his home state, and throughout America. (Although Fred had to go to law school in Ohio because black people weren't allowed to go to law school in Alabama at the time.)

I asked Fred a question that had my curiosity piqued: "When did you have your first white friend?" It is the only question I have ever asked Fred that seemed to stump him. He first had white people in his circle of life in law school but wouldn't call any of them friends. Before law school, he had studied for the ministry in Nashville but wasn't allowed in the white Christian colleges, so he had studied in an all-black school for preachers. He did remember well two white teachers who came and taught the Bible and the art of preaching. Once Fred started practicing law, he had to hang a shingle up because no Alabama firms would hire a black lawyer. Finally, a white lawyer stepped into his life as a legal mentor of sorts.

When I asked the same question of Fred's children, each near my age, I found out that one had his first white friends in college, although they weren't close friends. On this visit, I had one of the young lawyers at my firm with me. Davis (who is also my nephew) and I discussed the changing times. Davis' comment was that one of his earliest dear friends was black. Yet the times haven't eliminated all vestiges of discrimination, for one of Fred's current cases involves opening a park in the city to all races—the park was a gift for white people only in 1909, and the markers of that remain.

Paul's passage today indicates a fundamental truth of the Christian faith. Christ is the great equalizer. No one should allow color, national pride, economics, or gender to interfere with the unity of Christ. Christ unites all his people as one.

Lord, give me a heart for unity and a love for all. In Jesus, amen.

JANUARY 29

When the fullness of time had come, God sent forth his Son, born of woman, born under the law, to redeem those who were under the law. (Gal. 4:4–5)

The arrival of the Christian faith is a remarkably timed event. Some wonder how a faith in the death and resurrection of a thirty-three-year-old carpenter-turned-itinerant-teacher in the hilltop town of Jerusalem on the outskirts of the vast Roman Empire became a major religious force reaching into all areas of the empire in just a few decades.

One reason for Christianity's rapid expansion was the overwhelming and undeniable miracle that Jesus, following his death on the cross, was resurrected physically and appeared to hundreds of people. But even that itself doesn't explain the massive explosion of Christianity in an age when the internet, the telephone, and the automobile weren't even in anyone's imagination.

What happened? The timing was perfect! Rome had established a massive empire that included a network of roads, consistent laws, a coherent economy that transcended regions, and most importantly, the Pax Romana, or Roman peace. With troops stationed throughout the lands, Rome protected peace. This didn't make travel perfectly secure, but it made travel reasonably safe and easy. It allowed ideas and people to spread readily throughout the known world. It was also a time of literacy, since after Alexander the Great's world conquests centuries earlier, Greek had become a common language for the empire. Even the Jewish Scriptures had been translated into Greek. Everything was perfect for the church to blossom.

Today's passage speaks of God sending Jesus at the "fullness of time." God wasn't naïve about the world. He knew what was and wasn't available. Jesus didn't stumble onto the scene out of luck for the moment. The entirety of the Christian faith and church was intimately planned by God.

God's timing is best. Nothing else comes close. This was true two thousand years ago, and it is no less true today. God's timing was right for Jesus, it was right for the church, and it's right for you and me. I don't always see God operating life on my schedule, but I know that God's timing transcends mine. So I will wait and walk in his schedule.

Lord, I confess my impatience at times. Intellectually, I know your timing is best, but sometimes my heart overrules my head! Give me patience, in Jesus, amen.

JANUARY 30

God sent forth his Son, born of woman, born under the law, to redeem those who were under the law, so that we might receive adoption as sons. And because you are sons, God has sent the Spirit of his Son into our hearts, crying, "Abba! Father!" So you are no longer a slave, but a son, and if a son, then an heir through God. (Gal. 4:4–7)

With four daughters and seven granddaughters (as of the time I am writing this), I am sensitive to those who speak of the world as a "man's world." I work hard to use language that includes my daughters, so I don't write about "mankind" as much as I write about "people." Recently, I was addressing "manpower" needs at my law firm, knowing many of those spots would be filled with women. But what is an inclusive word for "manpower"? I decided to use "workforce."

My sensitivity arises in passages like today's. Paul writes that the believer in Christ will receive "adoption as sons." What about my daughters? Is this Paul being a chauvinist, as some claim? Is this Christianity being a male-centric religion, as some critics assert? Absolutely not! This is an important, culturally timed teaching.

In most Greek and Roman legal circles, adoption was well known, and it gave full rights to the adoptee. But inheritance rights differed based on gender. The sons received full inheritance rights, not so the daughters. The sons could step into the full rights as heads of the family, property owners, and more.

This is Paul's point. Paul has already indicated that in Christ, there is no male or female, but in Roman law, there was. Paul emphasizes that the full adoption rights given to sons under Roman law are given to every believer, regardless of gender.

So everyone has the Spirit indwelling, crying out to God in the intimate way of "Abba." *Abba* was an affectionate Aramaic word for "father." It isn't quite as informal as "daddy" in modern English, but it does carry a special intimacy. Intimacy with the Almighty God is an awesome thing. It is the right and destiny of all believers. It includes full rights of inheritance to males and females alike.

We are all heirs of God and given an inheritance. Let's live like it! Our position as heirs should affect all we say, think, and do.

Abba Father, thank you for my adoption into your family in Jesus. Amen.

JANUARY 31

But now that you have come to know God, or rather to be known by God, how can you turn back again to the weak and worthless elementary principles of the world, whose slaves you want to be once more? You observe days and months and seasons and years! I am afraid I may have labored over you in vain. (Gal. 4:9–11)

The churches in Galatia had a problem. They had learned of the death and resurrection of Jesus Christ. Paul had taught them in their synagogues and in the streets that Christ had broken down the barriers between people and God. Paul explained that in Christ, all were given full inheritance rights into God's family.

Then Paul left. Paul moved on, and the people were left trying to live this transforming faith without his watchful presence and teaching. Inevitably, the people were soon influenced by others, and they began to go back to old habits and belief structures. Being mostly Jewish, they returned to the Jewish celebrations of their earlier life, now finding them infused with great meaning by the arrival of Jesus but still maintaining the old forms.

Paul heard about this and couldn't leave it alone. He had to write them. Paul knew of the danger that faces almost everyone. We tend to lapse into the comfort of what we know. Change comes with difficulty. After doing the same things our whole lives, giving up those habits and traditions can be difficult.

Paul didn't want the people to lose their heritage and traditions, but Paul wanted those to be tools for the people in their walk of faith. For these Jewish believers, the old *ways* of the pre-Christian walk were feeble efforts to please or, at least, mollify the hard-to-reach God.

Yet Christ had transformed all of that. The old religion of people trying to reach up to God had been supplanted by God reaching all the way down to people. A relationship with God was no longer based on rituals and processes. The relationship was a true and permanent one based on the finished work of Jesus on Calvary. Hence Paul's concerns expressed in today's verse.

God must be bigger than my tendency to fall back into my comfort zone. From food to attitudes, God calls me to live for him in fresh ways based on his love expressed in Jesus. This requires my daily attention and commitment!

Lord, help me focus on your love in Christ as I live for you today. In him, amen.

FEBRUARY 1

For you were called to freedom, brothers. Only do not use your freedom as an opportunity for the flesh, but through love serve one another. For the whole law is fulfilled in one word: "You shall love your neighbor as yourself." But if you bite and devour one another, watch out that you are not consumed by one another. (Gal. 5:13–15)

One of my earliest memories was when I was three years old. Mom had an old-fashioned small, white alarm clock about the size of a box of Pop-Tarts with a ringer on top. Mom was throwing the clock away. When I asked her why, she said it was broken. I asked if I could have it, and she said, "Sure," handing it down to me. Somehow I got into my dad's tools—I don't remember how, but I distinctly remember sitting on the kitchen floor and somehow managing to take the back off the clock. I was convinced if I could take it apart, I could put it back together and fix it.

In my own small way, my mind wanted to know the *how* of things, hoping I could apply that knowledge to make life better. That story comes to mind as I read today's passage. Paul was a practical theologian. Paul liked to know and write about God and his working among us. Paul writes on "theology," and many of the first half of his letters explore his important theological concerns.

But Paul didn't do theology for theology's sake. Knowledge about God was important to him and his writings because it directly impacted life and behavior. Paul knows what we believe affects what we do. The two are tied.

So Paul writes about the "freedom" we have in Christ, a "freedom" that sets us right before God not based on our meritorious behavior but based on the merit of Christ. Paul then explains that the purpose of our freedom isn't rebellion against God but the liberty to serve him better. Our service to God proceeds from a purer heart. It isn't a required service; it's a service of love. That is transformational.

Paul explains the transformation in practical terms, teaching his readers to love one another—not to get right with God but because God has given us the freedom to do so. As John would say, "We love because he first loved us" (1 Jn. 4:19)! Paul, the practical theologian, reminds me of my young experience with the clock. Except I never got mine working!

Lord, may I show your love to others today in real, concrete ways. In you, amen.

FEBRUARY 2

But I say, walk by the Spirit, and you will not gratify the desires of the flesh. . . . Now the works of the flesh are evident: sexual immorality, impurity, sensuality, idolatry, sorcery, enmity, strife, jealousy, fits of anger, rivalries, dissensions, divisions, envy, drunkenness, orgies, and things like these. (Gal. 5:16, 19–21)

If I were to list the top ten spiritual influences in my life, without a doubt, one would be Don Finto. I had heard of Don as a fifteen-year-old boy in Lubbock, Texas. Don had been doing something at Abilene Christian University, and word got back to Lubbock. His teaching was transformational. I went to see Don preach a series of meetings in Roswell, New Mexico, while I was still fifteen. Don took time to meet with me over lunch, and he encouraged me to start memorizing large passages of Scripture. I went home and immediately went to work on Philippians.

Later, when I went to Lipscomb University in Nashville, I attended the church where Don preached. I remember so many of his sermons and teachings over forty years later. While in my twenties, I asked my local Houston church to bring Don in to speak about worship. Fast forward to when I was sixty, I knew that Don was still quite active. Although he had long retired from preaching, he was involved in training up and placing missionaries in Muslim countries. I reached out to Don and asked him to come lecture at our library in Houston. I wanted him to speak about how to grow old gracefully before God. He titled his message "Don't Retire, Refire!"

In that message, Don went through Paul's list of vices in today's verses. Don explained that these sins needed to be dealt with as a young person, or at least by middle age. Don said that if you don't deal with anger as a young man, you grow into an angry old man. If you don't deal with bitterness early, you grow into a bitter old man. If you don't deal with sexual immorality, you grow into a dirty old man.

How do we deal with these things? Paul explains it, as Don echoed centuries later: we walk by the Spirit. What does that mean? The Spirit convicts us of the truth of Christ's forgiveness on the cross. We bring our "desires of the flesh," as Paul calls them, to God in Christ. We pray and work with the Spirit not only to *not* do them but to do the good deeds of the Spirit instead. "Idle hands are the devil's workshop" isn't a quotation from the Bible. But it's certainly true!

Lord, keep me busy doing right before you, and grow me out of the desires of the flesh, please. In Jesus, amen.

FEBRUARY 3

But the fruit of the Spirit is love, joy, peace, patience, kindness, goodness, faithfulness, gentleness, self-control; against such things there is no law. And those who belong to Christ Jesus have crucified the flesh with its passions and desires. (Gal. 5:22–24)

Buying fruit at the grocery store is too easy, especially with watermelons. You can't pick up just any melon; instead, you look at the stem (is it still green or old and shriveled?), thump the melon for a ripe hollow sound, and check to see how wide any stripes might be. But if the melon is in the store, the odds are it is edible. Not so much the melons you might grow at home. I have had a watermelon patch for years, and I still struggle to figure out when they are ripe. All of them have their stems connected, so that won't do. As for thumping, I'm sorry, but I find they often all sound the same. I rely primarily on size, but I confess, I have picked many that aren't ready and are inedible.

Fruit grows from the inside out. That is one reason I find it hard to see which melon is ripe. While that makes watermelon picking tough, it also provides insight into Paul's agricultural metaphor in today's passage.

Paul speaks of the "fruit" of the Spirit. These are traits that grow from the inside out of those who walk by the Spirit. God's Spirit indwells the believer. One of his tasks is to transform us from who we are into who we can be. Jesus promised the Spirit would come to help us keep God's instructions (Jn. 14:15–17), adding that the Spirit would convict the believer of sin and righteousness (Jn. 16:8). The Spirit guides the believer into truth (Jn. 16:13). These works of the Spirit occur inside each believer, but their evidence is seen by others in how we act, in what we prioritize, and in our efforts to treat others as Jesus would.

So Paul writes of the evidence of the Spirit on the outside of a ripe, mature believer. The world will readily see one who loves God and others. Christians should be known by their love. They should grow through the Spirit in joy and peace. Mature believers treat others with kindness. They should be growing in being gentle and good. Hallmarks of believers should be self-control and faithfulness. As believers ripen and grow in these things, their fruit will become obvious to all. No one should have difficulty picking out a mature Christian.

Lord, grow your Spirit in me. I crave the Spirit's fruit! In Jesus' name, I pray, amen.

FEBRUARY 4

Brothers, if anyone is caught in any transgression, you who are spiritual should restore him in a spirit of gentleness. Keep watch on yourself, lest you too be tempted. Bear one another's burdens, and so fulfill the law of Christ. (Gal. 6:1–3)

Having four daughters can radically improve one's prayer life. I watched boys come and go in each of their lives as I prayerfully wondered who God had in mind for them. I can report that God put amazing men in the lives of each. A common thread that runs through all four sons-in-law is their quick desire and ability to see what tasks need help and jump in to do them. When my daughters' husbands are around, I must be on my A game, or they will unload every bag, open every door, go last in every line, fix every problem, and take care of anything else that needs attention. Amazing, really.

Community life can be a struggle or a blessing. Paul wanted his readers to find the blessing in community life. He wrote in previous chapters how Christians should grow in the fruit of the Spirit rather than feed on the desires of the flesh. Then as he turns to wrapping up his letter, he discusses how the community looks out for and takes care of one another.

Paul knew some would stumble in life. He wasn't referencing belligerent, high-handed, and defiant sin, like he does in other writings. Here, Paul writes of people getting caught up in sin. They had stepped wrong in life and lost their footing. This is the imagery for Paul's word translated "transgression" (*paraptōma*—παράπτωμα). Paul says that when this happens, true Christian community should see it and step in to help the transgressor.

Community life has a purpose. That purpose includes knowing others in the community well enough to recognize when they need help and then giving that help. Sometimes, even in our churches, we live insular lives where people aren't close enough to see the needs of others. Close fellowship takes cultivating, and it is important we do so. One day we might be the people in need; one day we may be the ones able to help others in need. Paul's concern was over missteps, but that shouldn't be the limit of community support. It rightly extends to other needs. Every community needs a tranche of my sons-in-law—people willing and able to step in and help wherever there is need. (I am remiss if I don't add that my sole daughter-in-law does so as well!)

Lord, thank you for helpers. Give me eyes where I can be an aid in Jesus, amen.

FEBRUARY 5

Do not be deceived: God is not mocked, for whatever one sows, that will he also reap. For the one who sows to his own flesh will from the flesh reap corruption, but the one who sows to the Spirit will from the Spirit reap eternal life. And let us not grow weary of doing good, for in due season we will reap, if we do not give up. So then, as we have opportunity, let us do good to everyone, and especially to those who are of the household of faith. (Gal. 6:7–10)

When I was young, I was a fairly decent player of speed chess—normal chess but with a time element. Each player had five minutes in which to complete the game. If one's clock ran out—that is, they spent all five of their allotted minutes—he or she lost. It was game over, regardless of who was ahead. As I have aged, my speed chess ability has taken a hit. Sometimes, in the flurry of making fast moves, I miss the most obvious move or make a genuine blunder. I have given away my queen by not seeing what was plainly before me.

Overlooking the obvious doesn't happen only in chess. Spiritually, we often miss what we should all readily know and acknowledge. I put Paul's passage today in that category. As I read it, I think, "Well, duh! Of course this is true. I know that!" Yet I find that my life doesn't always show that I know it. I blunder on this in the most obvious ways—repeatedly.

Paul points out the gardening maxim that you reap what you sow. If I put tomato seeds into my garden, I would be a fool to think I will one day harvest cucumbers. Tomato seeds make tomatoes. Cucumber seeds make cucumbers. Obviously.

This same maxim applies spiritually. For it to be otherwise would make a mockery of God. God certainly isn't short on vision or attention. Nothing we do goes unseen by him. So Paul wants his readers to read the obvious: God watches, God knows, and God will see to consequences.

Today will provide many opportunities to interact with people. My deeds are seeds sown not only in the lives of those I see but also in my own life. This means that not only are my deeds important, but so are my attitudes. God is watching. The garden of my life needs more deliberateness than my speed chess of late. I want to make the right moves and sow a garden of joy and love. The harvest will be great!

Lord, help me sow love and joy around me today. In Jesus' name, amen.

FEBRUARY 6

But far be it from me to boast except in the cross of our Lord Jesus Christ, by which the world has been crucified to me, and I to the world. For neither circumcision counts for anything, nor uncircumcision, but a new creation. And as for all who walk by this rule, peace and mercy be upon them, and upon the Israel of God. (Gal. 6:14–16)

Dr. Harvey Floyd, one of my Greek professors, told us a parable once: A good man died and found himself in line before Saint Peter, standing at the pearly gates. The good man overheard the interactions between Peter and the fellow before him in line. Peter told the fellow it took one thousand points to get into heaven. Overhearing this, the good man felt relieved. He had been, after all, very good in his life.

As the good man reached his place before Peter, Peter told him, "It takes one thousand points to get in here." The good man replied with a great list of things he had done in his life—helping the weak and the poor, loving his neighbor as himself, conducting his business affairs with honesty and integrity. Just to be careful, the good man listed two thousand good deeds. Peter was gobsmacked! With eyes open wide, Peter exclaimed, "Wow! That is incredibly impressive! We haven't had anyone this good in a long time! I'm going to give you a point for that!"

The good man was stunned. He had listed thousands of truly good deeds, and he only got a point. He started to sweat a bit but then remembered that he failed to list all the sins he avoided. The good man said, "Oh, and also, I didn't do any of the big ones. No murdering, no adultery, no gossiping . . ." On and on the man listed sins he avoided, and Peter's mouth dropped open. All Peter could reply was "Your memory is truly amazing. I'm giving you another point!" The man was at a loss. Realizing what he'd left out, starting with his family and moving to his church, he listed even more good deeds he'd done. Stunned, Peter offered one more point. The exasperated man said to Peter, "I've given you a lifetime of millions of good deeds, and all you've given me is three points. I need one thousand? How but by the grace of God does anyone get in there?" At this, Peter said, "And now you have your one thousand points."

God's grace, which is the death of Christ in our stead, is our sole ground for pride in this life. Nothing else accords for anything. To God alone be the glory.

Lord, I boast in the cross, in your unlimited love for me. I live and pray in Jesus, amen.

FEBRUARY 7

To the church of the Thessalonians in God the Father and the Lord Jesus Christ: Grace to you and peace. We give thanks to God always for all of you, constantly mentioning you in our prayers, remembering before our God and Father your work of faith and labor of love and steadfastness of hope in our Lord Jesus Christ. (1 Thess. 1:1–3)

Another Dr. Floyd story: For decades, Dr. Floyd taught Japanese students better English by using the Bible. He grew quite close to many of them, and in his older years, Dr. Floyd had a chance to visit several of them in Japan. After one nice visit, Dr. Floyd was to take the train to another city for another visit. The student he had been seeing insisted on not only taking Dr. Floyd to the station but actually riding the train with him to make sure he got off at the right stop. "It is my obligation," the student explained. After Dr. Floyd completed the next visit, that student too insisted on accompanying Dr. Floyd not only to the station but to the next city. Rather than describing it as an obligation, however, this student exclaimed, "It would be my honor."

Dr. Floyd noted the difference in how those two interactions made him feel. With the first, Dr. Floyd felt bad for imposing on the student. With the second, Dr. Floyd felt joy over the student finding honor in accompanying him. Dr. Floyd said he had applied this principle at home—when his wife Virginia asked him to do something, he noted that the reception was much different if he replied, "Virginia, it is my obligation," versus, "Virginia, it is my honor!"

Dr. Floyd told us this as he asked us to focus on these verses penned by Paul. Paul doesn't say, "Work and labor as your obligation to the God who saved you!" Paul fondly remembered the Thessalonians noting that the work they did for God proceeded from their faith and trust in God. Their labors on God's behalf came out of their love for God.

I like this theologically. Paul's theology is tight here, as our works before God never merit us God's love or salvation. God chose to love us and save us in Christ long before we were even born. Practically, I like this as well. I want to serve God out of loving faith, not obligation. Aside from being good theology, I find this attitude changes me!

Lord, I give you my day, my energy, my thoughts, my opportunities, and my service. It is my honor to do so in Jesus, amen.

FEBRUARY 8

For we know, brothers loved by God, that he has chosen you, because our gospel came to you not only in word, but also in power and in the Holy Spirit and with full conviction. (1 Thess. 1:4–5)

We used to play a lot of basketball at work. At the time, our firm was in two different locations in Houston, Texas. Each location would gather up a team of five, and we'd head to the gym shortly after work. It had gotten quite competitive.

Then, one day, I got a call from the athletic director at Texas Tech. He mentioned that one of Tech's top basketball players had recently retired after a decade as a pro player. The fellow had moved to Houston and wanted to get a job coaching high school basketball. The AD wondered if I might help with contacts. I explained I would be glad to help, but first I needed the ex-pro to bring his basketball shoes and shorts and come to my law firm about an hour before quitting time. I was going to put him through his paces.

The affable fellow showed up, and I explained the setup. I wanted the man to make a copy of a document for me. Then we were going to head to the gym. We were going to play five on five against my other law office, and I was going to introduce him as a new fellow we had working in the copy room. He was to wait till the time was right and then take over the game. Take over the game he did!!! He was *awesome*! The AD had told me he was good, but "good" doesn't do justice to what he could do. He would have won a game of five on one.

That experience reminds me of Paul's passage today. Paul had personally preached the gospel to the Thessalonians. This gospel related the truth that in Jerusalem, almost one thousand miles away and over a decade earlier, Jesus Christ was crucified and, three days later, resurrected by the power of God! Jesus did this to redeem people from sin, dying as a substitute and as a sacrifice for others.

The Thessalonians received this message, but not in words only. The message came with life-changing power and conviction of the Holy Spirit. This is the way of God's truth. God isn't after our brains alone; God wants to transform our lives. God's Spirit works powerfully in our lives. Not unlike our basketball that day, one can *see* a real difference when God is present and allowed to work in us.

Lord, come into my heart in powerful and transforming ways. In Jesus, amen.

FEBRUARY 9

For not only has the word of the Lord sounded forth from you in Macedonia and Achaia, but your faith in God has gone forth everywhere, so that we need not say anything. For they themselves report concerning us the kind of reception we had among you, and how you turned to God from idols to serve the living and true God, and to wait for his Son from heaven, whom he raised from the dead, Jesus who delivers us from the wrath to come. (1 Thess. 1:8–10)

Most people have five senses—sight, hearing, smell, touch, and taste. These senses gather information from the world around us and send that to the brain. The brain then processes the data to understand what is around us. In this way, our brains figure out danger and safety, our brains learn and grow, our brains instill in us drive, emotion, plans, ideas, inspirations, and much more.

Two of those five senses are especially adept at gathering data about other people. We can hear what others are doing. As I type this, I have a high school reunion around the corner. My fellow alums are populating social media with efforts to locate people and get them to the reunion. Once there, a good deal of conversations will occur as we find out what others have been doing and how their lives are going. We will hear, but we will also see. We can see how people have aged and get clues to how their lives have unfolded.

Paul knew that what people do—how they live, their priorities and convictions—not only is distinct to everyone but also is observed by others. Other people will be watching and listening. They will gather data about you and me and process that data. That data will transform them, for better or worse.

Paul had brought a life-transforming message about Jesus to the community of Thessalonica, which is in northern Greece. Paul had been forced to leave rather abruptly and was having to keep up through what he heard about the Thessalonians. And the reports that came to Paul were great! The faith of the Thessalonians was seen and heard by their neighbors and many others. God was at work in mighty ways. Their faith had grown strong. More and more were learning about Jesus and seeing the way God could transform their lives. Paul rejoices over this news.

Not only do we assimilate data in our brains and change our own lives, but those around us receive data on us too. We change their lives for better or worse. I want to do better.

Lord, let me live in ways that draw others to you. May I shine Jesus, I pray, amen.

FEBRUARY 10

We had boldness in our God to declare to you the gospel of God. . . . For our appeal does not spring from error or impurity or any attempt to deceive, but just as we have been approved by God to be entrusted with the gospel, so we speak, not to please man, but to please God who tests our hearts. For we never came with words of flattery, as you know, nor with a pretext for greed—God is witness. Nor did we seek glory from people, whether from you or from others, though we could have made demands as apostles of Christ. (1 Thess. 2:2–6)

Throughout decades of practicing law, I've seen it all—or at least a lot of it! I've seen people lie for money, manipulate out of greed, and preen in their pomposity. You find a motive for personal gain at others' expense, and I've seen it.

I'm sure the first century was no different. Thessalonica was a bustling port city in northern Greece. While today, ships sail directly to their destination, in Paul's day, the ships would hug the coast, stopping in a port almost every night. So any port city like Thessalonica typically received a great deal of traffic. With that traffic came salesmen—people hawking one idea or another and selling secret elixirs or secrets to life. When Paul showed up, he might have seemed like "just another one."

But Paul was different. Paul's pitch was unusual. He spoke of a Jewish man named Jesus, who was killed in the far away city of Jerusalem and resurrected to live again. This Jesus was the answer to life and its problems in the here and now and for eternity. Jesus had ascended to heaven but would be coming back, ending this age and bringing eternal life or eternal judgment to everyone.

Paul's difference from the daily supply of hucksters wasn't just his unusual message but also what came at the end of the message. Paul never asked for a dime. Paul didn't seek anything from anyone except a repentant and trusting heart in God. Paul wasn't getting praise or glory himself. He sought only God's glory. Paul's message, as absurd as it might sound, was confirmed by his actions, but the real reason the message was received was that the Holy Spirit would scream its truth into the hearts and minds of the Thessalonians.

As I read and reflect on this passage, it challenges me to examine my motives for today. I should live for God's message, not for what I get out of it.

Lord, give me insight into serving you with pure motives. In Jesus' name, amen.

FEBRUARY 11

But we were gentle among you, like a nursing mother taking care of her own children. So, being affectionately desirous of you, we were ready to share with you not only the gospel of God but also our own selves, because you had become very dear to us. . . . For you know how, like a father with his children, we exhorted each one of you and encouraged you and charged you to walk in a manner worthy of God, who calls you into his own kingdom and glory. (1 Thess. 2:7–8, 11–12)

Becky and I have five children of our own, a son and four daughters. We treasure them, as my parents treasured me and my two sisters. Parent-child relationships are unique. No other relationship is quite like them.

I find it interesting that Paul quickly, in just a few sentences, compares his sentiments toward the Thessalonians to those of a parent, using the analogy of both a mother and father. Like a mother, Paul was gently teaching about Jesus, seeking the best for his "children"—those who came to faith. Like a father, Paul exhorts them to live and go about their business in a holy way before God. The two parental roles were natural analogies for Paul, as he felt great affection for those who knew Jesus as Lord. Faith is a transformational process. Because he played a role in God's calling to others, Paul participated in their spiritual birth, resulting in a special bond with the Thessalonians.

Through that bond, Paul worked to help the Thessalonians grow in holiness and righteousness before God. Paul's parental affection was expressed not only in how he treated them but also in his letter. The letter reflects Paul's deep love for them. He didn't simply hammer out an email or draft a quick note of encouragement. He had to obtain writing supplies, and he likely found another to help him write the letter. Once written, he had to find a trustworthy messenger who would travel over 350 miles from Corinth (where scholars believe he wrote the letter) to deliver the letter to Thessalonica. Paul cared a great deal.

Paul's care challenges me to work harder on this book. I wrote my first devotional/teaching book for my children, wanting to gift them a thought each day from their dad. Baylor grabbed the book and published it (*Psalms for Living*), which led to a second, third, fourth, and now this fifth. Each is a book of love, seeking to bring God's message to you and others. May we all live with family care and concern for the kingdom of God!

Lord, give us a heart for your message and those who hear it. In Jesus, amen.

FEBRUARY 12

And we also thank God constantly for this, that when you received the word of God, which you heard from us, you accepted it not as the word of men but as what it really is, the word of God, which is at work in you believers. (1 Thess. 2:13)

We were building a "learning center." This facility would have over forty thousand square feet of classrooms and meeting spaces. During construction, we were asked whether the building could be used to host an upcoming conference of 350 college professors set about six months out. We boldly agreed to do it, expecting we could get the building done. In retrospect, we had a good nine months of work to be done in that six-month period. The crews were often working day and night trying to get the building ready.

Sometimes the work was frustrating. Watching it moment by moment, it seemed it would never get done in time. Yet gradually, as the crews labored long hours, the building began to take shape. I can report we finished with eighteen hours to spare!

The hard work of building the learning center comes to mind as I meditate on today's passage. Paul explains that the "word of God" is at "work" in the life of the believer. The Greek verb Paul chose, *energeō* (ἐνεργέω), comes into modern English in our word *energy*. The word denotes putting one's capabilities into operation. It means working, being active, and being effective. It describes what our crews were doing with the learning center, but here in Paul's letter, it is no human being doing the work. It is the word of God.

Something profound happens as we learn and pray through God's word. It is why each devotional starts with a passage of Scripture. This book isn't a selection of stories and metaphors to aid one in better living. I seek to produce a book that draws focus to and elucidates God's word. The word has an amazing power to work in the life of the person who brings it into their mind and heart.

Like a building project that may last for years, we may not notice the transforming power of God's word in the moment. But we can be sure that over time, God uses his word to create a changed life. As I spend time in God's word, I am changed. God is at work in me and you. God works to accomplish God's plans, intent on shaping us into what we can become. I am committed to spending more time in God's word.

Lord, put your word to work in me. Create in me what you will, and put me to work as you see fit, all to your glory and in Jesus' name, amen.

FEBRUARY 13

Therefore when we could bear it no longer, we were willing to be left behind at Athens alone, and we sent Timothy, our brother and God's coworker in the gospel of Christ, to establish and exhort you in your faith, that no one be moved by these afflictions. For you yourselves know that we are destined for this. (1 Thess. 3:1–3)

Cognitive psychology fascinates me. The field probes how people think and make decisions. Those working in that discipline have developed the phrase "status quo bias." Using the common Latin phrase *status quo*, which literally means "where things stand," the phrase describes the human tendency to prefer things remain the same. To varying degrees, many people don't like change. Some even fear it.

But the Christian life is one of change. God finds each of us where we are and takes us to where we are meant to be. Change doesn't come easy, nor is it accomplished overnight. Think about what God needs to change in your life.

When people place their faith in Jesus as their Lord, their commitment to follow Jesus will change their attitudes and priorities. That change can alter relationships—even family dynamics. As priorities shift, where you go, what you do, and how you do it will be different. You no longer treat others the same. You seek to serve and love in new ways. Life is no longer about *you* but about your neighbor. Accountability takes on a new meaning. You find a need to apologize and make up for the ways you have hurt others. You try to forgive those who have wronged you, knowing forgiveness is a hallmark of a Christ follower.

These changes are difficult, running contrary to that psychological makeup that finds comfort in the status quo, even if the present isn't great. Yet God sends his Holy Spirit to aid the believer in making these changes. The Holy Spirit works in the believer's heart as a comforter. Jesus promised, "I will ask the Father, and he will give you another Helper, to be with you forever" (Jn. 14:16). The noun Jesus used for "Helper" comes from the same roots as the verb Paul uses in today's verse of sending Timothy to *exhort*—a form of helping—the Thessalonians in their faith. God works directly in the believer, but God also works through others all for the purpose of helping each believer better walk and grow in Jesus.

Change may not be easy, but I know change is coming. God will not leave me as I am. He is going to make me better. He will grow me in holiness.

Lord, thank you for change, even though it is hard. Work in me in Jesus. Amen.

FEBRUARY 14

But now that Timothy has come to us from you, and has brought us the good news of your faith and love and reported that you always remember us kindly and long to see us, as we long to see you—for this reason, brothers, in all our distress and affliction we have been comforted about you through your faith. For now we live, if you are standing fast in the Lord. For what thanksgiving can we return to God for you, for all the joy that we feel for your sake before our God. (1 Thess. 3:6–9)

Social media has made me adjust my language. A recent example comes to mind. I asked a friend if they had talked to so-and-so recently. My friend said, "No, I haven't." I replied, "I wonder how so-and-so is doing." My friend said, "Well, quite well, it seems. So-and-so got a new job, moved to Cincinnati, and is really embracing life." I asked, "How do you know all this?" to which my friend replied, "Oh, I follow so-and-so on social media!" Well, of course.

Paul wrote in an era before social media. If Paul wanted to know how someone in another city was doing, he had to ask another person to go find out. It was a big ask: to interrupt one's life to travel by foot many miles and weeks just to determine how someone else was doing. Yet Paul sent Timothy, likely from Athens or Corinth, back to Thessalonica to check in on the new believers there. Paul wanted to know how they were doing. Paul wanted to know if their faith stood strong against the winds that seek to unmoor us in life. Paul was invested in the Thessalonians. They were important to Paul.

As I read today's passage, I reflect on the lives of those around me. Many people are points of contact that seem to come and go. But I am invested in some. God placed certain people in my life with whom I have deeper connections.

With these people, it is important that I stay plugged in. I'm not good at it. I'm one of those people who attends to what is immediately before me. Out of sight can mean out of mind if I'm not careful. Even when time is scarce, a simple note of encouragement, a text checking in, a quick call, or an email can show interest and care for others. It also can aid me in my prayers for others.

Paul knew that investing in others brought not only change in their lives but also joy and encouragement to Paul. This is part of God's system of community. It needs to be a bigger part of my life.

Lord, help me be better at plugging in and loving others. In Jesus' name, amen.

FEBRUARY 15

Now may our God and Father himself, and our Lord Jesus, direct our way to you, and may the Lord make you increase and abound in love for one another and for all, as we do for you, so that he may establish your hearts blameless in holiness before our God and Father, at the coming of our Lord Jesus with all his saints. (1 Thess. 3:11–13)

Recently, at a men's retreat, I observed firsthand how two godly men spend their mornings. Both arose and immediately went for two things: coffee and the Bible. Each would find a quiet place alone to read, pray, and take notes—much like I start my day, although you can keep the coffee. I have no use for that.

One of these men, Jarrett, stopped his reading to show me something. In his Bible, he had made extensive notes over the years. He often dated the notes. Jarrett showed me a passage in the Psalms that he had prayed over and over, noting his prayers in the margins.

Praying the Bible is a marvelous thing. Mechanically, it is quite easy. One finds a meaningful passage and turns those phrases into prayers. With some passages it is easier than others, but all these prayers can be significant and meaningful. Today's passage is an easy one to pray.

Paul prays for the Thessalonians today. Paul offers a prayer that we can easily pray for those important to us. As I write on Paul's prayer, I ask that you, the reader, internally ask God, "For whom can I pray this?" See if God doesn't put someone on your mind, and then read on as you internally pray for that person.

Paul prays that God will give him more future interaction with the Thessalonians. But whether God does or not, Paul asks God to help them grow in their love and community. Paul wanted them to have good relationships that aided their walks with the Lord. Paul prayed that God would "establish [their] hearts blameless in holiness." In other words, Paul wanted those for whom he prayed to be purified in the ways they think, feel, and behave.

Paul offers us a model for our prayers for others. Let's pray for those dear to us.

Lord, I pray for [fill in the blank]. Give me chances to interact with them to your glory. Grow them in your love for all. Give them hearts and minds to follow you more closely. Bless them in Jesus, I pray, amen.

FEBRUARY 16

Finally, then, brothers, we ask and urge you in the Lord Jesus, that as you received from us how you ought to walk and to please God, just as you are doing, that you do so more and more. . . . For this is the will of God, your sanctification: that you abstain from sexual immorality; that each one of you know how to control his own body in holiness and honor, not in the passion of lust like the Gentiles who do not know God; that no one transgress and wrong his brother in this matter. . . . For God has not called us for impurity, but in holiness. (1 Thess. 4:1–7)

My sister is a potter. She can take a lump of clay and turn it into almost anything. Watching her work at her wheel is amazing. Her hands shape and mold the clay into a plate, a bowl, a pitcher, or even a sculpture. If the clay has a fault, and the result isn't what she needs, Kathryn can always remold the clay, taking it back to a lump shape and refashioning it into what it is supposed to be.

Kathryn at the wheel reminds me a bit of the Christian walk. God created humanity in his "image" or "likeness" (Gen. 1:27). People were made to walk around and reflect God's likeness. Look at Adam and Eve, and you were to see a reasonable reflection of God. Yet sin entered the scene, and the image was marred. Humanity took a turn for the worse, and one could barely see God in Adam and Eve rebelling, in Cain murdering Abel, and in people's multitude of sins. God's holiness was basically gone.

Yet God didn't leave flawed clay. God set about giving humanity a new birth, making people a new creation in Christ. This means that you and I in Christ are being reshaped by God into a more perfect representation of his holiness. So Paul tells the Thessalonians in today's passage, "Keep up the good work!" But Paul adds that they are to grow more and more.

God cares about us. We aren't simply lumps of clay that he leaves to dry in a flawed shape. A master potter, he sets before us his instructions for growing into what we can be. Paul knew that we aren't passive clay but active participants in this process. So Paul urges his readers to pay attention. Sexual purity is his first example in this chapter. Paul reinforces his earlier teaching that life isn't about what we want. We live to please God. As we do so, as we follow his morality, we begin to reflect his image more accurately. This transformation is good and right.

Lord, help me walk in purity, seeking to model you in my life. In Jesus, amen.

FEBRUARY 17

Now concerning brotherly love you have no need for anyone to write to you, for you yourselves have been taught by God to love one another, for that indeed is what you are doing to all the brothers throughout Macedonia. But we urge you, brothers, to do this more and more, and to aspire to live quietly, and to mind your own affairs, and to work with your hands, as we instructed you, so that you may walk properly before outsiders and be dependent on no one. (1 Thess. 4:9–12)

I had a zealous friend who wanted to be so in sync with God's will that he would even pray to ask what God wanted him to order at Whataburger. He thought that God had a specific and perfect plan for the smallest detail of each day. His job was to find out what that was and then do it. I think my friend was missing out on what it means to be a human.

Yes, as a follower of God, I agree we should always seek God's will in big things and small things, but I also think that many times, God gives us the ability to make choices—and assures us he will bless us in our choices. God will set up principles and guidelines, but he wants us to learn to use our minds in godly ways to put those principles to work. Hence I know I should eat healthily, and Whataburger might be a treat, not an every-meal affair. But whether I get one type of burger or another might be up to my discretion, not a target of God's will.

Think of Adam and his early job before God. Adam was given the chance to name all the animals: "Whatever the man called every living creature, that was its name" (Gen. 2:19). God wasn't intent on picking the particular name for a zebra. Adam got to make that choice.

In today's passage, Paul gives instructions for following God's will in everyday life, but Paul doesn't tell the reader to determine which color tunic to wear on Tuesday as per God's perfect will. Paul gives important guidelines that help believers live holy before God. Paul's first guideline is about attitude: love and serve one another more and more. Paul then urges the people to seek a life of satisfied and quiet accomplishment. Their lives were to be set not on flash and brilliance but dedicated holy work, doing what was before them each day. This was important for their growth and for their ministry. People should see that our goal in life isn't to have a marquee name but to serve God. Here we find godly zeal in walking each day focused on God and his love and loving others.

Lord, open my life to loving others and working to your glory. In Jesus, amen.

FEBRUARY 18

But we do not want you to be uninformed, brothers, about those who are asleep, that you may not grieve as others do who have no hope. For since we believe that Jesus died and rose again, even so, through Jesus, God will bring with him those who have fallen asleep. . . . Therefore encourage one another with these words. (1 Thess. 4:13–14, 18)

History flows at its own pace on earth. God promised Abraham that through his offspring would come one who would bless all nations. This was a prophecy of the coming of Jesus Christ. Yet Jesus didn't come for two thousand years.

Then Jesus told his followers, as he ascended to heaven, that he would come again, bring this world to its conclusion, and take his people into eternity with him. That was almost two thousand years ago, and it has yet to happen.

Paul started the church in Thessalonica, explaining to the fledgling believers that Jesus had died, was resurrected, ascended to heaven, and would come again to take his people with him. The believers thought the return of Jesus was imminent. They hadn't contemplated it might be a few thousand years away. As a result, some hit the panic button when some believers died before Jesus returned.

The Christian grief suddenly could turn more severe than that of their unbelieving neighbors. The Thessalonians thought that Jesus would return for the living but thought the dead might be gone forever. Paul wrote to disabuse them of this notion. The Christian shouldn't be grieving like the world. Jesus didn't abandon those who predeceased his return. They were resurrected. Although their physical bodies were decaying, Paul uses the metaphor that their bodies were merely sleeping. These people weren't lost to God. They were secure in God.

This should encourage all believers. God not only works in this life but secures us in Jesus for eternity. When the believer dies, it is as Jesus instructed the thief on the cross: "Today you will be with me in paradise" (Lk. 23:43). The body may be still, seemingly asleep, but God is holding the believer in ways we can't fathom. Then one day, we will experience a resurrected body when Jesus returns to claim all his people—those alive and those who are dead. Be comforted!

Lord, I still grieve the death of many loved ones, but I do so with joyful confidence that you hold them dear and will one day gather us all together in Jesus! Amen.

FEBRUARY 19

So then let us not sleep, as others do, but let us keep awake and be sober. . . . For God has not destined us for wrath, but to obtain salvation through our Lord Jesus Christ, who died for us so that whether we are awake or asleep we might live with him. (1 Thess. 5:6, 9–10)

It is 3:09 a.m. as I write this. That is early for some; it is typical for me. I might claim 1 Thessalonians 5:6 as my life verse—"Let us not sleep"—and admittedly, it fits well enough that I have memorized it in Greek. But Paul isn't indicating I should awaken early. I am taking his point out of context to apply it here. Paul is using a metaphor for being alert in this life.

Yet Paul has another line buried in today's passage that does belong in an important biblical context. Paul speaks of "living" with God, in life and death (i.e., "awake or asleep"). This is important to the overarching biblical narrative of God's purpose and destiny for human beings.

We were not made as disposable paper towels, here to serve God while we exist and then disposed of into the trash. We have massive value, being made in God's image so that we can walk with him, talk with him, love with him, and grow in him. This was the setting for Adam and Eve before sin entered the picture. It is the curse of sin that drives humanity from life with God.

God was never content to leave you and me in isolation, alive but spiritually dead, walking this earth for a moment in history, aimless and without his care. God knew all along he would need to come on a rescue mission, redeeming you and me from sin and its curse. God did so in the form of Jesus. In Jesus, God took on our sins and paid the eternal just price for that sin. God died in our stead.

God performed this act of love in Christ because he has a certain future for his people, whom he rightfully calls his "children." God our Father desires to dwell with us eternally. We are indwelt with his Spirit, and there will be a day when we can declare, "Behold, the dwelling of God is with humanity, and he will dwell with them" (Rev. 21:3; my translation).

This biblical narrative runs throughout the Bible. This context remains true, even at 3 a.m.!

Lord, I am stunned you want to live with me. "Thank you" is too meager. I love you. In Jesus, amen.

FEBRUARY 20

Be at peace among yourselves. And we urge you, brothers, admonish the idle, encourage the fainthearted, help the weak, be patient with them all. See that no one repays anyone evil for evil, but always seek to do good to one another and to everyone. Rejoice always, pray without ceasing, give thanks in all circumstances; for this is the will of God in Christ Jesus for you. Do not quench the Spirit. Do not despise prophecies, but test everything; hold fast what is good. Abstain from every form of evil. (1 Thess. 5:13–22)

I often go to the grocery store with a list of things to get and come home without everything. Typically, this happens because I fail to either check the list or cross off items as I get them. When I don't cross off the items, things get a bit fuzzy as to what I have and haven't gotten. My eyes tend to glaze over the list. Confession: I tend to do the same thing with passages like today's. Paul is nearing the end of his letter, and so in almost a written staccato, Paul machine-guns out a list of instructions. They come so rapidly and without explanation that I must force myself to read each carefully so I don't fuzz over the instructions.

Paul's final instructions don't need much explanation. They are plain. With the Holy Spirit's aid, we just need to do them! Look at them this way:

- Be at peace with others.
- Admonish the idle.
- Encourage the fainthearted.
- Help the weak.
- Be patient with everyone.
- Don't repay evil with evil.
- Seek to do good to all.
- Rejoice always.
- Pray without ceasing (keep an ongoing dialogue with God).
- Give thanks constantly.
- Don't quench the Holy Spirit.
- Hold fast to what is good.
- Abstain from evil.

Those instructions are a pretty good list for every day! That is a list I need!

Lord, remind me and strengthen me to walk in godliness today. In Jesus, amen.

FEBRUARY 21

Now may the God of peace himself sanctify you completely, and may your whole spirit and soul and body be kept blameless at the coming of our Lord Jesus Christ. He who calls you is faithful; he will surely do it. (1 Thess. 5:23–24)

My sister Kathryn is an artist. In the main, she makes her art with clay. Her sculptures grace our home and garden, as well as my office. To make those art pieces, she takes clay and fashions it with precision. Out of the same clay, she also makes a mean pot or set of dishes. She can sculpt the clay for whatever purpose she determines. By itself, the clay isn't suitable for art or dishes, but with her touch, it transforms into something special.

What my sister does with clay is a great way to look at the biblical word *sanctify*. In today's passage, Paul prays that God himself will "sanctify" the Thessalonians "completely." The idea behind the word *sanctify* (in Greek *hagiazo*—ἁγιάζω) is to make something suitable or appropriate for use before God. As something is sanctified, anything incompatible with purity or holiness is removed. To use a gardening metaphor, it means pulling out all the weeds in one's life.

Paul's prayer is that God himself would work in the Thessalonians to shape them into holy vessels. He is asking God to work in their lives to pull out the weeds and make them pristine. Paul prays this with confidence that God will do that very thing. Paul knows God is reliable to do that to which he sets his hand.

This means that you and I are positioned marvelously. God doesn't merely forgive us of sins and take us into his presence. God works in our lives to clean us up. He wants us to be better and better each day. He sets himself to the task of giving us clean hearts. He works transformation in our minds.

This explains a lot in life. Some of the work God does involves chopping off lumps of clay that don't fit in the final sculpture. When my sister does this, the clay doesn't resist or yelp in pain! I find that I'm not so pliable. Sometimes I complain to God, as growth doesn't always come easily or without pain. But despite my occasional whining, he teaches and grows me, and I am deeply grateful.

Lord, thank you for staying involved in my life. Please do your work to make me suitable for your purposes. I live to love and serve you. In Jesus' name, amen.

FEBRUARY 22

Paul, Silvanus, and Timothy, To the church of the Thessalonians in God our Father and the Lord Jesus Christ: Grace to you and peace from God our Father and the Lord Jesus Christ. (2 Thess. 1:1–2)

In 1971, four sisters in Philadelphia, Pennsylvania, got together to form a singing group, Sister Sledge. The Sledge girls hit it big with the top-ten-hit song "We Are Family" in 1979. The lyrics are great: "We are family; I got all my sisters with me. . . . We walk together as we walk on by, and we fly just like birds of a feather, I won't tell no lie. All of the people around us, they say, 'Can they be that close?' Just let me state for the record, we're giving love in a family dose."

Family is important to people today, and it was in Paul's time too. In the Greek/Latin culture of Paul's day, the family unit rotated around the oldest living male, who was called the *pater* in Latin (or "father"). The father had authority *over* the family as well as responsibility *for* the family. Termed the *paterfamilias* in Latin, the father of the family had absolute rule over the household and held the title to all the family property. No matter their ages, sons couldn't own family property until their father died. The father even had the authority to keep or abandon a child born into the family.

Paul's address of this letter wouldn't go unnoticed by his readers in the Greek and Latin world. Twice, Paul terms God as "our Father." This is an awesome affirmation, worth contemplating. God is not a poor Father who abandons his children. God is a loving and caring Father who provides for his children. God gives instruction and teaching. He protects and guards his children. That doesn't mean nothing hurtful befalls a child of God, but it means that God works with whatever happens and that God doesn't allow more than his children can handle *when they rely on him!*

Paul's affirmation of God as "our" Father goes even a step further. Paul loops all the believers together in one big family under the Paterfamilias, the Father of the family. Like Sister Sledge affirms, we are family! We walk together, fly together, and live life together. This is a blessing that makes life's highs higher and gives aid and support in the low times. Paul's affirmation wasn't new to Paul. Jesus himself taught his followers to pray to *our* Father. This is family life!

Father, thank you for taking us in as children. May we proudly bear your name before a watching world and do so united as your children. In Jesus, amen.

FEBRUARY 23

We ought always to give thanks to God for you, brothers, as is right, because your faith is growing abundantly, and the love of every one of you for one another is increasing. . . . To this end we always pray for you, that our God may make you worthy of his calling and may fulfill every resolve for good and every work of faith by his power, so that the name of our Lord Jesus may be glorified in you, and you in him, according to the grace of our God and the Lord Jesus Christ. (2 Thess. 1:3, 11–12)

I am writing this in the summer, and it is so blistering hot outside. (Yes, I realize this devotional is set to be read in the middle of winter, but stick with me here!) The thermometer reads 104 degrees. Now the thermometer reading 104 degrees isn't what makes it hot outside. It's hot whether or not I have a thermometer. The thermometer simply shows what is already there.

In the same way, looking at one's prayer life can indicate much about that person's spiritual life. People's prayer lives reveal insight into their walk with the Lord, priorities in life, cares and concerns, and more. This is why I tend to focus in on passages like we have today.

Early in this second letter of Paul's to the Thessalonians, Paul details two areas of his prayer life. First, Paul prayed thanks for the Thessalonians and their growing faith and love. Paul knew that faith is the source of a good and vibrant life in the Lord. The more we trust God and his guidance in life, the richer and more fruitful our lives will be. Paul sees this abundant faith being expressed in the growing love and fellowship of the church. They were plugging into one another's lives in ways that made everyone better.

Second, Paul prays that God would work in these believers to grow their holiness. Paul wants them to be all they can be before God and do all they can do for God. Paul sees this as a way Jesus will be glorified and lifted up in each person, in the church, in the community, and in the world.

These are good prayers for me, but they are also good goals. I want to thank God for the faithful and pray for them to grow. But I also want to be among the faithful growing to God. These prayers inspire me.

Lord, lift up the faithful, and strengthen us all in Jesus, amen.

FEBRUARY 24

This is evidence of the righteous judgment of God, that you may be considered worthy of the kingdom of God, for which you are also suffering. (2 Thess. 1:5)

Almost every workday finds me doing something associated with a courtroom trial. I'm not actually in court each day, as most work for the courtroom happens outside the courtroom. But I am constantly accumulating evidence and analyzing and evaluating it for trial. I must figure out how to get that evidence before the court so that a just result can occur in each of my cases.

Paul was trained as a lawyer—albeit the first-century Jewish court system was very different from modern courts in the Western world. Paul well knew judicial language and concepts. It isn't a coincidence that Paul assembles three judicial words in rapid order in today's passage.

Paul speaks of "evidence" of God's "righteous judgment." *Evidence* was then what it is today. It is facts and data that indicate the truth of one thing or another. *Righteous* is the adjective form of what is considered "just" or "fair" in a courtroom setting. *Judgment* refers to the legal decision in a courtroom case.

These three courtroom terms in rapid succession capture my trial lawyer's attention. I find something remarkable here. Paul finds evidence of God's righteous judgment in the way suffering is manifested and in the way God handles it. Paul's subsequent sentences detail that God isn't going to allow those who afflict others to escape his punishment. A day will come when Jesus returns, and those who aren't found repentant in Jesus will suffer for the ways they hurt others. God will be just in his judgment.

Likewise, those who know God, who are found in an intimate relationship with him by hearing the gospel of Jesus and responding in faith, will have a different end from this world of suffering. The faithful will find God's comfort amid hurt, pain, and difficulty. God intervenes and brings rest to the weary.

God's intervention for his children is also evidence of God's just judgments. For God has already punished the sins of the faithful by substituting the death of Jesus on everyone's behalf. This gives me a fresh perspective on our just God.

Lord, as the just judge, I pray for forgiveness in Jesus. Please work in my life to help others discover his love and forgiveness for them. In his name, amen.

FEBRUARY 25

The coming of the lawless one is by the activity of Satan with all power and false signs and wonders, and with all wicked deception for those who are perishing, because they refused to love the truth and so be saved. Therefore God sends them a strong delusion, so that they may believe what is false. (2 Thess. 2:9–11)

Some people reading this book will believe in "predestination"—that God determines who will receive and respond to his gospel with saving faith. Others who read this book will believe that everyone makes the individual choice of whether to trust in Jesus for redemption. The choice is ours, not God's. Still a third group of readers will not care one way or the other. Today's passage is instructive to all three groups.

Paul addresses a perplexing problem about Christian faith. Why is it that everyone doesn't accept the glorious truth that there *is* a God who loves us; God's nature is pure, and to live with God we must be equally pure; Jesus died on the cross to pay a just penalty for our sins; as we trust in the death, it becomes attributed to us; and we then join in the resurrection of Jesus? Why do some people decide to live in a false reality that denies the truth of God and his love expressed in Christ?

Paul indicates that God sends people a strong delusion so that they might believe what is false. If Paul said that in isolation, it might make us question God's love for all people. Yet Paul first explains that this delusion is sent *to those who refuse to love the truth and so be saved.* God is at work, but God's work is based on choices made by each person. No one need ever think God is unfair, for anyone who wants salvation can have it simply by believing in the truth of the gospel.

Aside from informing the predestination-versus-free-choice debate, this passage teaches another lesson. Paul contrasts the power of deceit with the love of truth. This contrast is important every day. We speak and live in a world where we can aggressively love and pursue truth or encourage and promote falsehoods and deceit. The people of God should not only speak and live in truth but should love truth. This love should compel us to be honest with others but also respect, even appreciate, when others are honest with us. Deceit is not to be a tool in the arsenal of the believer.

Lord, give me a deep love for truth. Help me live a true life, authentic to you as I walk in this world. In Jesus, the true one, I pray, amen.

FEBRUARY 26

But we ought always to give thanks to God for you, brothers beloved by the Lord, because God chose you as the firstfruits to be saved, through sanctification by the Spirit and belief in the truth. To this he called you through our gospel, so that you may obtain the glory of our Lord Jesus Christ. So then, brothers, stand firm and hold to the traditions that you were taught by us, either by our spoken word or by our letter. (2 Thess. 2:13–15)

As a pre-teen I must have hit a rebellious stage. I had disobeyed my mom in some rather blatant way. I don't remember precisely what I did, but what followed made a huge impression on me. Mom came to me in my room to confront me about my behavior. I expected Mom to point out my disobedience and then punish me accordingly. But Mom did something different. Mom explained that she loved me more than life itself, and she didn't understand, since she loved me so much and had invested herself so heavily in me, why I would show a measure of contempt for her by dishonoring and disobeying her. It shook me to my core.

Genuine and true love of one for another rightly promotes responsive love and appreciation. This truth extends to our relationship with God. Significantly, Paul emphasizes that his readers are "beloved by the Lord." Paul's word choice in the Greek is the verb *agapaō* (ἀγαπάω). This type of love emphasizes a cherishing and affectionate love rooted in service and deliberate actions.

God loves you. God cherishes you. God goes to bat for you. God works in this world for your best. God calls us, saves us, purifies us, and prepares us for eternal glory. God willingly gives of himself for your betterment. God doesn't do so because you or I are worthy. God does so out of choice.

This truth of God's love *should* motivate us and change how we act. Mom made that point to me, and Paul makes the same point to his readers. Paul ends his paragraph of thought by explaining that because of this ("So then . . ."), the readers should hold to what they have been taught. God's beloved people should have the greatest regard for God and his work in our lives. We should be living faithfully to him, as his love stirs in our hearts a responsive love. When our love for God seems to ebb, it is time to refocus on God's great love for us. That love rightly speaks to us.

Lord, move my heart to understand the depth of your amazing love, and bring my responsive love into full flame as I live for you. In Jesus, amen.

FEBRUARY 27

Now may our Lord Jesus Christ himself, and God our Father, who loved us and gave us eternal comfort and good hope through grace, comfort your hearts and establish them in every good work and word. (2 Thess. 2:16–17)

Twofer is now a word in the dictionary! Typically defined as getting two of an item for the price of one, you can find *twofer* in the context of shopping, construction, political speech, and this devotional book. Yes, today's passage is a twofer!

In today's verses, Paul does something that is a bit of a pattern for him. He closes a section with a wish-prayer (see similarly in 1 Thess. 3:11–13). He wishes and prays for God to do the very things that Paul has set out in his letter up to this point. Paul can write about God's love, the eternal comfort and hope that come from grace, and the importance of living right, but he knows it takes the power of God to produce those results.

Bundled into Paul's prayer are notable insights into his theology. Paul's prayer is uttered to both God *our* Father and to *our* Lord Jesus Christ. Paul wrote before Christian scholars fleshed out the doctrine of the Trinity, yet Scripture has a widespread tripartite pattern of referring to God. Here, there is no doubt that Paul saw God the Father and the Lord Jesus Christ as both divine. Jesus was not a secondary being; he took primacy along with the Father (and Spirit, as we'll see in later writings).

But beyond the note of Jesus' divinity, this passage's twofer informs us of Paul's wish and prays to the source of that wish's fulfillment—God our Father and Jesus our Lord. Paul links his wishes for comfort and hope to "every good work and word." "Work and word" is an important Greek phrase. In Greek thought, everything could be divided into either work (*ergon*—ἔργον) or word (*logos*—λόγος). Everything is either something done or something thought of.

So in this passage, Paul wants *everything* in the lives of his readers to be informed by the love, comfort, and hope we have in the Lord. Nothing you or I will do today should be done apart from God's love. It can motivate us, direct us, teach us, encourage us, strengthen us, calm us, and sustain us. God will do remarkable things in us and through us as we walk in his loving care. Paul's wish-prayer is a remarkable insight for us all.

Lord, I pray for a deeper walk in your love, comfort, and grace. I pray this for me as well as those I love. In Jesus, amen.

FEBRUARY 28

May the Lord direct your hearts to the love of God and to the steadfastness of Christ. (2 Thess. 3:5)

For generations some variation of the childhood note "I like you; do you like me? Check one: ___Yes ___No" has been around. Or it might have taken the form of "Ask so-and-so if they like me"—children have sought out warmth and fondness for ages.

But it isn't just children who want to be loved. I think almost everyone has that craving. We don't want a manipulative, self-serving love. We crave acceptance and genuine love. We dream that someone will know us fully—with all our warts, blemishes, weaknesses, mistakes, bad habits, and more—and still love us, still be affectionate toward us, and still desire to be with us.

That craving has driven people to great extremes of behavior, trying to find or win such love. It has also driven people into defeat and frustration, convinced that love will never exist for them.

That is the world for us today, and I doubt whether the world in the generation of Paul was much different. After all, the Miori rule that "people are people" transcends time. So when I read today's passage, I am struck that Paul wants his readers' hearts directed to God's persistent and genuine love. (As Paul writes of the "steadfastness of Christ," he is writing of God's love enduring through life.)

Dwell on the love of God. Let it wash over you. God loves you as his creation. You aren't an accident; he brought you forth. He did it knowing everything about you, for time doesn't exist for God as it does for us. He was able to die for all your sins and shortcomings before you even existed. In our timeline, God has reached into us with his Spirit and down to us through others to confirm this love. You are reading the fruit of God's love in this passage today.

God is shouting from heaven's highest hold that he *loves* you and wants the absolute best for you. He will rescue you from everything through his love. He will purify all that isn't compatible with his love. And he will take you to himself for eternity to live in his love. This should transform our day!

Lord, let your authentic and deep love wash over me today, bringing me into deeper faith and trust in you. In Jesus, amen.

FEBRUARY 29

For we hear that some among you walk in idleness, not busy at work, but busybodies. Now such persons we command and encourage in the Lord Jesus Christ to do their work quietly and to earn their own living. (2 Thess. 3:11–12)

Christian clichés abound. Some are true (i.e., "Jesus loves you!"); others are bogus ("When God closes a door, he opens a window"—false! Sometimes God closes the door to keep you from going there, so don't pry open the window!). One Christian cliché that I believe is very true (although it's not found in the Bible in these words) is this: Idle hands are the devil's workshop.

Nature abhors a vacuum. Emptiness longs to be filled. That is true with the elements but equally true in our minds and lives. We can't decide to think of nothing. Even if we do, we are thinking about thinking of nothing. So we need to decide what to think. Similarly, when we have nothing to do, we will do something to fill the time. It might be binge-watching shows. It might be something destructive.

Paul wrote of people walking in idleness. Rather than being busy, they had become busybodies. The English play on words is present in the Greek but with a little more punch. Paul says that rather than working (using the Greek *ergon*), the people became meddlesome (using the same Greek *ergon* but adding *peri-*, or "about," to the front). Paul notes that those who don't stay busy will go about doing other things that aren't fruitful.

Today's passage instructs me on my mind and body. I need to keep my mind focused on things of God. I want to think about others as God thinks of them. I want to make choices that are godly. I want to spend my mental energy growing in the knowledge and love of Christ. I also want to use my physical energy for good purposes. My body should follow my mind in service to God.

Importantly, Paul isn't confusing the need for rest with idleness. Nor should we. God rightly teaches that all people need times of rest and refreshment. That is the lesson of the Sabbath. Paul is speaking of times that should be spent in work and industry yet instead are spent in useless endeavors. The alert Christian needs to live deliberately with eyes open. After all, idle hands are the devil's workshop!

Lord, give me insight into how to walk today. I want to think in godliness as I live a holy and productive life for you. In Jesus, amen.

MARCH 1

Now may the Lord of peace himself give you peace at all times in every way. The Lord be with you all. (2 Thess. 3:16)

In the early years of my law firm, I hired a young woman as a receptionist for whom English was a third language. Already fluent in Vietnamese and French, she had developed her English by moving to the U.S. After a year at the front desk, she requested some secretarial work to further develop her skills. At the time, I would dictate letters onto a dictation tape that she would play while typing. Soon thereafter, she gave me a letter for proofing and signing. She had typed my sign-off as "Virtually yours" instead of my dictated "Very truly yours." I corrected it. I gave thought to how I signed off, and I never did it virtually.

Paul doubtlessly gave thought to how he signed off his letters too. Today's passage comes to the last few verses of this letter. Paul's thoughtful sign-off was a prayer for his readers to have God's "peace at all times in every way."

This prayer for peace focused on an important term for Paul. In Paul's native language and culture, peace was a core concept. The Hebrew idea behind *shalom*, or peace, isn't simply the elimination of conflict. Our English word "peace" is a great effort to translate the concept, but the concept is much more than any one English word.

One could as easily translate *shalom* in the Hebrew mind as "complete." In that sense, Paul is praying for his readers to find the fullness of life in how they live and develop. *Shalom* also denotes prosperity, health, safety, and well-being. Paul wants his readers to experience life in a good way. Who could ask for more each day than being healthy and safe while prospering in good endeavors?

Paul didn't pray for his readers' peace in a vacuum. This prayer wasn't thrown up in the air like a desperate last-second basketball shot. Paul followed the prayer with an affirmation of where peace would be found. His readers would have all experienced this peace through the presence of the Lord in their lives. God's presence in our lives is truly transformational. When I trust God and look to him in my decision-making, he will make my decisions straight paths for me to walk (Prov. 3:5–6). If anyone doubts the power of God's presence, they should reread Psalm 23! Paul ended his letter with power for every reader!

Lord, guide my life today, giving me your peace. In Jesus, amen.

MARCH 2

Paul, called by the will of God to be an apostle of Christ Jesus, and our brother Sosthenes, To the church of God that is in Corinth, to those sanctified in Christ Jesus, called to be saints together with all those who in every place call upon the name of our Lord Jesus Christ, both their Lord and ours: Grace to you and peace from God our Father and the Lord Jesus Christ. (1 Cor. 1:1–3)

Maybe you've been there. I desperately wanted the job. My interviews had gone well, and I felt qualified, although I had some doubts. I received a call later that day from the law firm's hiring partner, who offered me a job as an associate attorney. I could start at the time of my choosing after law school graduation. That call was formative in my life.

Paul had also received a call. His call wasn't by telephone; it was more direct. The call was job-related for Paul too. Paul was called through the will of God to be an apostle—one sent out to bear a message—of Jesus Christ. Paul's fulfillment of that call included around eighteen months of living and teaching in Corinth, a metropolitan city of about 145,000 people. Paul's time wasn't misspent. God used Paul to bring many Corinthians to faith. After Paul left Corinth, he returned to Ephesus, a coastal city in modern Turkey. From there, Paul likely wrote to the Corinthians.

Paul tells the Corinthians that he wasn't the only one who had gotten the call! The Corinthian readers were also "called." They were called to the glory of Christ, but not because they were powerful or wise (1 Cor. 1:26*ff.*). The Corinthians were "called to be saints" together with everyone who is a believer in Jesus. That includes those reading this letter today, if we have put our faith in Christ. Paul calls all believers "saints"—*hagios* (ἅγιος) in the Greek.

This calling to be *hagios* means being dedicated or set apart to God. The Greeks would know the idea in reference to utensils that were set apart for exclusive use in their pagan temples. Paul uses the term for someone who is "holy" or "saintly" in God's sight and is dedicated for exclusive service by the Divine One. This is the call you and I have. We, like Paul's first-generation readers, have been set apart to be used for God. Our lives are not meant for the ordinary and profane usage of simple everyday living. Our everyday lives are spent in service to and for the glory of Jesus Christ. This is a great, important call we all received!

Lord, may I walk today holy and dedicated to your service in Jesus, amen.

MARCH 3

I give thanks to my God always for you because of the grace of God that was given you in Christ Jesus, that in every way you were enriched in him in all speech and all knowledge . . . so that you are not lacking in any gift, as you wait for the revealing of our Lord Jesus Christ, who will sustain you to the end, guiltless in the day of our Lord Jesus Christ. . . . God is faithful, by whom you were called into the fellowship of his Son, Jesus Christ our Lord. . . . For the word of the cross is folly to those who are perishing, but to us who are being saved it is the power of God. (1 Cor. 1:4–9, 18)

Coaching my son's basketball teams for some nine years was a great joy and blessing. It also gave me insights into parenting and mentoring. I started when the oldest was in kindergarten and quickly discovered that if I told them to do something differently, they wouldn't always make the changes. But if I told them they were doing a great job at a task and they could do even *greater* if they modified how they did it, they responded amazingly. Something about being encouraged and built up with positives captured their hearts and attention and made them want to do even better. I'm not much different.

Paul begins his letter with the positives. As noted in yesterday's devotional, Paul assures the Corinthians they had been "called" by God to be holy in serving him. In today's passage, Paul adds to that call, explaining that God called them into a relationship with Jesus Christ, God's own Son. This is profound and not to be read over lightly. God *calls*; he is the "hound of heaven" who seeks out you and me to be in a relationship. If a high school girl can whirl around in circles over getting called to go on a date with someone special, the idea of the God of the universe calling us to a deep relationship is stunning.

Paul explains that the calls and the relationship—the power of God to call us, transform us, and make us his own—are rooted in the death of Christ. This encouraging start to Paul's letter is remarkable because the rest of the letter shows the Corinthians were a mess. They were divided into factions, disorderly in worship, misunderstanding spiritual gifts, troubled in theology, and more. Yet Paul doesn't begin by reprimanding and correcting them. Like coaching a child's basketball team, Paul starts with the positives. He affirms their identity in Christ and only then teaches them to do better. We need to learn this lesson. We aren't all we should be before God, but he is still calling us and teaching us! Be encouraged.

Lord, thank you for your call. Make me better for you. In Jesus, amen.

MARCH 4

But God chose what is foolish in the world to shame the wise; God chose what is weak in the world to shame the strong; God chose what is low and despised in the world, even things that are not, to bring to nothing things that are, so that no human being might boast in the presence of God. (1 Cor. 1:27–29)

On the playgrounds of my youth, we, like so many others, would divide up into teams by picking two captains. The captains would then alternate choosing players for their teams until all were chosen. The initial choices were predictable. Almost everyone knew who the best players were, and they went first. A certain level of humiliation fell on those left at the end, who went to a team by default.

I don't know whether Paul ever picked players for teams while growing up, but in today's passage, Paul shows that God would never follow that process. As indicated in the earlier two devotionals from 1 Corinthians, God had called all believers to his family and to service. God's manner of choice is revealed in today's passage.

God never assembled his kingdom by grabbing the VIPs of this world. God wasn't intent on getting the strongest, the best loved, the most talented, the bon vivants, the smartest, the wealthiest, or the most wonderful people of this world. God doesn't exclude them, but the core of God's calling is for the low people and outcasts who haven't received the accolades and societal trophies of this world. God builds his kingdom out of his own love and power. Let no one boast in anything but God! Then as God's kingdom is built, and as we are transformed in that kingdom, the glory should never reflect onto any one human. All glory should come back to God and his work in Christ. This isn't the way of human wisdom. We pick teams based on merit and strength. But God's ways aren't our ways. God doesn't need us to succeed. We need him to succeed.

What then of the privileged in society? What of those fortunate, advantaged few? Paul says that all too often, the world's smarties think of God's work through the death of Christ as foolishness. Many "good people" stumble over the cross of Christ, as they see no need for it personally. The work of God is most readily embraced by those who perceive they need it. Yet we all *desperately* need it; many just don't realize it. I want to be wise in Christ, not in the world. I need God.

Lord, I desperately need you. Please open my eyes to see that. Let me never grow complacent in leaning fully on you in my life. I live and pray in Jesus alone, amen.

MARCH 5

And I, when I came to you, brothers, did not come proclaiming to you the testimony of God with lofty speech or wisdom. For I decided to know nothing among you except Jesus Christ and him crucified. And I was with you in weakness and in fear and much trembling, and my speech and my message were not in plausible words of wisdom, but in demonstration of the Spirit and of power, so that your faith might not rest in the wisdom of men but in the power of God. (1 Cor. 2:1–5)

Horse blinkers or *blinders* are those semicircular cups that affix to a horse's bridle to aid in a horse's focus when running a race. Horses have broad peripheral vision, and blinkers force the horse's eyes to look forward. Horses then concentrate on the ground, hurdles, and other things that might affect their race. Blinkers keep a horse calm.

Paul had a sort of blinkers in his ministry. Nothing would distract Paul from the core of his message. For Paul, the fact that Christ was crucified to take away the sins of the world was the only thing he needed to know. His peripheral vision was not focusing on anything else. Paul knew that Christ crucified was the power of God to alter all human history. In the death of Christ, a new life comes. For the death of Christ for you and me means a sharing also in the resurrection of Christ. We are "born again" or "born from above" in a very real sense.

One might reasonably ask, But didn't Paul teach and speak of many more subjects? Paul wrote of the importance of unity, love, holiness, church polity, and more. But those writings of Paul make his bold statement here even more important. That Paul wrote and taught of so many different things yet affirmed that he was set to know only Christ crucified shows how the death of Christ is central to the entire Christian walk.

Nothing we do should ever be viewed apart from the death of Christ. That teaches us love, unites us, motivates us to holiness, and gives us direction. We are empowered in life by the Spirit that resurrected Christ from the dead. Paul could rightly wear those blinkers of Christ crucified. The focus of his life should be the focus of ours as well. If we dwell on the crucified Savior, life shines as it should. Our peace is made whole. We become who we should be.

Lord, may the cross of Christ be my focus and core in life today. In Jesus, amen.

MARCH 6

Yet among the mature we do impart wisdom, although it is not a wisdom of this age or of the rulers of this age, who are doomed to pass away. But we impart a secret and hidden wisdom of God, which God decreed before the ages for our glory. None of the rulers of this age understood this, for if they had, they would not have crucified the Lord of glory. (1 Cor. 2:6–8)

Somewhere between fourth and sixth grade, students are taught about negative numbers. My teacher used a line drawn on the board. The line had a zero, and to the right, the teacher wrote out the numbers as we called them: "One, two, three." Then the teacher moved to the *left* of the zero. The teacher explained that there is a "positive" one to the right of zero, and its opposite is a "negative" one to the left of zero. It made a huge impression on me, opening an unseen world of numbers.

I fear some might think of Satan and his evil powers as the "opposite number" to God. It is as if God is the positive seven (or choose any number), and Satan is the negative seven. So where God is good, Satan is evil; where God loves others, Satan is filled with hatred; and so on.

Yet this idea of Satan as the negative equivalent of God is wrong, especially when it comes to knowledge. God is all-knowing. Satan isn't. Satan's cluelessness is most obvious with the cross. Jesus died for the sins of humanity. This was God's plan all along, but Satan had no idea. During Jesus' earthly existence, Satan worked overtime to thwart God's mission. Satan tried tempting Jesus in the wilderness, seeking to lead him astray from God's plan. During Jesus' ministry, those tending to Satan's schemes frequently designed plans to ruin Jesus' work and influence. The ultimate misplaced and ill-informed work of Satan was to enter Judas and betray the Lord. In a real sense, Satan worked to see that Jesus died, thinking that evil had won the day.

But Easter came and, with it, the resurrection. It soon became clear that Satan had brought about his own demise as well as the demise of the sting of death and curse of sin. God won over all that is evil. Had Satan a clue about this, he never would have worked toward the crucifixion.

In my life, I need to remember that Satan isn't God's opposite number. He doesn't have God's power, wisdom, or control, nor does he rule in my life!

Lord, let me walk in confidence of your victory in my life. In Jesus' name, amen.

MARCH 7

The natural person does not accept the things of the Spirit of God, for they are folly to him, and he is not able to understand them because they are spiritually discerned. The spiritual person judges all things, but is himself to be judged by no one. "For who has understood the mind of the Lord so as to instruct him?" But we have the mind of Christ. (1 Cor. 2:14–16)

Dad picked me up from Greek class one day. Driving home, he asked what class I had finished. I told him, "Greek," and he replied, "When I was in the navy, I learned a greeting in every language except Greek." Although I should have known better, I bit: "Tell me 'hello' in Swahili." Dad replied, "That's Greek to me!"

Yes, you need training to be able to speak a language. In a similar fashion, Paul drives home a point in today's passage: you need the Spirit of God to understand God's spiritual matters.

The Bible translation used in this book is the English Standard Version. It translates Paul's term for the one lacking understanding as "the natural person"—a somewhat literal translation. The New International Version translates this Greek term as "the person without the Spirit." Perhaps the greatest influence on modern rational thinking, John Locke (1632–1704), in his posthumously published notes stated that he considered Paul to mean a man with only "animal powers, the human unassisted by the spirit or revelation" (*A Paraphrase and Notes on the Epistles of St. Paul*).

Without pinning down with precision Paul's full meaning for this type of undiscerning person, we can be certain of one thing: not everyone who hears of the finished work of Christ is going to grasp its truth or significance. Moreover, we who accept the sacrificial death of Christ by faith should be praying for God to grow us in our understanding. God's Spirit at work in us will give us greater insight into Jesus and his work on our behalf. Jesus had taught us as much, telling his apostles that the coming Holy Spirit would indwell them and "teach [them] all things" bearing "witness" about Christ (Jn. 14:26; 15:26).

This is the work of the Holy Spirit. Our role is to seek and accept the Spirit's help.

Lord, may your Spirit give me greater insight into the significance of your work in Christ. Teach me. Grow me in faith and understanding. In Jesus, amen.

MARCH 8

But I, brothers, could not address you as spiritual people, but as people of the flesh, as infants in Christ. I fed you with milk, not solid food, for you were not ready for it. And even now you are not yet ready, for you are still of the flesh. For while there is jealousy and strife among you, are you not of the flesh and behaving only in a human way? (1 Cor. 3:1–3)

Will is our firstborn. After bringing him home from the hospital, I began a tradition that lasted for much of his young life. Every Saturday morning, starting when he was five days old, I would take him to the donut store. This tradition had been ongoing for almost a year before he got to eat part of those donuts! Before that, in his infancy, he wasn't physically ready for donuts. He existed on milk and formula.

Paul's metaphor in today's passage draws from human growth. Becoming a Christian isn't like downloading an app on your phone, where you immediately have access to all the app has to offer. God will stamp a new believer with his Spirit and make that person a citizen in his kingdom. But every believer still needs to grow before God.

Paul had already written to churches in Galatia, and he used the phrase "the fruit of the Spirit." Paul's metaphor there also denoted the idea of something that grows in the believer. Here, Paul adds something important to the growth analogy. Paul explains that people play a role in how they grow. Paul is chiding the Corinthians for failing to grow as they should.

Paul's interest in how his readers grow isn't for growth's sake alone. Fragile spiritual infants who are new to the faith aren't ready to handle what life throws at them. Growth in the Lord gives us the strength for life. We have greater purpose and direction as we grow. Our opportunities to serve God expand. We can love deeper, forgive easier, withstand storms more securely, see through delusions more readily, and encourage more effectively those around us in need. We are better parents, spouses, children, and friends. We do better at work, in school, and in relationships. All of life is affected by our maturity in Christ. Growth is important, and growth is something we should all see from God's Spirit.

Lord, please grow me through your Spirit. Teach me. Instill greater faith in me. Let me see you more clearly than ever before. I pray in Jesus, amen.

MARCH 9

According to the grace of God given to me, like a skilled master builder I laid a foundation, and someone else is building upon it. Let each one take care how he builds upon it. For no one can lay a foundation other than that which is laid, which is Jesus Christ. Now if anyone builds on the foundation with gold, silver, precious stones, wood, hay, straw—each one's work will become manifest, for the Day will disclose it, because it will be revealed by fire, and the fire will test what sort of work each one has done. (1 Cor. 3:10–13)

Building or remodeling a home comes with loads of choices. Which kind of wood will you choose for cabinets, floors, or shelving? Which appliances will go in the kitchen? Which fixtures in the bathroom? Wallpaper or paint? What colors? The multitude of choices can almost be overwhelming.

Paul uses a building analogy to speak of how we grow and mature in our Christian walk, but Paul's directive is, in today's passage, directed at those who teach others. Through Paul, God had established his church in Corinth. Paul had stayed there for around eighteen months but then departed. Others came in and picked up where Paul left off, teaching the church as they saw fit. In the process, Paul had been relegated by some as "old school"—a nice way to start, but not of the level where the Corinthians had gotten. Some seemed to view themselves as super-Christian, taught by superteachers. This had led the church into error and division. Paul wrote to address this problem head on.

Paul's building analogy speaks of the choices we have in construction. Paul emphasizes that a day of accounting will register whether the building choices were sustainable or transient. His list of materials for a home reminds me of the story of the "Three Little Pigs," where one house was built of sticks, one of straw, and one of bricks, and when the wolf blew, the stick and straw houses crumbled. Only the brick house remained secure against the wolf. So the believer can build a life with sticks and straw that will crumble in difficult circumstances or build securely with stone and fine metals.

We want to learn and grow right before the Lord. Days of testing come for everyone. Time spent studying God's word isn't wasted. The person with a solid faith will endure through the challenges of life. Ones with a flimsy faith who don't grow in the truths God has taught in Scripture will be hurt in the trials of life.

Lord, I want to grow in your grace in ways that are right and true. In Jesus, amen.

MARCH 10

Let no one deceive himself. If anyone among you thinks that he is wise in this age, let him become a fool that he may become wise. For the wisdom of this world is folly with God. For it is written, "He catches the wise in their craftiness," and again, "The Lord knows the thoughts of the wise, that they are futile." (1 Cor. 3:18–20)

Some things are best learned through experience. Many Asian cultures are notable for their esteem of the elderly. Often traced back to the teachings of Confucius (fifth century BC), the idea is premised on the elderly gaining wisdom throughout life, as well as earning a station of respect. I am not endorsing the extent of "filial piety" maintained in many Eastern cultures, but I can attest that I have learned certain truths as I have aged, truths missing in my younger years.

Among these truths is the inadequacy of worldly wisdom in addressing certain aspects of life. It seemed easy to challenge the status quo as a child raised in the 1960s and 1970s. I grew up in the turbulent age of seeking civil rights to address society's social injustices. Vietnam War protests were common in my youth. I remember the rallies challenging why eighteen-year-olds could be sent to die in Vietnam but couldn't vote until the age of twenty-one.

But while challenging the system has value and can be important, I realized as I got older that there are things that are right even though they are not as avant-garde. The belief du jour isn't always right. Sometimes the world's philosophy and values are contrary to the truth.

Paul warns his readers that the wisdom of the world is folly with God. God's insight isn't transient. It doesn't change day to day. God sees with a clarity of being timeless. As the God of yesterday as well as today and tomorrow, God's insight is without equal.

God's timeless wisdom should lead everyone to seek his wisdom. Yes, we must often translate from the biblical culture to modernity, but the core teachings of Scripture should be our divining rod for right and wrong. Our tendency to like what seems right to us isn't a guaranteed path to what is true. We should seek God's truth.

Lord, I don't want my life built on what seems right to the world around me. I want your truth to mold, shape, and direct my life and thoughts. In you I pray, amen.

MARCH 11

But with me it is a very small thing that I should be judged by you or by any human court. In fact, I do not even judge myself. For I am not aware of anything against myself, but I am not thereby acquitted. It is the Lord who judges me. (1 Cor. 4:3–4)

Paul poured his life into the city of Corinth for about a year and a half. He had brought to the residents the message of the resurrected Jesus. Some members of the Jewish community welcomed the news of the Messiah, while others rejected the message and persecuted believers. Many Gentiles in Corinth also welcomed the message, although without a doubt, many lacked a great deal of understanding without a background in Jewish Scriptures.

Paul then left Corinth, and others came in to teach and share. The Christian faith was spreading around the Mediterranean world, and Corinth was an important port city. So it's unsurprising that Corinth received a number of preachers and teachers about Jesus and Christianity. Many of these teachers were likely great for the fledgling church, but some sought to elevate their teaching while dissing Paul. Moreover, many in the church would disrespect Paul in favor of other teachers. You can hear echoes of this in many passages of Paul's letter, including today's.

Paul writes that the judgments of others had little effect on him. Paul didn't live worried about what others thought of him. Paul got his commission from Christ. What mattered to Paul was how he carried out what Christ entrusted to him. Paul cared about Christ's assessment and judgment, not that of some critical human.

In our lives, we will also be judged by others. How we conduct ourselves at work, in school, and even in social and family circles will get assessed by others. When others criticize us, our standing in their eyes should never matter compared to our standing in God's eyes.

This truth isn't a basis for living a life without regard for others and what they think. After all, we're to be a good influence on behalf of Jesus—a walking sermon, as some term it. But we must always keep it in focus. Our goal in life is to faithfully please God. This means being good to others. But it doesn't mean living under the judgment of another. We live under the judgment of God.

Lord, help me faithfully discharge your purposes for my life. Give me relief from living to please others as I live for you. In Jesus' name, amen.

MARCH 12

Already you have all you want! Already you have become rich! Without us you have become kings! . . . We are fools for Christ's sake, but you are wise in Christ. We are weak, but you are strong. You are held in honor, but we in disrepute. To the present hour we hunger and thirst, we are poorly dressed and buffeted and homeless, and we labor, working with our own hands. When reviled, we bless; when persecuted, we endure; when slandered, we entreat. We have become, and are still, like the scum of the world, the refuse of all things. (1 Cor. 4:8, 10–13)

Fortunately, I don't eat as much as I used to. But back in the day, there were many times I drove through a McDonald's saying, "One Quarter Pounder with cheese, french fries, and a Diet Coke—and supersize me!" I loved the food and wanted the extralarge fries and drink.

Paul's readers at Corinth predated McDonald's by centuries, but they might still have claimed the descriptor "supersize me!" They weren't thinking about physical enlargement. Their thoughts centered on spiritual enlargement. The church at Corinth had developed a problem, and today's passage illustrates it in a biting, sarcastic form.

Word had gotten to Paul, perhaps through a letter or maybe through personal testimony, that the Corinthians had decided that they had grown past Paul and his "elementary" teachings. Of course, we see Paul through the lens of history and know that his letters were inspired by the Holy Spirit and placed into Holy Scripture. They just saw Paul as the fellow who first taught them about Jesus and then moved on. Since Paul, they had had some super teaching, or so they thought. They thought they had arrived at super spiritualism.

Paul quotes some of the Corinthians as saying they had arrived; they had all they wanted. They were spiritually rich. They believed that Paul's life reflected the level of his spirituality. He was weak, was poorly dressed, was short on money, worked rather than enjoyed the support of churches, and endured ridicule and shaming. They looked down on Paul and viewed themselves as supersized spiritual Christians.

Time shows the truth. Paul sought Christ and his virtue. Jesus doesn't care how we dress. To suffer for Jesus is meritorious, not degrading. I clearly need to learn to value things as God does. That alone is super spirituality.

Lord, give me your priorities. Let me live humbly for you in Jesus. Amen.

MARCH 13

I do not write these things to make you ashamed, but to admonish you as my beloved children. . . . Some are arrogant, as though I were not coming to you. But I will come to you soon, if the Lord wills, and I will find out not the talk of these arrogant people but their power. For the kingdom of God does not consist in talk but in power. What do you wish? Shall I come to you with a rod, or with love in a spirit of gentleness? (1 Cor. 4:14, 18–21)

One of my high school friends had a mom who was quite active in her church. I was zealous for God and Scripture at an early age, and so I frequently engaged this mom in vigorous discussion over many Christian topics. One day, as we debated an issue, I quoted Paul as speaking definitively for my position. Her reply was "So? That is Paul! I have the benefit of almost two thousand years of Christian thought after Paul. I don't have to accept that he got this right!" Our argument then shifted to the authority and inspiration of Scripture.

My friend's mother had a biblical perspective, but not in the way she thought! As discussed in yesterday's devotional, some Corinthians thought themselves "beyond Paul," much like my friend's mom. Paul was fine as a starter, they reasoned, but if Paul were 101-level, they had since graduated and were taking master's-level classes.

Paul sent a reality check to those with such arrogant thoughts. Paul would be returning to Corinth, and the church would get to see who truly had the power and authority of God. Was it those who claimed it through their speech? Was it those arrogant souls who painted Paul as the introduction to Christian thought and no more? Or was it Paul himself? Remember that Paul came with the powerful workings of the Holy Spirit. Acts records Paul working miracles of healing (Acts 19:11–20) and even raising the dead (Acts 20:7–12). Paul was ready for a showdown between those who talked a big game and those who had the power of the Holy Spirit. It wouldn't be pretty for the arrogant talkers.

Paul wrote and taught some difficult things. Doubtlessly, some are tied to special events and some to cultural values. We need to read them carefully before applying them blindly. Yet we should also read Paul with reverence. He was speaking for God. He was teaching the word of the Lord. That should overtake any of our personal desires and interpretations of what we want and think.

Lord, I confess that sometimes I want your word to affirm what I believe rather than shape my beliefs around your word. Forgive me, and help me in Jesus, amen.

MARCH 14

When you are assembled in the name of the Lord Jesus and my spirit is present, with the power of our Lord Jesus, you are to deliver this man to Satan for the destruction of the flesh, so that his spirit may be saved in the day of the Lord. (1 Cor. 5:4–5)

In 1986, Roby Duke, a lesser-known artist from Mississippi, released the song "This Is Not a Game." He sang with a bluesy voice of one who was facing the temptation to walk in earthly ways, and he spoke into that life the truth, "We must face the music; this is not a game."

Life isn't a game; it is deadly serious. I don't mean there's no time for laughter, joy, and joking. There certainly is! But sometimes we forget the serious importance of living right before God. God isn't trying to limit our fun. He isn't an old man on a rickety rocking chair, wagging an aging finger as he proclaims, "We can't let them do *that*; it's way too much fun." Our moral instructions from God aren't arbitrary. The morality laid out for our lives is the very morality within the Godhead. God made humanity to display his moral virtue to the world. Instead, humanity embraced the wretched immorality of ungodliness—a.k.a. "sin."

Paul realized the true seriousness of life. He had special instructions for treating some in the church who simply weren't working on becoming holy but were consciously and deliberately living in absurd sexual sin. The sin was great even to the pagan community. Rather than being upset over it, the church seemed to tolerate it as a progressive freedom found in living under God's grace. In the church's view, anything goes to those who are already "forgiven."

Paul wanted this dealt with in a serious fashion. Paul sent the church a message to "deliver this man to Satan." Scholars have debated this phrase's meaning, but Paul's intent seems to set this unrepentant sinner outside the fellowship of the church. If the person wanted to live like a pagan and listen to the seductions of Satan, let him suffer Satan's consequences. This was to lead the person to repentance and a return to God's fellowship.

This passage reinforces Roby Duke's lyrics quoted earlier. Life isn't a game. God doesn't bring us into his kingdom for our worldly purposes. He brings us in love to transform us into who he made us to be.

Lord, I repent of my sin and pray for your holiness and forgiveness in Jesus, amen.

MARCH 15

Your boasting is not good. Do you not know that a little leaven leavens the whole lump? Cleanse out the old leaven that you may be a new lump, as you really are unleavened. . . . Let us therefore celebrate the festival, not with the old leaven, the leaven of malice and evil, but with the unleavened bread of sincerity and truth. (1 Cor. 5:6–8)

During the Islamic month of Ramadan, practicing Muslims fast each day from food and water. This fast lasts from sunrise to sunset for the entire month. I am not a Muslim. Nor have I practiced Ramadan fasting. I learned about Ramadan fasting in part because I was a huge Houston Rockets fan in the heyday of Hakeem Olajuwon, who managed to play exceptional world-class basketball without food or water consumed on game day. I absorbed this basic Muslim knowledge as a fan.

In Paul's world, most Jews certainly had familiarity with their Scriptures. Some Gentiles would have likely had a degree of general familiarity with them—much like what I know about Ramadan—and Christian Gentiles who received Paul's letter would also accept the Old Testament as their Scriptures. This is important because Paul is using a common Old Testament metaphor in today's passage.

The Old Testament establishes a metaphor of sin being like leaven (or yeast, as we more commonly call it today). Leaven was an old "sourdough" substance, not a package purchased in the store. It was fermented dough—dough that had gone sour. Leaven thus readily became identified as the corrupter of the bread dough, and while it made the bread light and tasty, it stopped bread from being the pure "unleavened bread" commonly associated with the nomadic ancestors of the Jews.

The illustration of sin as leaven works well. Sin is a corruption of what is good. For example, eating is a good thing. Eating in excess is a corruption of the good thing; it's the sin of gluttony. Marital sexual intimacy is a good thing. Sexual intimacy outside of marriage is fornication or adultery, both sins. Desiring holiness is a good thing. Desiring worldly things is covetous and greedy, which are also sins. Trusting in God is faithful obedience. Trusting in riches or the world is deceitful idolatry.

Paul urges his readers to seek out the sins in our lives and bring them to God to be purified. We ought to live pure, uncorrupted lives before our God.

Lord, purify my heart and life to follow you better. In Jesus, amen.

MARCH 16

For Christ, our Passover lamb, has been sacrificed. (1 Cor. 5:7)

Just as all of Paul's readers would have understood the metaphor of leaven as sin, of which I wrote in yesterday's devotional, so converted readers who accepted the Old Testament as Scripture would have understood the Jewish celebration of Passover, or *Pesach.* This Jewish celebration centers on remembering God liberating the Israelites from the bondage of Pharaoh and Egypt.

Key to Israel's liberation was the night that the angel of death covered the land of Egypt, killing the firstborn of each household. But certain households were spared death. The angel would "pass over" the houses that had the blood of a sacrificed lamb smeared on the lintels and doorposts. This celebration set Passover night apart for all generations of Jews, including those in Paul's day. Present among the items in a Passover feast was a *z'roa,* a roasted lamb shank bone (although many Jews today use a chicken neck as a substitute on the seder plate).

The lamb chosen for sacrifice on the first Passover in Egypt was a pure, unspotted lamb. The earliest church understood this as a pre-Christ image of God's true redemptive work. The angel of death comes to visit all who live in bondage to sin. No exceptions exist save for those who have put themselves under the blood of the lamb. This lamb, Paul explained, is Christ: truly unspotted by sin and pure as pure can be.

In today's passage, and in the larger context of 1 Corinthians, Paul is making the point that the death of Christ to cover our sins is a true turning point both in history and in the life of the believer. Because of Jesus' sacrificial death and subsequent resurrection, death passes over us, and we are a changed people. We no longer must live as slaves to the harsh taskmaster that is sin. We are set free to live under God's Spirit—a life of love, freedom, and joy.

This free life doesn't mean we have no accountability. Nor does it mean that we don't care about holiness and sin. We are free from sin's bondage so that we can pursue God and flee sin. To wallow in sin is to return to slavery. We have been set free and should live freely—that is, in holiness. This truth in Paul's day is no less true today.

Lord, thank you for the sacrifice of Jesus, my Passover lamb. May I live a life that pursues you in love, seeking to be free from sin's bondage. In Jesus, amen.

MARCH 17

Or do you not know that the unrighteous will not inherit the kingdom of God? Do not be deceived: neither the sexually immoral, nor idolaters, nor adulterers, nor men who practice homosexuality, nor thieves, nor the greedy, nor drunkards, nor revilers, nor swindlers will inherit the kingdom of God. And such were some of you. But you were washed, you were sanctified, you were justified in the name of the Lord Jesus Christ and by the Spirit of our God. (1 Cor. 6:9–11)

In 1984, Amy Grant released the song "The Now and the Not Yet." It is a marvelous song that captures the biblical idea that believers in Christ are new creations, declared holy and eternally God's, even though they still live imperfect lives in an imperfect world. The song begins, "No longer what we were before, but not all that we will be . . ." The song expresses an important recognition that we are being changed by God into the image of his Son, and this is a process.

Paul wrote some challenging lines in today's passage that align with this concept. Paul spoke of those who live persisting in sins, ranging from sexual sins to less sensational sins like greed and drunkenness. Paul's point distinguishes between those living unrepentantly in sustained sin and those fleeing from sin. His readers had previously lived in unrepentant sin, but they changed as they became washed, sanctified, and justified. In other words, as God removed the consequences of their sin, God transformed their behavior.

Grant's song adds the important thought "I'm caught in between the now and the not yet; sometimes it seems like forever and ever that I've been reaching to be all that I am. But I'm only a few steps nearer. Yet I'm nearer." This promise that God is transforming the believer into the image of Christ persists in Paul's teachings. The key is contained in Paul's explanation of how.

Paul says that the transformation, washing, sanctification, and justification were empowered by the "name of the Lord Jesus Christ" and "the Spirit of our God." In Paul's day, one's "name" meant one's résumé—what one did as well as the essence of that person. The "name of Jesus" references his atoning death on the cross where he bore the consequences of the world's sins.

By the death of Jesus, we are all made new. God takes us from our sinful lives, saves us, and transforms us into Jesus' likeness.

Lord, please purify my heart and life. In Jesus' name, amen.

MARCH 18

"All things are lawful for me," but not all things are helpful. "All things are lawful for me," but I will not be dominated by anything. "Food is meant for the stomach and the stomach for food"—and God will destroy both one and the other. The body is not meant for sexual immorality, but for the Lord, and the Lord for the body. (1 Cor. 6:12–13)

Email has substantially changed not only my life but how I write things. Historically, if someone wrote me a letter asking me certain questions or making certain points to which I wanted to respond, I would write back a responsive letter. Now with email, I simply hit reply and often intersperse my responses by using a different ink color to make my answers stand out.

Paul didn't have email, and sometimes it takes a bit of work to translate and understand parts of letters like 1 Corinthians where Paul is responding. In today's passage, for example, the translators have put quotation marks around three sections of the passage. This is because the translators have deduced that in those three clauses, Paul is quoting something the Corinthians have written or said to him ("All things are lawful" twice, and "Food is meant for the stomach"). Paul takes those quotes from the Corinthians and responds to each.

Based on Paul's responses, the Corinthians seemed to revel in the liberty and freedom that Paul taught. Paul didn't teach a legalistic faith where salvation and receiving God's love were performance based. God doesn't accept us because we earn his love. As a result, the Corinthians minimized the importance of godly living and distinguishing right from wrong.

Paul knew that right and wrong were important both now and in the future. Hence Paul could quote the Corinthians and say that "all things are lawful" but add the important understanding that "all things aren't helpful." Godly living was an essential part of comprehending God and the Christian life. Right and wrong are important navigation aids in life. Making wrong choices affects our internal joy and peace and also affects our external circumstances.

Reading this passage in context helps me maintain a good perspective on how to live. I want to live holy and right before God.

Lord, give me greater insight into your will for my life. May I walk in your holiness today. In Jesus I pray, amen.

MARCH 19

Flee from sexual immorality. Every other sin a person commits is outside the body, but the sexually immoral person sins against his own body. Or do you not know that your body is a temple of the Holy Spirit within you, whom you have from God? You are not your own, for you were bought with a price. So glorify God in your body. (1 Cor. 6:18–20)

Texas is loaded with ranches. Certain rules have arisen with respect to ranches. One such rule applies to gates: leave it like you found it. That means if you drive through the gate and the gate had been open, you leave it open. Livestock may need to move freely from one area to another. If you had to open a closed gate to drive through, you close it afterward. It might be imperative to stop livestock from moving where they shouldn't. While ranching and gates have the rule "leave it like you found it," borrowing something from another person has a different rule: leave it *better* than you found it. For example, if you borrow a car with half a tank of gas, you fill it up before returning it. This idea ties into today's passage.

Our bodies aren't ranch gates, where we leave them as we found them. Paul says our bodies belong to God. They are, in this sense, on loan from God to us. Our faith should help us leave our bodies better than we found them!

Paul applies his lesson to the context of sexual immorality, for the area of sex is one of intense personal perspective. Sexual drive ticks all the boxes of selfishness—that is, what we want, when we want it, and so on. Paul tries to move his readers past selfishness with the understanding that we—and our bodies—aren't our own. We belong to God. God has sent his Holy Spirit into our bodies to set up his residence. He dwells within each believer in Christ. As God's temple, then, we are God's dwelling place. We are his home. His rules apply as we live our lives. He has bought us by the precious purchase price of the death of Christ. Just as we might buy a home in which we live, God has bought us and lives within us. He is holy and he wants us to treat our bodies as holy.

So today, realize you belong to God. Let your life, including your body, reflect his glory. Leave yourself better than he found you. You have a chance to make a difference for him.

Lord, use me today. Give me the grace and presence to live my life for you, bringing you glory in all I do. In Jesus, amen.

MARCH 20

The husband should give to his wife her conjugal rights, and likewise the wife to her husband. . . . Do not deprive one another, except perhaps by agreement for a limited time, that you may devote yourselves to prayer; but then come together again, so that Satan may not tempt you because of your lack of self-control. (1 Cor. 7:3, 5)

The United States is a "common law" country. By that, I mean that not all law is passed by a legislature and written up in a legal code. Some law is created by the courts. This is most prominent in civil cases. The common law is a set of court-created general legal principles that apply to various factual situations, and then those situations are decided and become the law. For example, a general legal principle is that a driver cannot act outside what a "reasonably prudent person" would do when driving a car. If Person A fails to be reasonably prudent and thereby causes injury to Person B, then Person A is liable for the resulting damage. But the amount of damages isn't a set sum. It is determined case by case.

In much the same way, one can read today's passage and much of Paul's writing to the Corinthians. Paul wrote about specific issues that were endemic to that church. Paul addressed those specific problems with certain principles. We do the greatest justice to Paul's writings if we understand those underlying principles, for they apply differently to our factual situations today.

One of the issues that confronted the Corinthians was the idea some advocated that husbands and wives could find greater holiness by abstaining from sexual relations with each other. Paul sought to disabuse them of that notion. If they wanted to abstain from sexual intimacy, Paul put in conditions: abstaining must be mutually agreed on, it should be for the holy purpose of spending that time together in prayer, and there must be an end to it, where normalcy is resumed. Paul's guiding principle behind this teaching is simple: being together would help refuse Satan's strong temptations to sexual immorality.

The principle of "common law" I set out earlier is helpful here. All believers should remember that Satan is in the tempting business. He exploits all our weaknesses, wherever he finds them. We should work to minimize our exposure to his wiles. It is smart to take precautions and put up guardrails to stop him before he gets started.

Lord, give me eyes to see areas of vulnerability and grace to stop myself! In you, amen.

MARCH 21

Only let each person lead the life that the Lord has assigned to him, and to which God has called him. (1 Cor. 7:17)

One day when I was in roughly eighth grade, I was walking across the church parking lot when one of our youth ministers walked by. I was relatively new to town, and my church had hundreds in its youth group. As I passed by, he said, "Hi Mark." I was stunned. I never dreamed he knew my name. I was new, and I was one of hundreds. I was so touched; I remember it fifty years later.

The Bible is loaded with great stories about great (and not-so-great) people. These stories are centered on how those people related or failed to relate to God. We begin with Adam and Eve and then work through the stories of Cain, Abel, and Seth. We read about the call that God had on the life of Abraham and his call on Isaac, Jacob, Joseph, and others. The New Testament is loaded with stories of Jesus and his chosen apostles. Paul's call is dramatically told in multiple places.

I fear sometimes we default to the idea that the call of God is for the biblically great, for those who are at the pinnacle of faith. We might think that the rest of us are just one of the many who are Christians, but nothing special beyond that.

Today's passage is one of many that should put to rest any thought that we are only a number. Each believer is special, and each believer is called by God. God knows each person's name, character, talents, resources, wants, desires, options, opportunities, and more. God has a specific call on each person's life that is distinct to that person. God calls us all into a unique relationship with him.

Carl Cope was the man who called me by name decades ago in a church parking lot. I haven't seen him in at least forty years, and I never knew him well. But he was my youth minister, and I saw him lead singing and heard him teach for several formative years. I will not forget his name, nor will I forget that he knew mine.

The ways of God should be no less impressed into my brain. For God has my name etched on his hand, and he has a unique call on me. He has one on you too. We should find courage and strength for today as we live under the call of the Almighty God.

Lord, teach me to hear your call. Show me your ways. Let me walk before you with joy in the journey. In Jesus, amen.

MARCH 22

I want you to be free from anxieties. (1 Cor. 7:32)

I have a theory about worry that is totally unproven—there's no science addressing it, at least none that I have read. Yet I find it to be reasonably true. I call it the "percent-worrying syndrome," and I find it present in almost everyone. See if you find it true.

Almost everyone has a certain amount they worry. Maybe some are big worriers, and they spend 35 or 40 percent of their energy worrying. Some might not worry much, spending maybe 5 percent of their energy worrying. And if you ask someone to list the top ten reasons to worry, the 40 percent worrier will worry over however many items it takes to consume their 40 percent worrying quota. The 5 percenter will only worry over those few items that consume the 5 percent of emotional energy they expend on worrying.

Now you could resolve some of the listed items being worried over, but it wouldn't alleviate the worrying in general. The 40 percent worrier, out of habit, would just move down the list and find new items that will then meet their worrying quota. Likewise the 5 percenter.

We all worry, some more than others. Yet into this state comes this simple sentence from Paul: "I want you free from worry," free from "anxiety." Paul sets his wish amid a discussion on marriage, noting that one who is married focuses their energy more on family matters, while one who is unmarried can focus on matters of faith. Paul was addressing a particular situation and time relevant to his readers, but in our day and age, our faith should be fully incorporated into our marriage and parenting.

Paul's contextual focus is important, however, as it establishes the way we become free of worry and concern. We focus our efforts on God. In any context, when our lives are focused on serving God and on discerning and doing his will, we find ourselves empowered by him and our worries melt away. We live on mission for God, and he will see to our success. Why worry?

In practical terms, whether with my family, friends, job, situation in life, or anything else, I need to let all my worrying be about finding and doing God's will. I need worry about nothing else. God takes care of it all.

Lord, may I cast all my worries on you and do your will today. In Jesus, amen.

MARCH 23

Now concerning food offered to idols: we know that "all of us possess knowledge." This "knowledge" puffs up, but love builds up. If anyone imagines that he knows something, he does not yet know as he ought to know. But if anyone loves God, he is known by God. (1 Cor. 8:1–3)

Every driver is familiar with warning signs. I see them most often at curves in the road. Near our home is a sign that indicates that while the speed limit is sixty-five miles per hour, the curve should be driven at a maximum of thirty-five miles per hour to be safe. The driver is warned that higher speeds risk losing control of the vehicle.

In today's passage, Paul issues a warning sign for his readers on the road of life. In Paul's day, the warning came on trips to the butcher. Well, not a butcher like we might find in our grocery stores today—in Paul's day, the butchers were typically found at the various temples. People would bring an animal as a "sacrifice," and the priests would butcher the animal, keeping some of the parts for the gods (and the priest) and returning the rest of the butchered animal to be sold or eaten by the offeree. People would also eat at the temples.

The Christians knew it wasn't right to sacrifice to pagan gods, but an issue arose when buying meat, since that meat might have been butchered by a pagan priest as part of a sacrifice. Some of Paul's readers "knew better" than to think it was a problem because the pagan gods weren't real and they hadn't participated in the sacrificial system; they had just purchased the meat. Others were bothered by this. So the Corinthians had written Paul on the matter, and in their letter, some said something like "We know better" or "A group of us possess this knowledge." Paul seizes this context to warn his readers but does so in a way that warns all of us on life's road. When we think we know something, even something spiritual, we should beware. We are on the road to haughtiness and arrogance. We might be looking down on those who aren't "in the know." We might think ourselves superspiritual because of our knowledge.

The real goal in life isn't to know more than our neighbor, holding ourselves up high as a result. Life's purpose should be to know and be known *by God*! This is why we learn—so that we might know God better and he might have a greater hold on our lives. Read Paul's warning sign today. Seek knowing God, not knowing greatness.

Lord, help me know you better, in submission and service. In your name, amen.

MARCH 24

For although there may be so-called gods in heaven or on earth—as indeed there are many "gods" and many "lords"—yet for us there is one God, the Father, from whom are all things and for whom we exist, and one Lord, Jesus Christ, through whom are all things and through whom we exist. (1 Cor. 8:5–6)

When I teach lawyers how to try a case, I urge them to write down all the facts relevant to the matter at hand. Then from those facts, they are to write the one coherent story that includes all the facts. If some facts don't fit the story, then the story isn't right. Young lawyers often fall prey to telling one version of a story, allowing the other side's lawyers to tell their own story. But the true story contains all the facts.

Paul recognized that different people have different views of what is real. But only one story is the true story about reality. In today's times, rather than idols of supposed deities, people have other idols: the gods of money, pleasure, ease and comfort, popularity, fame, power, and more. These gods can be set up as the lords of life, dictating what one does and how one lives as a person seeks to achieve these goals.

Yet Paul knew the one truth. These gods aren't real. These lords are illusory. Only one true God exists and is worthy of our pursuits. God the Father and the Lord Jesus Christ are the ultimate reality. They are worth all our efforts, pursuits, and love. We exist because of God. We exist to praise and relate to God. God is the true beginning and end of all things and should be so for us. Each day should start with seeking God. Each day should consist of living under the lordship and instruction of Jesus. Each day should be filled with loving others in the love of Christ, serving others with the heart of Christ, praying for others with the fervor of Christ, and bringing praise and glory to God in the process.

At the end of a day like that, we can lie down in peaceful rest, knowing that the day was well and truly spent. No energy was wasted chasing after the illusion of gods and lords. And the true God was glorified.

I don't want to live a false story. I don't want my life built on false gods or lords. I want the one true story as the foundation and purpose of all I do.

Lord, may my day be spent in loving praise of you for all you are, all you've done, and all you will do. Be my one true Lord today and always. In Jesus, amen.

MARCH 25

But take care that this right of yours does not somehow become a stumbling block to the weak. (1 Cor. 8:9)

I overheard my wife on the telephone speaking to one of our daughters. They were talking about what to do for our son-in-law's upcoming birthday. Becky and I wanted to do something special to affirm our love for him. I couldn't hear our daughter's end of the conversation, just Becky's. But it was apparent from hearing Becky's end that the conclusion was a good one and that our son-in-law would be honored and feel loved.

In much the same way, we get to today's passage in 1 Corinthians. Paul wrote to address specific circumstances in Corinth, and we aren't there to see those circumstances. Much like hearing one side of a telephone conversation, we only get Paul's side of this discussion. Yet from this one-sided presentation, we can draw several confident conclusions.

The issue at stake is how the church should interact with what is considered acceptable by some (eating food left over from sacrifices to pagan gods) but is not acceptable for others. Those OK with it realize the gods are nonentities. But while others also know the truth about the pagan idols, their consciences still bother them when eating it. Paul doesn't want this person's conscience violated. For Paul, the question revolves around the point of focus. Are we to live our lives exercising our own freedoms, without regard to how we affect others? Or do we consider the results of our actions on those near and dear to us?

Food sacrificed to idols isn't much of a problem in our age. The closest we might come is eating meat that is "halal," which references meat killed in alignment with Muslim law in the Quran. Halal meat is butchered with a dedicatory prayer to Allah, the Muslim God. Most Christians aren't bothered by that meat and don't give it a second thought. But a Muslim who converts to Christianity might be bothered. If so, and if eating together, the conscience of the bothered sister or brother should rule over the one able to eat it. The same principle applies in other areas where there are legitimate differences among believers about certain practices. Whether under the circumstances of Corinth or today, we have a chance to live our lives to build others up. That is Paul's ultimate dictate in this passage.

Lord, let me focus on building up those around me in service to you. In Jesus' name, amen.

MARCH 26

For though I am free from all, I have made myself a servant to all, that I might win more of them. . . . I do it all for the sake of the gospel, that I may share with them in its blessings. (1 Cor. 9:19, 23)

In Lubbock, Texas, there used to be a restaurant named The Elephant. I never knew the source of the name, but this restaurant had a massive buffet, big enough to feed an elephant. I'm not sure the buffet would hold as much appeal to me today, but at the time, it was the most impressive lineup of food I could imagine.

The restaurant comes to mind as I read today's passage because Paul lists a full buffet of what he is willing to do to win people to Christ and his kingdom. In the part elided by the ellipses above, Paul says he will become a Jew to the Jews, he will be under the law to reach those under the law, he will be as one outside the law to reach those outside the law, and he will become weak to reach the weak. He sums it up by saying he will become all things to all people just to save some people.

Paul makes himself an Elephant-style buffet to feed and reach the tastes and dispositions of anyone with whom he comes into contact. Paul is driven by two motives. First, Paul is driven by the call of Jesus on his life. It is so important to Paul to affirm God's direction that Paul will uproot his life, subjugate his own preferences, and live in whatever condition is necessary to fulfill his calling.

Paul's second drive is his compassion for the lost. Paul has a strong desire to reach those who don't know Christ as their Lord. Paul cares for their here and now as well as their eternity. Paul loves reaching the lost.

These two drives in Paul are powerful. They push him to be a "slave" or "servant" to all. I wonder how deeply those two drives affect my life. Am I willing to set aside my comfort, tastes, preferences, desires, and more because I so clearly want to follow God's directives for me? Do I have such love for strangers that I am ready to alter my life to reach them for the gospel? Will I set aside my personal rights to be winsome to others? Will I do so with the goal of wooing them to the gospel? These are serious questions that deserve an answer.

Lord, help me focus on your call and seek to live it. May your purposes for my life exceed my personal desires in life. May I care and love others in ways that make my first mission reaching them with your tender love. In Jesus, amen.

MARCH 27

Do you not know that in a race all the runners run, but only one receives the prize? So run that you may obtain it. Every athlete exercises self-control in all things. They do it to receive a perishable wreath, but we an imperishable. So I do not run aimlessly; I do not box as one beating the air. (1 Cor. 9:24–26)

I have friends who are sports nuts. Certain sports they all follow—typically football, baseball, and basketball. Most also follow a good bit of soccer. Several are avid boxing fans. A few of them follow tennis diligently. You can talk to them about various players, past and present. You can discuss sports strategy as well as trivia. They may not all play sports, but they have a passion for sports nonetheless. I think the apostle Paul was a sports nut. He readily uses sports analogies in multiple letters, including 1 Corinthians, as seen in today's passage.

Sports analogies were especially fitting for a letter to the folks at Corinth. Corinth was on an isthmus in ancient Greece, and every other year, Corinth would host the "Isthmian games," a festival of athletic and musical competitions. During the time Paul wrote, the winner of each event would receive a pine wreath. People came from all over Greece to enter and compete. It was a mini-Olympiad in its day.

Paul used the athletic analogy to speak of the way a Christian should live. Athletes don't just stumble into a competition; they prepare and train hard. Just like athletes today, they had workout regimes, dietary habits, and thorough practices. This put all athletes at their best come competition time.

In the same way, Christians should live deliberately. Life shouldn't be stumbled through one day at a time. Rather, we should consider thoughtfully how to live. Each day should be carefully tuned to an active lifestyle that grows us in holiness and obedience to God.

The ancient athletes would work hard to compete in Corinth and win a pine wreath. Paul notes that Christians are living a life that will result in an eternal wreath or award. Of all people anywhere, Christians have the best reason to live careful and deliberate lives. How we spend our time, treat others, set our priorities and goals, talk with others, protect our minds, and care for those under our influence—in all these aspects of life, we should be thoughtful, living with care and attention.

Lord, give me focus for today to live thoughtfully for you. In Jesus' name, amen.

MARCH 28

Now these things took place as examples for us, that we might not desire evil as they did. Do not be idolaters as some of them were. . . . We must not indulge in sexual immorality as some of them did. . . . We must not put Christ to the test, as some of them did . . . nor grumble, as some of them did. . . . Now these things happened to them as an example, but they were written down for our instruction. (1 Cor. 10:6–11)

"'Will you walk into my parlor?' said the spider to the fly, ''Tis the prettiest little parlor that ever you did spy.'" Mom read this 1829 poem to me over and over as a child. She urged my sister Kathryn and I to commit it to memory. In the poem, the fly knows to refrain from the spider's invitations. That is until the spider plays on the vanity of the fly, explaining that she has a mirror for the fly to see his brilliant eyes and handsome wings. This the fly can't resist, and you can guess the poem's gruesome ending.

Mom taught us this poem as a moral lesson. She wasn't ready to teach an eight-year-old the moral truths more important for a young adult, but the power of temptation and the need to resist were appropriately taught in the easily understood poem.

In much the same vein, Paul explained that certain Old Testament texts had a teaching use beyond a simple history lesson. In Paul's fuller text, without the ellipses, he uses the exodus stories of Israel as a warning to live a godly life. The idolaters were more concerned with eating, drinking, and playing in the name of a golden calf than they were with worshiping the one true God. The sexually immoral people brazenly brought a pagan woman into their midst for sexual favors, all under the eyes of a permissive Israel. The grumblers whined that they were better off dying in Egypt or the wilderness than trying to invade Canaan.

These were all examples of people living self-centered lives rather than pursuing God's plans and his ways. Self-centeredness didn't work for them, and it doesn't work for us. As tempting as sin can be, Paul knew it was like the fly venturing into the spider's web. It doesn't end well.

Paul wants his readers to learn from this. Live for God today. Not for ourselves.

Lord, I confess that my actions and intent often lean into my desires. Forgive me. Grow my heart for your love and your ways. In Jesus, amen.

MARCH 29

No temptation has overtaken you that is not common to man. God is faithful, and he will not let you be tempted beyond your ability, but with the temptation he will also provide the way of escape, that you may be able to endure it. (1 Cor. 10:13)

Passages like today's give me pause. I struggle with them. I am bothered because I have sometimes found temptation seemingly too strong to conquer. Over and over, temptation has won in my confrontations, and a passage that seems to suggest I should always win isn't borne out in my life. Am I defective? Or am I misunderstanding the passage?

Today's passage shows the importance of reading Scripture in context. Paul isn't stating that the Christian should be able to live completely free from sin. Verse 13, which is set out above, is strategically placed between verses 12 and 14. In other words, there is a specific context through which we must first understand the verse before applying it to ourselves.

Paul is in the middle of addressing a major problem in the Corinthian church. The members were struggling to determine whether it is wrong to eat food sacrificed to idols. The craving to be accepted by others seems to be dictating their actions, which should rather be dictated by a desire to please God. So Paul teaches them that they don't have to succumb to the pressures of doing what everyone else does. Each believer can flee from acts that boost paganism. God always provides a way to live without compromising our faith in him.

This passage teaches us that our motives and desires should be centered on living the Christian life. As we understand it within its context, we gain better insight into its application to us.

Paul knows all sin. He sinned; we sin. Paul isn't setting up the normal Christian life as one where we are able to refrain from sinning. But Paul knew the importance of walking in God's path. He also knew that our temptations to fit in can lead us to do things we shouldn't. Paul drives home the point that we should never put pleasing others in front of pleasing God. God will give us an avenue to live better in this world by pursuing him above ourselves and loving others.

Lord, I confess my sinfulness. I struggle and often seem unable to be who I want to be. But I pray for your strength and the courage to do what is right. Show me your ways today, and embolden me to pursue you vigorously. In Jesus, amen.

MARCH 30

"All things are lawful," but not all things are helpful. "All things are lawful," but not all things build up. Let no one seek his own good, but the good of his neighbor. . . . So, whether you eat or drink, or whatever you do, do all to the glory of God. Give no offense to Jews or to Greeks or to the church of God, just as I try to please everyone in everything I do, not seeking my own advantage, but that of many, that they may be saved. (1 Cor. 10:23–24, 31–33)

The United States of America is known as a country of freedom. The First Amendment to the U.S. Constitution ensures people free speech. It also ensures freedom of religion and freedom of assembly. People are not only allowed but encouraged to pursue the job of their passion. We are a nation of self-directed people, choosing what we want in life and pursuing it.

Into that modern readership comes today's passage, one that describes how a Christian should view their freedoms in Christ. In Christ, the dietary laws of the Old Testament (eating "kosher") are gone. The Old Testament instructions for religious festivals and holy days are gone. The Old Testament system of sacrifices is gone. There is great freedom in the Christian life. Moreover, the progressive freedoms in Christ didn't simply substitute a new set of rules to update or replace the old ones. Those rules are gone.

But the freedoms that accompany the Christian aren't to be understood or expressed based simply on what pleases each individual. The freedoms aren't in place to allow believers to selfishly choose their own direction. Those freedoms exist to enable believers to live in ways that win others to Jesus. Christians should not exercise their freedom by doing whatever they want. Instead, Paul wants to woo others to faith, to grow people in faith, and to encourage people in faith by using their freedoms wisely. Freedom comes so one can serve, modeling Jesus in life: "For even the Son of Man came not to be served but to serve, and to give his life as a ransom for many" (Mk. 10:45).

Living in a free country is a huge blessing. Not worrying about going to jail for what I say, how and when I worship, and when and with whom I meet has become so commonplace, I often don't realize those liberties are unknown in parts of the world. Yet that same freedom mentality needs to be checked in me. I need to heed Paul's intense focus on living for Christ in ways that reach others.

Lord, give me a burning desire to serve those around me. In Jesus, amen.

MARCH 31

Be imitators of me, as I am of Christ. (1 Cor. 11:1)

As of the time I am writing this, I have walked with the Lord for about fifty years. For forty-five of those years, I have worked to read the Greek text of the New Testament and the Hebrew text of the Old Testament. For over forty years, I have taught in churches. I have led innumerable retreats and given lectures at events, and I have presided over more weddings and funerals than I can count. Although I am far from perfect, I try hard to live faithfully to God and model the Christian faith to others.

Yet with all of that, I find an important truth. There are faithful followers of Christ who inspire me and are examples for me. Recently, I went on a trip with two such men. They are younger than me by decades, yet they have a godly walk that encourages me to live better before God. The three of us stayed almost a week together in the same home in a foreign country. I watched how they spent time in prayer and the Word, how they valued others, how they spoke of their faith, and how they lived it. This time with my younger friends encouraged me. They touched my life, and I wanted to imitate them in many ways. I pray that I do the same for others.

You and I have unique walks with God. Our walks with God are always encouraged by watching and learning from the walks of godly people. This is true regardless of how long we have been believers or how much we know the Bible. Similarly, our walks with God should be such that others are encouraged when they see us. We should have a closeness with God such that others find it useful to "imitate" us in life.

In today's passage, Paul gives the key to such a life: imitate Christ. That is the fundamental for the Christian walk. As we imitate Christ, we can inspire others to live in godliness. As others imitate Christ, they can serve as models and inspirations to us. In Acts 11:26, we learn that in ancient Antioch, believers were first called "Christians." The idea behind the term is that they were partisans of Christ. By name, a Christian is like a "little Jesus." Let's live that way for the benefit of others, and let's learn from others who do so as well.

Lord, help me live as one who reflects Christ to others. Please place in my life strong influences for Christ. I want to grow in you as I pray in Jesus, amen.

APRIL 1

But in the following instructions I do not commend you, because when you come together it is not for the better but for the worse. For, in the first place, when you come together as a church, I hear that there are divisions among you. . . . When you come together, it is not the Lord's supper that you eat. For in eating, each one goes ahead with his own meal. One goes hungry, another gets drunk. . . . Do you despise the church of God and humiliate those who have nothing? What shall I say to you? Shall I commend you in this? No, I will not. (1 Cor. 11:17–22)

I love time travel shows. As a kid, I watched *The Time Tunnel.* Michael Crichton wrote *Timeline*, which also became a movie. *Dr. Who* is a longtime favorite. I do wonder what it would be like to go back in time, walk into Corinth in AD 55, and "go to church." My first problem would be finding the church.

The Corinthian church community met mostly in homes, likely those of the wealthier members. (The servant class generally had no homes, but lived with their owners.) The church wasn't a designated building, and it didn't have a sign out front. The worship times might well vary each week, but without real clocks for everyone, the time wouldn't be strictly adhered to. Church wouldn't start at "9:30 on the dot." Most of the time, church would start near a mealtime. In Corinth, it seems the church gathered around a general meal, often termed a "love" or *agapē* meal. The Lord's Supper, or Eucharist, would follow thereafter.

Gathering would have been an issue, for Sundays didn't become a day off until after the emperor Constantine became a Christian centuries later and made the Roman Empire Christian rather than pagan. So the slaves and working classes might well have been late to any service, coming in after the meal was underway or perhaps even finished by those with more control over their schedules.

Services at uncertain times and late arrivers created problems. Add that even the larger wealthier houses had dining rooms (*tricliniums*) that would allow only ten or so to recline at meal. Others would likely be standing in an inner courtyard, the late-coming lower classes eating the dregs left and maybe even cleaning up.

This created a problem. The people came together for their own supper, not the Lord's Supper. Jesus died to make one church, not a segregated church. Paul wanted the people to focus on the others at church, not themselves. I live two thousand years later, but my focus should still be on others.

Lord, give me eyes to see and the will to overcome division in Jesus' name. Amen.

APRIL 2

For I received from the Lord what I also delivered to you, that the Lord Jesus on the night when he was betrayed took bread, and when he had given thanks, he broke it, and said, "This is my body, which is for you. Do this in remembrance of me." In the same way also he took the cup, after supper, saying, "This cup is the new covenant in my blood. Do this, as often as you drink it, in remembrance of me." For as often as you eat this bread and drink the cup, you proclaim the Lord's death until he comes. (1 Cor. 11:23–26)

Jesus died for your sins and mine. Jesus was resurrected into a new life, one that we inherit and share. Jesus sits at the right hand of God the Father, and he will come again to bring judgment to humanity and eternity in his presence to his followers. The church declares these truths every time it takes communion or "the Lord's Supper" (also called the Eucharist).

Today's passage is a powerful reminder of why we come together to do church. Church is community life built around worshiping God. We worship him in song, prayer, the teaching of his Scriptures, fellowship with one another, and the Lord's Supper.

I grew up in a church where the Lord's Supper was celebrated each Sunday. Some churches today offer the Lord's Supper each morning of the week! Some churches celebrate it once a month, others once a quarter, and others less frequently.

Paul wrote about the Lord's Supper not to establish a schedule for taking it but to prescribe the meaning behind the Supper and how it was to be taken. The "how" is set out in the larger context of today's passage. The people were to come *together* to take the Supper. It was to be a uniting act, not a segregating one. The participants were to examine themselves, put themselves to the test, to make sure that they partook with proper attitude.

The proper attitude for the supper is a reflection on the historical death of Jesus, our sin and need for Jesus' death, the fact of his bodily resurrection, and the significance that we will likewise be resurrected and therefore will live with him eternally. We are to remember these things regularly. They should never be far from our minds. Thinking about them should be as regular as eating. Jesus instituted this reminder and worship. As Paul reminds us, it's his Supper we are taking.

Lord, be glorified. I need you. I wait for your return. I pray in your name, amen.

APRIL 3

Now concerning spiritual gifts, brothers, I do not want you to be uninformed. . . . Now there are varieties of gifts, but the same Spirit; and there are varieties of service, but the same Lord; and there are varieties of activities, but it is the same God who empowers them all in everyone. To each is given the manifestation of the Spirit for the common good. (1 Cor. 12:1, 4–7)

My buddy (and pastor) Jarrett Stephens says, with a smile, "My spiritual gift is hanging out!" My sweet wife, Becky, says her spiritual gift is DoorDash, a service from which she can order meals to be delivered to the door of others in need. Both speak with humor, but both make a real point. God gives a variety of gifts to his people, and those gifts have purposes.

In the verses that follow today's passage, Paul illustrates his point by identifying multiple gifts. God gives some the gift of sharing wisdom. Others receive the ability to learn and speak with knowledge. For some, their spiritual gift is a rock-solid faith. Still others receive the gift of healing, helping those with physical, mental, or emotional maladies find healthier lives. Some people have an ability to work miracles, while others can speak affirmatively the ideas and words of God. Some people receive a unique ability to tell the difference between what is godly and what isn't. Some can speak in different languages, and others can translate those languages! Paul's list isn't exhaustive; he adds other gifts elsewhere (see Rom. 12; Eph. 4). Ultimately, Paul is saying that God supplies the church with its needs for growing, evangelizing, and living in the will and purposes of God.

Today is a different day in the life of the church than the day of Paul. Today, we have Holy Scripture with words affirmed by the church as spiritually inspired. These words set out prophecy, knowledge, and wisdom. Today's gifts needed by the church include the ability to expound on Scripture as well as the capacity to apply it in our culture. Through God's gift of science and order in the natural world, most nations and people have access to medical care, which can deliver much of the needed healing for people.

But gifts are still needed for today's church, even if they take on a different color and hue than in Paul's day. God gives people an ability, a special gift instilled by God's indwelling presence in his Spirit, to build up, encourage, teach, love, and support the church. We should use all God gives us for those he and we love!

Lord, use me in serving others. Work in me to that end. In Jesus' name, amen.

APRIL 4

Therefore I want you to understand that no one speaking in the Spirit of God ever says "Jesus is accursed!" and no one can say "Jesus is Lord" except in the Holy Spirit. (1 Cor. 12:3)

I had a buddy named Eddie in high school who was a self-proclaimed atheist. (Eddie later became a strong believer and Bible teacher.) Eddie and I would frequently discuss whether God was real, whether the Bible was inspired, and other related topics. One day, Eddie came to class with today's passage in hand as a proof text that there was no God.

Eddie said to me, "Read this!" And I read the passage. Eddie said, "See where it says, 'no one can say "Jesus is Lord" except in the Holy Spirit'?" I said, "Yes." Eddie then said, "Jesus is Lord!" adding, "See? I said it, and I don't believe it. So I can say Jesus is Lord without the Holy Spirit! The Bible is wrong, and there is no God."

Careful reading of the context, as well as a better understanding of the Greek word translated "say," explains Eddie's misunderstanding of this passage. Paul doesn't write of what words form in one's mouth. The context makes clear that Paul is speaking of the words and actions that flow from one's heart and life. Some scholars call this a "speech-act." We understand this not only from Paul's context but also from the Greek verb in use (*lego*—λέγω). The word conveys a semantic range of meaning, including the ideas of recommending, directing, maintaining, and other activities of living that accompany a simple pronouncement.

Paul is clarifying that one can't say *and* live in a way that demonstrates and affirms the lordship of Jesus in life, except by the power of God's Holy Spirit. This was true in Paul's day, it was true for Eddie in high school, and it is true for me today. If I am going to live and proclaim the lordship of Jesus, I am going to need God's help. On my own, a holy life is futile. But by God's presence, direction, and empowerment, holiness becomes an achievable goal.

Daily, I need to seek God's assistance in living under the lordship of Jesus. This needs to be a pointed prayer for me today and every day.

Lord, empower me to live with Jesus as Lord today. Help me better understand how to live the truth of his love and holiness. I want to be a walking testimony of your lordship. In Jesus I pray, amen.

APRIL 5

For the body does not consist of one member but of many. . . . If the ear should say, "Because I am not an eye, I do not belong to the body," that would not make it any less a part of the body. If the whole body were an eye, where would be the sense of hearing? If the whole body were an ear, where would be the sense of smell? But as it is, God arranged the members in the body, each one of them, as he chose. . . . The eye cannot say to the hand, "I have no need of you," nor again the head to the feet, "I have no need of you." On the contrary, the parts of the body that seem to be weaker are indispensable. . . . But God has so composed the body, giving greater honor to the part that lacked it. . . . If one member suffers, all suffer together; if one member is honored, all rejoice together. (1 Cor. 12:14–26)

On a recent family vacation, one of our daughters had a complex puzzle of one thousand pieces out on a table for all to work on when they passed by. The puzzle had just been started, and the border wasn't finished. I was carrying one of our two-year-old twin granddaughters, who decided to try to put two pieces together. She took a center piece with knobs on all four sides and tried to put it on the outside border. Of course it wasn't right; the outside border requires one edge to be flat.

If you wish to complete a puzzle, you need every piece. The puzzle is not finished if one piece is missing, whether it is an end piece, a corner piece, or one of the many interior pieces. A full puzzle includes every piece.

The puzzle analogy is akin to the human body analogy Paul uses in today's passage. In both, the whole is made up of many parts. To emphasize one part over another is shortsighted. Each plays a role. Each is important.

So it is with the church. The preacher may be front and center, and the janitor may work behind the scenes, but both are important parts of the church's body. No one wants a church without clean restrooms!

I fear that in today's churches, many seem to think their role is to sit in a pew or seat. That misses an important part of Paul's analogy (and is why his is better than my puzzle analogy)! Every part of the body is intended to serve the greater body as a whole. So everyone who lives in Christ should be plugged into a church where they can minister and serve others in the church. Maybe it's greeting others each Sunday, helping people in need, comforting those hurting, and so on. But all are needed!

Lord, help me find my place serving the body of Christ, the church. In you, amen.

APRIL 6

And God has appointed in the church first apostles, second prophets, third teachers, then miracles, then gifts of healing, helping, administrating, and various kinds of tongues. . . . But earnestly desire the higher gifts. And I will show you a still more excellent way. If I speak in the tongues of men and of angels, but have not love, I am a noisy gong or a clanging cymbal. And if I have prophetic powers, and understand all mysteries and all knowledge, and if I have all faith, so as to remove mountains, but have not love, I am nothing. If I give away all I have, and if I deliver up my body to be burned, but have not love, I gain nothing. (1 Cor. 12:28–13:3)

OK, admit it: Who wouldn't want to have the gift of healing, where you could, with the aid of the Holy Spirit, walk up to someone paralyzed, pronounce them healed, and see them stand up? Or how about the more generic ability to work miracles, like walking on water or turning water into wine? Or what about, through the Holy Spirit, appearing one place and disappearing as suddenly as the resurrected Jesus?

In today's passage, toward the end of chapter 12 in 1 Corinthians, Paul whets his readers' appetites for these miraculous gifts. But then Paul puts this big claim to his readers—he says, "You might want those great gifts, but our earnest desire should be for an even greater gift." He then explains the greatest of all gifts.

The greatest gift is love. Not some romantic or sex-driven love but a commitment-to-serve-and-care-for-others love. In the Greek, this distinguishes an *agapē* love from an *eros* love. For Paul, the *agapē* love is the more excellent way of life. It is the greatest gift.

I can do lots of good things, but their value is minimal if they aren't accompanied by love. I can speak fifty languages, but if I don't speak to them with love, I'm just making noise. I could be smarter than a tree full of owls, but if I don't engage that brain power with love, then I am a waste of neural activity. If I can teleport mountains from one place to another but don't do so with love, I might as well be playing in a sandbox.

Our lives have meaning when they focus on caring for others. Our actions are right and proper when they center on serving others. Our talents are effectively used when they are used to help others. Serving in love is the greatest gift.

Lord, give me a heart to love others. In the name of the loving Jesus, amen.

APRIL 7

Love is patient and kind; love does not envy or boast; it is not arrogant or rude. It does not insist on its own way; it is not irritable or resentful; it does not rejoice at wrongdoing, but rejoices with the truth. Love bears all things, believes all things, hopes all things, endures all things. (1 Cor. 13:4–7)

In 1967, the "Summer of Love," the Beatles were chosen to be Great Britain's representative for the world's first televised satellite hookup between twenty-five countries. For the broadcast, John Lennon penned the Beatles hit "All You Need Is Love." The simple song is built around the title phrase, which is sung over and over. The song ends with the similar phrase "Love is all you need," sung by a chorus of many of the greats of the day, including Eric Clapton, Mick Jagger, Keith Richards, Graham Nash, and more.

Some critics have applauded the song as the Beatles' greatest. Others have panned it as naïve and "bloated with self-confidence." I can see the critics' concerns, but the power of the song is that it has a simple and easy-to-understand message. Love is a powerful force. Lennon was never one to proclaim Scripture, but the characteristics of powerful love have never been more clearly described than by Paul in today's passage.

I like to think of Paul's description of love in reference to different groups. First, I need to model Paul's instructions to those in my family that I love in unique ways. Do I love those I care for with patience and kindness? I shouldn't be irritable or resentful but should bear all things and endure all things.

Another group that comes front and center when reading Paul are those whom I don't count in my inner circle. Jesus said his followers should love their enemies. I wonder how I do with others in that or similar camps. Do I avoid envy and boasting? Are arrogance and rudeness found in how I behave? Do I refrain from rejoicing in wrongdoing but rejoice in and encourage truth? Do I seek to hope and believe rather than dismiss and reject? These traits are hard to find when dealing with those that aren't high on my "fondness list." Yet these are traits I need.

Passages like today's may seem a bit naïve, a bit like the rap on the Beatles song. Yet these are the very passages that bring me to my knees, knowing I need to grow before God in very real, core behavioral ways.

Lord, teach me true love. Help me love my friends and enemies in Jesus, amen.

APRIL 8

So now faith, hope, and love abide, these three; but the greatest of these is love. (1 Cor. 13:13)

In the 1987 classic movie *The Princess Bride*, Wesley pursues the captured Buttercup to rescue her from the evil clutches of the six-fingered man. Wesley gets caught and tortured, nearly dying before being rescued. His companions take him to see Miracle Max to revive him. Max at first refuses, asking why it is so important. Barely audible, Wesley whispers, "True love!" Max replies with a line ad-libbed by the actor Billy Crystal: "Sonny, true love is the greatest thing in the world—except for a nice MLT—mutton, lettuce, and tomato sandwich, where the mutton is nice and lean and the tomato is ripe. They're so perky; I love that!"

Paul would agree. Nothing is greater than a genuine godly love. That doesn't mean that other things aren't important. But something about love sets it apart, making it worthy of our best pursuits. Paul sets out this truth in today's passage.

Paul approaches the end of his opus on love by setting out three very important Christian virtues: faith, hope, and love. Faith is extremely important in the writings of Paul. We are saved through faith (Eph. 2:8–10). We walk by faith (2 Cor. 5:7). The righteousness of God is revealed from faith to faith (Rom. 1:17).

Similarly, the virtue of hope is integral to Paul's understanding. Paul terms God the "God of hope" (Rom. 15:13). Hope gives us boldness to walk in Christ (2 Cor. 3:12). We rejoice in hope (Rom. 12:12).

Yet as key as faith and hope are, they don't rise to the level of love. Paul wrote of this at the end of a paragraph where Paul spoke of eternity spent in the presence of Christ. In this context, we can readily see why love takes a preeminent position among these stalwart virtues. Once this life passes and believers spend eternity in God's presence, faith will have become sight. Hope will have been realized. Those two virtues will have finished their work in our lives. But love will last for eternity. We will love God, love his work, and love one another for time unending.

Love is indeed the greatest thing. With due respect to Billy Crystal, it is even greater than a nice MLT—or anything Chick-fil-A!

Lord, teach me to love as you love. I want to love you, my family, my friends, and even my enemies as Jesus loves. Through Jesus I pray, amen.

APRIL 9

Pursue love, and earnestly desire the spiritual gifts. (1 Cor. 14:1)

Much of hunting today involves preparation. People set up deer leases with deer feeders and deer stands that are a suitable distance from the feeders, and they set their gunsights for that distance. But in Paul's day, hunting was different. Hunters would travel to where they knew animals were likely to be found. They would look for signs of the animals and move decisively to get in range to kill their prey. This is relevant to today's verse.

On another note, the Greek playwright Aeschylus, who predated Paul by four centuries but whose plays were still performed and known in Paul's day, wrote in *Seven against Thebes* of the army of the white shield getting ready for battle and then rushing at full speed against the city.

In both situations above (a hunting description and the referenced play), the Greek writers would use the verb *diōkō* (διώκω) to describe the action of hunting or rushing at full speed. This is the verb Paul chose to use in writing today's passage. Paul wants his readers to "pursue" love, to chase after it as hunters did their prey. Paul wants his readers to rush at full speed to get love.

How does one do that? How does one work to get love? Many in the West believe that love is an emotional strike that might happen at first sight. But Paul is clearly writing about a different love. The love of Christ that Paul wants his readers to chase is a process. For this reason, Paul uses the present tense in his writing. To a Greek reader, Paul is saying, "Hasten after love every minute of every day! Do it right now!"

Scriptures give insight into how we can grow and give this godly love. One way is to spend time reflecting and appreciating the love Christ has for you (see 1 Jn. 4:19: "We love because he first loved us"). Jesus taught that as we put our time and efforts into a cause, we will find our hearts following (see Mt. 6:21: "Where your treasure is, there your heart will be also").

Daily, our efforts should go into loving and caring for others. We should invest our time and energy in them. We should reflect on Christ's love for others and seek to emulate that. Paul says we should rush to do this! Make it your priority today!

Lord, teach me to love as you love. In and for Jesus, I pray, amen.

APRIL 10

Brothers, do not be children in your thinking. Be infants in evil, but in your thinking be mature. (1 Cor. 14:20)

You've got to love a good metaphor. I do, and Paul certainly did. Our minds seem to think in metaphors. Grabbing one thing you know and understand and using it to understand another concept is fundamental to learning and retaining what we learn.

Aging in life is a great metaphor. Many ancient cultures mentioned aging in the form of a riddle. The ancient Greek Apollodorus wrote that Oedipus was bequeathed a kingdom by answering a Sphinx's riddle. (Many had tried and failed to answer the riddle, causing them to be gobbled up by the Sphinx.) The riddle was "What has one voice yet becomes four-footed, then two-footed, and then three-footed?" The answer was "a person," who crawls in infancy, walks in adulthood, then uses a cane in old age.

In this passage, Paul uses aging not as part of a riddle but rather as a metaphor for how one's attitudes and knowledge adjust in aging. Paul wants the reader to be grown up about what they think and do. Being grown up, ironically, includes the idea of being "infants in evil."

Having five children and (as of this writing) ten grandchildren makes me appreciate this metaphor. Our four-month-old granddaughter Zoey knows nothing of evil. She knows joy and smiles throughout the day. She knows her mother's voice and finds it soothing. She can call out (OK, she *cries* out, typically!), she maintains bodily functions, and she has recently discovered her hand belongs to her. But evil? She has no knowledge of evil. Evil motives and evil deeds are not found in her. Period.

That is how Paul wants the believer to be. By calling us to infancy in evil, Paul wants us to abstain from not only evil acts but also evil thoughts. Our minds should never be evil's playground. We shouldn't be flirting with evil. Evil should be shunned. We should be infants in evil.

Before closing this metaphor, note that Paul says to be "mature" in thinking. Maturity is akin to not being children in thinking. This is our growth plan!

Lord, grow me in mature thinking. Wash me from evil and renew my mind, bringing me back to infancy in evil. In Jesus' name, amen.

APRIL 11

God is not a God of confusion but of peace. (1 Cor. 14:33)

Recently, on a family vacation, we had all ten grandchildren, together with our five children and their four spouses. One morning, I was reflecting on this passage as the grandchildren were running around. It was a zoo. One granddaughter was playing make-believe that she was an alien and trying to discern who was human and who wasn't. Another set of grandkids was learning how to share a toy designed for ages two to three. (That is a polite way of saying they were fighting for the same toy.) Two of the grandchildren were singing at full volume. And several were just yelling so they could be heard above the din of the rest. It was a zoo.

All of this was happening on the morning my quiet time had me reading, "God is not a God of confusion but of peace." Our zoo was marvelous and draining all at once. But our zoo was appropriate for a family vacation with a passel of kids seven and under. Becky and I were smiling, and I suspect God was too.

Earlier that same day I had gone to a local church down the street. We were vacationing in England, and this church was noticeably different from our home church. The service was liturgically based, and the mood was contemplative and quiet. God was honored in the service, and I was edified.

With those two times of the same day in stark contrast to each other, I decided to write about today's passage. The Corinthians had a problem. Their worship services had descended into chaos. People were clamoring to be heard, with many speaking at the same time. Some were speaking in tongues—apparently some ecstatic utterance that no one else understood. Some of the women kept interrupting the service with loud questions about one thing or another. The church had no real focus in its services; it was a bit like my vacation zoo with the grandkids.

The reason my zoo took place was that all the kids were playing in their own worlds while occupying the same space as the others. So the space alien had to shout to keep her play going while the twins were singing "Happy Birthday" loudly to anyone they saw. Each was focused on their own goal. But in church, everyone is to have the same focus and goal. Our attention is on God, praising him and understanding him by serving others. For this we need order, not chaos. We must be single-minded about God in those times.

Lord, give me a proper focus on you and your heart for others. In Jesus, amen.

APRIL 12

Now I would remind you, brothers, of the gospel I preached to you, which you received, in which you stand, and by which you are being saved. . . . For I delivered to you as of first importance what I also received: that Christ died for our sins in accordance with the Scriptures, that he was buried, that he was raised on the third day in accordance with the Scriptures. (1 Cor. 15:1–4)

"Finish what you started," my dad would preach to me when I was young. "Too many people start things and then leave them before finishing!" I'd love to say I always took Dad's advice, but I haven't. His words echo in my head, however, as I study today's passage and all of chapter 15 in 1 Corinthians.

Paul is nearing the end of his letter, and his thoughts reinforce his mighty theme given in 1 Corinthians 2:2: "For I resolved to know nothing among you except Jesus Christ and him crucified." He is setting about finishing what he started. The entirety of chapter 15, the penultimate chapter in his letter, is centered directly on the crucifixion of Christ.

As Paul expounds on the crucifixion and resurrection, we get the most direct glimpse of a word that is almost uniquely Paul's in the Bible. Paul takes a compound noun, *good news*, and turns it into a verb. First Paul sets out the compound noun, which is translated as "gospel." Then Paul takes that word and puts it into a verb form—and here, the translators are at a bit of a loss, so they translate it "preached," for that is how Paul gave the good news. It wouldn't read as seemly saying, "I would remind you of the good news I good newsed to you!"

Of all the occurrences of this verb in the New Testament, around 90 percent are in Paul's writings. It is critical. It is core. It is the message of Christ crucified and resurrected on behalf of humanity. This is the key moment in the Bible's love story. It is the ultimate act of love by a God who pursues and woos you and me. It gives meaning and purpose to all of life. Paul is fresh from writing his magnum opus on love in chapter 13, and it is a natural time for Paul to expound on not only the good news of God's love but the greatest news any of us could receive.

If we fail to live each day focused on God's love and provision, as expressed for all time in the death and resurrection of Christ, we will miss much. God loves you.

Lord, give me a greater understanding of your love expressed in Jesus, amen.

APRIL 13

Christ . . . was raised on the third day in accordance with the Scriptures, and that he appeared to Cephas, then to the twelve. Then he appeared to more than five hundred brothers at one time, most of whom are still alive, though some have fallen asleep. Then he appeared to James, then to all the apostles. Last of all, as to one untimely born, he appeared also to me. (1 Cor. 15:3–8)

In my book *Christianity on Trial,* I titled one chapter "The Audacity of the Resurrection." I chose the word *audacity* carefully. Think about it. The Christian faith is based on the idea that in a minor corner of the ancient Roman Empire, a thirty-something-year-old carpenter-turned-itinerant-preacher from a small backwater village was killed by the authorities, buried under guard by the military, and on the third day, physically resurrected, proving himself to be the Son of God. That seems too preposterous to take over the Roman Empire and replace a millennia-old belief system in the Roman and Greek gods of myth.

Yet the Christian faith in the resurrected Jesus did just that—and grew like wildfire immediately. I don't see that happening with a fictional story. The odds are smaller than winning the lottery. The reason Christian faith grew was the testimony of eyewitnesses, the conviction of the Holy Spirit, the confirmation of prophecy, and the way it made sense of life and the wiring of the human heart and brain.

Paul himself was an eyewitness to the resurrected Jesus. He wasn't alone, as he says in today's passage. Hundreds were alive who could testify to seeing Jesus physically resurrected from the dead. Paul identified many eyewitnesses, including James, the brother of Jesus, who was a cynic about his big brother's messianic dreams before the resurrection but was willingly a martyr for the faith after seeing it with his own eyes. James wouldn't be the only martyr. Paul himself (along with most apostles) and so many others gladly gave their lives rather than recant what they knew to be true: Christ was resurrected.

The resurrection isn't just a cool miracle. It is the saving act of ultimate love by a wonderful and just God. Christ crucified was a just solution to the sin of humanity. Like an insurance company satisfies the debt someone owes when in a car crash, so Christ satisfies the debt of sin. The resurrection then confirms that those who share in the death of Christ will also share in his resurrection. Death becomes the door to eternity in God's presence. How audacious and grand!

Lord, thank you for the resurrection. Grow my faith in the resurrected one, amen.

APRIL 14

The sting of death is sin, and the power of sin is the law. But thanks be to God, who gives us the victory through our Lord Jesus Christ. Therefore, my beloved brothers, be steadfast, immovable, always abounding in the work of the Lord, knowing that in the Lord your labor is not in vain. (1 Cor. 15:56–58)

Dr. Harvey Floyd had a huge influence on me and many others. He was one of my Greek professors and also taught other classes in the Bible department at Lipscomb University. One day, a student who didn't know Dr. Floyd well asked before class began, "Dr. Floyd, we've never heard about the day you got saved. While we await others getting to class, would you tell us about it?" Dr. Floyd got a wistful look on his face. He looked toward the floor and took off his glasses while murmuring, "The day I got saved . . . ," and then he looked up.

Dr. Floyd said, "Well, it was a magnificent day almost two thousand years ago right outside the city of Jerusalem." He then began recounting the story of the death, burial, and resurrection of Jesus Christ, concluding with "I was saved on that day."

Dr. Floyd followed the footsteps of faith that Paul had. Paul knew where his victory in life came from. It came from the death and resurrection of Christ. In today's passage, we read the culmination of over fifty verses where Paul discusses the death and resurrection of Christ, the day all believers were saved. This day was transformational. It rocked all of history for all eternity. It changed my life.

Paul knew that the truth and power of the resurrection weren't simply a box ticked that meant life after death. The resurrection also speaks loudly into the here and now. It motivated Paul to turn his life upside down in response to the calling of God to share God's love with a world in need. Experiencing God and his love gave Paul the drive to live under the conviction that faith is true.

We can trust God in the present, as we have seen him secure the future. We can trust his will, his instructions and guidance, his claims of holiness, and his purposes for our lives. We can shun the seductions of the world in favor of the truth of his love. This love and truth make us steadfast, immovable, always abounding in the work of the Lord. Several thousand years ago, Christ not only saved me for eternity, but he also saved me for life today!

Lord, thank you for your saving and transforming love. In Jesus, amen.

APRIL 15

I will visit you after passing through Macedonia, for I intend to pass through Macedonia, and perhaps I will stay with you or even spend the winter, so that you may help me on my journey, wherever I go. For I do not want to see you now just in passing. I hope to spend some time with you, if the Lord permits. But I will stay in Ephesus until Pentecost, for a wide door for effective work has opened to me, and there are many adversaries. (1 Cor. 16:5–9)

What to do, what to do—everyone has twenty-four hours in a day. Each of those hours is loaded with sixty minutes, each minute with sixty seconds. How are we going to spend them? Two of our five children are intense planners. They not only get joy in making plans, but they also get uncomfortable if they don't make plans. That doesn't mean they can't be spontaneous; they just want to plan it first. You might say that for them, spontaneity has its time and place.

I'm a planner too, albeit not to their degree. My job requires a great bit of scheduling. Time is in high demand. I can work only a certain number of hours each day. This means I live with that concept taught in first-semester economics—*opportunity costs.* This term references that everything we do has a cost of not being able to do something else. If I chose to spend my hour doing Project B, then I cannot do Project A in that hour.

So how do we decide what to do with our time? How do we spend our precious minutes and hours? Paul's focus demonstrated in today's passage is instructive. Notice two things: First, Paul uses his brain. He makes plans that seem right and consistent with his godly desires. He intends to go through Macedonia and strengthen the churches there. These would likely be the Philippian and Thessalonian churches, at least. Paul then plans to walk south into Greece and visit the Corinthians. He notes he might even spend the winter season with them.

Second, Paul adds that important caveat: "If the Lord permits." Paul doesn't want to do anything with his minutes that God hasn't blessed. This instructs me. Paul didn't read God's hand as an excuse for ease of the day, either. Paul was staying in Ephesus to work because God had opened the door there for him before traveling. He worked there despite all the opposition he was getting.

Today's passage should challenge me and you. How are we spending today?

Lord, may I carefully align my plans with your will. In Jesus, amen.

APRIL 16

Be watchful, stand firm in the faith, act like men, be strong. Let all that you do be done in love. (1 Cor. 16:13–14)

I first translated this passage in my late teens as a college student. I don't remember thinking twice about it. The Greek was relatively easy; there are five imperative verbs. Those are verbal commands—"Do this," "Be that," and so on. I could translate this passage and teach this passage without a second thought.

But as life changed, my mind-set changed with it. Today I am far from that nineteen-year-old boy. Many decades older, I have an incredible wife, four amazing daughters, and seven granddaughters. My buddy Pastor Jarrett, who also has four daughters and a wife, says, "I could be president of my own sorority." I can relate.

This change in life circumstances doesn't negate Paul's instructions here, but it does give me pause as I write on it. Paul orders the Corinthians to "act like men." That seems, at first blush, to be unfriendly to the women in my life. At least it seems to disregard them. Yet here is where a more careful study of the text reveals the fuller meaning.

Dissect the five commands from Paul. First, "be watchful." In the Greek, the command is to be alert, alive, and ready to act (*grēgoreō*—γρηγορέω). We get the name *Gregory* from this word. Jesus used it when telling his followers to be ready and watch for his return (Mt. 24:42). The second command is to "stand firm in the faith." Our trust in Christ and his lordship should never be one of convenience. We find trusting in him a firm place to put our feet.

It is then that Paul orders his readers to "act like men." This and the next command to "be strong" are similar. They aren't sexist; they are expressions in the context of his age and culture to have courage. We might translate them to "be courageous," but there is no reason to flee Paul's words. He is instructing all his readers to be courageous, a trait not in the exclusive scope of a man's charge. Paul uses a colloquial expression to exhort everyone to courage. He then sums up that all is to be done in love. This returns the reader's mind to Paul's treatise on life in 1 Corinthians 13. I need to be courageous. The women in my life should be so as well!

Lord, give me the presence to live under these instructions. Help me with being ready for the moment, firmly trusting you with courage and strength. In love, amen.

APRIL 17

I, Paul, write this greeting with my own hand. If anyone has no love for the Lord, let him be accursed. Our Lord, come! The grace of the Lord Jesus be with you. My love be with you all in Christ Jesus. Amen. (1 Cor. 16:21–24)

For over 2,500 years, people have studied how to give a captivating presentation to an audience. Greek playwrights sculpted dramas to enthrall people, even staging competitions for the most entertaining and noteworthy play. Aristotle wrote his famous *Rhetoric* dissecting the elements of a good speech so that presentations would be informative and persuasive while holding the audience's attention. Paul's letter to the Corinthians is written in a style that is all the above.

Paul's letter wasn't intended to hit a copy machine for distribution. Neither was it written for inclusion in a book that would be edited, printed, and placed in the local bookstore. Paul wrote a letter that was to be read to the congregation. It would then be hand-copied. And while some might keep a copy at Corinth, other copies would expectedly be sent to other congregations for reading out loud in their gatherings.

This manner of presentation meant that the reading would culminate on a high note. The reader wouldn't fade into oblivion and rapidly pass over the final words with a "blah, blah, blah" attitude. Those words would be read as the crescendo of the piece. So we rightly pay careful attention to how Paul ends his letter.

Paul takes the quill from his secretary, who had been taking Paul's dictation in the letter, and writes the final verses with his own hand. That personalizes these verses in a way to grab the audience's attention. Paul then adds these two interesting phrases, one a curse for those who won't have a relationship with the Lord Jesus and one an Aramaic prayer put into Greek, calling for the return of Jesus. We might consider this Paul's concluding plea of "OK, you've heard this letter, you know what's at stake, you know what is called for—are you in or out?"

This is the real question we should all be asking each day. Do we side with the Lord in our life? Do we seek his coming into the moments of our day, even as we seek his second coming? Paul concludes trusting the answer is "Yes! We want Jesus!" with a prayer for God's grace and a declaration of Paul's love to end his letter. That is where I want to end each day.

Lord, I am in! Give me more of Jesus in my life. By your love and grace, amen.

APRIL 18

Paul, an apostle of Christ Jesus by the will of God, and Timothy our brother, To the church of God that is at Corinth, with all the saints who are in the whole of Achaia: Grace to you and peace from God our Father and the Lord Jesus Christ. (2 Cor. 1:1–2)

Miss Noack, my ninth-grade English teacher, instructed us in the form of paragraph writing. Each paragraph was to begin with a topic sentence. Paragraphs were to mark off different ideas, and each was to begin with a sentence that indicated that new point. Theme papers were to have introductions that were also topically driven, not for the first paragraph only, but also for the entire paper.

In Paul's day, letters like 2 Corinthians had some similar elements. The introduction or beginning of the letter would contain an identifier of the author(s), here Paul and Timothy; the recipients, here the church in Corinth and the surrounding region; and a prayer of blessing or greeting.

Yet in addition to the standard elements of a letter, Paul adds important modifiers that, like a theme paper for Miss Noack, set out important ideas that will later resurface in the letter. Consider several of these:

Paul self-identifies as an "apostle of Christ Jesus *by the will* of God." Paul's job as an emissary, a chosen one with a special message from God, is an important theme in the letter, for Paul's authority was under attack. Paul didn't apply for a job as an apostle. He didn't inherit it as a family occupation. His calling in life was fulfilling God's desire for him. Even reading these first words convicts me that I want my life to be driven by the calling of God. I want to do what he wills me to do today and every day.

Paul sends his letter not to individual Christians but to a church, which was an assembly, a body that gathered for a purpose (*ekklēsia*—ἐκκλησία). I need to be in a church body. Church attendance isn't optional for a growing and thriving Christian. We are expected to be in a church to worship God and hear his word.

Paul expresses God's grace and peace to his readers. I couldn't wish for a finer blessing in life. I want to walk in God's grace and peace.

Lord, may I hear your voice and do your will today as I walk in your grace and peace. In Jesus, amen.

APRIL 19

Blessed be the God and Father of our Lord Jesus Christ, the Father of mercies and God of all comfort, who comforts us in all our affliction, so that we may be able to comfort those who are in any affliction, with the comfort with which we ourselves are comforted by God. (2 Cor. 1:3–4)

One of my sisters is older than I am by almost two years. She went to kindergarten while I stayed home. After she'd return home, we'd play school. She'd be the teacher and teach me all the things she learned. Ditto for her first-grade year. When Kathryn was in second grade, I finally started kindergarten. Mom took me to class—a day I still remember because kindergarten lasted only one day. The teachers told Mom that I had already learned the kindergarten curriculum (thank you, sister!), so Mom might as well put me in first grade, which she did.

Today's passage reminds me of my experience. Paul explained that what we go through and what we learn are for us to use and teach to others. Paul's immediate example is for those who know God's comfort to comfort others who are hurting. I like this. It gives meaning and purpose to the troubles I've faced in life.

Paul describes God as not only "Father of the Lord Jesus" but also the "Father of mercies," a word that also conveys compassion and caring in regard to another's misfortunes. God isn't bent on making his children miserable. When we hurt, he cares. Jesus wept over the pain that Mary and Martha experienced when their brother Lazarus died. Jesus wasn't weeping for Lazarus, for he was about to raise him from the dead. Jesus wept over the pain of his friends.

Paul then labels God as the God of "all comfort." God can comfort the grieving, strengthen the weary, support the hurting, help the helpless. God comes to the rescue of those in need. I have experienced that over and over. I can testify that it is true. It doesn't make loss go away. Nor does it end pain and hurt. But it brings a soothing balm, a loving presence, and an assurance that one walks aided by a loving God.

This truth not only must be experienced but should be shared. Those with a story to tell about God's comforting love and mercy should speak up. It informs the healing process for others, giving them a confident hope amid life's difficulties.

Lord, thank you for your mercy and comfort. You have rescued me over and over. May I share your comfort with others in need. In Jesus, amen.

APRIL 20

You also must help us by prayer, so that many will give thanks on our behalf for the blessing granted us through the prayers of many. (2 Cor. 1:11)

I well remember the Friday night one summer when I was twelve years old. The next morning, I had a Little League baseball game, and to my twelve-year-old mind, it might more appropriately be called "Big League" baseball. There was nothing little about the game. Praying before I went to sleep, I included the rare request, "God, please help me hit a home run tomorrow!" I didn't think of it as selfish, nor was I hesitant to pray it; however, it wasn't a prayer I remember uttering before. The next day, I had forgotten the prayer. But as I stood up to bat in the first inning, on the first pitch, I swung, connected, and hit the ball over the centerfield fence, banging the Pepsi bottle cap on the scoreboard almost dead center. As I trotted around the bases, I suddenly remembered my prayer. Admittedly, I also thought, "I wonder if I'd have hit that home run if I hadn't prayed!"

Prayer changes things. Even the super holy apostle Paul, a man who prayed without ceasing (1 Thess. 5:16), sought the prayers of others. In today's passage, Paul sought the prayers of his readers—not so he could hit a home run in a baseball game but for much better reasons. Look carefully at how Paul writes.

"You also must help us by prayer": translators face a challenge putting this clause into word-for-word English. For "must help," Paul uses a verb that conveys the idea that the Corinthians should be working together. They should be uniting in prayer and working with Paul by praying on his behalf. The meaning of the verb can also include that they are working with God as they pray for Paul and the church. Paul puts the verb in present active participle form to indicate the church is to be continually helping by praying.

The prayers of the Corinthians would continue to bring Paul protection from the dangers he constantly faced. By praying, the readers not only aided Paul but advanced God's kingdom as more and more disciples were made, refreshed, and taught through Paul's ministry.

Paul needed others to pray. Prayer changes things. You and I should both pray for others and seek prayer from others. The world will be different when we do.

Lord, I pray for a more effective prayer life. Thank you for so many answered prayers. In Jesus' name, amen.

APRIL 21

For I wrote to you out of much affliction and anguish of heart and with many tears, not to cause you pain but to let you know the abundant love that I have for you. (2 Cor. 2:4)

Donatien Alphonse François, also known by the title "the Marquis de Sade" (related to the word *sadism*), lived from 1740 to 1814 and died in a mental asylum. He was repeatedly imprisoned for his degenerate mistreatment of others. Over a century later, some uphold his writings, which champion libertarian views that the government has no right to intervene in areas of sexual morality. In truth, however, his life was filled with appalling mistreatment of others. Inflicting pain was pathological for this man.

Modern psychology has identified a mental disorder termed *narcissism*, describing one with a grandiose self-view, a need for constant affirmation, and a lack of empathy. Narcissists don't really care how others feel. Life is all about the narcissist.

Paul modeled the opposite of these self-gratifying and self-centered emotional states. As today's passage indicates, Paul knew personal pain but lived his life to help others avoid pain in their lives. Paul was acutely aware of how his actions would affect others, and the emotional state of others mattered to him.

Some people believe their actions aren't to be moderated by the feelings of others. I remember a person close to me saying things that seemed intended to manipulate me emotionally so I would take a certain course of action. I stopped it by saying, "Don't make me feel guilty because I won't [ABC]." The other person commented, "I can't make you feel anything." The response reflected the view that we each choose how to feel, so others can act without regard to consequences. I corrected this person immediately. I said, "Yes, you can affect how someone feels."

Paul never sacrificed truth for another's feelings, but Paul clearly changed how he went about life to maximize his chances to teach about Jesus. Paul cared so much about his ministry, including the attitudes and feelings of those in his orbit of influence, that he was always tuned into the effects of his actions.

I need to pay attention to others. I shouldn't needlessly cause pain.

Lord, give me a heart for others while keeping healthy boundaries. In Jesus, amen.

APRIL 22

Anyone whom you forgive, I also forgive. Indeed, what I have forgiven, if I have forgiven anything, has been for your sake in the presence of Christ, so that we would not be outwitted by Satan; for we are not ignorant of his designs. (2 Cor. 2:10–11)

When I meditate on a passage of Scripture, I try hard to understand it in the context in which it was written. I work to understand the kind of writing (here, a letter from Paul written out of a need to address certain situations at the church in Corinth). I work through the original text in Greek to see what insights or nuances might lie beyond the given translation. But then the hard part comes. I prayerfully ask how the passage might apply to me and my friends today. The application typically produces a story that I use to introduce each of these passages to you, the reader. Today's passage poses a plethora of problems that arise from application.

Forgiveness can sound easy at times, hard at times, and occasionally, like a foreign term that I don't even understand. Without a doubt, it is a hallmark of Christianity. In my life, I have been wronged, I have been slighted, and I have borne abuse from people. I know I need to forgive them, but what does that forgiveness entail? I have a dear friend who decided he needed to forgive a brother and sister who had wronged him twenty years before. They hadn't spoken since, so he decided to write them letters of forgiveness. He wanted me to read them first. They read like a recitation of wrongs for two solid pages. Then at the end was the tagline "But I am a Christian now, so I forgive you. But I never want to speak to you again." He asked me what I thought.

What is forgiveness, and how does it work? These questions are core to faith. We all seek God's forgiveness of our many wrongs and the wholeness that comes from that, and I suspect that is part of the key to forgiveness. Jesus implied such in teaching about prayer to his disciples: "Forgive us our trespasses[/debts] as we forgive those who trespass against us" (Mt. 6:12; my translation).

Paul gives another important link to forgiveness in this passage. Forgiveness foils the designs of Satan. Failing to forgive works in tandem with him. Forgiveness doesn't mean staying where abuse can continue, but forgiveness is more than lip service. This is a Christian struggle, to find full forgiveness for others.

Lord, I have people to forgive, and I see it's a process. Please guide me in this, so I can forgive them in line with your plans, growing in Christ in whom I pray, amen.

APRIL 23

But thanks be to God, who in Christ always leads us in triumphal procession, and through us spreads the fragrance of the knowledge of him everywhere. For we are the aroma of Christ to God among those who are being saved and among those who are perishing. (2 Cor. 2:14–15)

As a young boy, we would go trick-or-treating every Halloween. We would knock on a door and, when it was answered, hold out our bags or plastic lanterns and proclaim, "Trick or treat!" But one year, I learned the enchanting version every young boy was proud to say: "Trick or treat; smell my feet; give me something good to eat!" I'm not sure why that struck us as funny, nor why we seemed so cool saying it, but who gets the mind of an eight-year-old boy?

Paul writes of the effect of an aroma, but not with the crassness of an immature boy trick-or-treating. Paul uses a metaphor to give insight into a reality of life and motivate change in his readers. Paul's metaphor of smell is profound. Aromas have an unseen effect on those within their reach. We have all been around smells that are offensive. But smells can also be marvelous! I can remember my friend Cynthia in high school tapping me in English class and saying, "I got a new perfume. Don't you like this smell? It's Bal à Versailles!" I realized then Cynthia was on a different level! Boy, it smelled amazing!

We need to understand that when we are around others, people discern what we are, in a sense, by what we are wearing, how we treat others, how we prioritize life, how we handle life's challenges and successes, and how we process what might be in the future—whether with worry, fret, and fear over the future or with faith that gives us confidence. These behaviors and attitudes will show others in the world what life is like in Christ.

For as Paul indicates, it is Christ who leads us in procession. We are lined up behind him, and he marches us through this world in our lives. As his followers, we should be wearing his cologne! Like Bal à Versailles with Cynthia, it should set us apart from the rest.

Let the world know who you are by how you are. Don't be a smelly testimony of what Jesus can do in life. Be a tribute, an aroma that makes people ask, "What is it about you that seems so great?" Then tell them about Jesus!

Lord, may my life be a testimony to the difference you make. In Jesus, amen.

APRIL 24

Such is the confidence that we have through Christ toward God. Not that we are sufficient in ourselves to claim anything as coming from us, but our sufficiency is from God, who has made us sufficient. (2 Cor. 3:4–6)

Keith Green's song "Oh Lord, You're Beautiful" came out when I was an impressionable college student. I was taken by his lyric "And when I'm doing well, help me to never seek a crown. For my reward is giving glory to you." In a culture where most strive for self-importance and where accomplishments are praised and awarded, it stood out to me that Keith wanted to make sure that his good works before God were not to his own honor and prestige but rightly giving praise to the one who enabled him to accomplish those things.

In today's passage, Paul exemplifies the attitude in Keith's song. The context stems from Paul having started the church in Corinth, staying and teaching for over a year. Corinth was a major port city in the day, and the town (and church) would regularly receive visitors from all over the Roman Empire. Some of those visitors brought with them letters of credentials vouching for them as bona fide teachers in the faith. But others denigrated Paul in their teaching. We don't know precisely how, but Paul's letters seem to indicate the visiting teachers considered Paul a bit superficial, a bit weak in appearance and demeanor, mildly unsuccessful, and even a bit askew in his theology.

Paul wasn't so concerned about it from a "Paul perspective." What bothered Paul was that the interloping teachers were denigrating the gospel. That is something Paul would not tolerate. So Paul wrote several letters, including 1 and 2 Corinthians. Paul explained that his sufficiency as a teacher was the sufficiency of God and Christ. Paul's letters of commendation were the very people that formed the church in Corinth. Anyone who was challenging Paul and the gospel were challenging God. Similarly, all the good Paul accomplished was the true accomplishment of God. So all glory went to God, not to Paul or anyone else.

As I go through life, my goal shouldn't be about me; my goal is properly God. I want people to be drawn to God by what I do and say. God is the playwright and director. My job is to follow his directions and give him all the glory.

Lord, I want to take your word and shine it all around, but help me first to live it. And when I'm doing well, help me to never seek a crown, for my reward is giving glory to you. In Jesus' name, amen.

APRIL 25

Since we have such a hope, we are very bold. (2 Cor. 3:12)

The courtroom was packed. Lawyers, press, and general visitors had lined up for over an hour to get a seat and avoid sitting in the overflow courtroom televising the proceedings. It was about fifteen minutes before I would give a ninety-minute opening statement for the plaintiffs. The defendant was a multinational corporation that had hired a stable of thoroughbred lawyers, well-paid and, some might say, the best money could buy.

A lawyer friend who also holds a PhD in psychology came up to me, saying, "I am sorry to interrupt your thought, but I have to ask, are you nervous?" I answered honestly, "No, not really!" She looked stunned, and she asked, "I have to know why. You should be petrified!" I told her that I had limited time before the judge took the bench, and her question deserved a much longer answer than I could give, but in brief, I could let her know my belief system that undergirded my confidence.

I explained that I really do believe there is a God. I believe that God made me and has an interest in who I am and what I do. Furthermore, I am convinced that what I was doing that day, I was doing in alignment with God's will for my life. So if God made me to do what I was about to do, if he gave me the gifts to do what he made me to do, and if I had worked hard to do right by those gifts and that opportunity, what reason could I ever have for fear? My only fears are whether I am correctly understanding what he wants me to do and if I am doing it to his glory to the best of my ability.

She asked, "But what if you lose?" I replied, "So be it. God doesn't promise me the outcome; he calls me to do what I am to do. He's in charge from there on." So again, no fear—just faith.

As today's passage indicates, Paul understood the role of hope in life. The Greek word for "hope," *elpis* (ἐλπίς), is not a pie-in-the-sky hope but a confident expectation of what is to come. When we have a confident expectation in God and his work, we can be bold in what we do. That boldness isn't limited to a trial in a courtroom but should extend to all of life. What I need to do daily is focus on God's will and purposes and give it my best. I can be bold there.

Lord, show me your will. Empower me. Embolden me. May my life be a walking exhibit of faith to help others seek you. In Jesus' name, amen.

APRIL 26

And we all, with unveiled face, beholding the glory of the Lord, are being transformed into the same image from one degree of glory to another. For this comes from the Lord who is the Spirit. (2 Cor. 3:18)

One of my earliest preaching experiences came at the Broadway Church of Christ in Lubbock, Texas, in the late 1970s. On the dais was a large, sturdy wooden pulpit. On the preacher's side of the pulpit was a plaque that could be seen every time one stepped into the pulpit to preach but not read by those in attendance. The plaque said simply, "Sir, we would see Jesus."

The plaque quoted John 12:21 from the King James Version. In John 12, Greeks approached Philip, one of Jesus' apostles, with the request to see and hear Jesus. The placement of that plaque was to remind everyone who stepped into the pulpit to preach that the goal of every sermon should be to show Jesus. Today's passage gives a good reason why.

The passage speaks to the radical transformation that happens in the lives of Christians who spend their days "beholding the glory of the Lord." They are genuinely transformed. God works in the lives of believers who spend their energy and efforts gazing upon, contemplating, and prayerfully reflecting upon Jesus and his love.

I know my need for this transformation. My mind needs rewiring. My motivations need modifying. My goals need to be reshaped based on better priorities. My discipline needs fortifying. My compassion needs fueling. My service needs energizing. My joy needs feeding. My patience needs revitalizing. My purity needs enhancing.

If instead of beholding his glory, I spend my time gazing into the darkness of life, I will find my transformation darkening as well. These simple truths are important. They are like eating. I won't get good nutrition and health by eating right once. It is a daily commitment and process. If I eat right day in and day out, over the weeks, months, and years, I will begin to see a positive transformation in my body. In the same way, a steady diet of Jesus will transform my heart and mind into his image.

Lord, I want to see Jesus. I want to know him and his love. I want to be transformed into his image little by little each day. I pray in his name, amen.

APRIL 27

Therefore, having this ministry by the mercy of God, we do not lose heart. But we have renounced disgraceful, underhanded ways. We refuse to practice cunning or to tamper with God's word, but by the open statement of the truth we would commend ourselves to everyone's conscience in the sight of God. (2 Cor. 4:1–2)

To some, Niccolò Machiavelli (1469–1527) was a political philosopher and writer. To others, he was an immoral atheist and a cynic. Today, his name is associated with manipulative behavior. His best-known work, *The Prince,* is a straightforward "how-to" book on ruling, dedicated to Lorenzo de' Medici, the ruler of Florence at the time.

The third section of the book focuses on the qualities a good ruler must have. Machiavelli argues that a prince must sometimes act with vice rather than virtue because lofty ideals do not always result in good governance. In chapter 18, he explains that appearing virtuous is important, but acting virtuously should often be shunned.

The chapter is entitled "Concerning the Way in Which Princes Should Keep Faith." Machiavelli is blunt. A ruler should pretend to have religious faith and fervor, but there's no need for that faith to be genuine. People are beguiled and want to believe their leader has faith. So pretend to be faithful, but discard any semblance of faith in actual ruling.

Paul did not get or keep his authority based on Machiavelli's philosophy. Nor did Paul use the philosophers of his day. (Machiavelli doesn't credit it, but much of what he contends is based on Cicero, a deceased Roman philosopher and writer who was still well known in Paul's day.) For Paul, no end would justify the means of vice. Paul believed in authenticity.

Unlike others, Paul refused to manipulate his readers with any backroom cunning or other sinful approach. Paul was direct, faithful, and true to the faith of Christ in conduct as well as teaching.

In my life, I make choices every day. My faith can be lip service, extolled when convenient or necessary to keep up appearances. Or my faith can be genuine, a rudder for life even when the waters are rough. I want to be like Paul, not those who are fake.

Lord, illuminate the way of true faith for me. Help me walk it. In Jesus, amen.

APRIL 28

The god of this world has blinded the minds of the unbelievers, to keep them from seeing the light of the gospel of the glory of Christ, who is the image of God. For what we proclaim is not ourselves, but Jesus Christ as Lord, with ourselves as your servants for Jesus' sake. For God, who said, "Let light shine out of darkness," has shone in our hearts to give the light of the knowledge of the glory of God in the face of Jesus Christ. (2 Cor. 4:4–6)

The Bible begins with an important story. God creates the heavens and earth, and they are without form and void. God then forms the heavens and earth for three days and fills what he has formed for three more days. As part of forming, God makes light, calling it out of darkness (Gen. 1:3–4). As part of filling, God creates humanity in his "image" (Gen. 1:26–27). As creation moves from the seven-day account to the particulars of humanity, Adam and Eve are placed in a marvelous garden and given responsibilities appropriate for those made in God's image, and life is good. Then sin creeps in, and death takes over. The image of God in Adam and Eve is marred. They lose their garden home and live under the curses of sin.

The impact of losing their purity is most apparent in the story of their sons Cain and Abel. Cain's jealousy and temper incite him to murder his younger brother, and God banishes him from the region. Adam and Eve undoubtedly grieve Abel's death as well as Cain's actions that damaged his reflection as God's image to the world. Humanity's distortion of God's image grows over time, and by the time of Noah, the whole world has run so amok, it seems all are past a point of redemption. They are suitable for destruction. By the time of Jesus, the world is still in a state where, although God's Spirit has worked in many, the authorities murder an innocent Jesus. And evil is so pronounced that a zealous Paul, before his conversion, tries to eradicate God's working church.

But Jesus has entered the world, has died a death for sins, and lives as the resurrected Messiah, ready to invade the hearts and minds of those who put their faith in him. When they do, the curse that followed sin in Genesis begins reversing! God begins to shine his light in darkened hearts, and the distortions of God's image begin to retreat. This is done as the light of knowing God's glorious act of redemption in Christ takes root and grows in our hearts and minds. God takes his true image in Christ and transforms us.

Lord, make the image of Christ real to me. May his face shine into my life and bring me into a greater likeness of you for all the world to see. In Jesus, amen.

APRIL 29

So we do not lose heart. Though our outer self is wasting away, our inner self is being renewed day by day. For this light momentary affliction is preparing for us an eternal weight of glory beyond all comparison, as we look not to the things that are seen but to the things that are unseen. For the things that are seen are transient, but the things that are unseen are eternal. (2 Cor. 4:16–18)

My buddy Mike tells me he is in "the winter of life." He adds, "I'm so old, in the mornings when I awaken, if I don't hurt anywhere, I breathe into my hand to make sure I'm alive!" I'm not as old as Mike, but I can often relate to his thoughts. As my brother-in-law Kevin explained to me, "It's like the warranty is out on body parts once you get past forty. You need to be careful!"

Paul lived a full human life. His writings are rife with common experiences of you and me. He experiences emotional highs and lows. He laughs and cries. He gets excited and exhausted. He even sees his body growing old. Today's passage is a marvelous illustration of that. Paul knows, as anyone who lives long enough recognizes, that our bodies age and deteriorate. That might seem contrary to the Christian faith on the surface. After all, in yesterday's devotional, I wrote about Paul teaching that Christianity is reversing the curse and bringing a new creation into the lives of believers.

Yet Paul doesn't want any reader to misunderstand. Our physical bodies are not being returned to their pre-fall state, at least not yet. That will come later, after death and the final judgment. But even as our bodies decline, God is already renewing and remaking our "inner self" (Greek *eso*—ἔσω, or "what's inside").

This "inside" work God is doing is work on the parts of a person that can't be seen. They aren't body parts, not even those under the skin. It is our thoughts, feelings, trust, and consciousness. Paul knows that God is working to change our essence, and this process of God is daily. God works on us 24/7 to make us more closely resemble what we were made to be.

I may not feel as well physically today as I did decades ago. But I can affirm that by following Christ, I am a better husband, father, and all-around person. God has done that in me, and he will do that in everyone—a daily transformation.

Lord, work in me. Help me see your hand in my life. Make me a better reflection of your love. In Jesus, amen.

APRIL 30

For the love of Christ controls us, because we have concluded this: that one has died for all, therefore all have died; and he died for all, that those who live might no longer live for themselves but for him who for their sake died and was raised. (2 Cor. 5:14–15)

In 1980, I was in Dr. Floyd's Greek class. We were looking at today's passage. Dr. Floyd asked the twenty or so of us sitting in class, "Tell me, please—ἀγάπη τοῦ Χριστοῦ [translated 'the love of Christ']—is Paul using a subjective or objective genitive?" Now if you're reading this book and you have a Greek or Latin background, you get that question. If you don't, you likely miss the import of the question. Yet the question is important if we are to understand this passage. Let me explain.

The translators tell us that we are controlled by "the love of Christ." Does that mean Christ's love for us, like we might speak of a mother's love for her infant child? Or does it mean the love that we have for Christ, like my love of apple pie? Does Paul find we are controlled by the love Christ has for us or by our devout love of Christ? This was the thrust of Dr. Floyd's question of Greek grammar.

All of us who had experienced Dr. Floyd knew he was looking for a specific answer, and we knew we would have to back that answer up. We discussed it after class. We thought we knew the answer, but we were all afraid to offer it, lest we be wrong or unable to support our view. After all, experience teaches that our love for Christ changes the way we behave. So should we affirm that it is an objective genitive—that is, that our love for Christ transforms us?

But we also knew that we love him *because* he first loved us (1 Jn. 4:19). Our love for Christ comes from understanding and experiencing his love for us. That could lend credence to Paul speaking of Christ's love for us, a subjective genitive. The class stayed mute, so Dr. Floyd answered himself, explaining that we should look to the context of the passage as well as Paul's usage in other places. When Paul references the love of Christ, Paul means Christ's love for us. In this passage, he speaks of the death of Christ on our behalf. Jesus died because "God so loved the world" (Jn. 3:16). This love of Christ transforms us, moves us to love, and changes us. Praise God.

Lord, thank you for your love in Christ. May I grow in it and respond in love. For the sake and through the work of Jesus, amen.

MAY 1

From now on, therefore, we regard no one according to the flesh. Even though we once regarded Christ according to the flesh, we regard him thus no longer. Therefore, if anyone is in Christ, he is a new creation. The old has passed away; behold, the new has come. (2 Cor. 5:16–17)

Scottish people may speak the English language, but they have their own complete set of slang words, foreign to any English I grew up speaking. One word seems to convey the idea of someone who, in my common English, we might term a *jerk*. (The Scottish word may have a bit of a vulgar spin; I'm not too sure!) In one Scottish television comedy, a new boy is brought into a high school, and an established student is charged with showing him around. All the host student does, however, is point out people, saying simply, in my English, "Jerk. Jerk. Jerk. Not a jerk. Jerk," wagging his finger and labeling everyone they see.

The humor in this show stems from the idea that people often view things simplistically, deciding who they like and don't like. It is human nature to place value judgments on people we encounter. This isn't always done expressly, as it was in the show, but most are careful with where to sit, to whom to speak, how to speak to others, whom to befriend, and on and on. Regrettably, most make these value decisions based on appearance, social status, behavior, success, and other similar attributes.

In today's passage, Paul admonishes people to stop this. The Christ follower isn't to judge or regard others "according to the flesh"—that is, by these typical indicators of value. The presence of Christ has changed all that. The immediate filter for everyone we see can be set into two buckets: (1) has Christ and (2) needs Christ.

The old way we might have assessed people before coming to faith in Christ is gone. We who have experienced the change Jesus makes in our lives should exercise that change in who and what we value. The old ways should be dead to us.

This truth is easy to write but hard to practice. To decide that we will treat people as Christ would, wooing the lost and encouraging the saved, will radically change our behavior daily. This changes how we treat people.

Lord, give me your eyes to see people as you see them. Change me so I can love others as you do. In Jesus, amen.

MAY 2

All this is from God, who through Christ reconciled us to himself and gave us the ministry of reconciliation; that is, in Christ God was reconciling the world to himself, not counting their trespasses against them, and entrusting to us the message of reconciliation. . . . We implore you on behalf of Christ, be reconciled to God. For our sake he made him to be sin who knew no sin, so that in him we might become the righteousness of God. (2 Cor. 5:18–21)

Aesop is famous for his fables—short stories (frequently of animals) that tell a larger truth. While scholars are uncertain if Aesop even lived, he would have been alive some six hundred years before Paul. At the time of Paul, a popular biography of Aesop was in circulation. Aesop was allegedly a slave on the Greek island of Samos. Aesop won his freedom by telling wise fables. Meanwhile, Croesus, the king of Lydia (modern Turkey), went to war to conquer the island of Samos. Aesop gave advice to the Samians, and they thwarted Croesus at every turn. Croesus got word that Aesop was the brains behind his defeat, so he offered peace to Samos if they sent him Aesop. The Samians refused, but Aesop went anyway of his own accord. Croesus found Aesop physically repulsive and decided to kill him.

Aesop got Croesus' attention by telling a fable of locusts and a grasshopper. The king was stunned and offered Aesop any wish he desired. Aesop wished for reconciliation between Croesus and the Samians, which brought the war to an end. Aesop returned home a savior.

Turn now to today's passage. Paul uses the same vocabulary found in Aesop's biography as he describes the work of Christ with the believer and God. Christ made the journey that ended the hostilities between God and the believer. As sinners, humans are rightly under God's wrath. Sin is a destructive and hurtful disease that destroys the works of God. God rightly brings death to sin and sinners. Yet Christ became sin and died the death of sinners to bring the hostilities to an end.

In Christ, Paul explains, the believer can become the righteousness of Christ. This is a practical truth. It means that God is on our side. God's mercy has triumphed over his judgment. Regardless of the extent of our sin, we have peace with God as we are given the righteousness of Christ. Like the Samians experienced peace through the work of Aesop, so we freely get released from sin's consequences by the work of Christ. "Reconciliation" is a powerful, life-changing truth.

Lord, thank you for reconciliation in Jesus. May I reflect your love. In him, amen.

MAY 3

Working together with him, then, we appeal to you not to receive the grace of God in vain. For he says, "In a favorable time I listened to you, and in a day of salvation I have helped you." Behold, now is the favorable time; behold, now is the day of salvation. (2 Cor. 6:1–2)

I didn't grow up wearing watches. My buddy Chip used to chide me for my failure to have one on my wrist, thinking it the height of irresponsibility. I didn't need a watch. I could always ask Chip what time it was. Of course, this was before cell phones functioned as timepieces. Still, my argument was that a watch could only tell you the time; it couldn't tell you the *time*! Let me explain.

The Greeks had two marvelous and different words translated as "time" in the Bible. One word was *chronos* (χρόνος), which pointed to more of a point or moment in chronological time. Hence our English word *chronological*. This is the word used, for example, in Matthew 2:7 when Herod summons the wise men to determine what "time" the Bethlehem star had appeared.

But the Greeks had a second word for time: *kairos* (καιρός). The distinction in this word is that it emphasizes time that is fit for something. We might call it a "propitious moment." It is akin to what we today would refer to as "good timing." It is the right or proper time for whatever is referenced.

Here Paul uses this "propitious moment" word in describing the "favorable time" when God helped as the "day of salvation." Paul isn't worried about on which calendar day or at what hour God came to his rescue. Paul is speaking of God coming at the *right time*.

This speaks to me 24/7. At any time of day, any day of the week, any month or year, I can be assured that God will listen to me. More than that, God will respond in his good timing, and that timing will be right.

I don't need a watch to tell me when God will arrive. He will arrive at the right time. In that, I can live today in faith, knowing my God will be there. This gives me confidence in times of doubt, faith in days of trouble, encouragement when I am down, and strength as my resolve weakens. It gives me what I need today.

Lord, hear my cry and come to my aid. Save me in this day in your good timing. I pray in Jesus, amen.

MAY 4

As servants of God we commend ourselves in every way: by great endurance, in afflictions, hardships, calamities, beatings, imprisonments, riots, labors, sleepless nights, hunger; by purity, knowledge, patience, kindness, the Holy Spirit, genuine love; by truthful speech, and the power of God; with the weapons of righteousness for the right hand and for the left; through honor and dishonor, through slander and praise. We are treated as impostors, and yet are true; as unknown, and yet well known; as dying, and behold, we live; as punished, and yet not killed; as sorrowful, yet always rejoicing; as poor, yet making many rich; as having nothing, yet possessing everything. (2 Cor. 6:4–10)

The trial was important—certainly for the clients I represented as plaintiffs but also for a larger litigation of thousands of others who had suffered from the same defective hip implant. My friend Ernest had found a star witness for us, a doctor to explain why and how the artificial hip was defective. I put the doctor on the stand to testify. Initially, I asked him his qualifications so the jury and judge would realize he was no ordinary witness. The doctor had headed orthopedic surgery at a premier medical center in the United States. He had invented surgical techniques that are now commonplace. He had put artificial hips in two presidents, countless sports figures, and America's top evangelist. Then to top it all off, he had worked as a rocket scientist *before* medical school, doing the calculations for NASA to help return Apollo 13 to earth after its catastrophic failure.

Paul also had a résumé. So do you and I. Paul's résumé wasn't like the résumé of my testifying doctor. Paul's résumé recounted the many difficulties, trials, tribulations, sufferings, and abuses he experienced for the sake of the gospel. Anyone familiar with Paul's past would know of his earlier, far different résumé. Paul was on track to be one of Israel's greats. He had been a star pupil of the top rabbi, Gamaliel. Paul had been the chosen prosecutor of the ruling body of Israel. Paul came from a top family, one with wealth and reputation. Paul had dual citizenship, in Tarsus (no small city) and in Rome itself.

Yet for Paul, his real stud-sheet was that he had endured hardship and even ridicule for the kingdom and purposes of God. Reading his self-written credentials makes me wonder how well I endure hardship for God. Do I find value in walking difficult roads? Do I treasure the moments I get to sacrifice comfort, security, or ease for the sake of following Jesus? I need to work on my résumé!

Lord, give me a heart to value serving you above all else. In Jesus, amen.

MAY 5

Do not be unequally yoked with unbelievers. For what partnership has righteousness with lawlessness? Or what fellowship has light with darkness? . . . What agreement has the temple of God with idols? For we are the temple of the living God; as God said, "I will make my dwelling among them and walk among them, and I will be their God, and they shall be my people. Therefore go out from their midst, and be separate from them, says the Lord, and touch no unclean thing; then I will welcome you, and I will be a father to you, and you shall be sons and daughters to me, says the Lord Almighty." (2 Cor. 6:14, 16–18)

Playground basketball was common growing up. We didn't need uniforms. As we were just boys playing, we picked teams, and half of us took off our shirts as we played—"shirts versus skins." It was easy to spot your teammates.

Distinctions aren't only for the playground. God's people should have marks of distinction, ways that they are set apart from those not in the kingdom. This isn't something new. It was true even in ancient days, as God gave Israel certain instructions to set them apart from the nations that didn't know God. Prominent among those ancient distinctions were dietary laws like not eating pork. Paul wasn't concerned about keeping *kosher* as a mark of distinction for the church. His "unequally yoked" analogy employs a transportation or farming reference. You didn't hitch up an ox and a donkey together to pull a cart. You matched the two types of animals to share the yoke. The yoke that fit an ox wasn't made for a donkey. That wouldn't work.

Paul then extends his analogy to law abiders and criminals, then to light and darkness, then to God and idols. Paul's final reference is to exclusionary laws from the Old Testament—laws that referenced the behaviors God used to set apart Israel from its pagan neighbors. Paul uses a wide variation of distinctions to make an important point. The Christian is *not* like everyone else. How we act, what we prioritize, our gentleness, the way we respond to difficulty and tragedy, these things and more set us apart from those who aren't in a relationship with God.

Paul says our distinctions align us with God, not with those aligned with the world. This touches whom we marry, with whom we go into business, those friends who are close confidants, or anyone else that we share a yoke with. We can spot our teammates and play accordingly, just as we did on playgrounds decades back.

Lord, give me the faith to follow you living distinct from the world. In Jesus, amen.

MAY 6

Since we have these promises, beloved, let us cleanse ourselves from every defilement of body and spirit, bringing holiness to completion in the fear of God. (2 Cor. 7:1)

This morning, I awoke extra early. I needed to shower, get dressed, and be ready to fly to Indiana to have lunch with a government official. I prepared by putting on a suit and tie, a clean pressed shirt, clean socks, and appropriate shoes. I did so before reading today's passage. Then I sat down and went to work.

My early morning preparation seemed particularly relevant to the phrasing of Paul's concern in today's passage. Paul has just finished speaking to the ways God had instructed for Israel to show its unique affiliation with God. Referencing Israel's kosher dietary laws, Paul concluded by quoting the Old Testament assurance that God would be like a father to those who follow him. The followers would be sons and daughters to the Lord Almighty. This is an awesome thought. It proves Paul's lead-in to the verses I have set out above.

Paul uses a small three-letter Greek conjunction that is translated "since." It could also be translated "therefore" or even the more formal "thus." Paul is saying that based on what he has written previously, the readers should cleanse themselves from every defilement of body or spirit. This is a profound lead-in critical to understanding Paul's emphasis.

Paul says that our status as the Lord Almighty's sons and daughters should motivate us to clean up. Just as I showered and put on clean clothes this morning to meet the government official, so all of us who follow God should be at work cleaning up for our daily routine.

I like Paul's language. It makes sense to me, and it challenges me. I should not present to the world wearing the same dirt everyone else does. I am a child of the Almighty. I should be clean. This applies to how I think and speak, to how I treat others and treat myself, to how I spend my time and my money, and to how I love, forgive, minister, and serve. It should affect what I learn and allow into my mind. I want to be clean and properly present myself to God, my Father.

Lord, help me clean up today. Show me areas of dirt and grime. Cleanse my heart and mind to better represent you as your child. In Jesus' name, amen.

MAY 7

But God, who comforts the downcast, comforted us by the coming of Titus, and not only by his coming but also by the comfort with which he was comforted by you, as he told us of your longing, your mourning, your zeal for me, so that I rejoiced still more. (2 Cor. 7:6–7)

I was scheduled to speak out of town at a community breakfast. My assigned topic was my book *World Religions on Trial.* The day before, I became ill, and I slept fitfully. I awoke too sick to make the breakfast. I felt horrible about it. I frequently give speeches, and I can't remember the last time I missed a scheduled speech.

Realizing I couldn't make it, I asked my assistant to text the person who had arranged for me to speak to explain my inability. As bad as I felt physically, I felt even worse that I had failed to meet my commitment with basically no notice. I called my wife. There was nothing she could do about it, of course. I called just to let her know and commiserate. That brought me comfort.

Comfort is a marvelous thing. It spreads pain around in a way that seems to reduce its impact on the person hurting. Paul wrote in today's passage about the comfort God provided in getting Titus to Paul's side. The Greek word translated as "comfort" gives a picture. The word breaks down into someone who is called or asked to be at the side of another (*para* [beside] + *kaleō* [called to] = παρακαλέω). (The noun is used to describe the Holy Spirit by the apostle John.)

We all have times where stings in life are lessened by someone who cares being with us, even if they can't do anything specific other than be there. Paul knew this firsthand. What I find interesting—and yes, comforting—is that Paul saw the presence of another as a godsend. God was the one who was providing comfort through another, here Titus.

God wants to comfort the downcast. God can do so directly as the God who is always there. But God also uses his people to be a source of comfort for others. It is a proper calling for you and me to identify those who are hurting and provide God's comfort. It may just be dropping them a text or email. It may mean a meal. It might be a phone call or visit. But let's share God's comfort with all who need it.

Lord, thank you for comforting me. Help me be a comfort to others who hurt, and to do so in your name. Amen.

MAY 8

For godly grief produces a repentance that leads to salvation without regret, whereas worldly grief produces death. (2 Cor. 7:10)

I was watching a football game and was frustrated over my team's playing. As my team's winning chances dwindled to near zero, I decided to use a time-out to go to the restroom. I dawdled, got a drink, and returned to the TV. Everyone was celebrating. Evidently, my team made a touchdown off some incredible play, and that seemed to turn the whole game upside down. I missed it. But no worries; I hit the rewind button on the remote, and presto, I got to watch it. I love that rewind button.

The problem is that I don't have a rewind button for my life. If I did, I could relive the good moments over and over. But more importantly to me, I could take those mistakes I've made and redo them. I've made mistakes that I crave a chance to fix with a do-over. Instead, I have regret for those mistakes, and I need to live with that.

Into this truth of life comes Paul's writing today. Paul speaks of a "godly grief." Grief in the Greek (*lupe*—λύπη) refers to a pain or sorrow that one feels deeply. But Paul distinguishes a "godly grief" from a "worldly grief." A godly grief is one that produces repentance—that is, a turning around that proceeds from a changed mind. It is a grief that brings us to our knees in a cry to God for forgiveness. It changes how we live and what we do. We realize our mistakes and seek to live differently.

A worldly grief is different. We may feel bad about what has happened, but there is no real evidence of a changed mind. There is no turning around in our behavior. This is the attitude that might regret an action but not enough to behave any differently.

Paul explains that godly grief leads to salvation. It is the road of the believer. God comes to rescue those with godly grief. The worldly grief, in contrast, just leads to a dead end.

I don't have a rewind button to fix my big mistakes in my life. I wish so much that I did. But I do have a God who will hear my grief, see my repentance, and come to my rescue in love and forgiveness. What a mighty God we serve.

Lord, I repent of my sin, and I seek your forgiveness and healing in Jesus. Amen.

MAY 9

We want you to know, brothers, about the grace of God that has been given among the churches of Macedonia, for in a severe test of affliction, their abundance of joy and their extreme poverty have overflowed in a wealth of generosity on their part. (2 Cor. 8:1–2)

Baking soda tastes terrible. For that matter, so does flour. Drinking a cup of oil? No thanks! As for salt, it's fine on food but, by itself, rather stringent. I've never been one for raw eggs either. Milk? It has its time and place. Now while I am not a fan of any of those items on their own, when I mix them together in the right proportions, I have morning pancakes, and *those* are something I devour.

A crazy thing can happen with the right mix of ingredients. Today's passage sets up a surprising example from a spiritual perspective. Paul is telling the Corinthians about how the churches in Macedonia contributed to the church in need in Jerusalem. The Macedonians had combined an abundance of joy with extreme poverty to produce a wealth of generosity. What is more, this was done during a time of "affliction," or distress.

How did the Macedonians mix joy and poverty to find such a successful and productive result? Clearly it was the work of God in their hearts. A bit later, Paul will recognize that the Macedonians did this by giving themselves first to the Lord.

Amazing things happen in our lives when we give ourselves to God first. Things can turn upside down for us, in a good way. The Macedonians become a lesson for us as they were for the Corinthians. Believers can be distressed and afflicted yet have joy. They can be impoverished and yet have wealthy generosity. Their lives can find success and importance by serving God and watching him use them in a wonderful recipe, mixing their life experiences into a world-class dish.

As I go through my day, I need to see how the pieces mix. I need to make sure I find joy in the Lord by serving him first. I need to put him before any other want or desire. I need to pursue and even chase after his character over the seductive call of the world's desires. As I do so, he can stir generosity in me and bring to completion his work in my life.

Dear Lord, please have your way with me today. Help me place you first in my life and pursue you above all others. In Jesus' name, amen.

MAY 10

I say this not as a command, but to prove by the earnestness of others that your love also is genuine. For you know the grace of our Lord Jesus Christ, that though he was rich, yet for your sake he became poor, so that you by his poverty might become rich. (2 Cor. 8:8–9)

In 1970s Manchester, England, musician Eric Stewart found himself walking through slushy rain and snow to work out some issues with Gloria, his soon-to-be wife. The phone lines were down, and his love compelled him to get to her soon. A few years later, Stewart used that vivid memory to inspire the lyrics to one of his band's top hits: 1976's "The Things We Do for Love." This wasn't a giddy love song of gooey emotions. It was a practical love song proclaiming the notion that love compels us to do things we wouldn't otherwise do.

Paul presents love as a pure motive for the highest and best good. Love manifested in deeds is what Paul terms "genuine" love. The word (*gnesios*—γνήσιος) could also be translated as "authentic." It was frequently used to distinguish one who is a legitimate part of a family, as opposed to an impostor or interloper.

Paul's best illustration of genuine love is shown in the incarnate life of Jesus. Paul often wrote of the massive change Jesus embraced, an idea I will develop more in the devotional on Philippians 2:5–11. This is worth deep contemplation. Stop for a minute and think about it. Jesus willingly abdicated heaven's riches, setting aside his heavenly existence to become human. What is more, as a human, Jesus didn't choose earthly luxury. Jesus didn't even wait until humanity had invented air conditioning (stunning if you've spent summers in Israel).

But Jesus didn't come to earth on a tourist visa. He wasn't on holiday. Jesus came out of love, through more than rainy slosh. Jesus came into a life of suffering, tribulation, humiliation, and more out of his loving desire to make things right with humanity. As Paul says, Jesus became poor so that we might become rich.

Those of us who are enriched by Jesus and who follow him as Savior and as Lord are rightly moved in our own behavior. Our values shift. As Christ followers, we mature in love. The things we do for love are evident to all around us. We are modeling our Lord who first loved us.

Lord, I am deeply grateful for your loving care. I confess my own shallow, often unappreciative response. I long to be grateful and model your love in Jesus, amen.

MAY 11

With him [Titus] we are sending the brother who is famous among all the churches for his preaching of the gospel. And not only that, but he has been appointed by the churches to travel with us as we carry out this act of grace that is being ministered by us, for the glory of the Lord himself and to show our good will. We take this course so that no one should blame us about this generous gift that is being administered by us, for we aim at what is honorable not only in the Lord's sight but also in the sight of man. (2 Cor. 8:18–21)

A required course in most law schools centers on the ethical standards governing lawyers. In my school, the class was called simply "Professional Responsibility." Attorneys have ethical requirements in their practice. Unsurprisingly, the rules preclude lawyers from improper behavior. For example, you can't cheat your client. But another important rule goes a step further; it prohibits even the *appearance* of impropriety. Ethically, it's not enough to avoid doing wrong; one should also avoid even the appearance of doing wrong.

Paul could have written that rule of legal ethics. Today's passage gives details about how Paul is collecting the financial contribution of the Corinthians to be delivered to the church in Jerusalem. Anyone who knew Paul surely knew Paul was trustworthy in this regard. Yet Paul wanted to remove even an appearance of impropriety. So Paul sent three people to collect the contribution: Titus and two unnamed folks, one of whom Paul recognized as a "famous" preacher.

Paul's concern wasn't only his behavior before God but also the perception of his behavior before the watching world. I fear that often God's children are big on the first part (being honorable before God) but don't worry too much about how things appear to the world. After all, some surmise, if I am right before God, it's the world's problem if they don't see it.

Yet that isn't the case with Paul. Like the legal code of ethics, Paul saw a responsibility to live above reproach before a watching world. To the extent Paul could, Paul lived aware that his actions reflected on God. For Paul, his actions needed to be of the highest honor.

I wonder if I live as carefully. Do I make sure that the world sees an authentic, true faith in me? Do I rightly reflect a pure God? People are watching.

Lord, may I live above reproach before a watching world. To your glory, amen.

MAY 12

Now it is superfluous for me to write to you about the ministry for the saints, for I know your readiness, of which I boast about you to the people of Macedonia, saying that Achaia has been ready since last year. And your zeal has stirred up most of them. But I am sending the brothers so that our boasting about you may not prove empty in this matter, so that you may be ready, as I said you would be. Otherwise, if some Macedonians come with me and find that you are not ready, we would be humiliated—to say nothing of you—for being so confident. So I thought it necessary to urge the brothers to go on ahead to you and arrange in advance for the gift you have promised. (2 Cor. 9:1–5)

We were preparing one of our children (this story applies to *all* of them) for their birthday party. Our children were good-hearted and certainly excited and appreciative of the gifts they would receive. But we told them before their parties, "Be sure you look at each person who gives you a gift and you say, 'Thank you!'" We hoped our kids would, but we wanted to make sure!

This experience with our children comes to mind as I read this rather extended passage of Paul today. Paul had left Corinth and gone north into Macedonia, home to churches in Philippi, Thessalonica, and others. Paul's group was taking a much-needed contribution to the Jerusalem church, which was facing famine and want. The Corinthians had more resources than many, including the churches of Macedonia. As Paul was collecting from the Macedonians, he had told them that the Corinthians were preparing to give a gift as well. This was a motivation for the Macedonians to show a giving love, as the Corinthians were prepared to do.

Paul decided it would be wise to tell the Corinthians about this so that once the time came for Paul to collect, the funds would be ready. Paul knew that if his boasting about the generosity of the Corinthians proved wrong, he would be embarrassed, as would the Corinthians. Like us parenting our children, Paul decided it would be safer to give the Corinthians a last set of instructions about manners.

This gives me another perspective on God and his teaching me as a Father. Here God is teaching the reader about trust and faith. Reading this should alert us that God expects our lives to reflect faithfulness, and he isn't above warning us. This isn't simply about being honest or avoiding sinful acts. These are Christian manners and virtues. We should be ready to show giving and love every day.

Lord, teach me to show your love. May I be ready each day. In Jesus, amen.

MAY 13

Each one must give as he has decided in his heart, not reluctantly or under compulsion, for God loves a cheerful giver. (2 Cor. 9:7)

An infant only survives by the care of others. Even toddlers require others to tend to their needs. We grow up as needy people. So I am not surprised that as a young man, I thought God must be needy as well. Everything in me understood need. But what could God need? I decided God must need attention, so he made us to give him praise. Or maybe God needs entertainment, so he made us to be the functional equivalent of countless shows he could binge-watch.

Of course, I grew to realize that God is fully self-sufficient and has no need for you or me. As the Psalms say, if God was hungry, he wouldn't ever ask anyone. After all, "the cattle on a thousand hills" are his (Ps. 50:10–12). God has relationships within the Trinity; he certainly doesn't need us for relationships and love! Furthermore, God isn't some narcissistic divinity craving the applause or praise of fallen humans.

So if God didn't create us for what he got out of it, why did God create us? The best biblical answer I have found is that God made us to give. At his core, God is a loving God, whose love is often manifested in his giving: "For God so loved the world, that he gave . . ." (Jn. 3:16). God gave Adam and Eve paradise (Gen. 2–3). God gives the believer not only eternal life but spiritual gifts (1 Cor. 12). Jesus compares God to a Father who gives good gifts to his children (Mt. 7:11). God is a giver.

We are all made to reflect God to the world around us. This is part of what it means to be made in the image of God (Gen. 1:27). We are being transformed into the image of the loving and giving Christ (2 Cor. 3:18).

Considering these truths, I am not shocked to read today's passage. God loves a cheerful giver, someone giving from a loving heart, not from force, manipulation, guilt, or some ungodly motive. Sometimes I see this in me. Sometimes I don't! I know that it is an area where I need to focus—meeting the needs of others, giving cheerfully, thanking God for the opportunity to show his love amid the misfortunes of life that befall others. I have some more growing to do!

Lord, thank you for your giving to me. Give me your loving and giving heart. May I find joy in giving to others as you show me need and opportunity. In Jesus, amen.

MAY 14

The point is this: whoever sows sparingly will also reap sparingly, and whoever sows bountifully will also reap bountifully. . . . He who supplies seed to the sower and bread for food will supply and multiply your seed for sowing and increase the harvest of your righteousness. You will be enriched in every way to be generous in every way, which through us will produce thanksgiving to God. (2 Cor. 9:6, 10–11)

I have seen the faithfulness of God in today's verses repeatedly. As a young professional (the source of the word *yuppie*), I had a well-paying job yet also a house payment, a car note, mouths to feed, insurance to pay, a student loan, the need for clothes, and more. Each paycheck's outflow exceeded its inflow. How could I have such a good job and be so broke? I also attended church, and I went through a phase where I didn't budget the money to tithe. Then I heard a sermon that struck a nerve. God called me to tithe and to trust him to meet my needs. I tried it. He did it. It is that simple.

Now I certainly recoil at the idea that you can "name it and claim it." God's word doesn't teach that whatever we ask for in faith, God will supply. God teaches us that when we ask in faith aligned with his will, he will answer—but our asking must align with his will, not our own selfish desires. Yet it is biblically true that when God calls us to do his will, he will see that we are able to do so.

This passage today clearly teaches it, even more so when considered within the larger context of what Paul is writing. Paul knew that if the Corinthians (or any reader for that matter) would cheerfully give as God instructed, then God would see that the giver didn't suffer in ways outside the scope of God's will.

Does that mean that if you are in debt and you give to the Lord, you are in for a lottery win? No. If we are in over our heads financially (or in any other way), God is set to teach us discipline, good habits, and responsibility. Yet as he does so, he will do it in alignment with his will for us, which includes teaching us to be givers in faith, trusting God to meet our needs.

I have seen this over and over and can testify that God is faithful. God will meet and exceed our needs as we faithfully discharge our calling. That is nowhere more apparent than in his call to show that our possessions are on loan from him. We are to deal with what we have as he instructs. He will take it from there.

Lord, I desire to be faithful in giving. Give me that trust in you. In Jesus, amen.

MAY 15

I, Paul, myself entreat you, by the meekness and gentleness of Christ—I who am humble when face to face with you, but bold toward you when I am away! (2 Cor. 10:1)

Today, I am headed to Nashville to meet with some prospective clients. These are the CEO, general counsel, and a few other higher-ups within a major corporation. They are considering hiring our law firm to represent them in some big litigation. As I type, I am wearing sweats and a T-shirt. Before I go, I will put on a suit and tie. I need to look like a lawyer. My clothes won't change who I am. I would be the same person if I met them as I am currently dressed, but I would not look like a lawyer.

In similar fashion, Paul was having an image issue with some in Corinth. They believed that when Paul was with them, he was "humble" and passive, yet when Paul was writing, he was "bold" and strong. His opponents in Corinth mocked him for this and suggested he wasn't the stout apostle he claimed.

Paul explained his in-person persona was nothing less than the "meekness and gentleness" that Christ himself exhibited. These two words in Greek have some overlap, but they aren't perfect synonyms. They function together like our English words *big and strong* in that they fit well but convey some slightly different ideas. *Meekness* (*prautēs*—πραΰτης) conveys the idea of not being overly impressed with oneself or of being considerate in the presence of others. This is the same word used in the Beatitudes: "Blessed are the meek . . ." (Mt. 5:5).

To *meekness*, Paul added the word translated "gentleness" (*epieikeia*—ἐπιείκεια). This word gets a wide range of translations among scholars. It can be translated "kindness," "reasonableness," "fairness," "moderation," "consideration," "great-heartedness," "selflessness," "patience," "self-forgetfulness," and more. It is rooted in the idea of seeing that things are fair, even at one's own expense.

Paul lived traits lived by Christ himself. This was the right clothing for Paul to wear. It didn't stop Paul from addressing problems. It certainly didn't stop him from writing tough words when they were needed. Yet Paul conducted himself appropriately dressed as one who follows Christ. I can learn from this.

Lord, teach me to walk in the meekness and gentleness of Christ. In him, amen.

MAY 16

For though we walk in the flesh, we are not waging war according to the flesh. For the weapons of our warfare are not of the flesh but have divine power to destroy strongholds. We destroy arguments and every lofty opinion raised against the knowledge of God, and take every thought captive to obey Christ. (2 Cor. 10:3–5)

Confession: I am a bit of a chess nerd. The game has elements of math, art, logic, and more. It is centuries old and uses military metaphors from the ancient days in its pieces. There are kings that can't be captured. Knights that jump around in battle. Bishops that range the board to convert or kill. Pawns that are minions used for the aid of others except for the rare few that are promoted in the ranks to higher callings. Rooks can go to the corners of the board as towers of protection or used in offense. These military metaphors come to mind reading Paul's passage.

Paul uses military language in obvious ways, reading the passage as translated. But in the translation process, scholars are handicapped in their ability to capture the specialized military meaning some of Paul's language conveys. Paul uses words that were used not only in battle but specifically in siege warfare. These technical words include *siege engines*, translated "weapons"; *demolition*, translated "destroy"; *fortresses*, translated "strongholds"; and *rampart* and *raised rampart*, translated "opinion" and "lofty opinion." Paul uses these tools to *carry off to captivity* (translated as "take captive") the *opposing forces and battle plans* (translated as "thought") to be in *subjection* (translated "obey") to Christ.

What is driving Paul's colorful language? Paul uses both offensive and defensive metaphors in the sense of both attacking and defending a city. Paul's point wouldn't have been missed by the ancient reader. Paul was saying that godly living isn't always sunshine and roses. The struggle in life is real. This struggle can be to attack the evil one finds in life. It can also be to find defensive refuge against the attacks of others.

The key for Paul—and for me as I read this—is to be Christ's in all we do. We fight evil for Christ, but importantly, we do so by the power of Christ. Paul wrote of the "divine power" to achieve these gains. I will get nowhere in life's struggles if I fight solo. I need God, his Spirit, weapons, energy, direction, and plans to empower me to find good in this life. Unlike chess, this isn't a game. It is real.

Lord, empower me to do your will today, whatever I face. In Jesus, amen.

MAY 17

But we will not boast beyond limits, but will boast only with regard to the area of influence God assigned to us, to reach even to you. . . . "Let the one who boasts, boast in the Lord." (2 Cor. 10:13, 17)

Larry Bird is famous not only for his basketball prowess but for his trash talk. At the highest levels of basketball, Bird would tell the defender, "Here's what I'm going to do. I'm going to get the pass at the top of the key, dribble three steps left, and then shoot right over you and win the game." Then he would do it. He had a level of confidence (some might say arrogance) that left his opponents shaking their heads in disbelief.

Self-confidence can easily bleed over into arrogance and pride. We accomplish something big, and from the earliest age, we have an urge to say, "See? Look what I did! Aren't I important?" The desire to matter is not bad, but when it crosses over into arrogance, it becomes the biblical sin of pride.

Paul wrote in today's passage about boasting. His chosen Greek word for *boasting* speaks to taking pride or glory in something or someone (*kauchaomai*–καυχάομαι). Paul was not one to brag or boast about his accomplishments–which is quite something, looking back at his life and influence.

Some scholars reckon Paul to be the formative force behind the entire Christian religion. Paul took his top-level education and went throughout the Mediterranean world establishing churches, including that in Corinth. Paul taught a generation of evangelists, missionaries, and teachers who would come in his wake and further the work. Paul wrote the foundational letters that explained the core Christian doctrine of justification by faith and more. Paul had direct contact with the Lord Jesus in visions and dialogue.

Yet for all that, Paul typically (see the coming devotionals) refused to boast in his accomplishments. Paul didn't believe he was incredible for what he did. Paul knew that the Lord was incredible. The Lord was able to use even Paul to spread God's good news about the redemption and new life found in the death and resurrection of Christ. The Lord alone is worthy of our boasting.

Lord, may I bring glory to you. When you use me for good works, may my voice and attitude always show that you are the one due the glory. In Jesus, amen.

MAY 18

For I feel a divine jealousy for you, since I betrothed you to one husband, to present you as a pure virgin to Christ. But I am afraid that as the serpent deceived Eve by his cunning, your thoughts will be led astray from a sincere and pure devotion to Christ. (2 Cor. 11:2–3)

As I write this devotional, three of my four daughters are married (to wonderful men), and my fourth daughter is engaged. The proposal was quite a process. Her intended planned it with precision suitable for a rocket launch. He had both families in for the proposal, hid them until the critical moment, lured Sarah unexpectedly to the right spot, and then, in a surprise, dropped to a knee and proposed. Now the marriage is almost a year away, but the planning is in full swing. The venue has been selected, a wedding planner has been retained, and the wedding dress shopping has begun.

Weddings are typically cheerful and anticipated events. It seems they have always been so. This allows a wedding to serve as a wonderful metaphor. In the Old Testament, the wedding analogy typically featured God as the husband and the people of Israel as God's bride. In the New Testament, the metaphor is used of Christ (the groom) and the church (the bride). Paul uses this metaphor for Christ and the church, but he adds a new party! Paul inserts himself as the father of the bride.

Paul uses this analogy to emphasize how the church maintains itself in the lead-up to the marriage. The book of Revelation completes the metaphor of Christ as groom when the end of days comes and the wedding feast is held (Rev. 21). But until the end of days, the church (meaning the believers in Christ) lives in the preparation stage. We are "betrothed," to use the language of today's passage, but the marriage isn't yet consummated.

How we live in the period of engagement is critical. Paul wants us presented in the wedding as faithful to Christ. Paul's fear was that as Satan had lured Eve into rebellion and error, so his audience might be deceived into impurity. The impurity that was Paul's concern isn't necessarily the same impurity that believers face today. But the struggle is the same. You and I must each day be diligent in life, knowing our efforts are preparation for the wedding of eternity. Let us get ready. Our wedding day is coming.

Lord, I want a sincere and pure devotion to you. I pray you will guide and strengthen me to seek holiness above all else. I pray expectantly in Jesus, amen.

MAY 19

And what I am doing I will continue to do, in order to undermine the claim of those who would like to claim that in their boasted mission they work on the same terms as we do. For such men are false apostles, deceitful workmen, disguising themselves as apostles of Christ. And no wonder, for even Satan disguises himself as an angel of light. So it is no surprise if his servants, also, disguise themselves as servants of righteousness. Their end will correspond to their deeds. (2 Cor. 11:12–15)

When I was a young man, most of us in the neighborhood would go trick-or-treating each Halloween. The easiest costume each year was to buy and step into a one-piece costume that was finished off with a plastic mask held to your face with a piece of elastic string. One year, I remember the "devil" costume being particularly popular. Combining a red suit with a mask with horns was admittedly not too convincing, but it worked to get the candy.

False faces and altered appearances aren't only for Halloween. Paul has put Halloween in reverse in today's passage. He has Satan dressing up as a follower of Christ. But Satan is not about trying to fill a plastic pumpkin with candy. His mission is malevolent. He seeks to subvert the work of Christ, confuse and disorient Christ's followers, and wreak any havoc he can.

If Satan's actions aren't bad enough, at times, some people join him in his efforts. Paul calls them "his servants." The context of today's passage makes this troubling truth even more disconcerting. Paul wrote of traveling preachers—people who the larger context of Corinthians explains were denigrating Paul and, more importantly, taught false doctrine. We don't know whether these destructive people realized they were servants of Satan, but their work and words left no doubt as to whom they served.

My actions today will advance the purpose of God or of his enemy in a raging cosmic war. That may seem bizarre, in that I am likely to have a normal day with normal decisions, but it is true nonetheless. When I choose to walk in godliness, speaking with grace and kindness, God is glorified and his mission advanced. But when I walk in selfishness and sin, I might as well be donning a Halloween mask, as I am working for the enemy.

Lord, may I walk for you in your truth today. In Jesus, I pray, amen.

MAY 20

But whatever anyone else dares to boast of—I am speaking as a fool—I also dare to boast of that. Are they Hebrews? So am I. Are they Israelites? So am I. Are they offspring of Abraham? So am I. Are they servants of Christ? I am a better one—I am talking like a madman—with far greater labors, far more imprisonments, with countless beatings, and often near death. Five times I received at the hands of the Jews the forty lashes less one. Three times I was beaten with rods. Once I was stoned. Three times I was shipwrecked; a night and a day I was adrift at sea; on frequent journeys, in danger from rivers, danger from robbers, danger from my own people, danger from Gentiles, danger in the city, danger in the wilderness, danger at sea, danger from false brothers; in toil and hardship, through many a sleepless night, in hunger and thirst, often without food, in cold and exposure. And, apart from other things, there is the daily pressure on me of my anxiety for all the churches. (2 Cor. 11:21–28)

For over a decade, I tried to read a chapter of Proverbs each day. There are thirty-one chapters of Proverbs and thirty to thirty-one days in most months, so I would read the Proverbs chapter that corresponded to the day. The twenty-sixth of each month was often a stumper to me. Proverbs 26:4 says, "Answer not a fool according to his folly, lest you be like him yourself." I could get that. Don't answer a fool! But then the very next verse says, "Answer a fool according to his folly, lest he be wise in his own eyes." So now I am to answer a fool? Which is it? I walked away from those readings with my interpretation: you don't get far if you are dealing with fools.

Yet into that issue of foolishness comes today's passage, where Paul devolves into what he terms "foolish" speech. In the overarching context, Paul is addressing people who have heard others denigrate Paul and his message. These interlopers into the Corinthian church foolishly portrayed Paul as a bit ordinary at best, while they exalted themselves as a bit like "superapostles." Paul then enters his own brand of foolishness to address the foolish claims of these dangerous people.

Paul's history recounted for them and us a most impressive résumé, especially when considering that Paul gave up a life of wealth and success to pursue God's mission.

This moves me in two ways. First, I am challenged by how little I have suffered for Christ. Second, I am determined to pay attention to and appreciate Paul's text.

Lord, I am inadequate in so many ways. May I be a better servant in Christ, amen.

MAY 21

So to keep me from becoming conceited because of the surpassing greatness of the revelations, a thorn was given me in the flesh, a messenger of Satan to harass me, to keep me from becoming conceited. Three times I pleaded with the Lord about this, that it should leave me. But he said to me, "My grace is sufficient for you, for my power is made perfect in weakness." (2 Cor. 12:7–9)

Charles Hoyt wrote the lyrics to a song published in 1896 entitled "Some Things Are Better Left Unsaid." The subtitle was "Do you want to know the rest, or shall I stop?" Hoyt offered the gossip of the day but also probed into the character of the listener. The song comes to mind as I look at 2 Corinthians 12. In this chapter, Paul writes of being "caught up to the third heaven" (v. 2) and a "thorn . . . in the flesh" (v. 7), two ideas that have stumped many modern readers trying to figure out precisely what Paul meant.

I suspect the fullness of Paul's experience will not be known in this life; however, the points Paul makes from those experiences are both knowable and valuable. Those points are centered in today's passage.

Paul's glorious experience in the third heaven was so vivid that he couldn't tell if it was a bodily experience or not. But Paul informs the reader that when there, he "heard things that cannot be told, which man may not utter" (v. 4). This most profound experience might have easily led to conceit. To prevent that pride or self-importance, Paul received the unknown "thorn . . . in the flesh." This pestering problem seems to have been a physical malady that remained present despite Paul's fervent prayer.

Life may lead all of us into circumstances, experiences, accomplishments, and results that may cause feelings of self-importance. Paul's writing serves as an admonition to guard against such conceit. For all of us also carry afflictions in this life. Our afflictions might not be physical maladies, but we all struggle with sin despite our prayers to the contrary.

Into our world, then, we find a chapter of Paul that, though many would think it was better left unsaid, contains a critical teaching. As weak as we may be in life, as sinful and error prone, the grace of God is more than enough. In our weakness, God will win with his resurrection power.

Lord, be magnified in my life. Rescue me in your grace. In Jesus, amen.

MAY 22

Therefore I will boast all the more gladly of my weaknesses, so that the power of Christ may rest upon me. For the sake of Christ, then, I am content with weaknesses, insults, hardships, persecutions, and calamities. For when I am weak, then I am strong. (2 Cor. 12:9–10)

We all want to be special. We want to be loved. This is readily apparent in the young, who haven't grown enough to put filters on their words and behaviors. I saw it in my children and see it in my grandchildren: the quick "Watch this!" that precedes an act of daring, a dance of joy, or a simple deed of accomplishment. As we age, we get more subtle, but the temptation to show others our skills, brilliance, talents, accomplishments, and more still exists.

Today's passage comes near the end of an important section of Paul's letter where he has addressed the claims of false teachers who have come into Corinth dissing Paul and his message. Paul's Christian maturity is on full display as he handles the problem. For Paul, what was important wasn't his feelings of adequacy or self-worth. Paul's concern was how his detractor's teaching affected God's message. Moreover, Paul used their disrespect as a teaching point.

Paul could certainly list his qualifications as God's tool, and he did so earlier in the previous chapter. But Paul was quick to accept his shortcomings. As much as Paul could boast about what made him special, Paul wanted instead to boast of what made God special and how God had used his shortcomings.

Through all the difficulties, weaknesses, and challenges in Paul's life, Paul was able to proclaim the greatness of God. God was greater than Paul's hardships. God reigned over all, even amid the insults hurled at Paul. Paul might be persecuted, but as God walked with Paul through those persecutions, God was magnified. Calamity befell Paul, but God lifted Paul up. People might heap their insults on Paul, but God still shone brightly and purely.

Paul's bottom line that God's grace overcomes all our personal shortcomings and difficulties informs me today. I might want to show my accomplishments to feel special, but the truth is all of us *are* special to God. We are special because God made us that way. God's love pours into our lives to grow us into the likeness of Jesus. In the face of all the difficulties of life, God is strong in our weakness.

Lord, give me peace amid life. Give me joy in being yours. In Jesus, amen.

MAY 23

For he was crucified in weakness, but lives by the power of God. For we also are weak in him, but in dealing with you we will live with him by the power of God. (2 Cor. 13:4)

Research has indicated that as many as 25 percent of television commercials feature a celebrity endorsement of a product. Many reasons are given for this, but a common factor is the public's desire to have the traits of A-list stars. Many of us see someone we respect and daydream about what it would be like to be like them. Almost every student athlete has imagined themselves as Lebron James or Patrick Mahomes while on the court or playing field.

Similarly, in some ways, believers seek to be like Christ. But there are often some limits. We want the holiness of Christ, but few desire the sufferings of Christ. It wouldn't be a bad thing to be able to heal the lame, like Jesus and his apostles, but being persecuted for following God isn't high on anyone's list.

Paul here shows he had found a particular way his experiences charted the life of Christ in one of these areas most would avoid. He states Christ was "crucified in weakness." Christ was humiliated in his crucifixion, the worst kind of death imaginable. It was unfathomable for God to die, let alone in this horrible way. Yet the crucified one (past event) now lives (present tense) both by and in God's power. God's resurrection power is on full display in the living Christ.

That same contrast between weakness and resurrection power is in play for Paul and others. Paul might seem weak to those in Corinth. Indeed, as discussed in earlier devotional teachings, Paul was suffering a thorn in the flesh, was being humiliated and insulted by interloping teachers, and had many rough times in his preaching ministry. Some false teachers might assert Paul was lacking in the faith department because if Paul were really all that, wouldn't his life be "blessed" materially, physically, and generally?

No, Paul knew that those who follow Christ have the chance and obligation to pick up their cross and follow Jesus through difficulty. Our hard times do not mean God has turned his back on us. We experience weakness and find God's power!

Lord, walk with me in my weak times. Give me your strength. In Jesus' name, amen.

MAY 24

Finally, brothers, rejoice. Aim for restoration, comfort one another, agree with one another, live in peace; and the God of love and peace will be with you. Greet one another with a holy kiss. . . . The grace of the Lord Jesus Christ and the love of God and the fellowship of the Holy Spirit be with you all. (2 Cor. 13:11–14)

I hate long good-byes. Given the choice, I would like to say good-bye, then quickly get distracted by something else so I don't have to dwell on the separation. My wife is similar. Frequently in my job, I must spend a good deal of time away from home. If we are going to be apart for multiple days, and I bring that up a day or two before I leave, Becky will say, "I don't want to think about that now! Don't talk about it!" Long good-byes aren't our thing!

Paul isn't on a visit, but he is still bringing his letter to a close. Paul is burdened to say more than "Well, that's all I've got! See you guys soon, I hope!" Paul ends his letter with care. Paul gives a final exhortation or encouraging instruction for his readers. He wants them to (1) rejoice. Paul has been writing some strident words, scolding and upbraiding a few of the Corinthians. Yet like the discipline I received from my parents growing up, he too wants to end with a statement of restoration: "OK, we're done dealing with that. Now let's move on and enjoy life." (2) Aim for restoration. Paul gave them homework, starting with the assignment to work hard to draw closer to one another. (3) Comfort one another. For Paul, as they drew closer in restoration, they would have chances to minister care and solace/support/consolation to one another. (4) Agree with one another and live in peace. In English, this might best be expressed in the negative—try not to be disagreeable! Get along. Care about the peace. (5) Greet one another with a holy kiss. In modern parlance, hug it out! Paul wants genuine closeness among the church.

None of Paul's instructions truly work if we are chasing them out of our own strength. These are manifestations of God's Spirit at work in our hearts and minds, bringing us into a greater likeness of our Savior Jesus. So it is appropriate that Paul's final words be a prayer that God's grace, love, and fellowship be present with every reader.

Paul did a longer good-bye than I typically employ. His is much better! I want to heed his instructions, even though I am not a first-generation recipient of his letter!

Lord, be with me in your grace, love, and fellowship, to the glory of Jesus, through whom I pray, amen.

MAY 25

Paul, a servant of Christ Jesus, called to be an apostle, set apart for the gospel of God. . . . To all those in Rome who are loved by God and called to be saints: Grace to you and peace from God our Father and the Lord Jesus Christ. (Rom. 1:1, 7)

The church "began" in Jerusalem. Jews from all over the Mediterranean world came in to celebrate Pentecost. The Holy Spirit descended, Peter preached, and thousands were converted, among them Jews from Rome. As those Jews returned home, they took their faith in the Messiah and became the first church at Rome. Over time, the church in Rome doubtlessly grew, and even Gentiles came to faith, although the Jews would have likely been the stalwarts, those who knew the Holy Scriptures, and those from whom the faith originated.

History records that a fight among the Jews in Rome was such a community disturbance that Emperor Claudius expelled all Jews from Rome. This doubtlessly left the church in an unusual position. Those who started and likely ran the church, from its teaching to its budget, were gone, and only Gentile believers remained. Great teachers like Priscilla and Aquila left for Corinth. Yet for the year or so that the church was only Gentiles, it seems to have thrived.

When Jews were allowed to return to Rome, can you imagine the impact on the church? "We're home! Thanks for taking care of things while we were gone. We've got it now!" While the Gentiles were thinking, "Actually we did pretty good! We need to have more of a role than before." This doubtlessly brought into focus how the groups interacted and coordinated for the kingdom. Many church issues must have arisen.

Amid this scenario, Paul writes Romans. Paul hadn't yet been to the church, but he did have friends there. Paul writes to teach the church and to explain an important truth: *before God*, there is no difference between Jew and Gentile. To do so, Paul goes back to basics. Starting with creation, Paul moves through to the gospel, the salvation provided by Christ. Paul shows everyone has the same need for Christ. All are saved by his death, burial, and resurrection through faith. Paul begins this theological masterpiece noting his calling before God to preach and teach the gospel. He writes to the church calling them *all* saints, Jew and Gentile alike. Everyone embracing Christ in faith is a saint—that is, someone set apart for God and his service. No exceptions!

Lord, may I embrace your gracious love. Thank you for Jesus. In him, amen.

MAY 26

For I am not ashamed of the gospel, for it is the power of God for salvation to everyone who believes, to the Jew first and also to the Greek. For in it the righteousness of God is revealed from faith for faith, as it is written, "The righteous shall live by faith." (Rom. 1:16–17)

Dr. Floyd was an exacting Greek teacher. He cared about every nuance of grammar. Accent marks were to be learned with precision, minding each rule. Vocabulary was important as well. He would take words and not only help us find the range of meanings in Greek but also ensure we understood particular usage by certain authors. This verse was important to Dr. Floyd because it contained a pet word for Paul. That word is *euangelion* (εὐαγγέλιον), translated "gospel."

"Gospel" is a compound word in the Greek that combines "good" (*eu*) and "message" or "news" (*angelion*). Now, there is certainly a lot of good news we can discuss, but in Paul's mind, when he uses this word in its theological context, there is news that so surpasses all other news, there's no close second. That news is the salvation story wrapped in the death, burial, and resurrection of Christ on behalf of the world. No news compares.

Now to some, especially in Paul's day, this idea that Christ had to die to give them righteousness before God might be humiliating. After all, can't folks be good enough on their own? No. Paul wasn't ashamed that Christ had to die for his sins. Paul notes that the death of Christ, this greatest of news, is the ability or power of God to save anyone. This is where God's righteousness is revealed through our faith or trust (the Greek word conveys both "mental belief" as well as deep trust).

As Paul dealt with a church recently reuniting Jews and Gentiles (see yesterday's devotional), Paul points out that this powerful salvation is for *all*, even though the Jews chronologically received it first and the Gentiles subsequently accepted it.

Words matter. Paul explained that the Christian journey is rooted in the death and resurrection of Christ. The journey begins with a trusting faith in that historical truth, and the journey ends with that same trusting faith. This will not only make believers righteous before God, but it is God's tool for growing believers in righteousness. For Paul, the cross of Christ was the great justifier and the great equalizer. It remains the greatest news, the gospel for all humanity.

Lord, thank you for Christ and his sacrifice on my behalf. I pray in him, amen.

MAY 27

For the wrath of God is revealed from heaven against all ungodliness and unrighteousness of men, who by their unrighteousness suppress the truth. For what can be known about God is plain to them, because God has shown it to them. For his invisible attributes, namely, his eternal power and divine nature, have been clearly perceived, ever since the creation of the world, in the things that have been made. So they are without excuse. (Rom. 1:18–20)

An insightful young doctorate student at Oxford University had made the long jaunt to Texas with our son to tour the United States. The young man didn't believe God was real, at least as revealed in Scripture. In addition to being very smart, he was marvelously upright, caring deeply about right and wrong. I asked him how he logically believed so fervently that there is objective morality (i.e., some things are plain wrong, regardless of whether someone intellectually agrees they are wrong) if there is no God to define right and wrong. His reply was that wrong just exists in the universe, like mathematics. In his thinking, "Two plus two is four whether there is a God or not."

While I believe he loses the logical thread by trying to force what is true (objective morality) into a godless framework, he nonetheless has seen a fundamental truth. God is hardwired into our universe. Paul says as much in today's passage.

God's invisible attributes—his eternal power and divine nature—are on full display in the cosmos. For example, we can see how God is a God of cause and effect, a fundamental rule of the universe. That principle was on display when God announced to Adam, "If you eat of the tree, then you die." Cause and effect (if . . . , then . . .) is demonstrated in Scripture from Genesis to Revelation. Similarly, the laws of nature are consistent. Gravity doesn't exist only a few days a week. Physics textbooks can be safely written because of Newton's law of inertia and other unchanging rules of our world.

The unchanging laws of nature reflect the unchanging God who created nature. No one need worry that God is going to change. The God of compassion who cares for us will not decide tomorrow that he's taking back the sacrifice of Christ on the cross. He won't decide that he's going to be a selfish God instead of a giving God. He doesn't change, and we can rely on that. He's shown us in his creation.

Lord, I praise you as the unchanging God. I also rely on you, trusting you to be true to your word. I see that's who you are, and I am thankful. In Jesus, amen.

MAY 28

And since they did not see fit to acknowledge God, God gave them up to a debased mind to do what ought not to be done. They were filled with all manner of unrighteousness, evil, covetousness, malice. They are full of envy, murder, strife, deceit, maliciousness. They are gossips, slanderers, haters of God, insolent, haughty, boastful, inventors of evil, disobedient to parents, foolish, faithless, heartless, ruthless. Though they know God's righteous decree that those who practice such things deserve to die, they not only do them but give approval to those who practice them. (Rom. 1:28–32)

No one knows the origin of the phrase "Be careful what you wish for; you might get it." Some attribute it to Aesop's fables, others to an ancient Chinese proverb. Neither seems conclusive. While the phrase isn't found as such, the idea is conveyed in many old stories. The idea is commonplace today.

Paul could have used the phrase in today's text. Repeatedly in the first chapter of Romans, Paul explains that when people see and honor God, their lives are transformed in goodness and righteousness. But when one refuses to accept God and respond to him in faith, the repercussions are profound. If they wish to live in a world devoid of God's reign and lordship, they will get their wish. But the world without God's character is a world riddled with sin.

Paul's list of sins covers the gamut. He has the sins we rail against—murder, deceit, malice, and so on. But he also includes the "lesser sins" (in the eyes of some)—foolishness, gossip, bragging, disobedience, and so on. People inherently know these things are wrong, but when they don't worship the one true God, then these traits in some variation become their God. These traits rule their lives and actions.

I am struck by several things in today's passage. First, I realize that all sin is offensive to God's nature. I don't have to be a murderer to need God's forgiveness, for my sins nestle right next to the harsh ones on this list. A second aspect of this is that as I choose to wander from God, as I loosen the tightness of my grip on his hand, I will see it in my behavior. I will start to wander not only from his heart but from his character. If I want to live in one sin or another, I better watch what I wish for because I might get it. And where it leads is not pretty.

Lord, I want to grow closer to you each day. I want to love as you love, see as you see, value as you value, care as you care, and serve as you serve. Help me. In Jesus' name, amen.

MAY 29

When God's righteous judgment [is] revealed[,] he will render to each one according to his works: to those who by patience in well-doing seek for glory and honor and immortality, he will give eternal life; but for those who are self-seeking and do not obey the truth, but obey unrighteousness, there will be wrath and fury. (Rom. 2:5–8)

My expert witness was testifying about the effects of finding asbestos in baby powder. Under cross-examination, he was read one seemingly inconsistent sentence out of an article he had written. The lawyer pressed him, "You wrote this, didn't you?" My expert said, "Yes." The lawyer continued, "And you wrote the truth, didn't you?" To this my expert replied, "Yes, but you've taken it out of context." The lawyer pushed, "Well, but it is written precisely in the way I read it, right?" My expert calmly replied, "You have read that part of what I wrote, but you need to read the rest for context. Otherwise, it's like saying, 'It was a beautiful day,' and leaving out, 'until the tornado hit.'"

That story comes to mind as I read chapter 2 of Paul's letter to the Romans. As I set up in May 25's devotional, Paul is addressing a recombined church of Jews and Gentiles, and he is setting out fundamental truths of God's work in people through the death and resurrection of Christ Jesus. Paul here in chapter 2 and in a good part of chapter 3 sets out God's principles of judgment. If people read the dictates of God's justice in these verses, they may be left disturbed or even panicked. But that is taking Romans 2 out of context from the rest of the book.

After all, if on judgment day, God truly is going to "render to each one" according to their works, we are all in trouble. If those who are self-seeking and do not obey the truth but obey unrighteousness are set to receive wrath and fury, then we are all lost. For almost without exception, the best human deeds are tainted with at least a smidgeon of selfishness. By God's standard of judgment set out in these verses and this chapter, it is Christ alone who measures up to God and is worthy of eternal life.

Spoiler alert: in Romans 3, Paul sets out a means by which a just God can clear the sinful other than through our works. But for now, looking at this passage, we should all feel a need for forgiveness from God. No one measures up to God's standards.

Lord, I am too familiar with my moral failures before you. I am not who I want to be, nor who I need to be, save by the mercy in Jesus, through whom I pray, amen.

MAY 30

For all who have sinned without the law will also perish without the law, and all who have sinned under the law will be judged by the law. For it is not the hearers of the law who are righteous before God, but the doers of the law who will be justified. For when Gentiles, who do not have the law, by nature do what the law requires, they are a law to themselves, even though they do not have the law. They show that the work of the law is written on their hearts, while their conscience also bears witness, and their conflicting thoughts accuse or even excuse them on that day when, according to my gospel, God judges the secrets of men by Christ Jesus. (Rom. 2:12–16)

In my college days, as I was working through this passage in Greek, I thought, "Well, I'm going to Hell." Not that I was a bad person; by the world's standards, I was quite good. But my internal assurance before God was based in large part on my goodness. I had interpreted the reference to the "law" as being those instructions of the Old Testament that still apply today. I watered down the "law" into something that I could comfortably do. I could avoid the big sins of murder, theft, and the like. That seemed to me all the law a Gentile like me had to obey.

But Paul, as discussed in yesterday's devotional, declared that God's principles of judgment are basically as follows: if you are righteous, you have eternal life; if you aren't, you rightly receive God's wrath. Having set out God's basis for judging, Paul now focuses on God judging the Gentile. In tomorrow's passage, Paul shifts to cover God's judgment of Jews.

Gentiles were not blessed historically with the law given by God on Mount Sinai through Moses and secured by the prophets of the Old Testament. But that didn't give the Gentiles an excuse for sin. For God hardwired into everyone the sense of right and wrong. Everyone knows some sense of righteousness, and in that awareness, no one measures up to God's perfection. No one has the track record to stand before God and say, "I'm good. I'm not a lawbreaker."

If my reading of Romans stopped at today's passage, I would be a mess. Reading this passage as a Gentile, I am certainly not fit for God's eternity. I am set for his wrath. Fortunately, today's passage is one stop on a road that leads to Romans 3:16 and what follows—truths that are addressed next month. Keep reading!

Lord, I am lost without you. I am a sinner in need of your mercy. Help me in Jesus' name, amen.

MAY 31

But if you call yourself a Jew and rely on the law and boast in God. . . . You who boast in the law dishonor God by breaking the law. For, as it is written, "The name of God is blasphemed among the Gentiles because of you." (Rom. 2:17, 23–24)

Comparisons. We all make them. We compare one thing to another when shopping. We compare one person to another when deciding who to date, marry, work with, and hang with. We compare careers, deciding what to do, and then compare jobs, deciding where to work. We compare options for eating, options for vacation, and options for what to wear to what event. Comparisons are part and parcel of life. But problems arise in certain areas of comparison.

In Rome, as discussed in the May 25 devotional, the government had "compared" the people's heritage and expelled the Jews for a time. Those were the Jews who had started the church in Rome. Upon their return, the Jews were reintegrating into the church, but there seemed to be some divisions still percolating. Paul is in the middle of putting those divisions to rest, at least in eternal terms.

Paul explained in chapter 2 that God's principles of judgment are the same for Jews and Gentiles. They are no different there. As discussed yesterday, even though the Gentiles were without the revealed Law of Moses, they still had a hardwired law of God in their hearts and minds, and thus they were lawbreakers. Paul now shifts that focus to the Jewish readers and puts them in the same boat as the Gentiles.

For the Jews had the revealed law, and while they might find room for boasting in that law, the truth is that they were lawbreakers as well. They could proudly proclaim God's revelation, but they failed to live up to that revelation. Even in boasting of knowing God's law, a certain hypocrisy was present, as those boasting couldn't keep the law.

We are not able to satisfy God's perfection in our lives. It simply isn't possible. But God loves us anyway, and God establishes a path for us into his eternal fellowship based on his works of mercy and grace, as Paul will explain. None of us should ever think ourselves righteous before God because of how we compare with others. That is comparison gone awry!

Lord, I know my need for you. Forgive me any pride in life. In Jesus, amen.

JUNE 1

What then? Are we Jews any better off? No, not at all. For we have already charged that all, both Jews and Greeks, are under sin, as it is written: "None is righteous, no, not one; no one understands; no one seeks for God. All have turned aside; together they have become worthless; no one does good, not even one." (Rom. 3:9–12)

By the time Paul wrote Romans, Greek plays—notably tragedies and comedies—had been performed for centuries. The Greek tragedy followed a basic formula. After a prologue provided the necessary background for understanding the play and an opening song introduced the main characters, the play was broken into episodes. Each episode consisted of the characters and chorus acting and dialoguing. When each episode ended, the characters exited the stage, and the chorus sang a *stasimon*, a reflection of what was said in the episode that placed it into a larger framework of significance. Then another episode began.

Paul isn't writing a Greek play, but he does begin a bit of a "stasimon" here, in that he summarizes what he has already said in a way that facilitates a larger understanding. In the previous verses, Paul has set forth God's principles of judgment, explaining that sinners inure to wrath and punishment. Paul then applied that to his Gentile readers, noting their excuse "But we never had the Law of Moses" didn't hold water because fundamental principles of right and wrong are written on everyone's heart. Next Paul explained that the Jews also faced judgment, noting they had the law but failed to keep it. Now Paul summarizes with an important central truth: all have sinned.

Paul writes for every reader to relate. Everyone falls under his concluding ideas of sin and self-righteousness. Paul uses several Psalms to reinforce one objective and simple truth: everyone is a sinner. No one is righteous. No one truly seeks God as he or she should. No one is even capable of a good deed, if by *good* we mean done with the purity of motive and action that is found in God.

If Romans ended here, it would be a tragedy of immense proportions. But fortunately, as seen in tomorrow's passage, this foundational truth isn't the end. But before getting to tomorrow, I pause and reflect. I have zero basis for arrogance or haughtiness before God or any human. I am a sinner in need of a Savior.

Lord, I confess I am not adequate to live with you, to pray to you, to call for you. But call on you I do, seeking you through the grace of Jesus, amen.

JUNE 2

For by works of the law no human being will be justified in his sight, since through the law comes knowledge of sin. But now the righteousness of God has been manifested apart from the law, although the Law and the Prophets bear witness to it—the righteousness of God through faith in Jesus Christ for all who believe. (Rom. 3:20–22)

In legal circles, the phrase *kangaroo court* is often used to describe an egregious miscarriage of justice overseen by a judge who is either utterly incompetent or deliberately unfair and unjust. The judge might be dishonest, might be in collusion with one party or another, or might be subconsciously biased. A kangaroo court is the opposite of what a court should be—a place of fair and impartial decisions based on the merits and law.

Does God, the great judge, run a kangaroo court? That is modern terminology applied to an ancient question that takes front and center for Paul in Romans. Paul was legally trained as a lawyer. He had prosecuted Christians in his pre-conversion years. He knew the importance of a fair and just court. He knew well those Old Testament Scriptures (especially the "Minor Prophets") that railed against Israel and Judah for injustice in their court systems. He knew that God had visited judgment on Israel because God was a "just" God.

So if God is a just judge, and if God had proper principles of justice (as laid out in the previous chapters and devotionals), and if all humanity stands guilty before God, then how can a just judge (God) declare guilty people "not guilty"? How does God forgive sins without turning into a kangaroo court?

One might say, "God can't!" Others might say, "Well, he can just decide to." After all, "He's God; he can do anything he wants." All of these statements have a problem, however. They either leave humanity straddled with the full punishment for sin, or they turn God into an unjust God and require him to deny his true character.

Paul's answer begins unfolding in today's passage. It has one of the most powerful contrasting conjunctions—*but*—found in the Bible. Yes, God is just. Yes, people are all guilty. But—God can rightly declare people free and absolved of guilt by substituting Jesus Christ as the atoning price for sin. With the penalty paid, a just God will rightly declare the sinful no longer guilty. Period.

Lord, I need your redemption. I need your forgiveness. I seek it in Jesus, amen.

JUNE 3

All have sinned and fall short of the glory of God, and are justified by his grace as a gift, through the redemption that is in Christ Jesus, whom God put forward as a propitiation by his blood, to be received by faith. (Rom. 3:23–25a)

I was probably almost twenty years old before I ever used the word *propitiation*. I think I asked this: "What does *propitiation* mean?" I learned the word from one of my Greek professors, who explained its meaning in today's verse. I have never said or heard the word used except in biblical teaching.

This Greek word is unusual in the New Testament. It occurs twice: here and in Hebrews 9:5 (although a related word occurs a handful of times). The word is *hilastērion* (ἱλαστήριον). It denotes a removal of wrath—here specifically, God's wrath. Many translators dislike the word, for they do not like the idea of God having wrath, seeing it as a human emotion of anger that needs removing. Yet God does have a divine wrath against acts and omissions that hurt people. God's wrath isn't the same as the human emotion, but it is real. It is inherent in his justice and purity. If we minimize his wrath against evil, we minimize his character.

One of Scripture's most famous passages is John 3:16: "For God so loved the world, that he gave his only Son, that whoever believes in him should not perish but have eternal life." But John's train of thought didn't end in verse 16. The chapter's last verse says that those who hear but don't respond to Jesus (the meaning of the verb translated "obey") "shall not see life, but the wrath of God remains on him" (v. 36). God's wrath is real. It rightly sits on evil.

God seeks a just way to set aside his holy and righteous wrath. That is done by a propitiation. The specific way God's wrath is propitiated is by the blood of Christ. It is akin in some ways to the idea expressed in the Old Testament of the "mercy seat." This seat was built over the ark of the covenant. It was the place where God's mercy was symbolically applied over the sins of the people as the atoning sacrificial blood was sprinkled. The seat was termed a *hilastērion* in the Greek translation of the Old Testament. God has wrath on evil and evildoers. But God's love trumps his wrath and saves the evildoer by absolving the responsibility for sin through Jesus' death. It is still a courtroom analogy for Paul. Our sin is real. Our sin is evil. Our sin deserves judgment. But in Christ, the consequences are freely paid, and we stand whole before God, fully forgiven and free of all wrath.

Lord, thank you for the sacrifice of Jesus. I need your grace. In him, amen.

JUNE 4

All have sinned and fall short of the glory of God, and are justified by his grace as a gift, through the redemption that is in Christ Jesus, whom God put forward as a propitiation by his blood, to be received by faith. This was to show God's righteousness, because in his divine forbearance he had passed over former sins. It was to show his righteousness at the present time, so that he might be just and the justifier of the one who has faith in Jesus. (Rom. 3:23–26)

English can be a bit goofy in some ways. Our language is a bit of a witch's brew, with words from ancient Greek, Latin, German, Anglo-Saxon, Nordic, and more. Sometimes those words are aligned in meaning but not usage—think of *swine* (Germanic) and *pork* (Latin). Today's passage is another marvelous example, and I use a bit of yesterday's passage to add to the illustration.

Paul writes of people "justified" in a way that shows God's "righteousness" and his "just-ness" as the "justifier" (a predicament set out in yesterday's devotional). Those words stem from either Latin (the *just* words) or old Germanic roots of Old English (the *righteous* words). Yet at their core, they mean the same.

Why does this matter in today's passage? Because in Paul's Greek, Paul uses the same root word for all those English options. The words *just*, *justifier*, and *justified* are from the same basic Greek word as *righteousness* and *righteous*. The Greek words (from *dikē*—δικη) are generally rooted in judicial fairness but could also indicate the upright behavior of one who lives up to legal codes and standards.

In English, we use different words to translate this Greek concept, with different translations generally depending on whether Paul uses the root in the form of nouns, verbs, or adjectives. It would be awkward English to use the same term, even though it would show consistency with Paul's Greek. If we focus on this concept, however, we see that Paul says that while all sin before God (i.e., no one is righteous), we are made righteous ("justified") through the redemption in Christ. Christ's righteousness was to cover past sins as well as sins today. Hence Christ's death shows God's righteousness because he forgave sins in the past and passes over sins today and in the future. He righteously declares others righteous. God is a just/righteous judge who metes out just justice to those with faith in his Son.

Father, I don't merit your justice. I am fully sinful and inadequate. But I trust in your mercy shown in Christ, through whom I pray, amen.

JUNE 5

What then shall we say was gained by Abraham, our forefather according to the flesh? For if Abraham was justified by works, he has something to boast about, but not before God. For what does the Scripture say? "Abraham believed God, and it was counted to him as righteousness." Now to the one who works, his wages are not counted as a gift but as his due. And to the one who does not work but believes in him who justifies the ungodly, his faith is counted as righteousness. (Rom. 4:1–5)

I hired a fellow to do some yard work. My mom's house needed some serious landscaping help. The fellow designed a gorgeous set of beds with climate-appropriate and seasonally fitting plants and flowers. He brought a large crew with him, and they spent the better part of three days removing the old beds, building the new ones, and transforming my mom's yard from something you drive past without seeing into the yard of the month, where people stop, gawk, and appreciate its beauty.

When the man and his crew had finished, he presented me with his bill. It reflected the work performed, the plants purchased, and the soil bought. I was glad to pay the bill. He earned it.

Now, if someone else who had no involvement in the project had submitted a bill to me, I would have told them, "No, this isn't something I should pay. You did zero work for this invoice." I would be right.

Yet something unusual has happened between God and humanity. People have an opportunity to receive something they don't deserve. Paul recounts the Old Testament story of 100-year-old Abraham believing God's promise about having an heir and God counting that faith as righteousness (Gen. 15:6). Paul uses an accounting word of mathematical calculations to say the faith is "credited" or "counted" as righteousness. It is a word for paying a bill.

Importantly, Abraham didn't arrive at "righteousness" through deeds performed. He never earned it. It isn't like landscaping. No one gets into a relationship with God by working hard. Thankfully, it comes only through trust and faith.

Lord, I seek your righteousness that comes by faith. I trust you to redeem me. In your name, amen.

JUNE 6

That is why it depends on faith, in order that the promise may rest on grace and be guaranteed to all his offspring—not only to the adherent of the law but also to the one who shares the faith of Abraham, who is the father of us all, as it is written, "I have made you the father of many nations"—in the presence of the God in whom he believed, who gives life to the dead and calls into existence the things that do not exist. (Rom. 4:16–17)

Many churches have a children's song called "Father Abraham." It is more akin to a workout song than one built on theology, yet it is built on a kernel of biblical truth. The lyrics are simple: "Father Abraham had many sons, and many sons had Father Abraham; I am one of them, and so are you, so let's just praise the Lord." Everyone then says, "Right arm!" The song repeats word for word while everyone pumps their right arm in and out. At the conclusion of the second sing-through, people say "left arm" rather than right. Then as the song is sung a third time, both the right and left arms pump. This continues as the right leg, then left leg, then occasionally even the head are added and pumped, bringing the song to a conclusion.

The small grain of theology in the song concerns the idea of Abraham being the father of not only many genetic offspring but also many children who aren't his genetic descendants. These are children of faith rather than blood ties. Paul invokes this idea in today's passage.

Paul uses an encounter between Abraham and God when Abraham was ninety-nine years old as an example of faith. Before this encounter, Abraham was simply named *Abram*, Hebrew for "exalted father." God calls Abram to walk in fellowship and devotion, setting a course of righteousness for Abram. Abram agrees to follow God Almighty and falls on his face in worship. God then declares his covenant: God will bless Abram by making him the father of many nations. God changes Abram's name to the Hebrew for "father of a multitude," which is Abraham. By making this covenant, God promises to make Abraham fruitful—the father of kings and nations—and to honor the covenant forever.

Paul indicates that children of faith, regardless of genetics, are the fulfillment of God's promise to Abraham. The key for Paul isn't the DNA; it is the faith—bowing before God and trusting his promises. That is something to sing about!

Lord, I bow before you today. Be my Lord and God Almighty. In your name, amen.

JUNE 7

No unbelief made him waver concerning the promise of God, but he grew strong in his faith as he gave glory to God, fully convinced that God was able to do what he had promised. That is why his faith was "counted to him as righteousness." But the words "it was counted to him" were not written for his sake alone, but for ours also. It will be counted to us who believe in him who raised from the dead Jesus our Lord, who was delivered up for our trespasses and raised for our justification. (Rom. 4:20–25)

Most readers have never seen my wife pack her luggage. She gets more stuff into a small space than I would think possible. Her luggage springs open with no effort once unzipped. Similarly, Paul has packed a lot into today's verses.

Unpacking today's passage, one is struck by Paul's typical usage of the Old Testament Scriptures. Quoting Genesis 15:6, Paul sees the Scripture written *to* Jews in centuries past as written *for* readers of all time. Abraham's faith counted as righteousness takes on special significance to the reader after the death and resurrection of Christ.

Also striking is Paul's mention of Jesus being "delivered up," a reference to his crucifixion. Paul doesn't lay the crucifixion at the feet of the Romans, Judas, or the Jewish authorities. Paul uses what modern grammarians call a *divine passive*. Paul says that God delivered Jesus up. No human had the true power to crucify the Lord Jesus unless God willed it. Paul will say this clearly in Romans 8:32: God "did not spare his own Son but gave him up for us."

Paul echoes the prophet Isaiah out of the Greek translation of the Old Testament, where Isaiah refers to the Messiah making intercession for sinners (Isa. 53:12). God not only delivered up Jesus to death for our sins but importantly also raised him from the dead for "our justification." The Greek grammar is difficult for commentators looking for a precise meaning, but the import doesn't get lost. In the death and resurrection of Christ, one finds not only forgiveness but also a right standing ("justification") with God.

I need this. I need to know that even in the time of Abraham, two thousand years before Christ, God planned for my forgiveness. God paid the necessary price beyond measure to restore a relationship with us. What an awesome God!

Lord, praising you, let my life reflect my gratitude in Jesus, amen.

JUNE 8

Therefore, since we have been justified by faith, we have peace with God through our Lord Jesus Christ. Through him we have also obtained access by faith into this grace in which we stand, and we rejoice in hope of the glory of God. (Rom. 5:1–2)

In 1980, Keith Green put out an album called *So You Wanna Go Back to Egypt.* It became the soundtrack to my final college year. One song, based on today's verse and called "Grace by Which I Stand," was good then but over the decades since has grown in significance and meaning. In the song, Keith is struggling with his feelings about God and faith. Today's verse identifies the foundation for his hope for each day. It begins, "Lord, the feelings are not the same. I guess I'm older; I guess I've changed. And how I wish it had been explained that as you're growing, you must remember that nothing lasts except the grace of God by which I stand in Jesus."

Keith rightly drew this hope from Paul. By this point in his Romans treatise, Paul has set out the truths that (1) no one will achieve righteousness before God because of human effort and (2) people achieve righteousness before God based on faith and trust in God, not simple human merit, as demonstrated by Abraham. When Paul reaches the first verse of Romans chapter five, he starts explaining the ramifications of this faith in the current age.

Paul identifies the first ramification as the peace believers have when they are made right with God. When sin's price is paid, God's wrath is appeased, and believers stand solidly in the grace found through faith in Christ and find full peace in the Hebrew sense of that word (*shalom*—שָׁלוֹם). This peace is a completeness and includes the ideas of being safe as well as prosperous and sound in body and mind. It means contentment and even friendship. This peace with God comes through Jesus' sacrifice that fully atones for sin. It transforms human life.

At the birth of Jesus, the angels sang of "peace" on earth among God's people (Lk. 2:14). This peace allows rejoicing even in suffering (as Paul explains in the verses that follow today's selection). Peace with God lets one live in hope regardless of their feelings about or circumstances of life. Paul emphasizes that when one is right with the Creator, life has a fullness found nowhere else. From great days to rough weather, one can stand in the grace of God, knowing God will not abandon or forsake them. He will provide and sustain. I appreciate Keith's song more and more as I age.

Lord, I pray in faith, standing in grace through Christ. Sustain me, please. Amen.

JUNE 9

Not only that, but we rejoice in our sufferings, knowing that suffering produces endurance, and endurance produces character, and character produces hope, and hope does not put us to shame, because God's love has been poured into our hearts through the Holy Spirit who has been given to us. (Rom. 5:3–5)

If you stand on a four-wheel cart loaded with sandbags, and if you throw the sandbags off the rear of the cart, the cart, all on its own, will roll forward, the opposite way of where you threw the sandbags. This occurs because of a fundamental rule of physics: for every action, there is an equal and opposite reaction. Cause and effect are seen everywhere around us, and not surprisingly, they are also present within us.

Paul uses cause and effect to discuss suffering in the life of a Christian. Paul writes that suffering produces "endurance." The idea in the Greek word (*hupomonē*—ὑπομονή) is "fortitude," or an ability to bear up in the face of a difficulty. This makes sense. If when we suffer, we do so prayerfully, seeking God's strength and aid, then we will be able to walk through that suffering, knowing the power and love of a sustaining God.

Learning endurance grows our godly "character." Character in the Greek (*dokimē*—δοκιμή) speaks to real results in one's personality and makeup that come from enduring an ordeal or test. It can include the outward characteristics or indicators of a person's fortitude. As the Romans' suffering produced a fruit of endurance, or an ability to patiently walk through difficulties by leaning on God, their composure, attitudes, and overall godly character would be evident to themselves and others.

Paul's next link in his chain of cause and effect is the "hope" produced. Enduring suffering by leaning on God will change believers' character as they see God as reliable and trustworthy, proving God's presence, compassion, and strength. God's trustworthiness gives believers a confident expectation (the idea behind the Greek *elpis*—ἐλπίς, translated here as "hope") of the future. As one's character changes, one grows in confidence that God is real, God is love, and God is present in his love, which is how Paul ends his "cause and effect" chain. The key is walking in God's presence—or throwing the sandbags off the cart in the right direction! Otherwise, suffering won't have its useful effect. We'll go the wrong way.

Lord, sustain me in your love through life's difficulties. In Jesus' name, amen.

JUNE 10

For while we were still weak, at the right time Christ died for the ungodly. For one will scarcely die for a righteous person—though perhaps for a good person one would dare even to die—but God shows his love for us in that while we were still sinners, Christ died for us. (Rom. 5:6–8)

When I was fifteen, I listened to a sermon on marriage. Not being old enough to drive on a date, I certainly wasn't contemplating marriage anytime soon! Still, I paid attention to the sermon, figuring one day it might come in handy. The idea for the sermon came from Paul's letter to the Ephesians. Paul wrote, "Husbands, love your wives, as Christ loved the church and gave himself up for her" (Eph. 5:25). The preacher tied that instruction back to what Paul said in today's passage.

Today's passage gives a clear affirmation about God's love for his people and the expression of that love through action. God never waited for you or me to come to him seeking his forgiveness before paying the price for our sins through his sacrifice. Instead, Christ died while no one was righteous. Christ died to make us righteous, not because we possessed righteousness.

Our salvation, restored relationship with God, growth in holiness and godly character, and righteousness all stem from God's initiative in Christ. I liken it to the idea that humans can reach up to God as best and as high as they can, but God still must reach down all the way. It is a spiritual truth.

Paul's point extends to many areas of life, including marriage. When today's passage was tied to Ephesians 5:25 in my youth, it illustrated the principle that Paul gave to husbands to be initiators of love to their spouses. In practical terms, I don't need to wait for my wife, Becky; I need to hurry to reach out in love, forgiveness, caring, and more.

Beyond marriage, I need to relate this passage to my fellowship with the Holy One. God has initiated this relationship. I am responding. I determine what form that response takes. Understanding what God has done should move me not only in gratitude but in a desire to be more like him, including deeper holiness. I should grow into what God wants me to be. He initiated the opportunity so I could follow him.

Lord, thank you for your precious love, reaching out to me in my undeserving state. Please grow me in holiness as I learn to live before you. In Jesus' name, amen.

JUNE 11

But the free gift is not like the trespass. For if many died through one man's trespass, much more have the grace of God and the free gift by the grace of that one man Jesus Christ abounded for many. And the free gift is not like the result of that one man's sin. For the judgment following one trespass brought condemnation, but the free gift following many trespasses brought justification. For if, because of one man's trespass, death reigned through that one man, much more will those who receive the abundance of grace and the free gift of righteousness reign in life through the one man Jesus Christ. (Rom. 5:15–17)

Sesame Street used to have a song that easily stuck in one's head. The simple lyrics set up the scene before the child: "One of these things is not like the others. One of these things doesn't belong. Can you tell which thing is not like the other by the time I finish this song?" Concurrent with the singing, there might be displayed three squares and a circle. Or three apples and a banana. A young child readily learned to observe and distinguish things.

Paul doesn't sing the song, but he does give a strong contrast in today's passage. Paul's contrast is between the actions of Adam, the first human, and Christ, who in some biblical sense is portrayed as a "new Adam," or the first of a new humanity. Paul's contrast is rooted first in the results of the actions of Adam and Christ.

Paul's contrast starts with the value comparison of what Adam and Christ did. Adam's action was a "trespass" or an offense, a violation of moral standards that brought a curse. Unlike Adam, Christ's obedience produced a free gift of grace. The contrast continues, noting that Adam's sin spread death to his progeny. Juxtapose the righteousness of Christ that brought righteousness and life to his followers. Under Adam, the courtroom pronunciation is "guilty," one of condemnation. Under Christ, the courtroom resounds with the announcement "not guilty," one of justification.

Paul's point isn't limited to believers' eternal standing before God. Paul is also speaking of the here and now. The fruit of the righteousness of Christ is manifested in his followers growing in righteousness before God daily. We are no longer offspring of Adam and his sin. If we sing the Sesame Street song, the Christ follower isn't like the sons and daughters of Adam. Our actions should show we don't belong where we started out; we are part of new humanity in Jesus.

Lord, may my life better reflect your love and righteousness in Jesus, amen.

JUNE 12

We know that our old self was crucified with him in order that the body of sin might be brought to nothing, so that we would no longer be enslaved to sin. (Rom. 6:6)

Countless lives have been destroyed by addiction to drugs. Easily over a million people in the United States alone have died from drug overdoses in the last two decades. This doesn't include the vicious consequences of alcohol and tobacco, two extremely addictive substances. I've known addicts. I've kicked in a door to rescue an unconscious friend who had overdosed. I've escorted friends to rehab to help find a solution to addiction. It isn't pretty.

Paul writes of sin using cultural terms of his period, but the idea can easily transpose into addiction terminology today. In today's passage, Paul makes one of his references to being "enslaved" to sin. His word choice isn't accidental. Paul uses the standard verb for serving as a slave to describe the sinful state of humanity apart from deliverance in Jesus. To use the modern analogy, people are naturally addicted to sin and unable to overcome that addiction without God's intervention.

Sin is sticky and dirty. It beckons us with its siren song of joy for the moment, of satisfying our desires, of letting us forget the pains and woes of the world, of falsely making us feel confirmed or valuable, of distracting us from our lives, all the while increasing serotonin levels in the brain that make us feel really good. For the moment, that is. But reality always kicks in. The downside of sin appears. The long-term consequences become too obvious to ignore. Yet like a drug addiction, the solution too often is simply to sin some more, to get the kick again.

Paul says that in Christ, one gets a new nature—one that is no longer addicted or enslaved to sin. Christ not only died to forgive sins, but he gives his resurrection life to believers to empower us to new life. This was Jesus' teaching to Nicodemus about the need to be born from above or born again (Jn. 3).

It is, of course, true that Christians are still sinners and frequently stumble. But the power to conquer sin is different once Christians are empowered by God. A Christian's path is toward a greater holiness or Christlikeness. Believers have a deeper yearning to leave behind the ways of the world. The addictive power of sin is broken, and rehab has begun!

Lord, be my rescue from the power of sin, through the resurrection of Jesus, amen.

JUNE 13

For the death he died he died to sin, once for all, but the life he lives he lives to God. So you also must consider yourselves dead to sin and alive to God in Christ Jesus. (Rom. 6:10–11)

My mom was in a critical care hospital bed suffering from multiple life-threatening conditions. She had been rushed into the hospital with heart issues that would take most people's lives. All her children and grandchildren came to the hospital. In weakness, Mom managed to gather the strength to speak to each person. Mom had last words to give. By the grace of God, Mom survived those two weeks in critical care, and as I type, she still is an active joy in all our lives. But watching Mom live through what she thought might be her last days impacted me on many levels.

Mom had taught us early in life how to become a Christian by finding a personal relationship with God. Mom also taught us how to live as a Christian. While she was as imperfect as all of us, she was fully devoted to the Lord, and it showed. Her life was vibrant, using what we thought was her last strength and opportunity to again model for me the importance of walking daily with Christ.

Paul uses life and death as illustrations of how we should live with and for Christ. Paul emphasizes in today's passage that Christ died on account of our sins—sins that he bore as a substitute for you and me. Death didn't end Christ. In a sense, Christ ended death. God resurrected Christ. Paul knew that the resurrection of Christ was, in a sense, substitutionary also, in that we share in that resurrection.

This gives a new meaning to the life of a Christ follower. We follow Christ in his death by recognizing that the life we led before following him was a dead life. Those sins and the sinful nature are what were destined for death and what Jesus died for as our substitute. Why on earth, Paul wonders, would anyone think it right to live in that old way? Following Jesus means we follow him into a resurrection that brings a new and unending life.

Today I need to live like the new creation I am in Christ. As Mom directed us in that critical care unit, it isn't enough to become a Christian. We ought to live like a Christian, with all that entails. We seek to follow Christ in his death *and* in his resurrection.

Lord, I want to follow you. Give me your grace and strength to live for you today as the new creation I am in Jesus, by whom I pray, amen.

JUNE 14

For when you were slaves of sin, you were free in regard to righteousness. But what fruit were you getting at that time from the things of which you are now ashamed? For the end of those things is death. But now that you have been set free from sin and have become slaves of God, the fruit you get leads to sanctification and its end, eternal life. For the wages of sin is death, but the free gift of God is eternal life in Christ Jesus our Lord. (Rom. 6:20–23)

In complicated litigation where many law firms have a stake, courts often form committees designating which lawyers will make various decisions guiding the litigation. On these committees I have often served with my friend Richard. One time we were facing a decision, and the debate on what to do was thorough. Finally, Richard spoke up and resolved the debate by saying simply, "Let's take the high road; there's less traffic on it." Once he put it that way, no one could argue.

Paul sets out two roads in today's passage. One road involves a life bound up so tightly with sin that Paul calls it "slavery" to sin. Without Christ, even the best-behaved person is simultaneously captivated and oppressed by sin. Furthermore, even the best human deeds apart from Christ and his Spirit are motivated by at least a modicum of selfishness and self-interest. At the end of that road is death.

The second road is one found in Christ. It is a road that sets one free, redeeming them from the ownership of sin. It liberates everyone on it to a path free to pursue righteousness like never before. It binds one's heart to God and God's interests. To describe its impact on the life of a believer, Paul uses a metaphor of a growing fruit. Over time, this fruit is reflected in the holiness ("sanctification") that grows in the believer. When the fruit ripens and matures, its completion is eternal life.

Paul then gives the final assessment of these two roads. The payment earned by the road bound up in sin is death. But in contrast, the high road of walking with God through Jesus doesn't result in any payment at all because it isn't earned. This road is based entirely on the free gift God gives to those who walk with Christ.

I have chosen the Christ road in life. Paul says I need to remember that each day as I choose how to live. I shouldn't make the choices that belong on that old road. I should choose the high road bound up in service to my gracious God.

Lord, give me the wherewithal to follow you in holiness today. In Jesus' name, amen.

JUNE 15

But now we are released from the law, having died to that which held us captive, so that we serve in the new way of the Spirit and not in the old way of the written code. (Rom. 7:6)

As a youth, my understanding of God was much more limited than it is now. As we spend time with God in his word, we grow in understanding him. One example of my naïve view of life in Christ exploded when I came to understand what Paul is saying in today's passage. Earlier, I had thought that the death of Christ eliminated the Old Testament sacrificial law. I had heard that Christ had "crucified that law" on the cross, and sacrifices, the priestly system, and so on were gone. The extension of this, I thought then, was that Christ gave a new law. Certain aspects of the old law still bound me, like "Don't murder" and "Don't lie." Yet the weird laws about not wearing clothes of mixed fabrics or sacrificing a goat were gone.

What is more, when I examined the "new" law I believed Christ instituted instead of the old one, I found it was more difficult to keep! Before I couldn't murder; now I wasn't supposed to hate. Before adultery was a transgression, but now lust was. Mercy, keeping this new law was more than a full-time profession! It was impossible. So I figured the impossibility of it all was where the grace of God might make up for my shortcomings. I just hoped it would.

Then came the truth Paul expresses today. The Old Testament law was an illustration of the character of God expressed in the language and culture of ancient Israel. The teachings of Jesus also revealed the character of God in a later culture, preserved in a different language (Greek instead of Hebrew and Aramaic), and for all nations, not a select nation with a select destiny. But in both cultures, the character of God never changed.

Walking consistently in the character and morality of God was and is something I can never achieve, whether as an old law or a new one. My only hope is a life apart from trying to achieve God's holiness on my own. This is where Paul explains grace. The cross of Christ releases one from blind obedience to any law. It gives believers a complete relationship with God that allows us to serve God in the Spirit. It's not that God's character is different or has turned irrelevant. It is that the scorecard isn't kept. I have been forgiven for falling short, giving me the strength to succeed! Blessed be the works of the Lord!

Lord, give me peace of mind to pursue you in love in Jesus, amen.

JUNE 16

So the law is holy, and the commandment is holy and righteous and good. (Rom. 7:12)

When I set out to write a devotional book on the Torah, the second book in this series, many wondered, "Why write on the Torah?" After all, isn't the Torah, or as it is more commonly known, the Old Testament "law" (or simply Genesis through Deuteronomy), a Jewish book? Aren't I a Christian? One modern Christian preacher even expressed the need to "unhitch" Christianity from the Old Testament. Why then would I spend, or expect others to spend, 365 days studying and praying through the Torah?

I had many reasons for working carefully through the Old Testament law, all of which are wrapped up in Paul's passage today. The law is "holy," filled with commandments that are "holy, righteous, and good." These are important truths. The idea of the law being "holy" (*hagios*—ἅγιος) means it is sacred. It isn't an ordinary writing; it is one dedicated to God. As Paul says in a later letter, it is "breathed out by God" (2 Tim. 3:16). Therefore, it contains core instructions about life, purpose, and priorities and prophecies about God, his promises, and his Messiah.

Who wouldn't want to study pages laced by God with insights into life? Certainly, the law is not an easy thing to understand, as even Jesus had to explain it carefully. For example, Jesus explains in the Sermon on the Mount that the injunction of "Don't murder" (Ex. 20:13) goes beyond physical killing and speaks also to one's attitudes toward others. Jesus emphasizes this attitude almost immediately after saying he did *not* come to abolish the Law or the Prophets (Mt. 5:17–22). It didn't disappear; we just didn't understand its full ramifications.

Paul never writes off the law as irrelevant to a believer. Paul explains that the law is very good at pointing out sin. The law shows how woefully short we fall of God's perfection, especially when read in light of Jesus' teaching on attitudes. The key for Paul is that the law was never intended to be the basis for people's standing in restored relationship with God. Restoration of Eden's fellowship between God and people is based on faith and trust in God. Jesus' sacrifice has paid the just penalty for sin, and humanity can find restoration and redemption.

Paul knew the law was holy and important. Writing my Torah book was fulfilling.

Lord, thank you for your law. May it serve me in my walk in Jesus, amen.

JUNE 17

For I do not understand my own actions. For I do not do what I want, but I do the very thing I hate. Now if I do what I do not want, I agree with the law, that it is good. So now it is no longer I who do it, but sin that dwells within me. For I know that nothing good dwells in me, that is, in my flesh. For I have the desire to do what is right, but not the ability to carry it out. For I do not do the good I want, but the evil I do not want is what I keep on doing. Now if I do what I do not want, it is no longer I who do it, but sin that dwells within me. (Rom. 7:15–20)

Most every Christian I know, and many of my good Jewish friends, have asked the question, "Why do I do bad things when I earnestly wish to do good?" The distinction between what we wish to do and what we do is often stark. Some of the kindest people I know blow a gasket over the smallest things. I hear snarky things come out of the mouths of people who are genuinely loving to others. Even Jesus' brother James expressed that his readers had difficulty controlling their tongues. Everyone knows the importance of thinking about good and holy things yet finds their minds wandering into the trash heaps along life's road.

It comes as a bit of reassurance that Paul seemed to share this common experience. Although Paul was saved, holy, a missionary extraordinaire, and the writer of so much of the Bible, he also struggled as we do.

Paul knew and taught that the life of the redeemed isn't easy. Holiness isn't achieved through a single prayer of faith. For a lifetime, people have had their hearts, minds, and bodies ensnared and intertwined in sin. God's work of unweaving the intricately connected sin nature from the redeemed is a process that takes time.

But the saved shouldn't be faint of heart. The idea of throwing up our hands and saying, "Well, I just can't live right," or "There's no point; it's just who I am," is wrong. God does promise to work in us. God is going about his restoration of a good and holy mind, body, and spirit for each of his children.

We should never give up on pursuing God, despite our failures and sins. God comes with not only forgiveness in Christ but also loving work of his Spirit as he convicts us of sin and of righteousness. Because God is at work, we should not dismay.

Lord, forgive my sin, fortify my soul, give me mercy and strength in Jesus' name, amen.

JUNE 18

There is therefore now no condemnation for those who are in Christ Jesus. For the law of the Spirit of life has set you free in Christ Jesus from the law of sin and death. (Rom. 8:1–2)

Today's passage has traveled with me most of my life. When I was fifteen, my buddy Rick Reynolds took me to a week-long meeting in Roswell, New Mexico, where Nashville preacher Don Finto delivered a nightly message. Don preached on this passage. I was so blown away I got a cassette tape of his sermon and listened to it at least twenty-five times.

Four years after hearing it over and over and wearing out the tape, I got the joy of translating it in Greek. Learning some nuances in the passage heightened my love and appreciation of it. From there, my life took a legal turn, as I went into law school, but my legal training opened yet greater vistas of understanding. Here, many decades later, I find this passage still lights up my life and heart.

Paul began today's passage emphasizing the words "therefore now no." (In the Greek, the "There is" is implied, not written.) Paul draws a major point for the reader. "*Therefore now NO* condemnation for those in Christ Jesus" is a literal rendering of the Greek showing Paul's emphasis. Paul continues his use of legal language with the word "condemnation" (*katakrima*—κατάκριμα) in verse 1. This word was the judicial pronouncement of "guilty" that a judge (now usually a jury) would make at the conclusion of a criminal trial. We might modify Paul's sentence even further to read, "*Therefore now, NO* 'GUILTY!' from the Judge of the ages for those in Christ Jesus." Why? That is the meaning of the second sentence.

Paul explains that the "law" (*nomos*—νόμος) of the Spirit of life in Christ Jesus has set believers free in Christ Jesus from the "law" of sin and death. (The "in Christ Jesus" was only written once by Paul, but it can be applied grammatically to both phrases.) Here Paul gives two competing principles. First, if you sin, you die (the "law" or "principle" of sin and death). The second is the principle or law that life is found in Christ. This means no one in Christ is condemned. I am free to serve God without fear. I am eternally destined to live in his care. Is it any wonder I have here one of my favorite passages in Scripture?

Lord, I stay stunned by your gracious love, care, and provision in Jesus, through whom I pray, amen.

JUNE 19

For God has done what the law, weakened by the flesh, could not do. By sending his own Son in the likeness of sinful flesh and for sin, he condemned sin in the flesh, in order that the righteous requirement of the law might be fulfilled in us, who walk not according to the flesh but according to the Spirit. (Rom. 8:3–4)

Some 650 years before Paul, the prophet Jeremiah sought God's answer to an issue that particularly galled him. God was a righteous judge, and Jeremiah couldn't say differently. Yet somehow God's judgments didn't always *seem* righteous. Hence Jeremiah wrote, "Righteous are you, O LORD, when I complain to you; yet I would plead my case before you" (Jer. 12:1). Jeremiah's point isn't lost on Paul.

Paul addresses a serious legal and practical question in writing to the Romans. If God is the Judge of the universe and of eternity, a point made repeatedly in the Old Testament, then how can God be a *righteous* and *fair* judge and let guilty folks like you and me go free? How can a righteous judge take guilty people and announce, "Not guilty!"?

Paul answers this objection over and over in Romans, and today's passage is another emphasis of this point. God is a just God when he pronounces those in Christ Jesus "Not guilty!" because the sin itself was condemned in the flesh of Jesus the Messiah. Paul says God "condemned sin in the flesh"—using the courtroom term of guilt and judgment—but pronounced that condemnation upon the flesh of Jesus, who took it on voluntarily as a substitute for you and me.

The American legal system has different laws for civil and criminal justice, but a civil law gives a modern parallel. Most drivers are covered by insurance, so when they get into a wreck, their insurance company steps in on their behalf. If you blow through a red light and cause damage to another car, your insurance company should step in and defend you in court and pay the damages you caused (at least up to policy limits). This allows a fair and just judge to let you leave court without paying the penalty for your failing to obey the law and stop at the light. The insurance company steps in and bears the penalty.

God had Jesus step in and take the penalty of sin. This releases the follower of Christ from sin's penalty, freeing the individual to walk *post-judgment*, to use a modern legal term. Praise God!

Lord, I rejoice at the liberty that is mine in Christ Jesus. Thank you! Amen!

JUNE 20

For those who live according to the flesh set their minds on the things of the flesh, but those who live according to the Spirit set their minds on the things of the Spirit. For to set the mind on the flesh is death, but to set the mind on the Spirit is life and peace. For the mind that is set on the flesh is hostile to God, for it does not submit to God's law; indeed, it cannot. Those who are in the flesh cannot please God. (Rom. 8:5–8)

Imagine you are standing in a room with two doors before you. One door says "Death" and the other door says "Life and Peace." Which door would you choose? The answer in that form is obvious. Everyone in their right mind would opt for life and peace. In a real sense, those doors are framed in everyone's life, as Paul sets out in today's passage.

Paul explains that people can live a life of the "flesh" or a life of the Spirit of God. These are two stark doors before each person. Each door leads to a room. The room of the flesh is not a reference to a physical body, for no one can live without their body. Instead, Paul uses the word translated "flesh" (*sarx*—σάρξ) as a reference to the natural orientation of people to this physical world. The word was used by other Greek writers like Epicurus to reference the seat of one's emotions and desires. The flesh is our fallen nature passed from generation to generation. It fails to live righteously before God and needs redemption. That is the flesh that is put to death in the crucifixion of Christ. Believers who trust in the death of Christ as atoning for their own sins aren't forced through the door marked "Death." Death has already occurred, albeit vicariously through Christ.

This leaves a second door, one marked "Life and Peace." This is the door that is entered by those who belong to God through trusting in the death of Jesus. These people become a seat for God's Holy Spirit to dwell within them, changing their view of life, sin, and the world and empowering them to live in ever-increasing holiness to the praise of God.

Paul isn't just stating the obvious; he is challenging us to evaluate how we live. Do we live like we used to? Are our minds and emotions going through the wrong door? Do we realize the importance of living in God and with God living in us? These are stark choices we make every day in decisions large and small. We should live the reality of our existence in Christ—not to death but to life.

Lord, empower me in your Spirit to live to your glory and pleasure in Jesus, amen.

JUNE 21

For all who are led by the Spirit of God are sons of God. For you did not receive the spirit of slavery to fall back into fear, but you have received the Spirit of adoption as sons, by whom we cry, "Abba! Father!" The Spirit himself bears witness with our spirit that we are children of God, and if children, then heirs—heirs of God and fellow heirs with Christ. (Rom. 8:14–17)

Growing up, two of our daughters expressed an intent to adopt children when they got older. One of them was set on adopting out of compassion. She wanted to find children in need of a home and provide one. The other daughter planned to adopt because she dreaded the experience of childbirth.

In Paul's day, adoption wasn't a Jewish practice; the Old Testament created different laws for orphaned children. (They were raised by surviving family members.) Adoption was, however, a notable Roman practice and, as such, was remarkably useful to Paul for his metaphor in today's passage.

Adoption (*adoptio* in Latin) was common in Rome as a means of directing an inheritance. It wasn't really used for compassion purposes, as it is today. Hence even adults were commonly adopted to bring them into a family for inheritance rights. Up to Paul's day, adoption was by and large done only with males/sons. (Emperor Claudius is the first known person to adopt a female/daughter.) Knowing a bit more about Roman adoption practices unlocks several important parts to today's passage. First, Paul wrote of "adoption as sons." This wasn't a sexist moment; it was a factual metaphor. Male adoption was the practice. Paul clearly is including females, as we see in his shift to "we are children," which is a Greek word with no reference to gender. Moreover, Paul uses an analogy to explain that God brought us into a family to establish an inheritance. We become true children of God, calling him "Father." The "Father" in the Roman adoption process was the *paterfamilias*, the head of the family, with full authority over all in the family.

God didn't adopt you and me so that we could live in squalor. He adopted us to inherit the marvelous life he has for us. He becomes our authority, provider, and protector as well as the receiver of our allegiance. We are his children and are expected to both relish it and act like it! Heaven forbid that we should forget or ignore that.

Lord Father, thank you for adopting me. Thank you for the right to be your child. Give me strength, protection, and wisdom for the day. In Jesus, amen.

JUNE 22

For I consider that the sufferings of this present time are not worth comparing with the glory that is to be revealed to us. For the creation waits with eager longing for the revealing of the sons of God. . . . And not only the creation, but we ourselves, who have the firstfruits of the Spirit, groan inwardly as we wait eagerly for adoption as sons, the redemption of our bodies. (Rom. 8:18–19, 23)

I grew up thinking my body was a fleshly drape that enveloped my spirit/soul. Upon death, I reasoned, my spirit/soul would travel to some afterlife heaven filled with other spirits/souls who would then spend eternity there. Then I learned better. I was tenaciously asserting what I believed to be true after Greek class one day when a friend told me, "You're a Platonist!" He was right. My view was straight out of Plato—a pagan writer, not a biblical one!

Upon death, there certainly seems to be a nonphysical presence and awareness, but the destiny of the redeemed is a physical one, not a disembodied one. Paul wrote more about this in chapter 15 of 1 Corinthians, where he explains we don't know what our future physical body will be like, but we are assured that we will have a physical body and a physical earth in which to dwell. Paul makes that point also in today's passage.

The life to come is one filled with glory, and that should fuel our outlook today. Today isn't perfect for anyone. The world isn't perfect; it is filled with good things but also with famine, global warming, tornadoes, hurricanes, fires, blight, flooding, and many difficulties. Similarly, no one has a perfect life in a perfect body. We suffer sickness and disease. We struggle with weight and discipline. Our minds stray into areas forbidden and dangerous. We often do things that are destructive.

Yet we are "redeemed" and brought into God's family by being adopted as heirs (see yesterday's teaching). Paul puts all this into perspective by noting that the world and our lives aren't perfect right now. But we all can rightly and eagerly await when everything will be made right. We aren't going to be a disembodied spirit floating in a netherworld for eternity. We will become truly and fully human, living in a good and right world, as God intended from the beginning. That is a glorious expectation that should encourage and sustain us in our daily walk, especially in times of difficulty and suffering.

Lord, be with me today and instill me with faith for tomorrow. In Jesus, amen.

JUNE 23

Likewise the Spirit helps us in our weakness. For we do not know what to pray for as we ought, but the Spirit himself intercedes for us with groanings too deep for words. (Rom. 8:26)

The memories of our five children being born are etched in my mind. As the father, I had little to nothing to do with the birthing, yet I saw that the entire pregnancy has times of pain and difficulty! When God was announcing the curses of the fall to Adam and Eve, he singled out the woman: "I will surely multiply your pain in childbearing; in pain you shall bring forth children" (Gen. 3:16). Echoing that passage, the prophet Jeremiah spoke of the travails of the Jews being conquered by Babylon and carted off into captivity as he exclaimed, "For I heard a cry as of a woman in labor, anguish as of one giving birth to her first child" (Jer. 4:31).

Both of those passages (and the birthing experience with its great pain that produces guttural cries and moans) reflect a key part of today's passage. Paul wrote of the Spirit interceding on our behalf, tuned into our weaknesses even in our prayer life. Paul says the Spirit does so with "groanings too deep for words." Paul's word for "groaning" (*stenagmos*—στεναγμός) is the word used in both the curse of "pain" in bringing forth children in Genesis and the "anguish" of a mother giving birth to her first child.

The Spirit's role as our prayer-warrior is explained in a way that shows an intense involvement with and caring for our lives. This should come as a comfort to us all. For whom of us really believes that they pray adequately before God? As Paul has already described in the earlier verses, we all have reasons to groan inwardly—as our world seems to close in on us, as we don't have answers to life's problems, as we fear what may be or what may come, as we lose the ability to smile, and as our bad habits or traits seem to continue day after day. But we should all take courage. When we groan, God's Spirit groans with us. God knows our frailties and shortcomings. God doesn't abandon us in our weakness; he rushes to our aid.

I haven't given birth to a child, but my life hasn't been short of groaning. Importantly, life's travail should never lead to despair. I can rightly rejoice, knowing God is with me no matter how desperate the circumstances. God will walk with me through any fire.

Lord, I need you, every hour. May your Spirit bring your blessings in Jesus, in whom I pray, amen.

JUNE 24

And we know that for those who love God all things work together for good, for those who are called according to his purpose. . . . What then shall we say to these things? If God is for us, who can be against us? (Rom. 8:28, 31)

Albeit a long time ago, I took a course in computer programming. The language we used was called "basic." Computer code is a whacky business. Programmers type in loads and loads of lines that make no sense in and of themselves. But once the program is expertly written, it performs supremely complicated and magnificent functions.

Your life and mine are a bit like computer code. Events come and go, and like lines of code, they alter who we are, how we think, and what we do. We should always remember that our lives are not randomly coming together. God is working on us, in a sense writing—or at least editing—our code.

With that in mind, look at today's passage. Paul has been working through how we live in a fallen world with its great difficulties and challenges. Paul has noted that the world groans, we groan, and the Spirit groans with us. But those are lines of code! In isolation, they may make no sense. But God is the Master code writer, and he is at work! God takes life's events, takes our holy living, and works out his lines of code—lines that produce his masterpiece. God has set us up to handle life's challenges with his help. God has ensured we are able to walk through times of hurt. God will even take our own errors and sins, like bugs written into a computer program, and rework our code to sustain us and make us able to achieve his plans for our lives.

Paul explained that we have a destiny of eternity with God. The here and now can be quite bleak at times, but into the reality of life's hardships, Paul gives two assurances. First, all these things are going to work together for good. Not for pleasure, not for personal gain, but all things will work together for good as God sees goodness!

Second, we have the assurance that God is on our side. If God, with his knowledge, power, and compassion, is on our side—if he is writing our code—then no one and nothing will stop God's success on our behalf. We will be blessed through these hardships in the end, even if it is not until heaven. If we haven't been blessed yet, it isn't over yet. Praise God!

Lord, we are honored to be on your team. Work in our lives for your good, amen.

JUNE 25

Who shall separate us from the love of Christ? Shall tribulation, or distress, or persecution, or famine, or nakedness, or danger, or sword? . . . No, in all these things we are more than conquerors through him who loved us. For I am sure that neither death nor life, nor angels nor rulers, nor things present nor things to come, nor powers, nor height nor depth, nor anything else in all creation, will be able to separate us from the love of God in Christ Jesus our Lord. (Rom. 8:35–39)

In my life, I have known vastly more people than I can count. I cannot think of a single person that didn't need and want to be loved. Love is powerful. It is a balm to the soul. It takes the worst problems and makes them more bearable. It affirms one's value, even when one feels unworthy. It makes a house a home; it makes a marriage a union. Love builds up the one loved, gives courage for the day, and gives peace amid chaos. Paul rightly wrote the Corinthians that love is greater than even faith and hope (1 Cor. 13:13).

It is notable, then, that as Paul writes about the struggles and tribulations of life in Romans 8, he makes it a point to zero in on Christ's love for you and me. Christ's love is not some earned or deserved love based on someone's merits. It doesn't vacillate with the weather or come and go like the tides. It is constant and enduring. In fact, the greatest expression of Jesus' love for us is his willingness to step into a human body in real space and time and die a sinner's death on our behalf. That expression of his love happened *before* we ever asked him or sought his intervention. His love was never based on our earning it.

The love of Christ is so strong that nothing in existence is strong enough to break it. Nothing that we endure, nothing that we do, nothing that comes against us—absolutely *nothing* can separate us from the love of God expressed in Christ our Lord.

Reflecting on that fundamental bedrock truth changes the way I see the world today. Come what may, I have the response, "Well, God loves me." I can face whatever challenges me each day based on this simple yet powerful truth.

Yes, everyone wants to be loved, and everyone is loved. Regrettably, many go through life without being aware of this love. I know it and rely on it unceasingly.

Lord, thank you for your love, deep and abiding. It gives me hope for the day. I pray in Jesus, amen.

JUNE 26

I have great sorrow and unceasing anguish in my heart. For I could wish that I myself were accursed and cut off from Christ for the sake of my brothers, my kinsmen according to the flesh. They are Israelites, and to them belong the adoption, the glory, the covenants, the giving of the law, the worship, and the promises. To them belong the patriarchs, and from their race, according to the flesh, is the Christ, who is God over all, blessed forever. Amen. (Rom. 9:2–5)

I remember as a young boy *really* wanting a Bob Gibson baseball trading card. In those days, you had to buy your trading cards one pack at a time, each pack containing five cards along with a piece of bubble gum. I truly think I had every baseball card for every player that year *except* Bob Gibson. It was 1968, and Bob was having a year for the ages. I never got that card, but I would have traded my entire collection for one, had someone offered.

In today's passage, Paul writes of one of his greatest desires. It isn't lightweight like a boy's desire for a baseball trading card. It is a deep longing of a mature believer in God, one whose life is devoted to God's mission and service. Paul's deep yearning is for the salvation of the Jews.

God blessed the Jews spectacularly. They had been taken in as God's family, and he gave them the glory of his presence first in the tabernacle and then in the temple. God made his covenant with them at Sinai, gave them the Law of Moses, inspired the Psalms for worship, and messaged the prophets with insight. From the start of the Israelites with Abraham, Isaac, and Jacob to the manifestation of God incarnated as Jesus, the Jews were uniquely recipients of God's blessings.

Yet most of Israel stood opposed to the teaching that Jesus is the Messiah promised through Moses and the prophets. This disturbed Paul so deeply that he was willing to give up his personal calling to see his relatives find peace with God through Jesus as Messiah.

I pause at today's passage and ask myself what I care about as an older man. I have put away the baseball card desires of my youth and have more mature desires. Heaven forbid my greatest desire be a car, a house, a job, a career, or some success in the world. I want a deep passion for God and his people, my family, my friends, and loved ones. I want them at peace with God.

Lord, ignite in me a flame burning for the lives and souls of others. In Jesus, amen.

JUNE 27

What shall we say then? Is there injustice on God's part? By no means! For he says to Moses, "I will have mercy on whom I have mercy, and I will have compassion on whom I have compassion." So then it depends not on human will or exertion, but on God, who has mercy. (Rom. 9:14–16)

"Nature or nurture" is a debate of some consequence. Are people the way they are because of their genetic makeup, that DNA fingerprint unique to everyone? Or is it the environment in which they were reared? Does the conditioning of life produce behaviors, thoughts, and reactions, like Pavlov's dogs salivating at the sound of a bell? Most scientists will accept that both are at play, but a debate rages about how much free choice enters the equation. Some believe that the entirety of human behavior is based on either nature or nurture, with nothing else added.

At first glance, one might get the impression that Paul believes our choices are constrained by nature and nurture with no real human free choice. But in today's passage, Paul says God's mercy reaches people based on God's decisions, not based on "human will or exertion." Does this close the book on reaching others for God? Passages like today's reveal a flaw in my approach in this devotional. That format makes it nigh impossible to keep passages within a larger contextual flow. Today's passage, and most of Romans chapters 9 through 11 generally, requires review of the context of Paul's statements.

Paul has already spent a great deal of time walking through the importance of understanding and sharing the good news of salvation in Christ, a subject he will return to again and again. In today's passage, Paul addresses the question, "Is there injustice on God's part?" Paul wants to answer the question of whether we humans can rightly indict God for being unfair or wrongly partial.

Paul doesn't see things as we do. His focus is different. Paul sees the world as rightly condemned. Paul understands that no one on their own merit deserves God and his eternity. Instead, God has chosen some for his mercy, just as God chose Israel out of the buffet of Mediterranean peoples in the days of Abraham. Paul recognized that God's mercy was remarkable and an indication not of his unfairness but of his remarkable love. More context is needed and will come in the next few days' readings, but today we are reminded of God's remarkable mercy for his children. We are reached not by nature or nurture but by the heart of God!

Lord, thank you for your love. May I share it with this world in Jesus, amen.

JUNE 28

What shall we say, then? That Gentiles who did not pursue righteousness have attained it, that is, a righteousness that is by faith; but that Israel who pursued a law that would lead to righteousness did not succeed in reaching that law. Why? Because they did not pursue it by faith, but as if it were based on works. They have stumbled over the stumbling stone, as it is written, "Behold, I am laying in Zion a stone of stumbling, and a rock of offense; and whoever believes in him will not be put to shame." (Rom. 9:30–33)

Asleep in bed, I was suddenly awakened by the loud noise of walking right above my head. As I struggled to consciousness, I realized it wasn't an invader upstairs; it was closer. My home intruders were animals in the floorspace between the upstairs and our bedroom. The noise continued unabated, and I changed rooms! The next day, we set traps, catching the raccoons that somehow invaded our house. We used humane traps that included a trigger that led to them being ensnared so they couldn't escape. The ancient Greek word that would have been used to describe the trigger to that trap is *skandelon* (σκάνδαλον). Paul uses that word in today's passage. It is the rock of "offense" that caused Israel to stumble in Paul's discourse.

Paul was addressing a church that had struggled with the roles and places for their Jews and Gentiles. Jews present at Pentecost had started the church (Acts 2:10), but almost two decades later, Emperor Claudius exiled Jews from Rome (Acts 18:2). For roughly two years, the Gentile "newcomers" to the church had full responsibility and control over church administration, teaching, budget, and more. Once Jews were allowed back into Rome, the church was trying to figure out how to integrate itself back into a unified church, honoring the Jewish leaders who started it but also recognizing the Gentiles God used when the initial leaders left.

Paul wants all believers to focus on one truth that unites us: we have all received a righteousness that comes through faith in Christ. Even though Jews had been blessed with God's revelation and moral teaching in the Old Testament, that was a trap if they thought it made them worthy of God or produced anything like the righteousness of faith.

So it is with us today. Our standing before God is based on our trust in the resurrected Christ through life and death. Trusting our relationship to God on anything else is a trap. We aren't raccoons; we should know better!

Lord, I trust in the righteous resurrected Jesus alone for my walk with you. Amen!

JUNE 29

For Moses writes about the righteousness that is based on the law, that the person who does the commandments shall live by them. . . . But what does it say? "The word is near you, in your mouth and in your heart" (that is, the word of faith that we proclaim); because, if you confess with your mouth that Jesus is Lord and believe in your heart that God raised him from the dead, you will be saved. For with the heart one believes and is justified, and with the mouth one confesses and is saved. For the Scripture says, "Everyone who believes in him will not be put to shame." For there is no distinction between Jew and Greek; for the same Lord is Lord of all, bestowing his riches on all who call on him. For "everyone who calls on the name of the Lord will be saved." (Rom. 10:5–13)

Korean drama shows commonly include cliffhangers, but with a twist. One show might end with the star in seemingly dire straits, but then the next episode comes, and rather than simply replay the dire straits, the newer episode will go back chronologically *before* the cliffhanger and give new facts that cause one to realize the cliffhanger was a ruse. Everything was OK. The timeline in the prior episode contained facts that weren't revealed until the subsequent episode, and those new facts made sense of the whole thing.

Paul uses a similar approach in today's passage. Paul notes that the Law of Moses was to be the living code of Israel. Alluding to one of Moses' recap speeches found in Deuteronomy 30, Paul cites the idea that life for Israel was to be found in following God's law. But the story doesn't end there. For the Old Testament Scriptures also explained that God's word was in the follower's "mouth" and "heart." Paul explains that the one watching the sequel learns a new fact about Deuteronomy 30:14: God was referencing the "word of faith." In a sense, he is reading back into the passage what was there as an unwritten truth.

As we profess with our mouths this word of faith, and as we hold it in our hearts, we find ourselves standing firmly upon salvation's bedrock of Jesus Christ.

This reality speaks to us today. God's plan is greater in detail and reality than anything we could devise or imagine. God planned from the beginning to redeem and justify humanity through faith and trusting the redemptive work of Christ. Full forgiveness of sin is no accident. It was always God's plan.

Lord, I proclaim with my lips the faith of my heart. May Jesus save me. I pray in him, amen.

JUNE 30

How then will they call on him in whom they have not believed? And how are they to believe in him of whom they have never heard? And how are they to hear without someone preaching? And how are they to preach unless they are sent? As it is written, "How beautiful are the feet of those who preach the good news!" But they have not all obeyed the gospel. For Isaiah says, "Lord, who has believed what he has heard from us?" So faith comes from hearing, and hearing through the word of Christ. (Rom. 10:14–17)

I have a buddy who didn't really go to church the first roughly forty-five years of his life. He was kind, but he lived a rough life where he skated in and out of the dark corners of this world. After he came to Christ, his marriage soon dissolved, his finances took a 180 and were wrecked, and his health seemed to spiral downhill. He suffered in many ways like Job, which soon became a favorite book for him to study. Over time, God's work in his life became evident. He learned holiness as he shed bad habits, retrained his mind, and placed his life's difficulties before God. One day, my buddy emailed me and said, "I need to quit going to church." His reasoning? Every time he went, he came under conviction of yet another area of life to change in his pursuit of God. He said God's word was so powerful that even his old grudges were dissolving as he extended forgiveness to others.

God's word changes us. My buddy is living proof of it. So am I. So are many others I know. It has always been this way, and it will be this way until the end of time. It is important that we speak of God and his work in Christ and so bring others into a relationship with the Lord. But it never stops there. Even for believers, it is important to keep digging into God's word, seeking the insight from his Spirit that will convict us, guide us, and teach us.

My experience in this is a core reason I find myself at 3:55 this morning sitting at my computer, with a prayer on my lips, asking God to give me insight and understanding into the Scriptures I use for these devotionals. God's word has a power unlike any other. It is a means by which he works in our lives. Heaven forbid I not spend time hearing him. Side note: May God bless the work of those who speak his word into our lives. Take a moment and bless those in your life who spend time and energy seeking to share God.

Lord, thank you for good preachers and friends who speak your word into my life. May I diligently seek to hear you and come under your words in Jesus, amen.

JULY 1

Then Isaiah is so bold as to say, "I have been found by those who did not seek me; I have shown myself to those who did not ask for me." But of Israel he says, "All day long I have held out my hands to a disobedient and contrary people." (Rom. 10:20–21)

In today's passage, Paul is in the middle of some deep theology. Paul's Romans section (chapters 9–11) is difficult territory to navigate theologically. It is open to many interpretations and misinterpretations. My buddies and I in school used to joke that Peter clearly had a copy of Romans 9–11 because Peter wrote of Paul's letters, "There are some things in them that are hard to understand" (2 Pet. 3:16)!

Yet even amid difficulties, gems stand out that challenge, encourage, and direct the steps of the careful reader. Today's section is a prime example.

Paul identifies two groups that approached God differently. One group was the Gentiles, who were never seeking the God of Israel—the one true God. Yet by the work of Christ and the Holy Spirit working through the mission efforts of Paul and others, Gentiles were coming to faith by droves. Paul notes this, quoting the prophetic voice of Isaiah from six hundred years earlier: "I have been found by those who did not seek me; I have shown myself to those who did not ask for me."

The second group, the Israelites, were called out of Egypt by God. He gave them the prophet and leader Moses. God appeared to Moses (and indirectly the people) on Sinai, and God established a covenant with them. He gave them words of revelation through Moses and generations of prophets. Using relationships as an analogy, God was both a spouse and parent to Israel. Yet many Israelites lived in constant rebellion. As Paul says, again invoking Isaiah, "All day long I have held out my hands to a disobedient and contrary people." Finally, as prophesied, God was fully redemptive of his people through the death and resurrection of Christ.

This sets before me a stark reality. Yes, I am a Gentile, but I live in an age where I have also been reared before God, taught his Scriptures, and heard his voice. My personal question is where I land. Will I find God in this life? Or will I be a disobedient and contrary person? That is a real question everyone faces daily.

Lord, I want to be aware of your love and compassion. I confess that I am often disobedient and ask you to help my efforts to do better. In Jesus, amen.

JULY 2

What then? Israel failed to obtain what it was seeking. The elect obtained it, but the rest were hardened, as it is written, "God gave them a spirit of stupor, eyes that would not see and ears that would not hear, down to this very day." (Rom. 11:7–8)

Social scientists describe a well-documented way our brains process data, known as "confirmation bias." This tendency in almost everyone is that once we decide about something (or someone), we tend to filter future interactions and evidence so that we pay greater attention to what confirms our opinion, while we tend to discount or explain away things that are contrary to what we already believe. This mental bias is documented in matters ranging from politics to purchases, religion to relationships, courtrooms to careers. Philosophers have noted it for centuries, and modern science has proven (and labeled) it over the last seventy-five years.

Confirmation bias is not a coincidence in the human mind. I believe it explains passages like today's. Paul is trying to explain why so many more Gentiles seem to be in the faith in comparison to the Jews who accept Jesus as Messiah. Paul quotes from the Old Testament, combining words from Deuteronomy 29:4 with Isaiah 29:10, as he tells the reader that God has given many Israelites "a spirit of stupor," which he then explains as "eyes that would not see and ears that would not hear."

Paul is not blaming God for those who reject him, as if God confused the minds of true seekers. Rather, those who reject God will be hardened as they walk the path they've chosen. If we dull ourselves to God, we see life through those dimmed eyes and interpret events based on those beliefs. In a real sense, God gives an attitude of deadness to those who have chosen deadness as their belief system. This isn't a shifting of responsibility; it is a fact. An analogy is that of a drunkard trying to use his inebriation as an excuse to avoid responsibility for his drunken actions. Those who seek God find him (Mt. 6:33).

You and I must carefully guard our hearts and minds as we assess passages like today's. When we dull ourselves to God and his will, it doesn't have just a one-time effect on our well-being. It seeps into our brains in ways with much longer-lasting repercussions. We begin to see the world apart from God, and we begin to miss his hand moving in our lives. We should always seek to be ready for God, following his lead and will daily.

Lord, I want to serve you better. Remove any of my dullness, in Jesus, amen.

JULY 3

So I ask, did they stumble in order that they might fall? By no means! Rather, through their trespass salvation has come to the Gentiles, so as to make Israel jealous. Now if their trespass means riches for the world, and if their failure means riches for the Gentiles, how much more will their full inclusion mean! (Rom. 11:11–12)

Baseball great Yogi Berra expressed himself humorously so often that many of his expressions have become known as "Yogi-isms." Sayings like "Nobody goes there anymore. It's too crowded" and "Pair up in threes" have become legendary. But one that occurs to me in reading today's passage is Yogi's comment "It ain't over till it's over."

The historical context for Paul's first readers becomes important here. The church at Rome had its roots in Jews who heard Peter's sermon during a visit to Jerusalem at Pentecost and believed in the resurrection of Jesus (Acts 2:10). The church quickly grew, and Gentiles became included in the fellowship. At some point, the Roman emperor Claudius evicted the Jews from Rome, including those who were also Christians (Acts 18:2). This left the Roman church, which was started and likely initially run by Jews, in the hands of the Johnny-come-lately believers: the Gentiles. At some later date, the Jews were allowed to return, including the previously evicted Aquila and Priscilla (compare Acts 18:2 with Romans 16:3).

This historical context would have been understood by Paul's first readers, for what had happened on a microscale in Rome was analogous to what was happening on a macroscale in history. God's first chosen people were those offspring of Abraham called out from Egypt: the Israelites. Yet there came a time when they were seemingly removed from God's presence, as the Gentiles then came into God's kingdom. Yet God promises that the Jews will return, just as they did in Rome. A time will come when a greater inclusion with a fuller presence of Jews will occur.

Yogi was right, "It ain't over till it's over." This is true on macro- and microscales. It is true in history, and it's true in your life and mine. As we struggle and find life's difficulties almost insurmountable, we need to remember that God is at work and the difficult moment is not the end of the story. We can live in that difficulty, trusting in the God who isn't finished yet.

Lord, give me strength to live each day trusting you. In Jesus' name, amen.

JULY 4

Oh, the depth of the riches and wisdom and knowledge of God! How unsearchable are his judgments and how inscrutable his ways! "For who has known the mind of the Lord, or who has been his counselor?" "Or who has given a gift to him that he might be repaid?" For from him and through him and to him are all things. To him be glory forever. Amen. (Rom. 11:33–36)

Francis Schaeffer was fond of saying, "We can know God truly, but we cannot know him fully." This has stuck with me for decades. God has revealed himself through Scripture, and that revelation of God is a true one. We can know God in truth. But God never revealed himself fully. I don't think the human mind can fully comprehend God, and if we could, God would take more books than could ever be written to give us that *full* revelation.

Passages like today's emphasize Schaeffer's point. Paul has been trudging through deep theological snow in the previous chapters, and as he draws this section of Romans to a close, he speaks decisively on what everyone should be able to agree: God's wisdom is beyond our ability to understand. God's knowledge is all-encompassing. God's treasures are deeper than the seas. I have good and true glimpses into the character of God, most clearly through his incarnation in Jesus, but I don't know him completely.

I love Paul's quote from Job, a book most don't quote from! (At least not the middle chapters!) "Who has been God's counselor?" Who has instructed God or told him how he needs to handle a crisis, as if he can't figure that out? This rhetorical question shouts the answer, "No one!" Or how about Job's next rhetorical question, "Who has given God a gift that he might be repaid?" Or as I would have worded it, "Who figured out what God needed for his birthday that he couldn't get for himself?" Of course, no one.

While we can't know God fully, we can truly know that he is beyond our comprehension in many ways. Our job is not to question his judgments, nor cross-examine his processes. Our role is to trust him, walk with him, lean on him, seek *his* help, and then give him all glory, gratitude, and praise.

God is the source of all good things. God is only good. God loves us enough to pursue us through death and beyond. We are rightly in awe and say, "Thank you!"

Lord, I rest today in your wisdom and provision. I seek to serve you in Jesus, amen.

JULY 5

I appeal to you therefore, brothers, by the mercies of God, to present your bodies as a living sacrifice, holy and acceptable to God, which is your spiritual worship. Do not be conformed to this world, but be transformed by the renewal of your mind, that by testing you may discern what is the will of God, what is good and acceptable and perfect. (Rom. 12:1–2)

With each of these devotionals, I will frequently try to find a story or illustration to begin with, tying the ideas in the Scripture passage to something modern. For me, this is the hardest part of writing each day. That's not to say that working through the passages is not challenging. I read and reread them, research what others have said, and weigh what I think. But application? That is always the harder part.

Somewhere, someone termed Paul a "practical theologian." I like that label; it fits. Over and over in Paul's letters, he spends a great deal of time writing profound theology, but then he shifts, and his letters become practical exhortations of application. Most of his missives can be split into the theology section and the application section. Today's passage marks that split. For eleven chapters, Paul has deeply delved into matters of profundity concerning the world, the work of Christ, the changes in the believer, and the struggles of God's process for rescuing his people. Now Paul uses the word *therefore* to begin explaining the implications of all these theological chapters on our day-to-day living.

Paul appeals to people not to let the theology sit only in their mind but to bring their entire lives, their "bodies," as something given to God for his usage. Paul wasn't a Platonist who separated the body from the soul. Paul was a Hebrew who thought of the body as all-encompassing. He says we are to give ourselves fully to God. He wants us to understand that "spiritual worship"—that is, giving God the value and worth he is truly due—begins by entrusting ourselves to God.

Paul says that this is an active process for us. We have our minds in our bodies, and we are to get to work on "renewing" our minds. We should make decisions to be different from the world. We shouldn't think like the world; we shouldn't feed our minds the world's fare; we should think on godly things and see God work to rewire our brains. God wants to remove our mental sin ruts and habits, redeem our bad memories, and train us in ways that seek his good will. This is practical and real.

Lord, take me, transform me, and make me what I can be for you. In Jesus, amen.

JULY 6

For by the grace given to me I say to everyone among you not to think of himself more highly than he ought to think, but to think with sober judgment, each according to the measure of faith that God has assigned. (Rom. 12:3)

In college, my buddy Carlus needed to change the oil in his car. I offered to help. Our problem was that neither of us had ever changed oil before. We had no real idea of what to do. We pulled the car up halfway on a curb so we could get under it. We found the bolt to remove so the oil drained out of the oil pan. We were feeling pretty good about that; it had taken us a long time to find it. We then opened the hood of the car and poured the new cans of oil in where you fill the car with oil. We did great, with one small exception: we never replaced the bolt for the oil pan. All our new oil was pouring out of the pan below the car just as fast as we poured it from above. We needed some instructions!

Instructions are especially useful on important topics. Today's passage comes on the heels of yesterday's, where Paul instructed the reader to set about being "transformed by the renewal of your mind." A nice thing to say, but it could use an instruction manual! Paul begins giving those instructions here. Using the word *think* (*phroneō*—φρονέω) in four forms in one small sentence, Paul says, "Don't *think* of yourself more highly than you should *think* of yourself, but instead *think* with *right thinking*" (translated by the ESV as "sober judgment"). We begin getting our minds right by thinking rightly about ourselves.

God calls us into reality. In his truth, we leave the lies and falsehoods that our minds readily concoct about ourselves and the world around us. His true truth is centered on the death, burial, and resurrection of Christ. That single redemptive act of the ages tells all of us what we truly are: people in need of God. Apart from Christ, all of us live in some degree of personal rebellion against God and his goodness. God calls us into relationship through that singular event of death to the world and rebirth to eternity. This reality is the object of our faith.

When we understand this common ground for all of us, God works to rewire our brains. We begin to better realize who we are and what we are about. Pride, arrogance, thoughts that we are better, more important, or more worthy of focus than another—they all fly out the window. This allows God to fill us, and real renewal begins. Paul's instructions continue, but this is step one!

Lord, forgive my baseless pride, and give me a right mind. In Jesus, amen.

JULY 7

Let love be genuine. Abhor what is evil; hold fast to what is good. Love one another with brotherly affection. Outdo one another in showing honor. Do not be slothful in zeal, be fervent in spirit, serve the Lord. Rejoice in hope, be patient in tribulation, be constant in prayer. Contribute to the needs of the saints and seek to show hospitality. Bless those who persecute you; bless and do not curse them. Rejoice with those who rejoice, weep with those who weep. Live in harmony with one another. Do not be haughty, but associate with the lowly. Never be wise in your own sight. Repay no one evil for evil, but give thought to do what is honorable in the sight of all. If possible, so far as it depends on you, live peaceably with all. Beloved, never avenge yourselves, but leave it to the wrath of God, for it is written, "Vengeance is mine, I will repay, says the Lord." To the contrary, "if your enemy is hungry, feed him; if he is thirsty, give him something to drink; for by so doing you will heap burning coals on his head." Do not be overcome by evil, but overcome evil with good. (Rom. 12:9–21)

Did you skip over reading today's Scripture passage? Don't skip! This is the longest quotation I have put in the entire book, but it is here for a reason. Like the rat-a-tat of a clacking keyboard, Paul delivers a barrage of instructions, all centered on making us "think rightly" as he set out in yesterday's passage. Among the many important instructions are several nougats that I want to discuss.

Paul urges genuine love. Genuine love includes hate for evil. Love and hate are not opposites but reactions of what we treasure. We should treasure rightly, loving good but hating evil. Our love for others includes showing them honor as a part of thinking of ourselves humbly (from yesterday's passage). This isn't natural and won't come to us without diligence, so we should be fervent, carefully pursuing this love. It means rejoicing in what we hope for others, being patient while we await God's promises, and constantly praying for one another. Where people need practical help, we give it. As Jesus said, we are to bless not only those who bless us but even those who are set against us. We aren't about keeping or evening the score. God is the one who sorts out such things. We seek, to the extent that it is within our power to do so, to live with peace, trusting in God. In doing so, we seek to be overcomers who let good defeat evil.

Today's passage has important instructions for us all. We can't skim it; we should read it with care, slowly and deliberately.

Lord, renew my mind to live as I ought. Grow virtue in me through Jesus, amen.

JULY 8

Let every person be subject to the governing authorities. For there is no authority except from God, and those that exist have been instituted by God. Therefore whoever resists the authorities resists what God has appointed, and those who resist will incur judgment. (Rom. 13:1–2)

Claudius was a bit of a dork. His family didn't think much of him and made fun of him. Shockingly, in AD 41, when Emperor Caligula was murdered, Claudius was made emperor of Rome. He worked hard as emperor, accomplishing some notable things at home and abroad. But Claudius attracted horrid women, eventually leading to his death. His first wife, Messalina, had countless affairs and was rumored to be plotting his overthrow with one of her lovers. The lover was killed, Messalina died shortly thereafter, and Claudius married his niece, Agrippina. In AD 54, some three years before Paul wrote Romans, Agrippina successfully plotted her husband's assassination, and her seventeen-year-old son, Nero, took the throne in Rome.

Nero reigned when Paul wrote today's passage. Paul told his readers *in Rome* to submit to the governing authorities, adding that they have been instituted by God. In a city rife with poor leadership, with assassinations and coups setting up and taking down emperors, Paul's words must have been mildly surprising. In the succeeding verses, Paul calls the authority the "servant of God" multiple times. Paul says that the authority's job is to punish wrongdoers and approve those in the right. Paul then gets very practical and says that as part of subjecting themselves to the government, his readers should be paying their taxes!

Roman government was certainly far different from ours in the United States. The Constitution of the United States establishes a government of the people, by the people, and for the people. Hence to extend Paul's reasoning, U.S. citizens are the ultimate rulers, and they are to be obeyed. It is fully appropriate to exercise constitutional rights of protest, free speech, and lobbying for legal changes, as well as the right to vote people in and out of office. But Paul still makes an important point for today: once enacted, those rules are to be obeyed until we succeed in changing them.

Submission isn't easy. God set up authority structures to teach Christians to live in submission. (Paul uses the same language when teaching believers to submit to leaders; see, for example, 1 Cor. 16:16; Eph. 5:21; Tit. 2:9.) As I learn to submit to earthly authorities, I will more readily be able to submit to the Lord himself.

Lord, teach me submission to you, as I learn it to others. In Jesus, amen.

JULY 9

Owe no one anything, except to love each other, for the one who loves another has fulfilled the law. For the commandments, "You shall not commit adultery, You shall not murder, You shall not steal, You shall not covet," and any other commandment, are summed up in this word: "You shall love your neighbor as yourself." (Rom. 13:8–9)

Did you ever fall in love? That question will generally conjure up the idea of a great emotional joy and longing for another, perhaps even a commitment. Do you love pizza? That question takes the idea of liking something and propels it to another level. The superlative of the word *like* to describe liking something greatly needs another word—hence the word *love* (used in phrases such as "I love my car"). Do you have a pet, perhaps a dog or cat, that you love? Here, one generally means an emotional tie has developed where you care for the animal.

None of my modern English expressions does an adequate job of wrapping up Paul's uses of *love* in today's passage. Among the many Greek words captured by our English word *love*, Paul here uses the Greek *agapaō* (ἀγαπάω), commonly referenced as "*agapē* love." While the word in Greek can certainly refer to warm regard or romantic feelings for another, at its root it also implies a level of service or work for another's good. It is an action word, not merely an emotional one.

In today's passage, Paul emphasizes this action aspect of *agapē* love. Paul begins the passage by instructing his readers to be responsible with debt. Often assumed to mean "Don't ever borrow," a difficult concept for those who seek a home or car in modern times, Paul has something else in mind. He uses a Greek construction (the present imperative) that might be more effectively understood here as "Don't continue owing." In other words, the Christian is to repay debts promptly in accordance with the terms of the loan.

But what Christians should consider a debt never to be fully repaid is the obligation to love others. This obligation Paul cites, much like Jesus did, as the ultimate fulfillment of the law's commands to not steal, covet, adulterize, and so on.

When we put into action a commitment for another's good, we are walking in the steps of Jesus. His entire life was one for the service and welfare of others—"For God so *loved* the world," John wrote (3:16). This is my daily obligation to *all*.

Lord, show me how to love everyone in my path today, as Jesus does. Amen.

JULY 10

The night is far gone; the day is at hand. So then let us cast off the works of darkness and put on the armor of light. Let us walk properly as in the daytime, not in orgies and drunkenness, not in sexual immorality and sensuality, not in quarreling and jealousy. But put on the Lord Jesus Christ, and make no provision for the flesh, to gratify its desires. (Rom. 13:12–14)

I sit in my office and type this devotional, having gotten up at 4 a.m. Looking out the windows, it is still quite dark. Soon, however, the early rays of sunlight will begin to creep near the horizon as the night ends. After I arose this morning, I showered and got dressed. Today I have legal meetings, so I'm wearing a suit. I don't always have the same dress code when I awaken, but I can't think of a day except when I was ill that I didn't change out of my sleeping clothes into daytime clothes (even during COVID!).

Paul knows the common experience of waking up and getting prepared for the day, and he uses this metaphor to talk about the importance of our daily attitude and actions. Paul's metaphor is placed in the context that as believers in Christ, each day we are closer to our final redemption, and our lives should reflect our growing closer to Christ.

Paul gives a few practical examples of holy living, and in his typical fashion, he begins with moral failures that most of his readers will readily acknowledge—no orgies, stay sober, avoid sexual immorality. But then Paul shifts to matters that hit closer to home for most of us: don't quarrel. Don't be jealous of another's life or success. Then Paul gives a catchall that certainly challenges all readers, "Make no provision for the flesh" (*flesh* is a term Paul uses to reference the selfish nature that we all carried before giving our lives in dedication to God).

How this is to be done is a nice touch in Paul's metaphor: take off your works of darkness, and get ready for the day. He says to put on your "armor of light," using a soldier's dress code. He indicates that the Christian will be at odds with much she or he sees in the day and will need to be ready to battle, to do what is right, pure, and holy. Paul then uses language of getting dressed, telling his readers to "put on Christ." Paul uses the same Greek word that was used to say, "Put on your shirt!" As believers, we are to wear Christ, changing who we are and what we do day by day, week by week, year by year. This is as right as getting dressed in the morning!

Lord, help me wear Christ and live today for your glory. In Jesus, amen.

JULY 11

As for the one who is weak in faith, welcome him, but not to quarrel over opinions. One person believes he may eat anything, while the weak person eats only vegetables. Let not the one who eats despise the one who abstains, and let not the one who abstains pass judgment on the one who eats, for God has welcomed him. (Rom. 14:1–3)

My friend Ernest had a favorite horse named Fletch. This horse knew Ernest better than Ernest knew himself. These two, working in tandem, won the world cutting horse championship. Fletch and Ernest were both one of a kind. As age was going to get the best of Fletch, Ernest made the monumental decision to use science and make a clone of Fletch. I think it was both a tribute to Fletch as well as a chance to keep part of Fletch in Ernest's life.

Cloning is a late twentieth-century scientific breakthrough, but the idea of similarity has long been a factor in various social groups. We relate well to other like-minded people and move into neighborhoods with people with similar professions, education, or socioeconomic status. Even in high schools, people gravitate toward the tables with their friends, who often have similar mind-sets and habits.

Yet the church was never intended to be this way, and we rightly lament where it has failed. God's house is built on diversity. Christians were never meant to be clones of one another. We have different skin colors, different heights and weights, different educational and social backgrounds, different places within society at large, and different personalities. But all these people, with all this diversity, gather in unity joined under the crucifixion and resurrection of Jesus Christ.

Paul wrote to a church that had become fragmented by Emperor Claudius' decree expelling Jews from Rome. Once those Jews returned, the differences among the people could easily have been magnified, creating deep divisions within the church. Many aspects of Christian life are based on opinion (how God wants us to celebrate special holidays and how and what we eat seemed to be issues for the Romans), yet the church should have room for different opinions on such nonessentials. Rather than being destructive, the variety adds greater flavor and opportunities for growth. We learn more about God and become better people when we have mixes of all sorts recognized and respected among us. This should challenge and change my views on church. Save cloning for horses, not church!

Lord, help me live with love outside my comfort zone. In Jesus' name, amen.

JULY 12

The one who observes the day, observes it in honor of the Lord. The one who eats, eats in honor of the Lord, since he gives thanks to God, while the one who abstains, abstains in honor of the Lord and gives thanks to God. For none of us lives to himself, and none of us dies to himself. For if we live, we live to the Lord, and if we die, we die to the Lord. So then, whether we live or whether we die, we are the Lord's. For to this end Christ died and lived again, that he might be Lord both of the dead and of the living. (Rom. 14:6–9)

In 1623, facing a serious illness, the English poet and dean of St. Paul's Cathedral John Donne wrote one of his most famous pieces, "No Man Is an Island." Found in his book of devotions, the short poem expresses the truth that all people are connected. We are pieces of continents, not islands unto ourselves. Donne may have been inspired by an older Greek saying, εἷς ἀνήρ οὐδεὶς ἀνήρ, fairly translated as "one man is no man."

In today's passage, Paul might seem to be making the same point, but in fact, Paul refers to something even more significant. Paul isn't saying that all people live in relationship to other people. Paul knows that all believers have their existence tied to the Lord. "None of us lives to himself, and none of us dies to himself" is Paul's reminder that God is always a part of the life and death of every believer.

Paul speaks of the reality of both living and dying in relationship with God. God determines when we live and when we die. Our lives are tied to God each moment and breath. Importantly, even death will not separate the Christian from this relationship with the Lord. Paul uses the illustration of the Lord Jesus himself dying while incarnate and then living again. Our lives and deaths are similarly existing in reference to God.

You and I aren't islands. But our ultimate tie isn't to the rest of humanity, as John Donne wrote. Our decisive tie is to God. It is God who will walk with us each breath. It is God who is present to rescue us in crisis. God is present to teach us, to grow us out of who we are into who we can be. God is ever present amid whatever today he has for you and me. In that truth, I can live and die boldly, confident in the ever-present God who loves and secures me.

Lord, thank you for making this life living in your presence. You give joy and peace that radically change my life. May I live to honor you in that truth. In Jesus' name, amen.

JULY 13

We who are strong have an obligation to bear with the failings of the weak, and not to please ourselves. Let each of us please his neighbor for his good, to build him up. For Christ did not please himself, but as it is written, "The reproaches of those who reproached you fell on me." (Rom. 15:1–3)

Paul's writings are good for me. Yes, I find them theologically enlightening, doctrinally instructive, and intellectually challenging, but they also stop me in life and make me assess who I am and how I live. Prayerfully reflecting on his thoughts brings me into greater alignment with God's thoughts and ways.

Today's passage illustrates this power of Paul in my life. In almost any age of civilization, in all cultures, and with most people, the strong live competitively, hardly taking notice of the weak and often taking advantage of them. Rarely will you find someone who lives with a burden for helping the weak among us.

In this passage, Paul continues his theme from the last chapter about those who are theologically strong living with those who aren't, but his principle extends past theology. It is a general principle that changes the outlook for the believer. Classifying himself emphatically in the Greek as among the strong (it would be fair to translate it "We who are strong, *we* . . ."), Paul says the strong looking out for the weak is not an option; it is an obligation.

Paul then uses a notable metaphor. He says that the strong person's obligation toward the failings of the weak is to "bear" them. Paul's word for "bear" (*bastazō*—βαστάζω) is a word speaking to carrying a load. This is the same word that John used to speak of Christ carrying the cross (Jn. 19:7). Paul's travel buddy Luke also used it when quoting Jesus' admonition that his followers should "bear" their own crosses and follow him (Lk. 14:27).

Fittingly, Paul uses Jesus as the ideal example of this lifestyle and attitude. Jesus never lived for personal pleasure. He didn't spend his days chasing money, seeking fame for personal glory, or amassing toys. He didn't time his incarnation with the age of pizza, ice cream, and air conditioning. He—the strongest of the strong—left his heavenly throne to live in service to humanity, the weakest of the weak. Paul will later say this is how we "glorify the God and Father of our Lord Jesus Christ" (Rom. 15:6). Such service and sacrifice are for God's glory.

Lord, give me your heart for those I can serve and help. Following Jesus, amen.

JULY 14

For I tell you that Christ became a servant to the circumcised to show God's truthfulness, in order to confirm the promises given to the patriarchs, and in order that the Gentiles might glorify God for his mercy. As it is written, "Therefore I will praise you among the Gentiles, and sing to your name." And again it is said, "Rejoice, O Gentiles, with his people." And again, "Praise the Lord, all you Gentiles, and let all the peoples extol him." And again Isaiah says, "The root of Jesse will come, even he who arises to rule the Gentiles; in him will the Gentiles hope." (Rom. 15:8–12)

My sister Kathryn is the world's best wrapper of presents. Any present she wraps gets pretty paper and is well cut, folded, and taped. But the wrapping is rarely done until Kathryn adds a bow or ribbon. Her final touches finalize the full beauty. In today's passage, Paul reminds me of Kathryn's wrapping. Paul is approaching the end of his letter, and he isn't going to finish without returning to his original purpose of writing and putting a bow on top of what he has already said.

As I discussed in several earlier devotional teachings, the Roman church was trying to adjust to an unusual situation. The church had started more than two decades earlier when Roman Jews who had heard Peter's pentecostal sermon in Jerusalem returned to Rome with the gospel. The church then began receiving into fellowship Gentiles who came to faith, but that process would take time. Meanwhile, it would have been the Jews who handled the church finances, teaching, leadership, and so on. Then after two decades, Emperor Claudius evicted Jews from Rome. For several years, the Gentile believers would have been running the church. They would teach, oversee the budget, and lead the church. Then the Jews returned, leading to a new problem: Who was to be in charge? And who was to teach? Paul writes to set straight everyone's obligation, beginning with the status each group has before God.

Paul then returns to this problem as his writing draws toward a close. Yes, Christ came to the Jews, the circumcised. But using four different passages from Jewish Scriptures, Paul shows God was always doing it to also reach the Gentiles.

We are part of God's big plan. We aren't to fuss for significance. We are to live to God's glory—at church, at work, at home. It is all about him.

Lord, give me a supple heart for seeing your mission everywhere. In Jesus, amen.

JULY 15

Greet Rufus, chosen in the Lord; also his mother, who has been a mother to me as well. (Rom. 16:13)

My friend Fred Gray was receiving an honorary doctorate from Texas Tech University. Fred was about to turn ninety-three and was an important part of American history. He had been the lawyer for Rosa Parks in her bus arrest during the early stages of the civil rights movement. From there, he went on to represent Martin Luther King Jr. as well as many other notable people and causes associated with destroying segregation in America. Among the many things that stood out to me was Fred's insistence that Ms. Parks and Mr. King (and indeed Fred Gray himself) were just ordinary people trying to do the best they could each day.

Something amazing happens when everyday people do what is set before them. Some become notable icons of history. Others may never be known apart from the few in their close circle. But everyone becomes part of the fabric that becomes the tapestry of history, whether well known or anonymous. Today's passage illustrates that point.

Rufus was a common slave name in Paul's day. The passage tells us little about him other than that he was in Rome and his mother had been helping Paul in ways unknown but worthy of the epithet "She has been a mother to me as well." The passage does add that Rufus was "chosen in the Lord," but Paul uses that language for all Christians. It likely shows a special tip of the hat to Rufus, but that description doesn't really provide us with any more information about him.

But this isn't the only biblical reference to someone named Rufus. A Rufus is also mentioned in Mark 15:21. As Jesus hauled his cross to Golgotha, he faltered under its weight. The Romans order a passerby named Simon of Cyrene (northern Libya near the coast facing Greece and Italy) to carry it. The Gospel of Mark, which Bible scholars believe was written first for a Roman audience, identifies Simon as the father of "Alexander and Rufus."

No one knows if the Rufus is the same. The pages of history do not record who most people are or what they do. Yet everyone is important in their service to God. Everyone—the most ordinary people—does their part in making God's history. This challenges me to live differently today.

Lord, help me live to your glory today, step by step in Jesus, amen.

JULY 16

I appeal to you, brothers, to watch out for those who cause divisions and create obstacles contrary to the doctrine that you have been taught; avoid them. For such persons do not serve our Lord Christ, but their own appetites, and by smooth talk and flattery they deceive the hearts of the naive. For your obedience is known to all, so that I rejoice over you, but I want you to be wise as to what is good and innocent as to what is evil. The God of peace will soon crush Satan under your feet. The grace of our Lord Jesus Christ be with you. (Rom. 16:17–20)

Some people have an innate sense of direction. Almost like a bird flying south without a GPS or cell phone to help, they can tell you which direction is north, south, east, or west. Others are directionally challenged. They need a cell phone to help them get five minutes away from their home. When I was young, in the pre-smartphone era, more people learned how to use a compass. The needle on this small instrument always points true north. I may want north to be one direction or another, but north is an objective direction, and the compass needle will correct my own druthers.

In the same way, Paul writes of those who are living based on their own directional preferences rather than the true north direction that a compass would give them. In Paul's case, the church was plagued by those who participated in church activities as believers, all while feeding their own appetites and desires. They weren't following Christ; they were following their own moral compass.

Paul says that God sets our course, and we are to follow him, not our own fancied route. Paul then calls back to the original story of sin. Adam and Eve opted for what they thought was best and selfishly wanted rather than live in obedience to God's instructions. They ate of the tree of knowledge of good and evil. Paul wants his readers to be wise to good but innocent to evil. As the believer in Christ follows the trail blazed by the Savior, the prophetic promise of God in Genesis 3:15 to crush Satan is manifested in our lives. God had promised Adam and Eve that he would crush the head of the serpent under the feet of the offspring of woman. God did that in Christ, but we walk in victory when we follow that path Christ set out.

I don't want to be living for myself and my desires. Too much is at stake. May God give me the wisdom to follow Christ, not my own ideas.

God, please give me insight and wisdom to identify my own selfishness and to follow Jesus. I want to live for you. In Jesus' name, amen.

JULY 17

Now to him who is able to strengthen you according to my gospel and the preaching of Jesus Christ, according to the revelation of the mystery that was kept secret for long ages but has now been disclosed and through the prophetic writings has been made known to all nations, according to the command of the eternal God, to bring about the obedience of faith—to the only wise God be glory forevermore through Jesus Christ! Amen. (Rom. 16:25–27)

As a lawyer, I spend a lot of time writing letters, emails, and notes to others. In my early practice, I worked at a large, well-established firm that had protocol for such things. We were taught to sign off letters with either "Sincerely . . ." or "Very truly yours . . ." Over time, as the internet came into common use, emails took the place of hard "snail" mail. An air of informality crept in with emails, as the back-and-forth nature of them removed the more formal endings. Some are now signed off with simply a name or, even less, with initials. Others have more thoughtful sign-offs that are still more commonplace than the formal ones. Some I see often include "Best wishes . . ." and "With appreciation . . ." One friend would always sign off his emails with friends by writing, "Blessings . . ."—the idea being a prayer of blessing on the recipient. With text messaging rapidly replacing emails, sign-offs have become even more brief (if they are even present).

Writing almost two thousand years ago, Paul is deliberate in today's passage as he ends his letter to the Romans. Paul isn't signing off with "Very truly yours . . ." or even with "Blessings . . ." Paul ends in magnificent praise to God. The sound that should ring in echo in the reader's ears is one that lifts high the only wise God who has unmatchable glory demonstrated in the Lord Jesus Christ.

Paul's sign-off is worthy of careful notation and consideration. Paul knew that for millennia, God's plan to rewrite eternity by rectifying what was destroyed and lost in the fall was in place yet was unknown to people. Paul calls this the "mystery" of the redemptive work of Jesus. God had spoken of it through his prophets and had set up signs so that those with a genuine desire to find God would find his loving work in Jesus.

Walking in the love and sacrifice of Jesus isn't just life changing; it changes eternity. This is the way to end a letter! This sets up the truth of God's glory, a glory unequaled in space or time—a glory we walk in and share.

Father, I marvel at your redemption in Christ. Thank you for bringing me from death to life. May I live to praise you eternally. In Jesus, amen.

JULY 18

Paul and Timothy, servants of Christ Jesus, To all the saints in Christ Jesus who are at Philippi, with the overseers and deacons: Grace to you and peace from God our Father and the Lord Jesus Christ. I thank my God in all my remembrance of you, always in every prayer of mine for you all making my prayer with joy, because of your partnership in the gospel from the first day until now. And I am sure of this, that he who began a good work in you will bring it to completion at the day of Jesus Christ. (Phil. 1:1–6)

Perhaps you've heard the phrase "An attitude of gratitude isn't simply a platitude." It's a nice, singsongy expression that is true. Attitude is important. It reflects one's outlook on life as well as one's convictions and priorities. It comes into sharp focus as I think through Paul's letter to the Philippians.

Paul traveled to and established a church in the important Roman town Phillipi, which is located in ancient Macedonia (now northern Greece), during his second missionary journey. While working in the community to grow the nascent church, Paul was arrested and imprisoned, as described in Acts 16. That imprisonment led to the conversion of his jailer and his family following an earthquake. Paul was released from the imprisonment, and the police, who had wrongly incarcerated him, persuaded Paul to leave Philippi.

Paul's history with the church made for a delightful reading of his letter, at least among the family of the jailer. For Paul was writing this letter from another imprisonment precipitated by Paul's faithfulness to preaching. Yet in this letter, almost every verse expresses Paul's joy, a joy that sustained him through the roughness of his incarceration. The jailer knew from his firsthand observations of Paul's genuine service to God and his attitude of song and gratitude in prison. Indeed, it was Paul's very attitude that had led to the conversion of the jailer and his family. Paul links his attitude of joy to the sharing in the faith that was the cornerstone of his relationship with the believers in Philippi. Paul knew that God didn't stop working in believers' hearts after they came to faith. Rather, God continued that important work, growing them in their faith.

This is what God is doing in all his followers. He draws us to him and then works in us to grow us in our relationship with him. Regardless of our circumstances, knowing this, we can keep an attitude of gratitude! God is at work!

Lord, thank you for working in my life, even with all that is going on. In Jesus, amen.

JULY 19

And it is my prayer that your love may abound more and more, with knowledge and all discernment, so that you may approve what is excellent, and so be pure and blameless for the day of Christ, filled with the fruit of righteousness that comes through Jesus Christ, to the glory and praise of God. (Phil. 1:9–11)

The start of college was tough on me. No, it wasn't so much the attendance, the studying, or the exams. My biggest difficulty was deciding which courses to take. I began college at Texas Tech University, a campus then of over twenty thousand. The course catalog was huge. I wanted to take everything. I wanted to take classes in at least seven different languages, economics, math, business, science, literature, political science, and more. There were at least five different majors I wanted to declare. It was a tough choice, but one made easier as I thought through what I wanted to do in life. For different paths brought different results.

That is the nature of life. All roads lead somewhere, and we should often think that through as we decide which road to take. This principle causes today's passage to make me think and consider my road.

Paul's "destination" set out in this passage is a life that approves and confirms the things that are excellent—that really matter. It is a life that is pure and blameless. Paul sets the goal of being filled with the fruits that rightly accompany the righteous child of God. This kind of life redounds to the praise and glory of God.

With that stellar destination, Paul identifies the path to get me there. That path is rooted in love for others and God. Love combined with knowledge and discernment lead to the life Paul has described. In a metaphorical sense, Paul is telling me which courses I am to take if I am to graduate into the life that is glorious service to the King of kings.

Paul prayed for his friends to grow in this love, loaded with awareness and understanding. This is a prayer I rightly pray for those near and dear to me. It is a personal prayer as well. Growing in God's love transforms life for everyone. This is not a naïve or blind love. It is a conscious and mature love, growing in knowledge and discernment.

Lord, please grow your love in me, loading it with knowledge and discernment. I pray the same for [fill in the blank with a host of friends and loved ones]. I ask in the name of Jesus, amen.

JULY 20

It is my eager expectation and hope that I will not be at all ashamed, but that with full courage now as always Christ will be honored in my body, whether by life or by death. For to me to live is Christ, and to die is gain. If I am to live in the flesh, that means fruitful labor for me. Yet which I shall choose I cannot tell. I am hard pressed between the two. My desire is to depart and be with Christ, for that is far better. But to remain in the flesh is more necessary on your account. (Phil. 1:20–24)

When I was eleven years old, I had great difficulty sleeping one night during a visit to my grandparents' house. For some reason, I kept thinking about the fact that (statistically, at least) my parents would likely die before I would. This bothered me so much that I remember praying, "God, please don't let my parents die first. Either return and take us all, or let us all die at the same time."

I write this fifty-two years later, and my mother is still alive, but my father died twenty years ago. Yes, I still miss him today, and assuming my mother predeceases me, it will be a tough grieving process. Yet I view things differently than I did that night. I know that when my father, a stalwart believer in Christ, departed this life, it was a better thing for him than living. This is a life of difficulty. The ravages of sin are apparent in almost every aspect of life, including economic challenges, relationship conflicts, struggles with personal holiness, and various trials and hardships. There are also great joys and mercies evident all around us, along with beauty, happiness, opportunities, and joy. So life is a mixed bag, no doubt.

But the assurance of Scripture, as so eloquently put by Paul in today's passage, is that it is certainly better to depart the difficulties and limitations of this life to find unbridled joy and peace in the presence of God. This doesn't make the death of a loved one without grief. For even Paul noted that one reason he knew it best for him to stay in this life was to minister to the Philippians.

This truth makes the death of a Christ follower different. Living in this world is an important opportunity to love and serve others in relationships. But dying is a better thing, a "gain" for the Christian. It is as if we get all the good of this life without the pain and misery. While many fear death, believers can be assured that we will find new meaning and joy with God in his kingdom.

Lord, thank you for this life. May I live it in daily service to you. In Jesus' name, amen.

JULY 21

Have this mind among yourselves, which is yours in Christ Jesus, who, though he was in the form of God, did not count equality with God a thing to be grasped, but emptied himself, by taking the form of a servant, being born in the likeness of men. And being found in human form, he humbled himself by becoming obedient to the point of death, even death on a cross. Therefore God has highly exalted him and bestowed on him the name that is above every name, so that at the name of Jesus every knee should bow, in heaven and on earth and under the earth, and every tongue confess that Jesus Christ is Lord, to the glory of God the Father. (Phil. 2:5–11)

British playwright William Congreve (1670–1729) was known in his day for his brilliant comic dialogue. Today, however, he is perhaps most famous for sculpting one line, although that line is generally misquoted. In *The Mourning Bride*, Congreve wrote, "Music has charms to soothe the savage breast" (not *beast*). Music does that and more. It also exalts and magnifies the substance of what is written.

According to most scholars, Paul here quotes from an ancient song. The song spoke of Christ pre-existing before the incarnation. The song then walks through the significance of Christ exchanging his equality with God by assuming the form of the created: a human. We don't know the depths of what this entailed, but it included his choice to empty himself of aspects of his existence as God. For example, Christ explained that there were things God in heaven knew of which Christ on earth didn't (Mt. 24:33–36).

Becoming human was a huge sacrifice, but it was far from the end of Christ's sacrificing. He suffered human humiliation by his obedience to God's will to the point that he died a most embarrassing, dishonoring, and painful death: crucifixion. But the song and the story don't end there. God exalted the crucified Savior and bestowed on him the name above all other names. In Greek, like Hebrew, the idea behind a name includes a person's reputation. In a modern sense, it would include one's résumé. Paul's song is spot on. For who has a better résumé than Jesus Christ, who walked the path of humiliation and death before being resurrected and bringing with him a redeemed kingdom of rescued masses?

Yes, this song isn't one to soothe the savage beast or breast. It is one to inspire people to praise God and follow him in living for others.

Lord, thank you for giving of yourself. May I follow you in Jesus, amen.

JULY 22

Have this mind among yourselves, which is yours in Christ Jesus, who, though he was in the form of God, did not count equality with God a thing to be grasped, but emptied himself, by taking the form of a servant, being born in the likeness of men. And being found in human form, he humbled himself by becoming obedient to the point of death, even death on a cross. Therefore God has highly exalted him and bestowed on him the name that is above every name, so that at the name of Jesus every knee should bow, in heaven and on earth and under the earth, and every tongue confess that Jesus Christ is Lord, to the glory of God the Father. (Phil. 2:5–11)

"*Hold the phone!!!*" you may be saying. "Didn't you do this passage yesterday? Have I found a *major* mistake in this devotional?" Yes, I did this yesterday, but the repeat isn't a mistake! This passage in Philippians is maybe my favorite passage in the Bible, and having spent so much time on and in it in my life, I want to get two teachings/devotionals out of it!

Paul's song, as I explained yesterday, wasn't crafted out of thin air. This song, an ancient hymn of the first century, is crafted in part from Isaiah 45, especially verses 21–23. In the Isaiah passage, the prophet is the mouth of the Lord God, speaking the words of "Yahweh," the Hebrew name of God given to Moses at the burning bush. The name Yahweh is signified in Old Testament passages by placing the word "LORD" in all capital letters, using a smaller font for the "ORD."

Isaiah 45 speaks of God being the only Savior, the only righteous one: "Was it not I, the LORD? And there is no other god besides me, a righteous God and a Savior; there is none besides me" (v. 21). The prophet says there is *none* besides him, or other than him. Then he adds, "Turn to me and be saved, all the ends of the earth! For I am God, and there is no other" (v. 22). How does God accomplish this? He follows the previous claim with "By myself I have sworn; from my mouth has gone out in righteousness a word that shall not return: 'To me every knee shall bow, every tongue shall swear allegiance'" (v. 23). Here we have part of the basis for Paul's song.

Jesus is the incarnate word of God, issued from the Father. He is one and the same as Yahweh God, for there is no other. It is to Yahweh God, to the Lord Jesus, that every knee shall bow and every tongue swear allegiance and confess him as Lord. Jesus is God and worthy of all our awe and worship.

Lord, you amaze me as wonderful, and I stand in awe of you. In Jesus, amen.

JULY 23

Therefore, my beloved, as you have always obeyed, so now, not only as in my presence but much more in my absence, work out your own salvation with fear and trembling, for it is God who works in you, both to will and to work for his good pleasure. (Phil. 2:12–13)

Baking bread from scratch is one of my favorite activities; the process and smells of baking yeast products—from a basic sandwich loaf to bagels, pretzels, and English muffins—give me deep joy. For the yeast to work in a bread, it requires many things. Among them is the working of the yeast into the dough in a way that ensures the development of gluten in the bread. As the yeast is worked into the dough, the yeast causes the dough to rise as the yeast feeds on the dough's starches and emits gases as a by-product. Those gases give the lift to the bread and keep it from being a cracker.

Baking is a helpful background for reading today's passage. Paul urges his readers to "work out" their salvation. Paul's word is *kataergazomai* (κατεργάζομαι). Among its usages were the grinding of corn for cooking, the chewing and digesting of food, and the ripening of fruits for eating. In the sense of kneading yeast into bread, Paul wants his readers to live in ways that respect what God will do in the believer's life. As we work godliness into our lives so that it exudes into all our dough, God is working in our lives (dough) to bring us to our best, which is his desire and pleasure.

Naïvely, some think this passage runs counter to much of Paul's writings, which state that we do not work for nor earn our salvation. A works-based salvation is not the spirit of what Paul is saying. Paul sets out the simple, practical truth that we are working out what God is working in. When we follow God in the nuts and bolts of daily living, we find God transforming our hearts and minds to look more like Jesus.

Life has red-letter days of great significance—marriages, graduations, childbirths, deaths, and more. But most of life isn't a red-letter day. It is the steady humdrum of going to the grocery store, going to work or school, being with friends or family, and so on. But it is in walking in godliness in everyday life that God develops and grows the character of Christ in us. Those are the times where our dough rises. It may not be obvious watching, but it happens. God works in as we work out.

Lord, work in me for your good purposes as I work to follow Jesus in this life. In his name, amen.

JULY 24

Do all things without grumbling or disputing, that you may be blameless and innocent, children of God without blemish in the midst of a crooked and twisted generation, among whom you shine as lights in the world, holding fast to the word of life. (Phil. 2:14–16)

The power God expressed when he brought Israel out of Egypt is hard to grasp. Well in advance, God sculpted Moses through a unique and difficult life and then called Moses through a burning bush experience unlike any other. By performing repeated miracles through Moses and Aaron, God brought Pharaoh to his knees and forced him to release the Israelites. When Pharaoh changed his mind and sent one of the world's greatest armies after the fleeing Hebrews, God divided the Red Sea and effectuated their escape and the army's demise. God then gave Israel a law of revelation and entered a covenant with them.

After all those miraculous displays of God's power and care for Israel, they reached the promised land of Canaan and sent spies out for forty days to assess the challenges and opportunities before them. The spies came back, and all but two reported the greatness of the land but also the fearsomeness of the inhabitants. The people got scared. Instead of following God's instructions and leadership, they rebelled and began "grumbling" against Moses and Aaron (Num. 14:2). But that grumbling was really against God, who had instructed Moses and Aaron.

In translating the Hebrew text of this verse, the Jewish scholars chose the Greek word *gogguzō* (γογγύζω). This word speaks of expressing oneself in low tones of discontent. It means muttering under the breath or whispering. Often the word is translated as "grumbling" or "complaining." Paul uses the same word in today's passage.

Paul's instruction is that Christians are not to be grumblers and complainers. Paul also used the word in harkening the Corinthians back to the Numbers 14 story of Israel (1 Cor. 10:10). We are not to grumble or complain. After all, we, like those early Hebrews, are beneficiaries of God's care and concern. Before the ages began, the Triune God planned the sacrifice of Jesus. God has worked a miraculous resurrection to affirm and show his sacrificial love for the world. How dare any of us complain about any aspect of this life? The God who brought us here isn't going to abandon us now!

Lord, forgive my grumbling. Give me strength and faith in Jesus, amen.

JULY 25

Look out for the dogs, look out for the evildoers, look out for those who mutilate the flesh. For we are the circumcision, who worship by the Spirit of God and glory in Christ Jesus and put no confidence in the flesh—though I myself have reason for confidence in the flesh also. (Phil. 3:2–4)

Confession time: I'm a math geek. I love math and always have. Math enables one to do cool things. Mathematical formulas can make interesting drawings when graphed out. When as a child I was asked, "What's your favorite number?" I had none. I loved them all!

In antiquity, numbers functioned as they do today but with a twist. Numbers were also symbolic. Among the symbolism, the number three in the Jewish world (and many surrounding cultures) was considered a divine number. It had a special heavenly punch, and one sees it over and over in threefold repetitions in the Bible. The classic is Isaiah 6, which is echoed in Revelation 4, as God is called "holy" three times, then labeled as the God who "was, is, and is to come," another triad.

Paul uses a triad here, with rhetorical flourish! He says (1) look out for dogs, (2) look out for evildoers, and (3) look out for flesh mutilators. Paul is referencing those teaching that Gentiles had to be circumcised to be Christians. This thinking betrayed an underlying error of the faith that is bedrock to true Christianity.

Circumcision was a rite that set Israel apart from the other nations. It showed Israel as a people uniquely chosen by God to receive certain covenants and promises, including the provision of the Messiah. The Gentiles would be blessed by the Messiah and would be incorporated into many of the promises of Israel, but they didn't have to become Jews to become Christians. For Gentiles, the marks of being God's people aren't marks of Judaism; they are marks of faith. Paul goes on later in Philippians 3 to speak of his incredible Jewish pedigree and accomplishments. But they all pale in comparison (he says they are "rubbish") to knowing Jesus as Messiah and Lord. Our relationship with Christ is based on faith, not being Jewish! So it was in Paul's day, and so it is today.

God doesn't love me because of what I am doing. He loves me because that's who he is. That is why I have confidence in Christ as my Lord and Savior. I didn't earn his love, but I couldn't live without it. That is worthy of saying three times!

Lord, thank you for your enduring love by which I stand in Christ, amen.

JULY 26

Not that I have already obtained this or am already perfect, but I press on to make it my own, because Christ Jesus has made me his own. Brothers, I do not consider that I have made it my own. But one thing I do: forgetting what lies behind and straining forward to what lies ahead, I press on toward the goal for the prize of the upward call of God in Christ Jesus. (Phil. 3:12–14)

A Nobel Prize for literature? Yes, it was bestowed on Bob Dylan, and rightly so. His lyrics can weave magnificent narratives and stories. He can take ideas and express them in brilliant poetry. He finds amazing rhyming schemes and superlative turns of phrases. Yet to cite him for only his lyrical mastery might miss the subtle power of his musical prowess. Bob can shape melodies that align with the lyrics in potent ways, delivering and sustaining the message with near permanence in the memory. Bob's snarling voice can accentuate what might otherwise be lost. A clear example for this is today's passage, memorialized in Bob's tremendous song "Pressing On."

Paul prompted the song by explaining that as Christians, none of us have arrived. We are all on a journey, termed *sanctification* by theologians. We are God's works in process. We are clay he is molding to become the vessel he wants, silver and gold he is refining to get it to a greater purity, and children he is rearing to grow into responsible adults. Each of these metaphors is found in the Bible. But Paul expresses this concept of growth in practical terms rather than metaphorical.

Paul explains that while we haven't yet achieved being like Christ in living righteously, we are growing daily. That growing process is enhanced through, as Paul instructs, forgetting what lies behind and pressing on to this higher calling of our Lord. This is what Bob echoes so powerfully in his song (to which I strongly urge everyone to listen!).

I need Paul's instruction. The older I get, the more regrets I seem to accumulate. I have made so many mistakes, sinned so many sins, and failed to measure up to even meager expectations. Yet my God is faithful. He rescues me time and time again and continues to work in my life to transform me. I'm not perfect, but I'm a lot better than I used to be! I need to remember Paul's admonition to forget the past and let God work as I join Bob and Paul in pressing on!

Lord, give me the grace to forget the past and pursue the present and future with you in Jesus, amen.

JULY 27

Brothers, join in imitating me, and keep your eyes on those who walk according to the example you have in us. For many, of whom I have often told you and now tell you even with tears, walk as enemies of the cross of Christ. Their end is destruction, their god is their belly, and they glory in their shame, with minds set on earthly things. (Phil. 3:17–19)

Growing up Protestant, we followed very few "church calendar days." Of course, Easter and Christmas were big-letter days, and I had some Protestant friends who honored Ash Wednesday and even a few who kept Lent. But by and large we stopped there. We certainly didn't keep the calendar our Catholic friends did.

I was reminded of this in emails with a friend of mine who is a devoted Catholic. He was telling me how much he personally finds feast days enriching. (In the church calendar sense, a "feast" isn't a big meal but rather a day of recognition or honoring.) Over time, the church has assigned feast days to several well-known and lesser-known saints. The Protestant in me is tempted to think, "So what? Why honor some dead Christian in this way? Let's honor Christ instead." But today's passage explains an important truth.

Paul says we *are* to value the faithful who walk before God. Paul wanted his readers to "imitate" him and to also "keep [their] eyes on those who walk" in godly ways. Paul isn't limiting this to those who are alive, and I dare say we shouldn't either. I seek even now to imitate Paul in many aspects of my Christian walk.

There is power in following models of faith. No one we follow is perfect, save the Lord himself. No other human will measure up to God's perfection, but even recognizing that, something important can be understood. I can see in the foibles of others how they respond. As Paul wrote in the verses discussed in yesterday's devotional, I need to learn to forget what lies behind and press on to what lies ahead. Those types of teachings are most powerful coming from holy people who have failed.

I want every chance to grow before the Lord. I want to find stellar examples of walking in faithful obedience to God and learn from them. Paul taught his readers to do this. It's a rich area for me to work on!

Lord, give me wisdom in watching and learning from others. In Jesus, amen.

JULY 28

Rejoice in the Lord always; again I will say, rejoice. Let your reasonableness be known to everyone. (Phil. 4:4–5)

I was ten years old. Rummaging through the pantry, I found a brownie mix. Brownies sounded good! I was also a bit bored, and the idea struck me, "Maybe I could make the brownies!" I asked Mom if I could, and she said, "Sure, just follow the instructions on the box!" I began to work, assiduously following the box's instructions. A few minutes into my culinary endeavor, Mom came in and found me with both hands in the batter, running it through my fingers. Stunned, Mom asked me, "What are you doing?" I said I was just following the instructions. I explained, "The box said to 'mix by hand.'" She couldn't stop laughing. I didn't think it was funny. I decided the box didn't have clear instructions.

In today's passage, Paul gives meticulously clear instructions. Even better, the reward for following his instructions is better than a pan of hot brownies. Paul instructs the readers to "rejoice in the Lord." This is such an important step that Paul repeats it. Joy, the root of the word *rejoice*, should be a key birthmark that shows on those born again.

Telling someone, "Be full of joy," sometimes isn't the most useful thing, for sometimes joy might be hard to find. Here context matters. Paul writes this instruction after writing over three-fourths of his letter already. We need to consider his prior comments that God is working in us, that persecution and difficulty can lead to good things, that death in the presence of Jesus beats life in the presence of others, that we find strength in being united with other believers in purpose and attitude, and most importantly, that Christ willingly gave of himself in inconceivable ways out of his love and compassion for us.

So Paul gives an instruction that should be the daily goal of every Christian. Live in the moment, knowing that the God beyond time also lives in the moment with us. We shouldn't forget that Paul has the unique right to say these things, as he is writing from a prison, certainly not a great place in first-century Rome.

I mixed the brownie batter by hand, thinking that I had seen my mom do the same when she made meatloaf. I missed the context of the brownie mix. I can do better with Paul's instruction!

Lord, give me your joy each day as I walk with you. In Jesus, amen.

JULY 29

The Lord is at hand; do not be anxious about anything, but in everything by prayer and supplication with thanksgiving let your requests be made known to God. And the peace of God, which surpasses all understanding, will guard your hearts and your minds in Christ Jesus. (Phil. 4:5–7)

We live in a connected age, but it hasn't always been so. When I began working after law school, I frequently had to leave town for one legal matter or another. When I was gone, I would have to frequently call the office to check on messages. If I left for several days, I would need my assistant to open my mail and via phone tell me what had come in and what hadn't. Sometimes when something important was pending, I would worry quite a bit between calls back to the office. I would wonder if "the call" or some ruling from a court had issued since my last call.

Today, email and smartphones alleviate much of that uneasiness. I know at a moment's notice when a ruling issues. It comes via email. I get my phone calls or messages immediately. If something notable occurs at home or work, I get a text in real time.

Those are modern times of life, different from a few decades back. Yet on those most important matters, in a real sense, modernity reaches back into antiquity. Today's passage illustrates my meaning. "The Lord is at hand"—God is within reach. This wasn't on a particular day or week. Paul is writing about twenty-four hours a day, seven days a week, every day of the year. God is *right there*, wherever we are. So we needn't be worriers; we need to be pray-ers, as in people who pray.

With God ever present, we can reach to him with all our cares and concerns. Moreover, we needn't worry about whether we matter enough for him to listen or care. For the death and resurrection of Christ answer any such concerns. He guards our hearts and minds "in Christ Jesus." God loves us enough to die for us. Our unworthiness is great enough that he paid for the unworthiness of *everyone.*

So today should look different for all thinking through Paul's passage. It means that with God at hand, we can speak with him about whatever concerns us. In our relationships, finances, health, opportunities, griefs, worries, and more, God is ready to give wisdom, direction, and solace. The God of peace is at the ready to give that peace.

*Lord, my needs are many [*list them!*]. Be with me, bringing peace in Christ, amen.*

JULY 30

Finally, brothers, whatever is true, whatever is honorable, whatever is just, whatever is pure, whatever is lovely, whatever is commendable, if there is any excellence, if there is anything worthy of praise, think about these things. What you have learned and received and heard and seen in me—practice these things, and the God of peace will be with you. (Phil. 4:8–9)

The preacher Don Finto spoke into my life in notable ways growing up. One was his challenge to me to memorize Scripture. Not just a verse here or there, but Don wanted me to memorize large chunks. He was my impetus to memorize the book of Philippians in high school. I worked on one verse every day, starting with Philippians 1:1 and going to the end. As I memorized a new verse, I would always repeat everything up to that point. When I hit today's passage, I struggled at first with the words and orders of Paul's instructions.

I was memorizing the book in the New American Standard Bible version. It read much like today's selection quoted out of the ESV, except the word translated above as "just" was translated "right." So in the version I was memorizing, I had to keep and order the instructions to think about whatever is *true, honorable, right, pure, lovely.* I took the first letters of each—*thrpl*—and realized if I used a bit of a cartoon affectation to my voice, I had "thriple," as in that baseball rarity, a thriple play! OK, it is a triple play, but I had my memory point. I had each word in the thriple play: true/honorable/right/pure/lovely.

From there, this has been an action verse in life. Anytime I find myself struggling or straying, worrying or fretting, purposeless or adrift, distracted or unfocused, I go to my thriple play. I force myself to think of something that is true. Jesus is my first go-to here, for he is the truth (Jn. 14:6). Thinking about Jesus as truth makes it easy to transition to what is honorable. Jesus is eminently worthy of respect, but so are many others, both living and historical. I find their lives inspiring as they handle great difficulties. Things that are right and just always take me back first to God. His rightness and justice are fundamental features but go hand in hand with his mercy. *Pure* has the same root in Greek as *holy* (*hagnos*—ἁγνός). It is an attribute of the divine in Greek. *Lovely* includes ideas of being amiable, pleasing, or delightful. As all these terms are rooted in the character of God, unsurprisingly, thinking about each brings the God of peace front and center in my mind, and that is always transformational!

Lord, guide and refine my thoughts through this thriple-ness in Jesus, amen.

JULY 31

Paul, an apostle of Christ Jesus by the will of God, and Timothy our brother,
To the saints and faithful brothers in Christ at Colossae:
Grace to you and peace from God our Father. (Col. 1:1–2)

Email simplifies things for me. I type in the name/address of whomever I am emailing; I put a subject in the appropriate place, and then I write my email. The software automatically puts me in as the sender. If I write a letter longhand, I must identify myself, write the recipient's name, and then insert my substance, although in a legal missive, I may still handwrite a "re" line indicating the subject.

Our Western world didn't invent forms for writing letters. They existed in the time of Paul. I have set out today's passage in a way that shows a modern equivalent of Paul's usage of the ancient form of letter writing. Letters in Paul's day typically consisted of the identity of the author, the identity of the recipient, and then the greeting.

Today's passage begins the series of devotionals through the book of Colossians, a church inland from Ephesus where Paul himself hadn't been but Paul's assistant Epaphras had. Paul's way of using the current writing conventions is worthy of note. Paul writes as "an apostle by the will of God." This addition to his name indicates several important matters. First, Paul is acting with God's authority in this message. Paul is carrying God's message. Second, all of us have our godly callings in this world because of God's will. Whether we collect garbage, teach students, or work in an office, we are to seek to do what God intends for us in life.

Paul addressed his readers, this fellowship of believers in Colossae, as "saints" (holy ones in Jesus) and "brothers and sisters" (the Greek word for *brothers* had a generic usage for both genders, much like our word *mankind*). This informs me of the intimacy and family tightness one believer should have for another.

Paul deviates slightly from the typical greeting of his day. The typical greeting to a Jew would be "peace" (*shalom*) or maybe "mercy and peace." The typical Greek greeting would be "grace." Paul sets them together.

We often live ordinary days in ordinary lives. But even in that, we can be inspired by Paul's writing. We should infuse the ordinary with the extraordinary God, seeing our purpose before him and extending that out to those we meet.

Lord, give me your eyes to see life rightly. In Jesus, amen.

AUGUST 1

Of this you have heard before in the word of the truth, the gospel, which has come to you, as indeed in the whole world it is bearing fruit and increasing—as it also does among you, since the day you heard it and understood the grace of God in truth. (Col. 1:5–6)

In law school, my moot court coach, Don Hunt, called an initial session after the team was chosen and announced. At that meeting, Coach explained that he expected everyone to put their faith and family first and their schoolwork second, but then he wanted all the rest of our time. I lived with those priorities until my buddy and pastor Jarrett helpfully suggested to me a better model. He suggested that we think of life as a wheel with faith at the center. Then all we do—family, school, work, and so on—becomes spokes that are led by and infused with our faith.

For Paul, all of life was wrapped up in the truth that Jesus Christ was crucified for our sins and then resurrected into a new life. The believer joins that new life through faith. Hence Paul wrote to the Corinthians that he had resolved to know nothing among them except Christ crucified (1 Cor. 2:2). The death of Christ applied to all aspects of life, enduing it with meaning and purpose. Today's passage echoes that truth, albeit in different words.

Paul writes of the "word of the truth, the gospel." He also calls it the "grace of God in truth." Both are references to the death and resurrection of Jesus. *Gospel* is the translation of a Greek compound noun meaning "good news" or "good message" (*eu-angelion*—εὐ-αγγέλιον). Now certainly there is a spectrum of good news—for example, the birth of a child, landing a new job, and so on. But that all pales in comparison to the ultimate good news: because Jesus died for our sins, we have been declared by the Judge of the ages "not guilty," and the door is open for us to walk in fellowship with God for eternity.

This greatest of news is functionally equivalent for Paul to "*the* grace of God." Paul uses a word (*charis*—χάρις) that speaks of a "favor" God has done for or given us. The death of Christ was no accident. It wasn't simply the fruit of a Roman system of justice run amok. It was a deliberate favor God did on our behalf. We find, in the death of Christ, ultimate love that infuses us with love, direction, gratitude, purpose, comfort, security, confidence, and joy. It changes everything.

Lord, I embrace the grace of Jesus for my sins, in gratitude and love. In him, amen.

AUGUST 2

He is the image of the invisible God, the firstborn of all creation. For by him all things were created, in heaven and on earth, visible and invisible, whether thrones or dominions or rulers or authorities—all things were created through him and for him. And he is before all things, and in him all things hold together. And he is the head of the body, the church. He is the beginning, the firstborn from the dead, that in everything he might be preeminent. For in him all the fullness of God was pleased to dwell, and through him to reconcile to himself all things, whether on earth or in heaven, making peace by the blood of his cross. (Col. 1:15–20)

When a judge enters the courtroom, a bailiff typically announces, "All rise!" Everyone stands. If John Doe walks into a room and someone announces, "All rise," the situation is vastly different. Rise for whom? Is the person worthy or qualified for honoring?

A similar question exists for God and Jesus. Is God worthy of honor and obedience? Does or should Jesus make any real difference in life? If so, what is the difference? The answer to these questions requires a scrutiny of who Jesus is.

Paul gives an expansive résumé of Jesus. Jesus is a visible image of the invisible God. See Jesus, see God. Jesus existed before creation. He is the Creator. Beyond creation of everything, Jesus is also the Sustainer. Without Jesus holding existence together, all would cease to exist. Jesus has, then, critical cosmic importance. Beyond that, however, Jesus is also present in personal ways.

Jesus heads up a collection of souls that compose his "church." Jesus—God incarnate—died and was resurrected for eternity, something theretofore unknown. His death and resurrection are something his collection of followers will share. Not because they (we) won a lottery ticket. It isn't simply our lucky day. We share in his resurrection because the Triune God agreed and planned in eternity past that his death be a substitute for our many rebellions against God. Our hostility toward God is removed, and peace reigns. This is part of the résumé of Jesus.

Jesus rightly commands our faithfulness and trust. He is rightly our Lord, the one whom we follow in obedience. This Jesus will transform our lives through his death and our simple obedient faith. We will never be the same. Amen.

Lord, words can't describe your awesomeness. But I live in awe of you. Thank you for your love and life, and may I better live for you today. In Jesus, amen.

AUGUST 3

Now I rejoice in my sufferings for your sake, and in my flesh I am filling up what is lacking in Christ's afflictions for the sake of his body, that is, the church, of which I became a minister according to the stewardship from God that was given to me for you, to make the word of God fully known, the mystery hidden for ages and generations but now revealed to his saints. (Col. 1:24–26)

When I was young, I would often roam the aisles of our local Christian bookstore looking for something interesting, educational, and inspiring to read. I stumbled on a book on Colossians by William Barclay, entitled *The All-Sufficient Christ.* I grabbed it, studied it, and grew from it. But the title, an encapsulation of Barclay's view of Paul's letter to Colossae, struck me as odd considering today's passage. Is Paul writing that something is missing in Christ? Paul says his own suffering is "filling up what is lacking" in the suffering of Christ. Did Christ not suffer enough? Does Christ need Paul, or anyone, to fill up for his lacking? I asked these questions in a bit of a shortsighted or at least naïve mind-set. I was thinking like a twentieth-century westerner and not as a first-century Jew!

Christ was and is all-sufficient in his life, death, and resurrection. As the very image of God, Christ is everything we need. Yet Christ left humanity with work to be done. God calls each of his followers to deny themselves, take up their crosses, and follow him (Lk. 9:23). We follow Jesus and obey his commands not because he is lacking. In fact, we are living with his Spirit within us. The life we live is *his.* Instead of thinking that Paul is writing about us filling some inadequacy of Christ, we should understand that we are fulfilling the mission and purpose of Christ. We are his hands and feet, walking and working on earth.

This leads Paul into calling Christ the "mystery hidden for ages" revealed. Since the fall in the garden of Eden, prophecy has pointed to Christ as the sacrifice to restore justly those who should rightly be destroyed as marred, sinful, and broken. Christ suffered to bring about this restoration, and now as his people, we continue his work, proclaiming his good news and the mystery of God's redemptive work. God often uses suffering in our lives as a way of teaching us to understand others, as a path to God's comfort, and as the necessary instrument by which God's kingdom comes. That isn't Christ insufficient; that is what Christ made possible.

Lord, I give you my life in good days and bad. Empowered by your Holy Spirit, may I live for your glory in Jesus. I thank you that he is fully sufficient to and for me. I pray in his holy name, amen.

AUGUST 4

Christ, in whom are hidden all the treasures of wisdom and knowledge. (Col. 2:2–3)

As a young lawyer, I was handed a slim book on writing by two lucid professors, William Strunk and E. B. White. The book, *Essential Elements of Style*, set out simple principles to make someone a better writer. Rule one was "Omit needless words." I remember reading that and trying to think of a way to rewrite it with just two words rather than three. I couldn't. I think they reduced the rule as far as possible.

In today's passage, Paul not only omits needless words, but he also omits needless theology! Paul makes a succinct and powerful affirmation of a critical truth about Jesus. In Christ are hidden all the treasures of wisdom and knowledge! Consider the implications of Paul's important affirmation built into five of his words.

Paul writes that Jesus is all "wisdom and knowledge." These two somewhat related yet distinct words are important. "Wisdom," especially as used by a writer like Paul conversant with the Hebrew concept (*ḥokmāh*—חָכְמָה), can be thought of as seeing reality and life the way God sees it. It is a rich term in the Hebrew and is rooted in God, his perspectives, insights, and so on. "Knowledge" carried more of an intellectual element—not excluding wisdom but changing the emphasis a bit. Together, these words speak of knowing what one needs to know and having it in right perspective for life.

Paul wrote not of "limited" wisdom and knowledge but of "all" wisdom and knowledge. These two "treasures" are all available in Jesus. Paul uses the word for the ancient equivalent of bank deposits, what one might store in a treasury. True wisdom and knowledge are invaluable commodities to anyone trying to successfully traverse the complexities of life. All that we need to understand, live, and succeed is found hidden in Christ. Yet for the Christian, they aren't simply stored in Christ. Instead, Isaiah 45:3—which in the Greek uses the same words translated as "hidden" and "treasures"—assures us that God will give his people "hidden treasures" so they might know that he is the Lord God calling us by name!

So today, I am assured that all I need for life is found in Christ. That truth drives me to know Christ better, one of the reasons I previously wrote my devotional *Jesus for Living*!

Lord, teach me Jesus, with all the treasures he gives even as I pray in Jesus, amen.

AUGUST 5

Therefore, as you received Christ Jesus the Lord, so walk in him, rooted and built up in him and established in the faith, just as you were taught, abounding in thanksgiving. See to it that no one takes you captive by philosophy and empty deceit, according to human tradition, according to the elemental spirits of the world, and not according to Christ. (Col. 2:6–8)

We were staying right outside Oxford, England, in a small country house. I had gone into town to get some needed groceries. I arrived at the store and went through the aisles filling my shopping cart, only to find that I had left my wallet at home! Whoops! That made for a needless back-and-forth, wasting a good bit of my time.

My memory of that day echoes in my mind as I think through Paul's message in today's passage. As was noted yesterday in discussing Paul's preceding verses, all the treasures of wisdom and knowledge are found in Christ. Christ doesn't hold those treasures in an inaccessible bank vault; he imparts them to those of us who have received him. Christ dwells in the hearts and minds of his followers. Because of that, his followers have access to the wisdom and knowledge of Christ as we live. It is a bit like me having in my wallet all the money and plastic I needed for groceries.

Paul then gives a very important instruction. He tells his readers to "walk in Christ." In other words, don't leave home without him! Don't let the world beguile you into thinking that the necessary wisdom and knowledge of life can be found in your own wisdom, strength, or anywhere else other than Christ.

All around us, we are bombarded with messages about how to think and live. Watch the ads on TV. How often does society urge us to value things over people? The message is to store up earthly treasures, with no consideration to divine ones. Countless television shows hold up asserting our own rights over the rights or needs of others. Constant messages of the value of power, the attraction of beauty, and the affirmation of popularity are boldly before us, as well as subtly disguised.

Yet the Christian can and should slice through the empty deceits of the world, taking Christ with us as we go. We are to be rooted in Christ, built up in Christ, and walking daily in Christ. Our focus is no more or less than to glorify God by walking in godliness all our days. We have all we need; let's take it with us in life!

Lord, walk with me and teach, encourage, and guide my life today. In Jesus, amen.

AUGUST 6

For in him the whole fullness of deity dwells bodily, and you have been filled in him, who is the head of all rule and authority. (Col. 2:9–10)

Earlier in the day, I was ordering a teapot to go with some teacups. I am an occasional tea drinker, and I like a pot that will hold about four cups of tea. I will pour from the pot, drink a cup, and repeat three times. It works great.

The teapot ordering is fortuitous timing with today's passage. Paul wrote of "the whole fullness of deity" dwelling in Christ's body. The meaning of "fullness" in Greek is akin to filling a teapot to the brim (*plērōma*—πλήρωμα). Mark used it to refer to how much bread and fish were left after Jesus fed the five thousand: "twelve baskets *full*" (Mk. 6:43).

Jesus wasn't simply a good fellow. Followers of Jesus aren't simply following an ethical teacher of good morality. Jesus was truly God. As Paul had written earlier in this letter (quoting an early church hymn), "For in [Christ] all the *fullness* of God was pleased to dwell" (Col. 1:19). Jesus had referenced much the same thing in his final night praying that his followers would have unity as Jesus had unity with God the Father: "That they may be one even as we are one" (Jn. 17:22).

But Jesus doesn't just possess the "fullness" of God as a teapot full of tea. For Paul explains that God sees that the followers of Jesus are also filled (same word in the Greek as that for "fullness"). Believers don't contain the fullness of God as Jesus did, but as teacups are filled by a teapot, so Jesus fills his followers.

This changes life. We have the divine Jesus imparting his presence in believers and appropriating gifts to them. This echoes Jesus' prayer in John 17 that his followers "may have my joy *fulfilled* in themselves" (Jn. 17:13). Jesus was praying that his full joy would be poured out, filling his followers. ("Fulfilled" in John 17:13 also has the same Greek root as the word Paul used in Colossians.)

As I live day to day, I need to remember that God seeks to fill me with all I need. Feeling pressed? Ask Jesus to fill you with patience. Struggling with sin? Ask Jesus to fill you with forgiveness. Besieged with loneliness? Ask Jesus to be your friend. Whatever your needs today, Jesus is full of God and can fill you up!

Lord, fill me with your love, peace, and holiness. Rule over my head and heart. I pray in Jesus, amen.

AUGUST 7

And you, who were dead in your trespasses and the uncircumcision of your flesh, God made alive together with him, having forgiven us all our trespasses, by canceling the record of debt that stood against us with its legal demands. This he set aside, nailing it to the cross. (Col. 2:13–14)

After a barrage of tests at the doctor's office, I was emailed a bill. The tests and visit cost a certain amount, but I didn't have to pay it all. Insurance paid some of what was due, and I paid the rest. No one likes paying debts, but they are part of life. Bills come due and need to be paid.

Paying bills and obligations are nothing new. The same were part of life in Paul's day. Today's passage calls on that practice to explain what happened in a cosmic, eternal sense when Jesus died on the cross. The passage begins by explaining that apart from Christ, people are "dead" in their trespasses. Paul doesn't say folks are sick or terminally ill; they are *nekros* (νεκρός). That is the word used for a corpse! Dead people can't accomplish anything. Dead people can't pay their bills. Dead people can't negotiate. Dead people are dead!

Yet something unheard of happened. God brought life back to the dead. God made dead people "alive with Christ." God did so by seeing that our debts were fully paid. God didn't pay part of our debt, as the insurance company did for my medical tests. God paid the whole bill. All the legal demands associated with the owed debt are fully satisfied. God paid the debt he didn't owe because we owed the debt we couldn't pay.

This profound truth has deep ramifications. It means that I am no longer a zombie, the walking dead. I have in me the real and eternal life that is found only in Jesus. This fact changes the way I see life. No one can strip me of the love Christ has for me, nor the value he assigns to me. Regardless of what the world throws my way, I know that I am treasured by one who has already purchased my new life. I have a Lord who is not only God but also my friend. His love for me is unsurpassed. He has shown it in transformational ways.

I rightly sing songs of rejoicing, reveling in my debt-free status. Alive in Christ, owing no one, but having a chance to show love to all, just as God has loved me. What a marvelous life God has given his children!

Lord, thank you for paying my debts and bringing me to life in Jesus, my amen!

AUGUST 8

If then you have been raised with Christ, seek the things that are above, where Christ is, seated at the right hand of God. Set your minds on things that are above, not on things that are on earth. For you have died, and your life is hidden with Christ in God. When Christ who is your life appears, then you also will appear with him in glory. (Col. 3:1–4)

In 2023, we moved my New York City office from one building to another. Our new offices were high enough in the building to command a great view of Madison Avenue. The offices were newly fitted out with the latest in electronics, a spotless new kitchen, fresh carpet, fresh paint, and new furniture. It was *nice*! The first time I went, walking in from the street, I stopped at the security desk. The woman behind the desk, Jenine, was nice. The lobby was relatively stark and, other than security, not notable. I guess I could have stayed in the lobby, but why would I? My office was high up in the towered building. It was where I could do the work needed.

My experience helps me better apply Paul's passage for today. Paul wasn't speaking of offices, but he was speaking of the life of a Christian. Christians no longer live or work where they did before coming to faith. We are on a higher level. We have been "raised" with Christ. So we are to seek the things above, the things where Christ sits.

Paul makes a pun of sorts, as he wrote of "raised with Christ." Paul uses a word that harkens back to his earlier discussion of dying to the things of this world and being baptized into his death and raised with him in his new life. Yet Paul does so with a word that also speaks of being "higher up" or above the old life.

For Paul, this idea of being "above" with Christ means we should no more be living as we did when we were lower than I should be officing in the lobby of my new building. All the good stuff is higher up! Similarly, the Lord Jesus himself is up above at the right hand of God. That should be where we live and operate.

Practically speaking, this means I shouldn't live as I might live apart from Jesus. In God's presence, there is no room for our anger, wrath, malice, slander, obscene talk, lying, immorality, impurity, coveting, or evil desires or passions. We should resemble our God and Lord, living with compassion, kindness, humility, patience, love, and forgiveness. No lobby living for those who are living on high!

Lord, give me the presence of mind to live rightly in your presence. In Jesus, amen.

AUGUST 9

And whatever you do, in word or deed, do everything in the name of the Lord Jesus, giving thanks to God the Father through him. (Col. 3:17)

"Don't make me tell you twice," my dad was famous for saying. It came after he asked us as kids, for example, to clean up our rooms. Or if he instructed us in some other task or chore and later found that we never budged from watching cartoons on the television. I do remember, with a hint of guilt, thinking that his mere statement "Don't make me tell [or ask] you twice" was, in a sense, asking or telling a second time. Regardless, if something is said once, it should be enough. Twice is sometimes merited. But when someone says something three times, it certainly shouldn't go unnoticed!

In today's passage, Paul repeats an instruction three times, or at least in three ways. The core idea expressed is that Christians don't have a list of rules for behavior but rather have an attitude that is guided by the ethics and morality seen in Christ. So Christians are to live Christlike. The actions, character, and life of Christ (ideas all wrapped up in the expression "the name of the Lord Jesus") should be our guide for living.

This core idea of living in reference to Christ is what Paul says three times. First Paul says, "Whatever you do." Paul uses the Greek word *pas* (πᾶς). It means totality within the individual parts referenced. It could be translated as "whatever" or "all." It references anything one does. But Paul doesn't stop there. He then adds, "In word or deed," a common Greek expression that covered all of life. In Greek thought, everything fit into one of those two things, either something thought (existing in the world of words) or something physical (existing as something done). This common Greek expression is seen in the New Testament, as Jesus was "mighty in deed and word" (Lk. 24:19). Moses was also seen as powerful in word and deed (Acts 7:22). Paul is saying a second time, "Whatever." Even having said it twice, Paul then adds a third time with "Do everything."

What does this mean? No longer should we divide life's actions into three categories: (1) holy (things like church and evangelism), (2) normal (like doing dishes and driving to work or school), and (3) sinful. For the believer, everything is done to God's glory in Jesus. True spirituality includes how we wash dishes, change diapers, drive to the store, and more. We live *all of life* to God's glory!

Lord, may I give you every moment, in the profound and mundane. In Jesus, amen.

AUGUST 10

Wives, submit to your husbands, as is fitting in the Lord. Husbands, love your wives, and do not be harsh with them. Children, obey your parents in everything, for this pleases the Lord. Fathers, do not provoke your children, lest they become discouraged. Bondservants, obey in everything those who are your earthly masters, not by way of eye-service, as people-pleasers, but with sincerity of heart, fearing the Lord. . . . Masters, treat your bondservants justly and fairly, knowing that you also have a Master in heaven. (Col. 3:18–22, 4:1)

Mom and Dad taught us to play bridge at an early age. Kathryn and I didn't always want to play, but our parents figured out how to get us to the card table. I remember in third grade being given the choice. Mom declared, "Well, it's bedtime, so y'all go get ready and hop in bed." Then Mom paused, letting it sink in that the fun of the day was over. Mom then declared, "Although, if y'all want to play some bridge, we could let you stay up a bit late!" Saved by bridge!

Bridge is dependent on the hand of cards dealt. You can't stack the deck. You must bid and play off the cards you have. It reminds me of Paul's passage set out above. Paul wrote into the social institutions of his day. He didn't write seeking to rewrite society's established foundations. In a card sense, he played the hand that was dealt. That does *not* mean, however, that Paul didn't work within those institutions to bring the Christian ethic into them.

Roman society in Paul's day was built on the *familia*, or "household." The Greek societies had functional equivalents. Almost always the head of the household was the oldest living male, called the *paterfamilias*. This man held authority over the wife, the children (even adult children), and the servants. While the law afforded the *paterfamilias* extraordinary rights, Paul didn't. Paul insisted that husbands love their wives (an unusual command not found elsewhere in the society of Paul's day), not provoke their children (remember, this included adult children in the familias), and be fair to servants.

Paul was, in my card analogy, playing the hand dealt—but playing it well! He knew these actions within society's structures were based on who God is. It was "fitting in the Lord," came from "fear of the Lord," and recognized that we all have "a Master in heaven." God doesn't ignore the everyday aspects of life. God speaks into them, seeking to transform every believer into the godly people we can be.

Lord, help me better model Jesus in all arenas of life. In him I pray, amen.

AUGUST 11

Continue steadfastly in prayer, being watchful in it with thanksgiving. At the same time, pray also for us, that God may open to us a door for the word, to declare the mystery of Christ, on account of which I am in prison—that I may make it clear, which is how I ought to speak. (Col. 4:2–4)

My buddy Skip is a man of prayer. If you speak to him about any issue, problem, opportunity, or important moment, you will frequently hear him stop and say, "Let's pray about that right now." Similarly, I get emails frequently from two others who almost daily note that they have prayed for me that day.

Prayer is important. It is a difference maker. Today's passage contains both a practical call to prayer as well as insights into prayer. Consider these and weigh them with how prayer features in your own life.

Paul urges his readers to "continue steadfastly" in prayer. Paul used the Greek present tense to express the constancy of his instruction to pray. The idea is to "pray without ceasing," as Paul wrote elsewhere (1 Thess. 5:17). Paul then adds to be "watchful" in it. Paul wants his readers to be alert in prayer—aware of what is in need of prayer and praying with the mind, not mindlessly. Partnered with this petitioning of God in prayer is thanksgiving to God. This extends faith into prayer, as we can seek God's actions with confidence and appreciation for what God will do.

Paul then moves from the general instruction to pray to a specific instruction to pray for his ministry. Paul requests prayers that God would open doors for Paul to speak of Christ and to speak clearly of him. There is theological profundity wrapped into this. Surely it is God's will that doors be open for Paul to teach Jesus. That is not only God's will; it is the work of the Holy Spirit (Jn. 15:26; 16:8–14). Yet it is still something that causes Paul to call for prayer. Paul teaches, through his own life, that we need to pray for God's will. We cannot do the things of God that we are called to do without God stepping in and working within us. When we pray, we release God to do the things he wills to do. This is a profound interworking that Jesus anticipated as he explained that the Holy Spirit "will bear witness about me. And you also will bear witness" (Jn. 15:26–27).

My praying friends are great examples for all. Take time right now to pray God's will for open doors to speak of Christ. Seek to partner with God in his will.

Lord, please open doors and help me teach of Jesus by my words and deeds. Amen.

AUGUST 12

Walk in wisdom toward outsiders, making the best use of the time. Let your speech always be gracious, seasoned with salt, so that you may know how you ought to answer each person. (Col. 4:5–6)

Rebecca and Dan returned from a date to a Lebanese restaurant in New York City, proclaiming, "That was one of the five best meals we've ever had!" I asked what made the experience so great, and it wasn't the atmosphere. Nor did they recount the quality of their time together on the date. The service wasn't mentioned, and they didn't cite the value or cost. The meal stood out because the food was seasoned exquisitely. It was extraordinarily tasty.

The experience of Rebecca and Dan should be the experience others have when they hear the words and see the life of Christ followers. Today I will be in front of a watching and listening world. I need to take advantage of every moment I have to show that Jesus is Lord and that it makes a difference to me.

Many tend to isolate church manners from everyday lifestyle manners. We can be nicer, speak gentler, and demonstrate a bit more patience when in church or around Christians, but when in the world, the manners might flip, the language gets rougher, the patience wears thin, and the gentleness evaporates.

This shouldn't be. Each day has twenty-four hours. Most days we get very limited time interacting with folks. I might have a few sentences in conversation, or I might have an afternoon conference. Either way, Paul knew and taught that as believers, we are to live and speak carefully. We should be seeing each encounter as a chance to proclaim Jesus as Lord. Paul's comment here comes right on the heels of his asking for prayer that God would open doors for him to speak of Jesus and do so clearly. If we see every encounter as God answering a prayer, giving us a chance to show Jesus, then we might find our Sunday manners apply each day.

Self-examination is tough. We can easily deceive ourselves and not realize where we can improve. By aiming to make each encounter one where we have the goal of exalting Jesus as Lord, we are setting ourselves on a path to live as Paul instructed. Rebecca and Dan had one of their best meals because of how the chef seasoned the food. Let's season our lives to give others the best experience of Jesus!

Lord, help me live a winsome life for Jesus to your glory. In him, amen.

AUGUST 13

I have sent [Tychicus] to you for this very purpose, that you may know how we are and that he may encourage your hearts, and with him Onesimus, our faithful and beloved brother, who is one of you. They will tell you of everything that has taken place here. . . .

Paul, a prisoner for Christ Jesus, and Timothy our brother, To Philemon our beloved fellow worker and Apphia our sister and Archippus our fellow soldier, and the church in your house . . . (Col. 4:8–9; Philem. 1–2)

I bought some white tennis shoes. Gorgeous. The white was so stark and clean, both in the leather and on/around the sole. I wore those shoes for months, almost wearing them out. Over time they yellowed a bit. I would get them dirty and wash them. I knew they weren't as clean as they had been when brand-new, but I never realized quite how dingy they were until I got a new pair. Then seeing the level of grime and dirt, they became almost unwearable.

Life can be a bit like those old shoes. Live long enough, and you will have a backstory of grime. Some trudge through more mud than others, but no one has sports-white tennis shoes after much living. We all carry varying degrees of filth and muck. Today's passage sets that up but with an encouraging affirmation.

Today, I selected two verses that are near the end of Paul's letter to the church at Colossae and combined them with the first two verses of a short letter Paul wrote to Philemon, a leader in that church. Those two letters were likely delivered at the same time. In the larger letter to the whole church, Paul speaks of "Onesimus" as a "faithful and beloved brother." Onesimus was from Colossae, but Paul chooses to word it as Onesimus "who is one of you." Onesimus came out of Colossae but in an unusual way. Onesimus was a runaway slave! He had fled the household of Philemon and as such, under Roman law, was subject to capital punishment.

In the accompanying letter to Philemon, Onesimus' owner, Paul asks forgiveness for Onesimus and subtly seeks his release from slavery. Paul sees the now-saved Onesimus as a Christian brother, not as Philemon's personal property. Onesimus had a backstory of grime—a runaway slave. But something happens with God. He takes our backstories and makes us new and shiny in Christ. I am glad. I need that too.

Lord, please wash me, clean me, and make me new in Jesus, amen.

AUGUST 14

I thank my God always when I remember you in my prayers, because I hear of your love and of the faith that you have toward the Lord Jesus and for all the saints, and I pray that the sharing of your faith may become effective for the full knowledge of every good thing that is in us for the sake of Christ. For I have derived much joy and comfort from your love, my brother, because the hearts of the saints have been refreshed through you. (Philem. 4–7)

If something frustrating or unfortunate happened—say one of us dropped a glass of water and broke it—my dad would usually say, "Well, if that's the worst thing that happens, you're going to have a good day!" I loved the way that thinking put life's events into perspective. Suddenly the unfortunate event didn't seem so bad.

Perspective is important, and we do well to align our "todays" with the reality of God's eternity. In today's passage, Paul helps his friend Philemon do that very thing. Paul writes from imprisonment. While under arrest, Paul encounters a young runaway slave, Onesimus. The slave comes under Paul's influence and the power of the gospel transforms the slave. The slave becomes a Christian.

Paul sends the slave Onesimus *back* to the household from which he had fled. Under law, the penalty could be as severe as the slave owner wished—even death. Paul doesn't send Onesimus bare but gives him a letter to give to his owner, Philemon. In that short one-chapter letter, Paul puts the runaway slave's actions into perspective. He had fled a rebellious lad, but he was returning a full-fledged Christian brother, indwelt by God's Spirit and born again into God's kingdom.

So in these early words of this important letter, Paul writes of the "love" and the "faith" that Philemon has not only for the Lord Jesus but for "*all* the saints." That now includes the runaway! Paul, who has shared faith with the runaway, now sends him back, praying that Philemon will also be sharing his faith "*for the sake of Christ*"! Paul continues noting his personal joy and comfort from Philemon's refreshing "the hearts of the *saints*," which also now includes Onesimus.

Perspective can change our attitudes and actions. We should all live cognizant of God's eternity and God's purposes. They are more important than our temporary comfort, our entitlements and rights, and our treatment from others. Our lives should reflect our faith in God's eternal plans.

Lord, give me your insight for life today. May I live for you in Jesus, amen.

AUGUST 15

I appeal to you for my child, Onesimus, whose father I became in my imprisonment. (Formerly he was useless to you, but now he is indeed useful to you and to me.) I am sending him back to you, sending my very heart. . . . Confident of your obedience, I write to you, knowing that you will do even more than I say. (Philem. 10–12, 21)

Encounters with God alter you. Sometimes the encounters transform you and turn you from what you were into what you can be. A dear friend of ours struggled with addiction, strung out on heroin and prostituting herself to pay for her habit. She was part of a convenience store robbery that left a clerk wounded by a gunshot from her co-criminal. Following her arrest, she was defended by a very prominent lawyer whom she paid with sexual favors. She was sentenced to a facility rather than a jail. In the facility, she had an encounter with God. She met Jesus, and her life changed on the spot. In a moment, her addiction was gone, she was radically transformed, and now forty years later, she still lives on fire for the Lord.

Some encounters transform you in smaller ways. We make choices that bring us nearer to God and closer to who we can be as his followers. Nothing as radical as my friend but notable nonetheless.

In today's passage, we see both radical and notable transformations. Onesimus' transformation was radical. This slave, whose name in Greek means "useful," was far from useful to his owner Philemon. In fact, he ran away from Colossae and his owner, fleeing to the city of Paul's imprisonment. There he met Paul and then met Jesus. This useless fellow was radically transformed and ready to return and face his punishment for running away. He left useless but returned useful.

The more subtle transformation was coming to Philemon. Paul didn't tell Philemon to release Onesimus from slavery in direct or blunt terms. Paul said to treat him like the Christian brother he'd become. Paul said to put Onesimus' debt on Paul's account. Paul said to welcome Onesimus back, not punish him for his wrongdoing. Then Paul said that he knew Philemon would "do even more."

Every day is a chance for an encounter with God. He can radically change us or subtly transform us—either way, we are altered for the good when under the influence of our God.

Lord, change me today. Mold me as you will in Jesus, amen.

AUGUST 16

I appeal to you for my child, Onesimus, whose father I became in my imprisonment. . . . I would have been glad to keep him with me, in order that he might serve me on your behalf during my imprisonment for the gospel, but I preferred to do nothing without your consent in order that your goodness might not be by compulsion but of your own accord. For this perhaps is why he was parted from you for a while, that you might have him back forever, no longer as a bondservant but more than a bondservant, as a beloved brother—especially to me, but how much more to you, both in the flesh and in the Lord. (Philem. 10, 13–16)

Consider these three clichés: (1) life gives you lemons, and you make lemonade; (2) when God closes a door, he opens a window; and (3) with God, there are no coincidences. Each one can be nitpicked for inaccuracies, if not outright errors. However, each also contains a certain amount of truth, and hence they are somewhat commonly used expressions. Their usage stems from the complexities of life and how difficulties become fertile ground for blessings as life unfolds.

Those clichés lace through today's passage. Onesimus was a runaway slave from Colossae, the household of Philemon. Philemon was a respected pillar in the growing church there. As noted yesterday, Onesimus' name meant "useful." It was a common slave name, but records do not show its use among free children.

During his runaway period, Onesimus met Jesus and became a Christian. Paul sends Onesimus back to face the consequences of his fleeing and notes this phrase to his owner, Philemon: "This perhaps is why he was parted from you for a while, that you might have him back forever"—no longer a slave but a brother! Paul knew that God was at work, even in the lawbreaking of a runaway slave.

History doesn't directly tell us what happened to Onesimus, but we have some hints. Somewhat bizarrely, around the time Onesimus would have become an old man, assuming he ran away as an adolescent, an "Onesimus" became the bishop of the church in that region. This wouldn't be a position for a slave, so someone likely was born a slave, was freed, and became a prominent church leader. This was also the time and location where Paul's letters were gathered into the group of ten now in the Bible. Folks wonder why the personal letter to Philemon was included, and I reckon it's possible that the slave-turned-freedman had something to do with it. God works that way. I wonder how God is working in my life today.

Lord, work through the challenges in my life for the good of your kingdom, amen.

AUGUST 17

Blessed be the God and Father of our Lord Jesus Christ, who has blessed us in Christ with every spiritual blessing in the heavenly places, even as he chose us in him before the foundation of the world, that we should be holy and blameless before him. (Eph. 1:3–4)

Witty wordplay has been a hallmark of several of my friends. For some, like Kevin, it manifests in puns made with a humorous purpose. For others, like Joseph, it is almost a scholastic way of bringing interest to a written matter or subject. The apostle Paul was a fan of wordplay. A marvelous example unfolds in today's passage.

The passage above is part of the opening salvo in Paul's letter labeled in most Bibles as "Ephesians." (The scholastic community is divided over whether this letter was written to the Ephesians. It opens, "To the saints who are in Ephesus," but the words "in Ephesus" seem to be added after the original letter.) Paul blasts onto the scene with his threefold wordplay with Greek puns on "bless."

The God and Father of our Lord Jesus Christ is to be "*blessed*" or "praised." We bless and praise God because he has *blessed* us. How has he blessed us? Paul's third pun explains God has blessed us with every spiritual *blessing* in the heavenlies. Paul then details these blessings in the verses that follow. The blessings include choosing us to be holy and blameless; to be his sons and daughters, incorporated into the family he oversees, provides for, and protects; to be redeemed and forgiven (because we are *not* the holy and blameless people we were designed to be!); and to be aware of God's great design for the culmination of history.

Paul's wordplay isn't an accident. Nor is it for humor. Paul is weaving a beautiful tapestry that exalts the great plans of the one who is from before all time. Your life and mine are no accident. We didn't stumble onto God in some serendipitous moment. God didn't have a plan B to save us from our sins. All the blessings we experience from the Blessed One are intended. God decided to love you and me. God decided to rescue you and me. God decided to bring you and me to the proper fruitful eternity of existence that only he could make. This is indeed a cause for great praise.

Lord, I praise you for your work of love in my life—that you love me, save me, treasure me, re-create me in holiness, and more. I deeply thank you in Jesus, amen.

AUGUST 18

In him we have obtained an inheritance, having been predestined according to the purpose of him who works all things according to the counsel of his will, so that we who were the first to hope in Christ might be to the praise of his glory. (Eph. 1:11–12)

My daughter Rebecca taught me how to do Sudoku puzzles. These mathematical, logical exercises are great. They have a grid with rows of boxes going across and down, a bit like a crossword puzzle but with no black squares. A select few single-digit numbers are placed in what seems to be a random pattern. The puzzle is then to be "completed." Once completed, every row across and every row down will include the digits zero through nine. An added feature is that the boxes are also divided into collected squares, each of which will also have the digits zero through nine upon completion. When done right—that is, the puzzle has all the digits—there is only one solution. The puzzles are interesting but also a metaphor for God's plans and human activity explained in today's passage.

People choose how to live. Today I can choose whether to follow God or walk in sin. It is my real choice. No one makes me choose. Similarly, heading into the crucifixion of Jesus, Pilate, Herod, and others made real choices to indict and punish Jesus. In a sense, these choices of ours become digits placed in Sudoku boxes. The remarkable thing is that even when people make choices in life that are contrary to God's will, life unfolds according to God's master plan. Our sinful choices are fully considered as he sculpts history into his divine will. So for example, Herod's and Pilate's decisions, evil though they were, culminated in the death and resurrection of Christ, God's foreordained mission (Acts 4:27–28).

Thus, Paul says God "works all things according to the counsel of his will." Though people disobey God at every turn, history itself shows God using all decisions to bring about his divine purposes. This process of God letting people select their own "Sudoku numbers" and yet having the completed puzzle present the precise picture of his ultimate will is beyond remarkable. It is that complicated reality of free choice and divine will living in tension and truth.

Beyond being a theological reality, however, this truth has practical implications. Regardless of what happens in this life, I can rest assured that God will triumph in my life, bringing to reality his purposes in and through me. Praise God!

Lord, I praise you for your work through and even in spite of me! In Jesus, amen.

AUGUST 19

In him you also, when you heard the word of truth, the gospel of your salvation, and believed in him, were sealed with the promised Holy Spirit, who is the guarantee of our inheritance until we acquire possession of it, to the praise of his glory. (Eph. 1:13–14)

When I was courting Becky, I wasn't alone. I had three incredible children who joined me in that courtship. In almost a *Sound of Music* likeness, my children were as enamored of Becky as I was. So when I got ready to propose, the children accompanied me to the jeweler. While I picked out an engagement ring, each child picked out their own choice of jewelry to give Becky. Then with all of us in procession, we each gave Becky our gift of promise and asked her to marry me and, in a sense, the children. Becky tearfully said "yes," and you will still see that jewelry on her today.

Our engagement trip to the jewelry store as part of the proposal comes to mind in today's passage. In the verse prior to today's verses, Paul referenced Jewish believers in Jesus who were "first to hope in Christ" to the glory of God. Now Paul adds that Gentiles ("you also") who came to faith in Christ were "sealed with the promised Holy Spirit." Paul accurately recounts God's historical unfolding of the growing kingdom. Starting with the Jewish conversions on Pentecost, the church grew with Gentile conversions like that of Cornelius in Acts 10. The key to seeing the Gentile inclusion was the Holy Spirit coming upon Cornelius (Acts 10:44–48). Similarly, when the early Jewish church debated whether Gentiles could come into the church without first becoming Jews, the decision was rooted in the reality of the Holy Spirit indwelling the Gentiles without Jewish conversion (Acts 15:8).

The indwelling Spirit is the "guarantee" of our inheritance until we acquire possession after this life ends. Here Becky's engagement jewelry takes center stage. Paul's word for "guarantee" is an old Semitic word that made its way into Greek through commerce (*arrabōn*—ἀρραβών). It was a pledge or object a purchaser gave to be held by the seller until the final payment was made. Modern Greek uses a form of the word for an engagement ring (*arrabōna*—ἀρραβῶνα)!

God places his Holy Spirit in the believer. The Spirit isn't just for teaching and training us in righteousness. The Spirit is the real presence of God. He validates our faith with the promise of our inheritance in Christ. A wedding is in the offing!

Lord, I long for eternity in your presence. Thank you for your Spirit in Jesus, amen.

AUGUST 20

I do not cease to give thanks for you, remembering you in my prayers, that the God of our Lord Jesus Christ, the Father of glory, may give you the Spirit of wisdom and of revelation in the knowledge of him, having the eyes of your hearts enlightened, that you may know what is the hope to which he has called you, what are the riches of his glorious inheritance in the saints, and what is the immeasurable greatness of his power toward us who believe, according to the working of his great might that he worked in Christ when he raised him from the dead and seated him at his right hand in the heavenly places. (Eph. 1:16–20)

My buddy Skip eats sardines. So does my wife. I don't. I like a good piece of fish as much as the next person, but not a can of oily, eye-looking-at-you sardines. No thank you. That said, I do find it interesting how many sardines they cram into a can. "Packed like sardines" is a common expression for a reason. It is also an apt metaphor for today's passage.

Paul prays that the God of our Lord Jesus Christ, a full title for the Holy One, will give readers a Spirit of wisdom and revelation in the knowledge of Christ. I don't want sardines, but I do want that! The ever-expanding opportunity to know Jesus better and to have a greater measure of his wisdom is a prayer I keep in my own heart for me and those in my circle of influence. This is chock-full of implications. It includes having the eyes of our minds and hearts enlightened. We have greater insight, deeper faith, and an ever-growing awareness of the hope of our calling.

The word for "hope" in the Greek carries the meaning of a "confident expectation," not a pie-in-the-sky wishful dream. This confidence in God grows as we grow in our knowledge and wisdom. We begin to better understand his riches for us and his power working in us. God's power is no small thing. It's the resurrection power behind Christ's work.

As a teaching point, Paul's lesson today is instructive, but even more important, as a devotional point, it is powerful. This means that all the struggles and challenges in life are more readily met as I grow in loving, understanding, and following Jesus. In his wisdom and power are the resources needed to confront all aspects of life. I need have no fear, only faith. Doubts erase, and confidence takes root. As I know Christ, I become convicted and convinced of his interest in me, his plans for me, and his power to bring those to fruition. Praise God!

Lord, I stand amazed in your presence. I need your love and power today and every day. May your Spirit enlighten my mind and heart in Jesus, amen.

AUGUST 21

And you were dead in the trespasses and sins in which you once walked, following the course of this world. . . . But God, being rich in mercy, because of the great love with which he loved us, even when we were dead in our trespasses, made us alive together with Christ—by grace you have been saved. (Eph. 2:1–5)

COVID hit the world, and it affected my family, my friends, and me. Many of us got sick, some badly. My brother-in-law had long COVID with certain symptoms that lasted for months. One of my daughters lost her sense of smell for almost a year. Thankfully, they each recovered, but several friends died from COVID.

Although it seems obvious, it is worth noting there is a difference between being ill—even very ill—and being dead. Knowing this, Paul's verses used in today's devotional strike me for Paul's health metaphor. Speaking of his reader's spiritual life before coming into their Christian walk, Paul doesn't say they were sick. He doesn't say they were extremely sick. Paul says they were *dead.*

Paul's view isn't an accident; it is a biblically based truth. The fruitlessness of death, the uselessness of death, the directionlessness (if such were a word) of death are the condition of those who live apart from Christ. God had warned of these consequences when telling Adam, "Of the tree of the knowledge of good and evil you shall not eat, for in the day that you eat of it you shall surely die" (Gen. 2:17). Certainly, sinning against God began the physical death process, but spiritual death also occurred on the very day Adam and Eve ate and rebelled against God. Hence they began hiding from God, knew shame, and were set on the road that would lead to physical death as well.

Left on our own, we are not godly. We live, as Paul wrote, "in the passions of our flesh." We carry out selfish desires rather than living in God's realm of selfless love (Eph. 2:3). But for the believer, the story doesn't end in death. For just as Christ died but was resurrected, so the believer is made new in Christ. Christians are made alive by the grace of God in Christ, which infuses everything with new meaning and purpose.

I am loved by God, sought by God, forgiven by God, and transformed by God. Praise be to God!

Lord, thank you for the life I experience in Christ. May I live it daily in honor of you! In him, amen.

AUGUST 22

For by grace you have been saved through faith. And this is not your own doing; it is the gift of God, not a result of works, so that no one may boast. For we are his workmanship, created in Christ Jesus for good works, which God prepared beforehand, that we should walk in them. (Eph. 2:8–10)

Dr. Floyd turned and wrote on the blackboard three columns, with the titles "Cause," "Means," and "Result." He then invited the class to turn to Ephesians 2, and beginning with verse 8, he produced today's passage (albeit he was doing so in Greek!). Dr. Floyd explained that many of Christian history's errors came from confusing the three columns he had written on the board.

Under "Cause," Dr. Floyd wrote "Grace." He then explained that in Greek, this noun (*charis*—χάρις) is rooted in a beneficial action one takes, gift one gives, or favor one does for another. Dr. Floyd then drew a picture of a cross. He explained that Paul was referencing the death of Jesus on behalf of humanity, the death of Jesus "for our sins." "The cross of Christ is the cause of salvation, nothing more and nothing less. This is the pure gospel!" Dr. Floyd explained, adding, "Christ crucified is *the* grace of God."

Under "Means," Dr. Floyd wrote "Faith." He explained that Paul's Greek noun (*pistis*—πίστις) carries a deeper idea than only mental recognition. The word includes the idea of trust and deep conviction. It is a confidence and belief that transforms. Dr. Floyd then said that while the cross of Christ is the cause of salvation, the means by which that salvation is embraced by a person is faith and faith alone. Paul doesn't want anyone deceived on this important point. We aren't saved because we are good enough. No one is good enough to walk personally with God. God redeems people to walk by faith.

Under "Result," Dr. Floyd wrote "Good Works." He explained that one with a biblical faith in the atoning death of Christ will walk in good works. Good works are important, but never to be confused as the cause or means of salvation. However, if one doesn't have good works, a warning light should go off. Such a person should examine his faith in the work of Christ. For assuredly, if one is trusting in Christ, one seeks to walk in good works. God prepared those works specifically for each believer. We should all be seeking them and living in them to the glory and praise of God!

Lord, I trust you for my salvation. May I walk in your good works in Jesus, amen.

AUGUST 23

Remember that you [Gentiles] were at that time separated from Christ, alienated from the commonwealth of Israel and strangers to the covenants of promise, having no hope and without God in the world. But now in Christ Jesus you who once were far off have been brought near by the blood of Christ. For he himself is our peace. (Eph. 2:12–14)

The drive for segregation is endemic, at least for many. "Us versus them" isn't simply a college football rivalry. It manifests itself in society through race and ethnicity, nationalism, political affiliation, religion, age, cultural ideologies, socioeconomic levels, and more. My lawyer friend Fred Gray has spent seventy years battling segregation through the civil rights movement. He represented Rosa Parks, Martin Luther King Jr., and many other notable people on causes seeking to abolish segregation in all forms.

Fred draws his motivation for his calling from Scripture. Trained first as a preacher, Fred has been in pulpits teaching Jesus for more decades than he has been in courtrooms. Fred can find no greater example for destroying segregation than Jesus Christ.

Paul wrote at a time when the segregation of the day was especially notable between Jews and Gentiles. Jews were God's chosen people, a select race, and they knew it. As Paul said elsewhere, they were "entrusted with the oracles of God [Scripture]." They had the "sonship," experienced the "divine glory," received "the covenants" and "the law," were given "temple worship," and were promised the blessing of bringing forth the Messiah to bless the earth (Rom. 3:2; 9:4–5). The Gentiles, on the other hand, were basically everyone else. Many Jews, as part of their daily prayers, would thank God that they weren't born a Gentile.

Yet Paul saw that Jesus' death and resurrection result in a radical transformation in racial relationships. No longer was there a segregation of Jew from Gentile. Jesus united them both. Furthermore, as Paul noted elsewhere, Jesus united the segregated genders, socioeconomic classes, and more. People are one in Christ. In a dual sense, Jesus brought peace—peace among people and peace between people and God. The church should readily show great diversity united by the blood of Jesus. All believers are made one in Jesus, meaning one with one another and one with God. Unity is God's amazing work we should all seek to follow.

Lord, show me where to help your cause of uniting people in Christ. In him, amen.

AUGUST 24

For this reason I, Paul, a prisoner of Christ Jesus on behalf of you Gentiles—assuming that you have heard of the stewardship of God's grace that was given to me for you, how the mystery was made known to me by revelation, as I have written briefly. (Eph. 3:1–3)

My mom believes firmly in the premise "Treat someone like a dog, and they become a dog." She attests also to the opposite: treat someone special, and they become special. This is one reason that my mom, as we grew up, levied expectations of godliness and purpose in the lives of her kids. Mom wasn't trying to sculpt us into something we weren't; rather, she worked to rear us into what we truly should be—servants of the Most High King.

Because of Mom's influence, verses like today's jump out at me. They should jump out at all followers of Jesus. Paul lived with purpose. Paul originally believed he was serving God by fighting against the fledgling growing Christian community. While on a trip pursuing believers in the resurrected Christ, Paul was personally visited by Christ. Paul's life turned on a dime. God then began revealing to Paul the truth of who Christ was, what he did, and how that not only fulfilled Scripture but also contained the true destiny of humanity. Paul spent the rest of his life teaching God's truth as revealed to him.

Paul used the phrase "the stewardship of God's grace." His word "stewardship" (*oikonomia*—οἰκονομία) referred to work of a steward, one who had the role and responsibility of managing another's household or estate. This stewardship work included ordering and managing the estate or home, training the staff, putting necessary plans in place, and so on.

Paul understood that his journey of life had become "the stewardship of God's grace." Paul's life wasn't built around his own wants or desires. His life belonged to God and was, in a real sense, entrusted to him by God.

This understanding of Paul's applies to you and me. All believers in Jesus aren't simply saved people. We are saved and set apart for purposes of God. Paul referenced that earlier in Ephesians 2:8–10; we are saved "for good works, which God prepared beforehand." Mom was right to instill purpose in us kids. We do have purpose before God, and we should live in it!

Lord, help me see my purpose in your kingdom, walking in it through Jesus, amen.

AUGUST 25

To me . . . this grace was given, to preach to the Gentiles the unsearchable riches of Christ, and to bring to light for everyone what is the plan of the mystery hidden for ages in God, who created all things, so that through the church the manifold wisdom of God might now be made known to the rulers and authorities in the heavenly places. This was according to the eternal purpose that he has realized in Christ Jesus our Lord, in whom we have boldness and access with confidence through our faith in him. (Eph. 3:8–12)

One Christmas, Becky and I knew we had something special—all five of our children, their spouses, and all their kids (ten grandkids as of that year!) were coming home. From the West Coast to the East Coast, from the north and from the south, all our brood would be together under one roof. Becky and I decided no holds were barred on that Christmas. Santa came, gifts were aplenty, and joy was all around. When the holiday neared its end, I walked in on one daughter packing. She was trying to squeeze so much into her suitcase she needed to sit on it to zip it.

Her overpacked suitcase comes to mind reading today's verses. Paul packed so much into these few lines that one page can't do them justice. Paul writes on his theme of Christ being the "mystery" of God. Books are written on the ancient idea of "mystery" (*mustērion*—μυστήριον). For centuries before Paul, the word was used in certain religious and cultic senses. Also in Judaism, the word was used in pre-Pauline literature referencing secrets revealed by angels toward the end of days.

For Paul, the idea of "mystery" wasn't rooted in the ancient Greek cults, nor was it something purposely hidden and unable to be known by most. For Paul, the mystery was something akin to a box where God had placed his plan of redemption. For ages, that box had been closed, and while God had indicated the box had salvation's plan and gave prophetic hints, the plan wasn't understood until the box was opened. Then the mystery that was Christ crucified became known.

Like my daughter's suitcase, Paul's passage is overstuffed. He speaks of "mystery" as "hidden for ages" and built into the fabric of God's creation. It is now to be proclaimed to all. The secret is revealed, the box is opened, and all should see God's magnificent plan of unsearchable riches flowing from the divine Jesus Christ. This opened box changes us. It teaches us we can boldly come before God in Jesus!

Lord, in Jesus we ask in confidence for you to be our aid in all we do. Amen.

AUGUST 26

For this reason I bow my knees before the Father . . . that according to the riches of his glory he may grant you to be strengthened with power through his Spirit in your inner being, so that Christ may dwell in your hearts through faith—that you, being rooted and grounded in love, may have strength to comprehend with all the saints what is the breadth and length and height and depth, and to know the love of Christ that surpasses knowledge, that you may be filled with all the fullness of God. (Eph. 3:14–19)

Name three people you care about. Who comes to mind? As we think of people, it is an important biblical injunction to pray for them. Often we might not know what to pray for, and in those situations, passages like today's ride to our aid. Paul gives his prayer for his readers in words that can guide our prayers for others.

Paul prays for his readers to be "strengthened with power" through God's Spirit in their inner being. If the prayer had a full stop there, the prayer would be a great example to us. After all, God's Spirit had the power to resurrect Jesus from the dead. This is no ordinary power! It is unlike any known on earth. If this unique power were to strengthen the weak, the consequences would be unimaginable!

Paul prays that this Spirit-infused strength will be in his readers (and us) for a purpose. He wants them to grow in the faith of Christ dwelling in their hearts. When we rely on Jesus indwelling within us, when we understand and trust God's very presence within us, then our lives take on a whole different perspective. Fears fall, replaced by faith. Priorities are reordered. The impossible becomes possible. Despair dissolves and joy arises.

Paul prays his readers will be "rooted and grounded in love." Wow! What a game changer. Living life where love supplants anger, patience takes the place of frustration, and emptiness is inhabited with the purpose and comfort that come from a real presence of the Almighty. This prayer doesn't end without Paul affirming the great love of Christ, the full love of God, that guards and protects his people. This is a prayer to both quote and use as a model for our loved ones.

So with your three people in mind, or maybe more, pray with me: God, grant them strength through your Spirit in their inner beings. May Christ dwell in them through faith, rooting and grounding them in love to better comprehend your deep and abiding love in Jesus. May they be filled with your fullness. In Jesus, amen.

AUGUST 27

Now to him who is able to do far more abundantly than all that we ask or think, according to the power at work within us, to him be glory in the church and in Christ Jesus throughout all generations, forever and ever. Amen. (Eph. 3:20–21)

Do you have a "life verse"? Have you heard of having a "life verse"? I hadn't heard of one for most of my life but encountered the phrase first through my friends David and Beverly Fleming. When they had first gotten married, out of the 31,102 verses in the Bible, they chose today's passage as their "life verse." They had it engraved on a stone kept by their front door to see it daily. They prayed over it and made it the modern equivalent of a medieval coat of arms. More than a family motto, it was the verse that best described their experience with God.

Not having grown up with the concept of a "life verse," I've never had one per se. My favorite verse in Scripture varies daily. If I were to choose one, however, this would certainly be in the top ten! So much about this passage shouts off the pages of Scripture into everyone's life.

First, the passage is true. If our eyes are open to the hand of God, we see that he's able to do not only what we ask but even what we think. In fact, he's able to do *more*—exceedingly more, exceedingly *far* more—than anything we ask or anything we think. Paul's Greek piles on the ability or power of God in much the same way as I have in that sentence. This is the power of God, and that power is at work in us. Of course, God will not work to our harm or detriment, nor will he work in ways that damage his kingdom, so we shouldn't use this as an excuse to make God into a genie. But look at the stars at night in a vast universe. Consider the intricacies of the DNA genetic factory. These are the works of a powerful God.

Importantly, Paul isn't using today's passage to generate an affirmation like Philippians 4:13 ("I can do all things through him who strengthens me"). Paul in today's verses draws attention to the level of praise appropriately flowing to God. Because of God's inconceivable greatness and unfathomable power, we who experience that power, who have been called from sin and death into eternal life and fellowship, rightly give all glory to God for all time. We all ascribe and echo Paul's amen! We should all revel in knowing, belonging to, and worshiping such an amazing God! That is certainly "life verse" worthy!

Lord, I give you praise, honor, glory, and worship. I live in awe of you and your exceeding greatness. Thank you for knowing me and loving me. In Jesus, amen.

AUGUST 28

There is one body and one Spirit—just as you were called to the one hope that belongs to your call—one Lord, one faith, one baptism, one God and Father of all, who is over all and through all and in all. (Eph. 4:4–6)

My friends Michael Card and John Michael Talbot are gifted musicians with hearts and minds for the Lord. Mike worships in a Protestant expression of Christianity. John Michael is a Roman Catholic Christian. In 1996, they released a joint project, *Brother to Brother.* It has the unifying song "One Faith," whose chorus uses today's passage. The chorus repeats, "There is one faith, one hope, and one baptism, one God and Father of all."

When the album came out, our daughter Gracie was seven. Becky and I heard Gracie one day walking around the house singing the chorus—but singing it through the ears of a seven-year-old: "There is one faith, one hope, and one bad visit . . ." We laughed, thinking in the vein of meatloaf, two out of three ain't bad! Gracie notwithstanding, the verses in today's passage are profound, and having them as the root of a joint song between two friends who come from different strands of Christianity magnifies their significance. We live in a world that often finds meaning and expression in disunity. An "us versus them" mentality permeates much of politics, nationalism, foreign policy, and even social relationships. We have adages like "Birds of a feather flock together" and "Like seeks like." The idea that "you are known by the company you keep" can be a driver to put people into different camps.

Yet the plea of Scripture, and the prayer of Jesus before his arrest, is that the people of God would be unified. Jesus prayed that his followers would be one—in the same unifying sense that God the Father and God the Son are one (Jn. 17:22). This doesn't just *seem* countercultural; it *is* countercultural. We may verbally acknowledge that "united we stand; divided we fall," but we don't often see this in practical expressions. That is why Jesus explained his unity desire as one that would show the world in unique ways that Christian faith is alien to the world's systems. It is of divine origin.

I may not agree with other Christians about everything. We may even have the occasional "bad visit." But I should seek to live with unity, not division.

Lord, teach me unity in love for all your people. In Jesus I pray, amen.

AUGUST 29

But grace was given to each one of us according to the measure of Christ's gift. Therefore it says, "When he ascended on high he led a host of captives, and he gave gifts to men." (In saying, "He ascended," what does it mean but that he had also descended into the lower regions, the earth? He who descended is the one who also ascended far above all the heavens, that he might fill all things.) (Eph. 4:7–10)

Bob Dylan's 1975 release "Simple Twist of Fate" speaks of the role that timing and fate may have in failed relationships. The song has a simple melody, but each verse's description of an encounter ends with "a simple twist of fate." That song plays in my head as I reflect on today's passage. Paul is writing about a successful relationship between God and his people, not a failed one. The relationship isn't failing; it is succeeding. The success is due not to fate but to the work of an all-knowing, almighty God. One might fairly ask why Dylan's song echoes in my mind when it seems so different from the passage. It's because Paul is making his point with a simple twist of Scripture!

Now, Paul isn't twisting Scripture in a bad way. Rather, he makes a twist to heighten its meaning. Paul's Scripture comes from Psalm 69:18. Paul quotes directly from the Greek translation of the Hebrew that was commonly used in his day. But Paul makes a change! The Greek he had likely read, "You ascended on high, leading a host of captives in your train and *receiving* gifts among men." That Psalms passage speaks of a king leading a processional with those he captured paraded before the throngs as the king received gifts.

Paul turns the picture upside down. After God as King came "down" to earth and conquered his enemies on the cross, he led a processional back "heavenward." But the King of kings, unlike the king in Psalm 69, doesn't receive gifts *from* humanity. Rather, he gives gifts *to* humanity! These are gifts to build his church, to meet the needs of his people, and to make the world a better place.

Paul didn't make this twist without a likely source. Scholars have found that this twist was present in some ancient Aramaic paraphrases of the passage. Paul's usage is no accident. Paul knows our God is a giving God who seeks to make our lives the best and most useful they can be. Let's thank God for his gifts!

Lord, thank you for your love and gifts. You have every right to receive, and yet you give over and over again. I pray in the name of Jesus, your greatest gift, amen.

AUGUST 30

You must no longer walk as the Gentiles do, in the futility of their minds. . . . They have become callous and have given themselves up to sensuality, greedy to practice every kind of impurity. But that is not the way you learned Christ! . . . as the truth is in Jesus, to put off your old self, which belongs to your former manner of life and is corrupt through deceitful desires, and to be renewed in the spirit of your minds, and to put on the new self, created after the likeness of God in true righteousness and holiness. (Eph. 4:17–24)

Life has few consistencies, but one is that every morning, almost without exception, I take off my pajamas and put on my clothes. I can't think of any day I have gone to work wearing pajamas. (Well, during the COVID lockdown, *maybe.*) Somewhere around age four, our kids learn to do this themselves—take off their pajamas and put on their clothes.

Paul uses the Greek words for that process in today's passage. Paul says that his readers are to "put off" their old self and "put on the new self." Paul's word for "put off" (*apotithēmi*—ἀποτίθημι) is the ordinary word for taking off one's clothes. Similarly, Paul's word for "put on" (*enduō*—ἐνδύω) is the typical word for getting dressed.

Our approach to life today and everyday needs to be not only one where we get dressed for our daily activity but also one where we get dressed for our Christian walk. We should not live as those who don't know Jesus. We have learned better (assuming we have learned about him). We take off the empty and purposeless existence of the world. We don't live without meaning, simply getting through each day trying to find our greatest happiness of the moment. Instead, we seek to live with holiness. We live right before God and people. We seek his purity. We live with purpose.

The "get dressed" analogy might break down if we aren't careful, hence the translators' hesitation to use blunt language of dressing. The breakdown can occur if we think it's right at the end of the day to get undressed and put back on our sleeping clothes. Paul doesn't want us to ever be undressed spiritually. Our Christian faith is a 24/7 journey. We are to follow God and live with purpose every minute of every day. So let's consciously walk in God's holiness, with purpose. Let's get dressed!

Lord, may I walk in your ways daily, with your kindness and love in Jesus, amen.

AUGUST 31

Therefore be imitators of God, as beloved children. And walk in love, as Christ loved us and gave himself up for us, a fragrant offering and sacrifice to God. (Eph. 5:1–2)

In the 1970s—an era of great transition and change, with bell-bottom jeans, big (and long) hair, polyester leisure suits, miniskirts, and more—came a Van Camp's Pork and Beans commercial with a fantastic jingle. The melody was memorable and the lyrics notable: "Life's simple pleasures are the best, all the little things that make you smile and glow, all the things you know; life's simple pleasures are the best in all the world." Simplicity has a great allure. Simple things are easy to understand, remember, and live.

In today's passage, Paul gives simple instructions for living the right Christian life. In a summation form, Paul explains we are to imitate God. It's that simple. Paul expresses that truth with the added statement "Walk in love." No greater expression of God can be found than love. Jesus came because "God so loved the world" (Jn. 3:16). Jesus died for others because "greater love has no one than this, that someone lay down his life for his friends" (Jn. 15:13).

Paul uses his famous word for love, *agapē* (ἀγάπη). This word for love denotes a regard for and interest in others. It includes esteem and affection but is also rooted firmly in the idea of serving and caring for others. It is seen in God's care for humanity. Paul explains it in the verses around today's passage.

Already, Paul has instructed the readers to be honest, not let anger turn to sin, work hard for what you get, not speak with words or tones that would hurt or corrupt others, use words to build others up, and eliminate bitterness, wrath, slander, and ill-will for others. Instead, be kind to others, with a tender, caring heart and ready forgiveness. Paul will go on to instruct his readers to stay far from sexual immorality, impurity, coveting, filthiness, crude joking, and foolish talking.

In short, Paul says it simply: imitate God. There is beauty in his simplicity. It gives a general principle to follow, even as he gives examples of what that following looks like. I need this to stick in my head like that old jingle I remember fifty years later.

Lord, imprint on my mind the rule to imitate you daily! In Jesus' name I pray, amen.

SEPTEMBER 1

Look carefully then how you walk, not as unwise but as wise, making the best use of the time, because the days are evil. (Eph. 5:15–16)

Some don't like to shop. I love it. It isn't so much walking through stores, looking at everything. That quickly turns to drudgery. I like buying—especially in bulk. I could be ground zero for starting a twelve-step program of those buying at wholesale clubs where I find I am getting things "I need" even though I no more need them than the man in the moon.

Perhaps that is why I am drawn to Paul's phrase "Making the best use of time." The New English Translation (NET) translates it as "Taking advantage of every opportunity." It's a fascinating phrase in the original Greek. The phrase in Greek is *exagorazomenoi ton kairon* (ἐξαγοραζόμενοι τὸν καιρόν). That first long word is a participle built off the Greek word for "market" (*agora*). The word has a core idea of purchasing or buying something. Paul combines it with one of two Greek words for "time." Importantly, Paul does *not* use *chronos* (χρόνος), with its emphasis on chronological time (dates, time of day, duration of activity, etc.). Instead, Paul uses *kairos* (καιρός), the word conveying the importance of the moment without regard to chronology.

If the last paragraph is a blur, let me put it in an appropriate metaphor apart from the Greek. Paul says life has placed you in a store. You are on the aisle that affords you a chance to buy something. You may not get on this aisle again. This is the time to make the choice of whether to buy it. What you are purchasing is the opportunity to live in this world in a way that draws you closer to God and his will while also pointing others in that direction. Your purchase is the choices you make, attitudes you hold, love and kindness you cultivate, and similar ways of following the Lord.

Paul carefully explains that time is unique to us all. We all must live with a conscious awareness of how we are buying our time each day. We don't want to fritter away our purchasing power. We want to use each moment carefully. This isn't buying in bulk. Nor is it window-shopping. It is living wisely in this world, moment by moment.

Lord, give me the wisdom to count the days and seconds. Let me live aware of you and with your holiness my first pursuit. Help me express this in love for others, with kindness and mercy toward all. In Jesus' holy name, amen.

SEPTEMBER 2

And do not get drunk with wine, for that is debauchery, but be filled with the Spirit . . . submitting to one another out of reverence for Christ. Wives, submit to your own husbands, as to the Lord. For the husband is the head of the wife even as Christ is the head of the church, his body, and is himself its Savior. . . . Husbands, love your wives, as Christ loved the church and gave himself up for her, that he might sanctify her, having cleansed her by the washing of water with the word, so that he might present the church to himself in splendor, without spot or wrinkle or any such thing, that she might be holy and without blemish. (Eph. 5:18, 21–23, 25–27)

Growing up in Lubbock, Texas, I frequently saw a bumper sticker that declared Lubbock "the hub of the Plains." In some ways that was true. The High Plains of the Texas Panhandle have countless small farming communities that all came to Lubbock for serious shopping, banking, health care, and more. Lubbock was the hub with spokes going in all directions.

For Paul, the incarnation, death, and resurrection of Jesus were the hub of all life. Years before he wrote Ephesians, Paul had written that his resolution among the Corinthians was "to know nothing among you except Jesus Christ and him crucified" (1 Cor. 2:2). From Paul's faith in Christ stemmed not only his preaching and teaching but also his understanding of Scripture, his purpose in life, and his entire ethic. Today's passage is a prime example.

Paul understood that the relationship between husbands and wives met its highest purpose and use in the light and focus of Christ. Paul sets that up with the general comment that all his readers should be submissive to one another, a concept he drove home earlier in his Philippians discourse of Christ submitting to humanity to the point of death so that he might save his people (Phil. 2:5–11). Here Paul speaks of Christ loving his church by giving himself up for her, something husbands should emulate for their own wives. Paul will continue to speak of Christ and the church as the most profound understanding of God's explanation of marriage in Genesis that the two "become one flesh" (Gen. 2:24; Eph. 5:31–32).

Think of this with Jesus at the center. God became human, dying for each of us, which rightly puts life into a different focus. Christ becomes the hub of all we think and do. His direction infuses life with rich meaning and purpose.

Lord, show me Jesus in ways to teach me a holy life. In him I pray, amen.

SEPTEMBER 3

Finally, be strong in the Lord and in the strength of his might. Put on the whole armor of God, that you may be able to stand against the schemes of the devil. For we do not wrestle against flesh and blood, but against the rulers, against the authorities, against the cosmic powers over this present darkness, against the spiritual forces of evil in the heavenly places. (Eph. 6:10–12)

As a young man, I devoured the teachings of Watchman Nee. Born in 1903, Nee (his Chinese name was Nee Shu-tsu) became a Christian in high school at age seventeen. The change was profound. He began writing and publishing at the age of twenty-two and traveled China preaching and teaching until 1952. His last three years of travel came as the communist government, the People's Republic of China, took power. In 1952, Nee was arrested for the sake of the gospel, and he died in prison in 1972.

Among Nee's better-known books is his explanation of Ephesians, entitled *Sit, Walk, Stand.* Compiled from a set of lectures Nee gave, the book's title is based on three postures Paul gives in Ephesians, with the instruction of how those should affect the Christian living in Christ before others and in battle with the enemy.

Nee first notes that Paul says the believer is raised with Christ to be "seated . . . with him in the heavenly places" (Eph. 2:6). This comes on the heels of Paul using the same word to describe how God seated Christ in the heavenlies after his resurrection (Eph. 1:20). The Christian must first understand his relationship with God in Christ if he is to sustain the Christian life.

Paul's second posture word is *walk.* This takes center stage in Ephesians 4:1. At that point in his letter, Paul has written "theology" and is moving to his "practical" instructions. They begin with the Christian who understands the position of being seated with Christ as walking in a manner worthy of that position. Nee wants the believer to get Paul's order. We don't walk to sit; we must first understand our position (sitting) before we are able to walk properly.

Only then does Paul get to the Christian's posture against the demonic and spiritual forces in life. Today's passage is the posture culmination with the injunction to "stand" against the devil's schemes. Nee explained that the first two postures—understanding our seat with Christ and walking in his holiness—enable us to stand against the enemy.

Lord, may I sit with you, walk before you, and stand against the enemy. Amen.

SEPTEMBER 4

Therefore take up the whole armor of God, that you may be able to withstand in the evil day, and having done all, to stand firm. Stand therefore, having fastened on the belt of truth, and having put on the breastplate of righteousness, and, as shoes for your feet, having put on the readiness given by the gospel of peace. In all circumstances take up the shield of faith, with which you can extinguish all the flaming darts of the evil one; and take the helmet of salvation, and the sword of the Spirit, which is the word of God, praying at all times in the Spirit, with all prayer and supplication. (Eph. 6:13–18)

My buddy Skip is a man of prayer. When you talk to Skip, any problem, issue, and opportunity is always met with "Well, let's pray about it!" followed on the spot with his prayers. So I wasn't surprised when I got an email from him one day talking about his daily prayers based on this passage from Ephesians. Inspired by Chuck Swindoll, Skip began praying for his armament each day. Paul walks through the various pieces of armor typical for a Roman soldier in that era.

Paul's use of a soldier is not accidental. The Roman soldier was the backbone of Rome's peace (the Pax Romana). In a day with no consistent police force, the Roman soldiers served to keep the Roman Empire intact. They were viewed as reliable and able to withstand greater numbers and forces arrayed against them. In this vein, Paul continues to use the "stand" language I discussed in yesterday's devotional, explaining the daily armor is what allows the believer to stand against the power of the evil day.

Paul does this in the spirit of Old Testament passages that teach that God arms himself with "righteousness as a breastplate" and "a helmet of salvation" (Isa. 59:17). Paul laces his metaphors with many defensive weapons but also with one offensive weapon: the "sword of the Spirit, which is the word of God." This was the weapon wielded so effectively by Jesus in responding to Satan's temptations in the wilderness (Mt. 4). Paul's words can be the basis of wonderful words of prayer, today and each day. Unsurprisingly, he uses them to bring his letter near the close.

Lord, clothe me in your armor so I might stand against the evil in this world. May my belt be truth, with no room for lies, my breastplate being the righteousness of Christ, my feet walking and proclaiming the gospel of your peace. Give me a shield of faith, a helmet of salvation, and the ability to wield your word. In Jesus, amen.

SEPTEMBER 5

Paul, an apostle of Christ Jesus by command of God our Savior and of Christ Jesus our hope, To Timothy, my true child in the faith: Grace, mercy, and peace from God the Father and Christ Jesus our Lord. (1 Tim. 1:1–2)

People who like lists can often cite their five favorite movies, but who can list the five most important spiritual influencers in your life? Authors don't count. Who are the five or so people that have spoken into your life in ways that have helped you grow and develop spiritually? I encourage you to write in the margin five people in your life, and thank God for them. For me, I had my family, of course, but beyond that, I think of certain preachers from my youth—Joe Barnett, Ken Dye, Charles Mickey, and Don Finto—all of whom gave love and lessons that formed me then and echo in my memory up to fifty years later. Rick Reynolds, Steve Robinson, and J. D. Hancock were ten years older than me and important mentors when they took an interest in my spiritual development. Even in adulthood, with pastors David Fleming and Jarrett Stephens, dear friend Louis Miori, and more, I have had the blessing of people speaking into my life in important spiritual ways.

These and many more come to mind, as they are important people I thank God for as I come to today's passage. This passage begins Paul's first letter to his younger coworker Timothy. Deemed by scholars over the last two centuries as a "Pastoral Epistle," this letter begins with Paul calling Timothy "my true child in the faith."

My mind goes in two directions thinking through today's passage: backward and forward. Looking back, I see those I mentioned above, and I am thankful for them. I pray God blesses those still alive, and I seek to give them honor. Looking forward, I think about those whose lives I might try to influence for good.

The world surrounds you and me with people old and young. It is easy to stay within a circle of comfort, spending our energy with those we know well. But today's passage calls us into relationships beyond our natural comforts. We should seek opportunities to speak into others' lives in positive, God-building ways. I don't mean we dictate a "Thus sayeth the Lord" instruction into how others live. But we should be trying to help others through winsome ways as we teach and model growing older in the Lord.

Lord, open my eyes to those I can influence for your good. Help me grow as a spiritual mentor, spreading your joy to another generation. In Jesus' name, amen.

SEPTEMBER 6

I thank him who has given me strength, Christ Jesus our Lord, because he judged me faithful, appointing me to his service, though formerly I was a blasphemer, persecutor, and insolent opponent. But I received mercy because I had acted ignorantly in unbelief, and the grace of our Lord overflowed for me with the faith and love that are in Christ Jesus. The saying is trustworthy and deserving of full acceptance, that Christ Jesus came into the world to save sinners, of whom I am the foremost. (1 Tim. 1:12–15)

Over the years, I have met multiple people who seriously doubted that God would forgive them. One was absolutely convinced that he had turned his back on God, and God would never allow him to return. In high school, he had turned his life over to the Lord but, in the succeeding years, had little to nothing to do with his faith. His early twenties were spent carousing, pursuing earthly pleasures, and ignoring the God of his youth. Then by twenty-seven or twenty-eight, he desperately wanted to return to his faith but believed God would have nothing to do with him.

I told my friend Jesus' parable of the prodigal son. This boy came of age, demanded the inheritance of his father, took it, went carousing, and wasted away every dime. My friend had done nothing beyond what this prodigal had done. Yet when the prodigal went home to beg for life with his father, the father ran to embrace him. Jesus wanted his disciples to know that God not only accepts sinners' return but even runs to receive them.

Despite that parable, my friend remained unconvinced. I then turned to Paul and today's passage. How can anyone think they sinned more than "the chief of sinners"? Christians were *dead* because of Paul. Paul denied Jesus in the most vehement fashion. Paul spent his energy seeking to destroy the work of God. Nonetheless, God took the chief of sinners, washed him clean, and set him on a mission to bring countless people into faith, establish churches around the Mediterranean, write ten books of Scripture, and nurture infant churches into sustaining and thriving fellowships. Ultimately, Paul would die a martyr's death, inspiring generations to come. Could my friend's sins outdo those of Paul?

God is in the saving business. He isn't seeking to exclude people from his love. He seeks out the lost. He wants all to be saved and working for his kingdom. How dare anyone think God lacks the power and mercy to use them for his service!

Lord, help me know and accept my forgiveness in Jesus, in whom I pray, amen.

SEPTEMBER 7

But I received mercy for this reason, that in me, as the foremost, Jesus Christ might display his perfect patience as an example to those who were to believe in him for eternal life. To the King of the ages, immortal, invisible, the only God, be honor and glory forever and ever. Amen. (1 Tim. 1:16–17)

Do you know the 1974 R&B classic by William DeVaughn, "Be Thankful for What You Got"? DeVaughn sang to folks with a catchy melody, "Though you may not drive a great big Cadillac, gangsta whitewalls, TV antennas in the back." When the song came out, I didn't even know what "gangsta whitewalls" were! (They are really cool tires!) But the song wasn't about driving. The car was an illustration of a greater truth. This came in the next set of lyrics: "You may not have a car at all, but remember, brothers and sisters, you can still stand tall. Just be thankful for what you've got." Fifty years later, I enjoy the song. Yes, it's catchy, but I like the point of being thankful in this life.

Paul has spent lines of ink speaking of his early life of sin before God. He culminates his memories of his rebellion with the fact of forgiveness, salvation, and purpose that came from the Lord Jesus. God saved Paul and put Paul on display to the world to show how a saving and merciful God loves and reaches into the darkest corners. When God reached Paul, Paul didn't have a life to be proud of. In the words of the DeVaughn song, Paul was reached at a time when he had no car at all. His life wasn't only worthless and sinful; it was seeking to wreck God's plans and church.

But God took Paul from sin, rebellion, blasphemy, arrogance, and more, and God washed him clean. Scales of Paul's fake holiness fell from his eyes, and Paul became God's tool for good. Paul might have wished to have always been on God's side, yet Paul knew that even his poor history with the Lord would become a means by which God reached others.

This rightly moved Paul to "be thankful for what you got." Paul ends his thought on his past with a proclamation of praise that is itself songworthy. The closing verse today was a song we sang in my youth group. It has served hymn writers through the ages. We would sing, "Unto the King of ages, immortal, invisible, the only wise God, be honor and glory forever and ever amen. Amen."

Lord, I join Paul in proclaiming you King of the ages, always alive though unseen, the only God rightly due my honoring and all glory for all time. In Jesus, amen.

SEPTEMBER 8

First of all, then, I urge that supplications, prayers, intercessions, and thanksgivings be made for all people, for kings and all who are in high positions, that we may lead a peaceful and quiet life, godly and dignified in every way. This is good, and it is pleasing in the sight of God our Savior, who desires all people to be saved and to come to the knowledge of the truth. (1 Tim. 2:1–4)

He had an inauspicious start. His mother killed her second husband and married her own uncle. That was how he came to marry his mother's stepdaughter. His mother then apparently orchestrated the murder of her uncle/husband. Thus sixteen-year-old Nero rose to the throne as emperor of Rome. Nero started out all right as emperor. He loved and fostered poetry, theater, and athletics, but he soon began using his power and position for personal pleasure. By age twenty-one (AD 59), his brutality was clear. He had his mother assassinated and had his wife killed three years later. If scholars accurately date this letter to AD 62–64, Paul wrote it within several years of his martyrdom under Nero's reign.

Yet with this dangerous, debased, tyrannical leader of the greatest empire known to the world at that time, Paul instructs his protégé Timothy to pray for "all people, for kings and all who are in high position." Paul wanted even Nero to be saved and come to the knowledge of the truth. I have no doubt Timothy did as Paul instructed. These prayers didn't cause God to make Nero a puppet. Nero could still refuse God, and history seems to indicate he did. Yet Paul knows that the responsibility of the believer is still to pray.

As I write this, we live in a politically divided time. The political parties are so polarized that at times, it seems if one party chooses the door, the other will exit via a window. Not all politicians are this way, nor are all voters. But I read Paul's letter and know that his instruction to Timothy applies to me as well. I am to pray for all people, those who agree with me and those who don't. Jesus even goes so far as to say, "Love your enemies and pray for those who persecute you" (Mt. 5:44).

I have a prayer list. Most on my list are family, friends, and those who have asked for prayer. Yet Paul tells me to pray beyond that. I have work to do.

Lord, I lift up to you all who are in power, our leaders from the president to the mayor. I lift up my neighbors, workers, and of course, family and friends. Bring them tightly to you, in Jesus, amen.

SEPTEMBER 9

For there is one God, and there is one mediator between God and men, the man Christ Jesus, who gave himself as a ransom for all, which is the testimony given at the proper time. (1 Tim. 2:5–6)

Certain commercial jingles I heard as a child still ring in my head decades later: "I am stuck on Band-Aids 'cause Band-Aid's stuck on me." Or Lay's potato chips—"No one can eat just one." Science explains how pathways form in our brains and we easily fall into those pathways, repeating songs, lines, and ideas.

Paul's brain was no different, and it makes a passage like today's jump off the page. Growing up a strong practicing Jew, Paul would have recited from his earliest memory the Shema three times daily. Named after the first word in Hebrew, *shema* (שְׁמַע), or "hear," Paul would have said for his whole speaking life, "Hear, O Israel: The LORD our God, the LORD is one . . ." (Dt. 6:4). When Paul begins today's passage with the affirmation "There is one God," Paul doesn't do so lightly. Paul is echoing his Shema, but with a twist!

Paul doesn't recite the entire Shema, which continues with the injunction to love the Lord with all one's heart, soul, and mind. Paul shifts to the way that God loves the world—that is, through the work of God in the incarnation of Jesus Christ. Paul explains that as God is one, so God has one way of mediating between himself and humanity. That mediation is done through the human work of Jesus Christ.

The divine God working through human flesh wrought a peace between God and humanity by overcoming the devastating and deadly consequences of sin. God tendered himself through Christ to pay for sin's wicked consequences. An eternal justice was met by Jesus Christ in human form "ransoming" you and me.

We must never forget the fact that Jesus was born, died, and was resurrected for a purpose. You and I are that purpose. Not because we are good enough, holy enough, caring enough, pretty enough, funny enough, popular enough, rich enough, successful enough, serious enough, driven enough, or any such thing. But simply because he loves us enough that he desires a just, holy, and eternal relationship with us. That unconditional love should change our day. It should alter how we see and treat others. It should put joy deep in our soul.

Lord, thank you for your love in Jesus. Thank you for your commitment to my good. May I respond in loving devotion by and in your grace. In Jesus, amen.

SEPTEMBER 10

I desire . . . that women should adorn themselves in respectable apparel, with modesty and self-control, not with braided hair and gold or pearls or costly attire, but with what is proper for women who profess godliness—with good works. Let a woman learn quietly with all submissiveness. I do not permit a woman to teach or to exercise authority over a man; rather, she is to remain quiet. (1 Tim. 2:8–12)

Optical illusions take advantage of the way our brain works when interpreting what we see. A famous one ("Rubin's Vase") has a picture that looks either like two people facing each other or like a vase. Which you see depends on whether your brain decides that the black is the background, while the white is the item of focus, or whether the background is white, and the black is the focus.

Our brains do a similar thing in reading a passage like today's. We must decide whether we read and interpret the rest of Scripture in light of this passage or whether, with the rest of Scripture as background, we understand and interpret this text accordingly.

Paul wrote in several other places about the role of women in the churches. To the Galatians, he said that in Christ, "There is neither Jew nor Greek, there is neither slave nor free, there is no male and female, for you are all one in Christ Jesus" (Gal. 3:28). To the Corinthians, he gave instructions on how women *were to preach and prophesy* in churches (1 Cor. 11). In an age where many Jewish leaders taught that it was improper for women to even study the five books of Moses (the ancient rabbinic teaching recorded in the Mishna in *Sotah Talmud Bavli* 21b says teaching your daughter the Torah is teaching them promiscuity), Jesus was emphatically clear that Mary was choosing a better thing by learning Torah over working in the kitchen (Lk. 10:38–42).

If these biblical passages serve as the background, then one sees here Paul addressing a prominent issue that must have arisen where Timothy was ministering. Paul describes women dressed in what was considered promiscuous clothing. Paul points out that these women weren't to dress as prostitutes or draw attention to themselves by how they looked. They were to learn quietly the virtues of being a Christian. In that, Paul has a lesson for all of us.

Lord, I honor your love for all. May my life reflect your values as I learn to walk holy in Jesus, amen.

SEPTEMBER 11

The saying is trustworthy: If anyone aspires to the office of overseer, he desires a noble task. Therefore an overseer must be above reproach, the husband of one wife, sober-minded, self-controlled, respectable, hospitable, able to teach, not a drunkard, not violent but gentle, not quarrelsome, not a lover of money. He must manage his own household well, with all dignity keeping his children submissive, for if someone does not know how to manage his own household, how will he care for God's church? He must not be a recent convert, or he may become puffed up with conceit and fall into the condemnation of the devil. Moreover, he must be well thought of by outsiders, so that he may not fall into disgrace, into a snare of the devil. (1 Tim. 3:1–7)

I'm a list guy. Give me a list, and I can get more done. I make lists of what to do each day, each week, and each month. If I go to the grocery store with a list, I can nail it. If I go without one, I wind up with a lot of stuff I don't need and inevitably fail to get something essential.

Passages like today's excite the list person inside me. Paul writes of characteristics one should find in an overseer of the church. While I don't seek to hold such office, Paul's description of the office as "noble" tells me the characteristics of its holders are important for anyone. Paul's word for "noble" (*kalos*—καλός) is rooted in ideas of beauty, goodness, and usefulness.

Paul then gives a checklist for traits associated with this beautiful and useful life. Several stand out to me as a married man. I should be loyal and faithful to my wife. My mind should think clearly, something that comes from learning about God, who renews our minds (Rom. 12:2). Self-control, gentleness, and kindness (not violence) are also fruits of the Spirit, things that come from walking in step with God (Gal. 5:22–25). Drunkenness, dissensions (in home and without), and divisions are works of the flesh that have no place in God's kingdom, among leaders or otherwise (Gal. 5:19–21). Paul also cares about how the church is perceived by a watching world. Paul not only adds traits that affect how the overseer fulfills the role in the church but also wants the overseer to be "well thought of by outsiders."

The list maker in me likes today's passage, although it also convicts me. These are noble and beautiful things I need to work on!

Lord, grow me in these traits to your glory and kingdom's good. In Jesus, amen.

SEPTEMBER 12

I hope to come to you soon, but I am writing these things to you so that, if I delay, you may know how one ought to behave in the household of God, which is the church of the living God, a pillar and buttress of the truth. (1 Tim. 3:14–15)

The household in the world of Paul was notably different from households today. Under the Greco-Roman society, a house was governed by the oldest male, who was considered the *paterfamilias* or "father of the family." This male was expected to establish the religion of the house, which all were required to follow. He also set up the house rules, which even the adult children followed. He provided for the house and its occupants and had virtually full authority to oversee all aspects of life for those under his authority. Even adult children were accountable to the *paterfamilias.*

Paul here writes of the household of God. He uses the structure of a well-known and long-established Roman society arrangement as a metaphor to explain the way Christians should walk in reference to God. Paul's term translated "ought to behave" (*anastrephō*—ἀναστρέφω) refers, among other things, to the rules and principles of conduct that a *paterfamilias* would put in place for his home. The household, however, isn't one found in contemporary society. Paul notes that the Christian belongs in the "household of God."

I pause reading this passage to ask whether I am living right in the household of God, in its full Greco-Roman sense. Do I identify as a member of God's household? Does the world see that I live under another's authority and that my God instructs me in my responsibilities? As a believer, I have the identity of one in God's family, and I also have his rules of accepted behaviors.

Paul extends his metaphor to ensure that all believers find their place in God's household, for the house of God is the assembly of those who belong to Christ. For Paul, there is only one church or body, even though it exists in any place where believers are found (Eph. 4:1–6). The church functions as the "pillar and buttress of truth" in this world. The church properly living under God's authority stands as a critical support for the truths in this world. In standing under God, the church can combat heresy within while also being responsible without to the world. These responsibilities all fall under living in the household of God as one "ought."

Lord, may I live readily thinking of you as my Father. May I identify as one of your household and care, following you in all you say as I live and pray in Jesus, amen.

SEPTEMBER 13

Great indeed, we confess, is the mystery of godliness: He was manifested in the flesh, vindicated by the Spirit, seen by angels, proclaimed among the nations, believed on in the world, taken up in glory. (1 Tim. 3:16)

I have a sister in the Lord, Lorraine, who regularly reads my daily devotion books. Almost without fail, she will send me an email with a note about the devotional she read and close the email with a link to a song that fits the devotional. Lorraine has songs in her soul. She thinks in song. Sometimes I think Paul did too. Paul often lapses into song verse, and he does so in today's passage.

Paul has spent the last few pages speaking of the roles various people have in the church and before the watching world. Paul wants people to understand the authority of God, the importance of following his instructions, and the keys to a godly life. Paul sums up his thoughts to this point with the lyrics to a hymn.

Before Paul sets forth these profound lyrics, he proclaims, "Great is the mystery of godliness." Paul's mystery idea for the church wasn't that one couldn't understand the truth. Rather, the mystery was something that had been hidden but was revealed by God in God's good timing. This mystery that was revealed in time is the subject of the song's lyrics.

The song contains three sets of two contrasting clauses. In the first set, Christ was "manifested in the flesh" and "vindicated by the Spirit," contrasting flesh and Spirit. Jesus was in fact born in flesh, even though his eternity and preexistence were shown by the Spirit's work in and through him. Set two has Christ "seen by angels" yet also "proclaimed among the nations," contrasting the angelic world's witness of the resurrected and reigning Lord with the proclamation of that resurrection before the world of people. The final set ends the song by noting the resurrected Christ is "believed on in the world" yet also "taken up" beyond this world "in glory." This is the revealed mystery of godliness—the crucified and risen Lord Jesus Christ.

Each of Paul's lyrics is written in passive voice. God is the one accomplishing the work in Christ. We see, proclaim, and believe, but God is the mover. God accomplished this work, hence our actions are rightly termed "godliness."

Lord, may I walk in concert with your actions in Christ, living to your glory. In Jesus' name, amen.

SEPTEMBER 14

Now the Spirit expressly says that in later times some will depart from the faith by devoting themselves to deceitful spirits and teachings of demons, through the insincerity of liars whose consciences are seared, who forbid marriage and require abstinence from foods that God created to be received with thanksgiving by those who believe and know the truth. For everything created by God is good, and nothing is to be rejected if it is received with thanksgiving, for it is made holy by the word of God and prayer. (1 Tim. 4:1–5)

In fourth grade, we began learning about negative numbers. It shocked me yet made perfect sense. On a line, going up one notch got me to a "positive one." If I went down one notch, I got a "negative one." The rules seemed basically the same; it was just going left instead of right, negative instead of positive.

People need to be cautious about applying rules of negative numbers to matters of faith. Some think of Satan and his demonic world as the negative or opposite of God and his kingdom. If God were a ten on the scale, some wrongly think of Satan as a negative ten. Yet Satan isn't God's opposite in strength, insight, or most any other thing. He is the opposite of God on only one point: Satan is evil.

In today's passage, Paul writes about the "later times," an expression akin to the oft used "in the last days." These are the times after the resurrection of Jesus—the times of Paul and the times today. But uniquely in Paul's time, the nascent church was without the New Testament or preachers taught in seminaries. The demonic realm was in overdrive, not knowing the future like God and hoping to destroy the fledgling church through heresy. Satan wanted the church neutered, if not outright obliterated. The heretic examples used by Paul included the apparently "spiritual" teachings that denied marriage as a holy calling and institution and that set up bright legal lines on what one could or couldn't eat. Paul told Timothy to combat such teaching and instead receive these things as the good gifts of God, pray in gratitude for God's blessings, and walk in true holiness.

We still live in the latter days, even though our Christianity is no longer embryonic. We have seminaries, millennia of thought and study, and the fruits that come from the Spirit's work through the ages. Yet we should still be on high alert for the schemes of the evil one who seeks to wreck what God makes. He may not be the negative number equivalent of God, but he still can do a lot of damage.

Lord, let me seek your truth and bring glory to you in Jesus, amen.

SEPTEMBER 15

Train yourself for godliness; for while bodily training is of some value, godliness is of value in every way, as it holds promise for the present life and also for the life to come. The saying is trustworthy and deserving of full acceptance. For to this end we toil and strive, because we have our hope set on the living God, who is the Savior of all people, especially of those who believe. (1 Tim. 4:7–10)

Our daughter Sarah started an email chain to her four siblings, Becky, and me. She urged us all to register for Disney's Dopey Challenge Run. This involved running a 5K through Disney World on a certain Thursday, then running a 10K on Friday, followed by a half marathon on Saturday, and finally, capping it off with a full marathon on Sunday. Yes, I thought, it is called the Dopey Challenge for a reason! This would take serious training!

Paul was from Tarsus originally, a city well known for its civic gym and the athletic endeavors occurring there. Over and over in his writings, Paul uses sports and workout metaphors and analogies. His language in today's passage is laced with exercise words.

Paul begins with "train yourself." The Greek word for "train" is the word from which we get *gymnasium*! It is pronounced "gym-nay-zo" (γυμνάζω). But Paul isn't referencing weight lifting or preparing to run the Dopey Challenge. Paul wants the training to be for "godliness," an idea of piety or showing respect to God by devoutly following him. Paul uses gymnasium language again, explaining that physical workouts ("bodily training") have value, but the value is limited to the body. But learning and growing in godliness have value in all areas of life, now and for eternity. So Paul willingly toils and "strives" (another workout word referencing an athletic contest) to the point of exhaustion, but Paul does so for godliness, something better than an earthly trophy. Paul's hope (confident expectation) was that God would bless his endeavors.

I like to work out, usually. I enjoy the discipline, the focus, and hopefully some results! But I need to take Paul's metaphor to heart. Christianity should never be something we merely wear as a label. It should be an opportunity to seek godliness and aim to grow in fitness for God's works and purposes. This type of training isn't dopey. It is wise!

Lord, give me insight and discipline to apply myself into growing in your love, your truth, and your mercy. Help me be more godly day by day. In Jesus' name, amen.

SEPTEMBER 16

Let no one despise you for your youth, but set the believers an example in speech, in conduct, in love, in faith, in purity. (1 Tim. 4:12)

As a fourteen-year-old kid, I had no business giving a keynote address to some seven hundred attendees at Lubbock Christian University's summer "Encounter." This annual multiday affair drew high schoolers from far and wide and typically featured the nation's best youth ministers as speakers. But for some reason, John King, the university's director of the camp, decided that I should (and could) give a keynote. My assigned topic was "Follow Me in Friendship." I spoke on the story of David and Jonathan. Certainly no one remembers that nearly fifty years later *except me*!

John wasn't my only encourager. Senior minister Ken Dye gave me numerous opportunities to preach and speak in our "big church." Our youth ministers called on me for various times of leading in prayer, teaching, and more. Doubtlessly I learned more in preparing for these tasks than anyone heard listening, but being in a community of faith that encouraged the young people to actively serve God was a developmental milestone that propelled me on the path where I stand today.

Paul was an encourager of the next generation, as today's passage boldly shows. Tucked inside a letter that assigned great responsibilities to Timothy, Paul exhorted Timothy not to let his age stand in the way. While Timothy was not a teenager, he was also not of the mature age that many would expect for one assigned such weighty tasks. But Paul knew Timothy was up to it. Timothy was a godly man, and he should be judged not on his age but on his conduct.

Therefore, Paul instructed Timothy to concentrate on basics. Timothy should be careful how he spoke, which would include not only the words he used but his tone of voice as well as when he chose to use those words. People listening to Timothy should not hear someone haughty, arrogant, or rude but someone kind, loving, and humble. The words Timothy spoke were closely linked to his overall behavior, on which he should also focus. His life was to reflect the love, faith, trust, and purity befitting someone who walks closely with the Lord.

You and I have a responsibility to pay attention to God, which should impact how we live. But it should also impact how we encourage others to live. We should all seek to embolden the next generation to live for Jesus. It is fitting and right.

Lord, give me eyes to see how to encourage others for your work in Jesus, amen.

SEPTEMBER 17

Honor widows who are truly widows. But if a widow has children or grandchildren, let them first learn to show godliness to their own household and to make some return to their parents, for this is pleasing in the sight of God. She who is truly a widow, left all alone, has set her hope on God and continues in supplications and prayers night and day, but she who is self-indulgent is dead even while she lives. Command these things as well, so that they may be without reproach. But if anyone does not provide for his relatives, and especially for members of his household, he has denied the faith and is worse than an unbeliever. (1 Tim. 5:3–8)

The social and familial world of the New Testament vastly differed from modern society in many ways, including the role and treatment of women. Dowries were paid by the women's family as an enticement into marriage, women were part of a larger household run by the presiding male of the house (the *paterfamilias*), and adult children often remained part of the household under the authority of the head of the house. Marriage, too, was often not for love but for practicality. Hence Caesar Augustus in AD 7 had no trouble enacting a law that *required* widows under age fifty to remarry within two years. It's not surprising, then, that many of the problems that happened in the first century, as well as the church's responses to those issues, don't readily translate in application to society today. But that doesn't mean valuable lessons can't be drawn from these ancient problems and solutions.

Today's passage is a great example. Paul is dealing with issues related to the way the church stepped into the gap that happened in the care of women who became widows. Paul expected children and grandchildren to support their widowed mothers. But if the widow had no such support coming, then the church stepped in to "honor" (a word that readily includes the idea of financial support) them. This was assuming the widow truly pursued God and was not simply looking for church welfare in an age where the state provided none.

Although our society is built differently, several applicable principles exist just as much today as then. First is the importance of the church to look after those who are disadvantaged. Second, as Paul summarizes, each family should provide for those members of their family in need. Third, Christianity addresses real-world problems with real-world solutions.

Lord, enable me to help those in need, then strengthen me to do so in Jesus' name, amen.

SEPTEMBER 18

In the presence of God and of Christ Jesus and of the elect angels I charge you to keep these rules without prejudging, doing nothing from partiality. (1 Tim. 5:21)

Most homes have coverings for their windows. Some have curtains, some shades, some even shutters, but most windows have something that can be drawn to stop people from looking into the house. Especially at night, when the house lights are on, inhabitants must guard against people on the outside having a clear view of the home. We once moved into a home before window coverings were installed, so we couldn't walk around in nightwear without being seen by any outsider looking in!

Window treatments don't exist with God. We might suppose we can hide our actions behind a curtain, but today's passage debunks that view. Paul has been instructing Timothy on what to do with church leaders/elders who are leading irresponsibly, if not outright sinfully. Paul gives practical instructions rooted in the Old Testament about the need for witnesses to wrongdoing. Paul explains the public rebuke that should follow clear sin in leaders' oversight of the church. Paul then instructs Timothy to keep these rules in a right manner. Paul's charge in this regard is serious; it is given "in the presence of God and of Jesus Christ and of the elect angels"!

Paul's description of a heavenly host observing our actions isn't without a biblical base. The Old Testament book of Job describes God within his heavenly court. Likewise, other Old Testament passages (as well as New) speak of God and his angels. But Paul inserts these as witnesses not only indicating the importance of what he was saying but also reminding us that when it comes to how we live and what we do, we don't have window treatments.

No matter how much we try to hide, God sees our every movement. God knows our every thought. God knows our past, our present, and our future. This is part of what makes him awesome. Yet for some reason, at times we think he isn't watching or, if he is, isn't paying attention. It's absurd to think we can draw curtains on our lives and keep God from looking in, but we still act as if we can.

Today, I want to live in the present awareness that God is watching. While his presence should make me check how to behave, it should also be a comfort. I am not alone. God is with me.

Lord, in your presence, I seek to live today to your glory. In Jesus I pray, amen.

SEPTEMBER 19

But godliness with contentment is great gain, for we brought nothing into the world, and we cannot take anything out of the world. But if we have food and clothing, with these we will be content. But those who desire to be rich fall into temptation, into a snare, into many senseless and harmful desires that plunge people into ruin and destruction. For the love of money is a root of all kinds of evils. It is through this craving that some have wandered away from the faith and pierced themselves with many pangs. (1 Tim. 6:6–10)

In his retirement years, my dad would say that he was "rich." This was notable because in money terms, Dad was far from rich. He worked a middle-class job all his life, and after raising three children and putting them through college, he was far from rich economically. But Dad wasn't banking on his savings when he said he was rich. Dad meant he was rich because he had his family, loving wife, and adoring children and grandchildren around him. Dad would say that was worth far more than all the money in the world. Money didn't make Dad rich; family did.

Dad exemplified the spirit of today's passage. Paul recognizes that having food and clothing are important parts of a good life. Like Proverbs 30:8–9, Paul knows life is good and fitting with "neither poverty nor riches." For we need enough food not to steal, but not so much that one quits relying on God. Riches, Paul says, are a snare or a trap. (Paul uses the word for animal traps.) Riches draw people away from pursuing godliness and into senseless and harmful desires.

Why is that so? Most people I know who wish for riches do so thinking they could do so much good with the money. Yet money can often change such noble desires. Instead of being a reservoir for God's work, money often becomes an addictive drug that makes people crave more and more. I am reminded of an old preacher who was approached by a church member who said, "Preacher, I used to tithe 10 percent to the church. But now I make so much that 10 percent is too much to give." The preacher replied, "I will pray to God that you make less, so you can more readily be obedient."

Paul doesn't say that money is the root of all evil. He says the *love* of money is the root. Later in the letter, Paul will instruct the wealthy not to be haughty but to use their riches for God and his purposes. He wants them "rich in good works . . . generous and ready to share" (1 Tim. 6:18). Money is God's tool. Period.

Lord, give me sensibility with the resources you've entrusted to me. In Jesus, amen.

SEPTEMBER 20

But as for you, O man of God, flee these things. Pursue righteousness, godliness, faith, love, steadfastness, gentleness. Fight the good fight of the faith. Take hold of the eternal life to which you were called. (1 Tim. 6:11–12)

When I was growing up, Muhammad Ali was front and center, the greatest fighter of all time, the heavyweight champion of the world. I never got to see any of his fights live while they were occurring. His fights were before the internet opened events worldwide to most anyone. Nor were these fights accessible on television. My best bet was trying to find them on a radio. Perhaps because I never saw the fights, I considered the athletic challenges not brutal but fascinating.

Paul uses the athletic, competition-based word for fighting in his illustration in today's passage. Paul instructs Timothy to "fight the good fight of the faith." These terms were not war terms as much as they were terms of a contest. The terms recognize that the Christian walk isn't one of complacency or ease. In our Christian journey (*or walk*), the believer is engaged in a struggle to do right and be right. Holiness doesn't come easily. God's indwelling Spirit makes it possible, but we must still choose the righteousness that should accompany our faith.

Part of that choice is also detailed in Paul's further admonitions in today's passage. Paul uses a common convention of ethical teaching in his day, contrasting the two words *flee* and *pursue*. Paul wants Timothy, as a man of God, to flee the many avarices he has recently recited in his letter. Timothy should flee greed, love of money, selfishness, laziness, corruptness—these traits and more Paul has spoken to in his letter. Instead, Timothy should chase after godly traits of right living and patiently trust God in love, resulting in a growing gentleness.

Each believer should follow Paul's prescription. It isn't always the easy path, but it is a fitting fight. Rather than chasing money, power, popularity, ease, prestige, fame, and comfort, rather than living to gossip about, backbite, denigrate, or hurt others, the child of God should be about God's business. God seeks to bring comfort and mercy to those hurting, supplies to those in need, faith to the doubting, and more. God is a builder of good things, and so should be his people. This is an important practical goal daily. Yet it is a fight. It isn't a sport to watch, à la boxing. It is a fight all believers should engage in.

Lord, give me the spirit of fighting for what is right. May I pursue goodness for the sake of Jesus, in whom I pray, amen.

SEPTEMBER 21

Keep the commandment unstained and free from reproach until the appearing of our Lord Jesus Christ, which he will display at the proper time—he who is the blessed and only Sovereign, the King of kings and Lord of lords, who alone has immortality, who dwells in unapproachable light, whom no one has ever seen or can see. To him be honor and eternal dominion. Amen. (1 Tim. 6:14–16)

Sitting with my friend, a PhD psychologist, I listened as she told me, "I figured out that at the root of all you do is your faith in God." "I can only wish," I thought. But then on further reflection, I realized it isn't so much my faith that is the center of my life but the real God who is the object of my faith. I am not who I am because I believe in God but because of God's work in me. As I believe in God and walk in that faith, I become who God makes me to be.

The core of all life really is God, whether we acknowledge it or not. Paul knew this truth, and his life and letters reflected it. As Paul nears the close of this personal letter to his protégé, we read Paul breaking out into praise of God. His praise is loaded, theologically and practically. Consider first the theology.

Paul puts forward core concepts of the majesty and awesomeness of God in the most supreme claims. God is the only Sovereign. In an age where Caesar reigned supreme with absolute authority, Paul's recognition of God as the true Sovereign puts God above any human being. He is the King of kings. He is the Lord of lords. All must bow before God. God is eternal. Anything or anyone existing into eternity shares the eternity of God. God brings his life into believers; believers share in the resurrection of Christ. This is true even though no physical eye can see God in his eternal form. Paul rightly gives all honor to God.

From a practical perspective, Paul's doxology in these verses calls out for a response. Our first response should be to voice all honor and dominion to the blessed God. But mere words don't suffice for the truth of who God is. God calls for our entire life. God wants to become the root of all we do.

Because there is truly a God as praised by Paul, my life isn't empty. I have purpose living for this awe-inspiring God. I can trust this King of kings with all I have. The Lord of lords can handle my worries and problems. Then when my life is over, I can trust the immortal God to keep me in his eternal care. What a God!

My Lord and King, my Ruler, Father, and Friend, I live for you in Jesus, amen.

SEPTEMBER 22

Paul, a servant of God and an apostle of Jesus Christ, for the sake of the faith of God's elect and their knowledge of the truth, which accords with godliness, in hope of eternal life, which God, who never lies, promised before the ages began and at the proper time manifested in his word through the preaching with which I have been entrusted by the command of God our Savior. (Tit. 1:1–3)

On a short runway, the airplane pilot announced, "Don't be alarmed, but I will be applying the brakes while I rev the engines. Then I will release the brakes, and we will accelerate very quickly. This is what we do on a short runway." The engines revved and roared, the brakes were released, and we shot out of there faster than I thought possible. I feel much the same way with today's passage.

The short letter of Titus begins with one long Greek sentence comprising these first four verses. The words spill forth before Paul even catches a breath. Like a jet plane, the letter launches with a greeting, theology, exhortation and encouragement, and preaching, all rolled into one massive sentence. Before Paul even mentions the recipient, Titus, Paul writes a letter's worth of material. Although not a precise parallel, it is almost like writing a letter and putting the first paragraph before noting, "Dear Titus."

I like this start. I can trace Paul's mind as he exuberantly dictated (or perhaps wrote), identifying himself as a "servant of God," an Old Testament title for one who is selected to serve God in unique ways, often with a word of revelation. He adds that he is an "apostle of Jesus Christ." Not leaving it there, he adds *why* he is an apostle, or why God sent him with a message. He was sent by God "for the sake of the faith of God's elect"—itself a loaded term. Paul's mission was to bring to and encourage faith in those who were no longer of the world but of God's kingdom. Not surprisingly, this letter will be one where the subject matter is care of and guidance to the church—that is, the elect.

Paul continues his introduction by noting the importance of knowing truth, which will produce godliness and hope. The core of this life-changing truth is rooted in a God who faithfully promised eternal life from earliest days and revealed his promise through the preaching of Christ crucified and resurrected. From its first sentence, the letter of Titus rightly commands my attention. Paul emphasizes the importance of faith and knowledge to God's people.

Lord, place people in my life to teach and encourage me in faith in Jesus, amen.

SEPTEMBER 23

Appoint elders in every town as I directed you—if anyone is above reproach, the husband of one wife, and his children are believers and not open to the charge of debauchery or insubordination. For an overseer, as God's steward, must be above reproach. He must not be arrogant or quick-tempered or a drunkard or violent or greedy for gain, but hospitable, a lover of good, self-controlled, upright, holy, and disciplined. He must hold firm to the trustworthy word as taught, so that he may be able to give instruction in sound doctrine and also to rebuke those who contradict it. (Tit. 1:5–9)

In high school, I had the privilege of working for Joe Stapleton. He owned a convenience store called Holiday Mart. He taught me about practical economics. For example, we would put chicken noodle soup cans on the bottom row of soups, while more bizarre kinds were placed at eye level. He explained that people would come in, look for, and stoop for chicken noodle soup but not cream of asparagus. He taught me good management.

In today's passage, Paul taught Timothy good church management. Paul had Timothy appoint caretakers using three different terms. Paul calls them "elders" (*presbuteros*—πρεσβύτερος), "overseers" (*episkopos*—ἐπίσκοπος), and "stewards" (*oikonomos*—οἰκονόμος). One might notice several theological words that, over history, became identifying words for churches and their polity or ecclesiastical structure. One can readily read *presbytery* and *episcopal* in the Greek words, as well, incidentally, as *economist* in the word translated "steward."

But the passage speaks beyond church polity. The passage should first be seen as emphasizing the importance of godliness. That godliness must certainly be seen in church leaders, but it is to be sought by all believers across all generations. Leaders for Jesus followers should deliberately seek to grow in traits of humility over arrogance, patience over a quick temper, sobriety over drunkenness, peace over violence, satisfaction over greed, and hospitality over inhospitality. They should care for others in need, treasure good, reject evil, control their passions and desires, and live upright, holy, and disciplined lives. Ministry leaders—indeed, all Jesus followers—should hold to truth, since Jesus is the ultimate revealer and embodiment of truth. That's a long and worthy list, one that we desperately need the Spirit's help to achieve.

Lord, in your Spirit may I grow in godliness. Grow your fruit in me in Jesus' name, amen.

SEPTEMBER 24

For there are many who are insubordinate, empty talkers and deceivers, especially those of the circumcision party. They must be silenced, since they are upsetting whole families by teaching for shameful gain what they ought not to teach. . . . Therefore rebuke them sharply, that they may be sound in the faith, not devoting themselves to Jewish myths and the commands of people who turn away from the truth. (Tit. 1:10–11, 13–14)

I never met the inquisitive explorers Lewis and Clark (they died in 1809 and 1838, respectively). Both were born on Virginian farms but died famous for the "Lewis and Clark Expedition." The two led an expedition that launched from St. Louis in April 1805, then explored the land acquired by the recent Louisiana Purchase, and then surveyed the Pacific Northwest, reaching the Pacific Ocean in mid-November.

The Lewis and Clark Expedition was trailblazing (literally) and undoubtedly fulfilling to adventurous explorers. I admire their drive, courage, and fortitude. That said, I believe some people often manifest a Lewis and Clark attitude when it comes to Scripture. Unlike the historical namesakes, however, a drive and desire to find obscure meanings, weird interpretations, or trailblazing innovations in Scripture can be a bit arrogant, if not destructive.

Novelty carries an allure for some. Others are often enticed by secrets. Church history holds innumerable stories of heresies arising from such people. I am not saying that there is no room for God to speak afresh in each age through his Spirit's work in opening Scripture to the believer. But we should always be on guard about someone bringing a "new insight" or "freshly discovered" understanding to passages that have been prayerfully studied by the church's holy and thoughtful leaders over nearly two thousand years.

Some basics exist, and they are clearly attested to by Scripture. God is infinite, personal, and moral. He made humanity in his image. People have been fallen since the age of Adam. God has redeemed fallen people through the death and resurrection of Christ. One is born again (or from above) by trusting in Christ. All believers should seek to live holy and righteous lives, serving God and his purposes in humility and love. Christ will come again in judgment and usher in a new heaven and earth. Beyond that, exploration of Scripture is great, but we should be mindful of our attitudes and approaches, keeping Lewis and Clark where they belong!

Lord, keep me growing in your truth in service to you and in Jesus, amen.

SEPTEMBER 25

Show yourself in all respects to be a model of good works, and in your teaching show integrity, dignity, and sound speech that cannot be condemned, so that an opponent may be put to shame, having nothing evil to say about us. (Tit. 2:7–8)

On rare occasions, I go into the prison system to take testimony from an inmate for use at a trial. When I go into the prison, they limit what I can bring. Usually, prison officials forbid taking money, and of course weapons are taboo. The inmates are in an isolated, controlled environment, and their rules of living are different from those in the outside world. "People are people," as my buddy Louis says, but those incarcerated live differently than those who aren't.

The letter to Titus wasn't written to people incarcerated, but it was written to people in a different world system than we live in today. Families were different, with strict limitations on what most women could do or be. Education was different, without mandatory schools for all genders. Safety in society was different, with little of what we now consider to be police. Law was different in how it applied to people, with some getting great legal protection and others having almost none. The economy was different, with slavery providing much of the labor force.

As Paul wrote into that culture and world of his day, he at times gave instructions that might seem out of place in our world today. The verses around today's passage are some of those. For example, earlier, Paul told women to be "working at home"—that might seem misogynist to modern readers, yet for Paul, it was simple. Women *were* at home. They could work or be lazy. He wanted them busy doing good things. Similarly, Paul gave instructions to slaves not because he was a fan of slavery but because there were slaves that needed instructions!

Regardless of culture, however, Paul explained the behaviors he taught were rooted in the moral goodness of God. Paul wanted the believer to be a "model of good works," a value that might be expressed differently in one place than another. Paul expected teaching to be full of integrity and dignity. Dignity in speech in Paul's day might look different from how it looks today. Paul knew that if believers live godly in their age and culture, then God is praised. But if believers don't, then people will speak less highly of God. The challenge for us today, within our culture, is to hold fast to the values and goodness of God. Believe it, but also live it.

Lord, give me insight, wisdom, and discernment to understand how to live your values in my world today. Let me live to your glory and kingdom, in Jesus, amen.

SEPTEMBER 26

For the grace of God has appeared, bringing salvation for all people, training us to renounce ungodliness and worldly passions, and to live self-controlled, upright, and godly lives in the present age, waiting for our blessed hope, the appearing of the glory of our great God and Savior Jesus Christ, who gave himself for us to redeem us from all lawlessness and to purify for himself a people for his own possession who are zealous for good works. (Tit. 2:11–14)

Dad traveled frequently when we were kids. When he was gone several nights, he often returned with a gift. We missed Dad while he was gone, but knowing we would get a treat gave us a bit of expectant eagerness even as he was leaving!

God never left humanity, but he did arrive in a previously unseen way by appearing through the incarnation of Jesus. When God came in human form through Christ, he did so bearing a gift. His gift wasn't a trifle or souvenir. God brought salvation, with all that it means, to his people. Salvation isn't limited to "going to heaven after we die." Salvation in Greek (*sōtērios*—σωτήριος) includes the idea of deliverance and preservation. God has brought us a gift that saves us from this world and delivers us into his eternity.

Accordingly, God's salvation and deliverance find their immediate effect in retraining our brains and will to godliness. We no longer value or pursue the passions of this age, with their negative effects on us. Chasing money, fame, pleasure, or other serotonin boosters are passions that the undelivered value. But those who have been blessed with God's gift of salvation and deliverance find value in self-control, holiness, and godly priorities. The old worldly stuff feels good for a moment, but like any drug working in your brain, the effect wears off and you feel worse afterward. The world's passions also lead down unprofitable roads, while the roads of godliness contain deep abiding joy.

God's gifts through Jesus inspire us and don't disappoint. For these are a "foretaste of glory divine," as the old hymn says. We know that Jesus will return to complete the deliverance and place us in the home of a new heaven and earth.

As I think through this life, I need to live in each moment, mindful of how God calls me to be different from how I would be without him. This is a great gift given.

Lord, thank you for the gift of salvation and all it means. May I live in your holiness and grace to the glory of Jesus my Lord through whom I pray, amen.

SEPTEMBER 27

Remind them to be submissive to rulers and authorities, to be obedient, to be ready for every good work, to speak evil of no one, to avoid quarreling, to be gentle, and to show perfect courtesy toward all people. For we ourselves were once foolish, disobedient, led astray, slaves to various passions and pleasures, passing our days in malice and envy, hated by others and hating one another. (Tit. 3:1–3)

Therapists' offices the world over are loaded with clients trying to change their behaviors. It is one thing to say, "I want to be *X*"; it is another thing altogether to be *X*. I may wish for patience, but I can't simply declare, "OK, I will be patient." Who we are deep inside surfaces, especially in times of anxiety, frustration, little sleep, and high pressure. I knew a lawyer who was nice until he got to trial. Then he would yell and even belittle those around him. I'm not sure he even realized it.

Yet in today's passage, Paul seems to be saying, "Do these things; don't be what you were before." Should we write this passage off as a platitude with no real chance of changing one's life? Absolutely not! A key is the first word in Paul's original, which is also the first word in the translation: *remind*! (*hupomimnēskō*—ὑπομιμνήσκω). If simply telling someone to change their disposition and behavior was sufficient, people wouldn't need to be reminded.

These traits encouraged by Paul—practicing submissiveness and obedience to authorities, doing good works, avoiding negative talk and quarreling, displaying gentleness and politeness—are akin to what Paul wrote of to the churches of Galatia, where Paul called them "fruit of the Spirit" (Gal. 5:22). These traits proceed over time, as a fruit grows and ripens over time. They also proceed from God's Spirit at work within us, just as a fruit grows from the inside out. But we aren't without a role in this important aspect of spiritual growth.

Hence Paul uses the word *remind*. We need to regularly think through how we should be as children of God. Paul draws a stark contrast between our life in God and the life isolated from God, with its foolishness, disobedience, malice, envy, and pursuit of passions and pleasures over the will of God. A reminder means that we should live mindfully and, as Paul adds later, "be careful to devote" ourselves to good works (Tit. 3:8). Our minds need to consciously work toward that which God is working within us. Then we will find that God rewires our brains, reshapes our will, and grows his fruit in us.

Lord, grow your traits in my life. I want to live as yours. I ask in Jesus, amen.

SEPTEMBER 28

But when the goodness and loving kindness of God our Savior appeared, he saved us, not because of works done by us in righteousness, but according to his own mercy, by the washing of regeneration and renewal of the Holy Spirit, whom he poured out on us richly through Jesus Christ our Savior, so that being justified by his grace we might become heirs according to the hope of eternal life. (Tit. 3:4–7)

The United States is a republic form of democracy with three branches of government. It doesn't have a king and can't in any way be described as a kingdom. We have politicians who take office and mostly (save federal judges) can be replaced via an election in the event they are deemed inadequate. In ancient times, people had to suffer through Roman emperors and other leaders without the ability to replace those who were inadequate. Language developed to describe virtuous rulers, and some of that language is co-opted here by Paul.

Paul speaks of God's "goodness and loving kindness." These Greek words were used of good rulers. They were what people hoped their leaders would be. "Goodness" (*chrēstos*—χρηστός) spoke of one who was worthy, decent, honest, upright, well mannered, of good character, kind and gentle, and even friendly. Interesting sidenote: this word in Greek has only a minor sound difference from the word for Christ (*christos*—χριστός), and since "anointed" (the meaning of "Christ") meant little outside Judaism, the Greek-speaking world often misunderstood the title of Jesus as "Christ" to be "Chrest." It made more sense to associate the regal aspirations of highest character with Jesus.

"Loving kindness" is also used regally when describing the optimal ruler's traits. It is more literally in the Greek someone who cares for and loves people (*philanthrōpia*—φιλανθρωπία). This word expresses God's concern for and interest in humanity. In its ancient Greek usage, kings were supposed to carry this godly trait as they exercised rulership.

These kingly traits rightly lie behind the King of kings, who in the highest and best way has sought out his people to populate his kingdom. God didn't do so for selfish, egotistical, narcissistic ambition. God reached out to save his people because of his kind, honest, caring essence. God is giving eternal life with him out of his own generosity. That, Paul knows, should move all of us in gratitude and love. What an awesome God we serve.

Lord, I praise you for your goodness, shown in your saving mercy in Jesus, amen.

SEPTEMBER 29

Peter, an apostle of Jesus Christ, To those who are elect exiles of the Dispersion in Pontus, Galatia, Cappadocia, Asia, and Bithynia, according to the foreknowledge of God the Father, in the sanctification of the Spirit, for obedience to Jesus Christ and for sprinkling with his blood. (1 Pet. 1:1–2)

Everyone is familiar with timelines. I frequently use them in courtrooms to help people keep track of the chronology of events as well as give structure to what the future projections are. We live on a timeline. We have a past, present, and future. Timelines help give perspective on the moment, as the past and future are placed alongside each other.

Timelines come to mind when reading the beginning of the letter "1 Peter," in these opening verses. Peter speaks of our past, describing the readers as "elect" exiles "according to the foreknowledge of God the Father." No one stumbles into God. God has known from the beginning who would choose to follow him, and his foreknowledge is part and parcel of God's election. While debates can rage over predestination and choice, there can be no doubt that all believers are in God's hands by his grace with full foreknowledge. God wants his people and goes to work for them.

God doesn't limit his role in our lives to our past timeline, as Peter makes clear in his next clause where he references the "sanctification of the Spirit." Sanctification speaks to multiple important parts of the Christian walk. It speaks to the fact that the saved are dedicated to God. This dedication also includes a cleansing as God through his Spirit works in each of us *today.* Whenever you are reading this, you can be confident that the God, who saved you, is working to purify you.

The future is found in Peter's timeline as well. Our dedication to God and purification by God are both in anticipation of future growth in obedience to Jesus and his commands. Peter was in a unique position because he walked with Jesus during his three-year ministry. Peter heard the Sermon on the Mount, listened to the parables, and observed Jesus' life of obedience to God to the point of death. Peter knew that obedience to Jesus was the greatest achievement for the believer. It is only possible by the dedication of Christ whose blood makes us holy.

Thank you, God. Thank you, Jesus. Work in me today and forever. In Jesus' name, amen.

SEPTEMBER 30

Blessed be the God and Father of our Lord Jesus Christ! According to his great mercy, he has caused us to be born again to a living hope through the resurrection of Jesus Christ from the dead, to an inheritance that is imperishable, undefiled, and unfading. (1 Pet. 1:3–4)

Chapter 3 of the Gospel of John tells the memorable story of Jesus' nighttime encounter with an important Jew named Nicodemus. In that intimate dialogue, Jesus told Nicodemus that a person needs to be "born again" or "born from above" (either translation is proper) to enter the kingdom of heaven. Nicodemus struggled to understand how someone might be born again. No one can reenter their mother's womb. In explaining the rebirth, Jesus spoke prophetically of his coming crucifixion and its role in this rebirth.

In today's passage, Peter artfully writes on the subject discussed by Jesus and Nicodemus, but Peter does it after the crucifixion and resurrection. While John wrote of the Nicodemus events using two Greek words, for "born" (*genenaō*—γεννάω) and for "again" or "from above" (*anōthen*—ἄνωθεν), Peter uses a compound word. Peter's compound word combines "born" with the root of "again / from above" (*ana*—ἀνά). Then in an artful turn on the words, Peter uses another compound word for resurrection that takes the same root as "again / from above."

No Christian should miss the import of what Peter is saying. The process of being "born again" is rooted in the resurrection of Jesus. We find a new life *in Christ.* This is how one is born "from above": by sharing in the resurrection of the Messiah, who himself was raised up from above. The resurrected Messiah lives eternally, having conquered death. So the new life of one born again through the resurrection is one that is imperishable, undefiled, and unfading. This gives a confidence in life that is a "living hope." Just as a child is born with hope of a great life, so a believer's rebirth in Jesus is accompanied by hope of a great life. This becomes important in Peter's letter, as the message is one of faithful endurance through suffering.

We Christians should always remember that our journey into God's kingdom is rooted in the trail blazed by the suffering Messiah, who, through his death and resurrection, made possible the new and eternal life that gives living new meaning.

Lord, I praise and thank you for my life in the resurrected Jesus. Amen.

OCTOBER 1

In this you rejoice, though now for a little while, if necessary, you have been grieved by various trials, so that the tested genuineness of your faith—more precious than gold that perishes though it is tested by fire—may be found to result in praise and glory and honor at the revelation of Jesus Christ. Though you have not seen him, you love him. Though you do not now see him, you believe in him and rejoice with joy that is inexpressible and filled with glory. (1 Pet. 1:6–9)

My friend Pastor Jarrett Stephens begins each day with a time of prayer and devotion, studying the Scriptures seeking to learn of and hear from God. For decades, Jarrett has journaled these times. His journal entries start with written prayer, and in those prayers he almost always tells the Lord, "I love you."

I grew up in a family where expressing one's love in words was common. Unlike some families where the phrase "I love you" is rare, our family was quite expressive. Our parents loved us kids, and they told us regularly. Many times, my dad said to me, as I have said to my own children, "You'll never know how much I love you until you have your own children." How right he was.

In today's passage, Peter speaks of loving Jesus. Peter loved him, which he exhibited not only through the life he led but also in that famous lakeside interchange between Jesus and Peter noted in John 21. Jesus asked Peter three times, "Do you love me?" Each time, Peter affirmed his love. This love was so deep that, as Jesus indicated in the John 21 dialogue, Peter would die a martyr's death for Jesus.

But Peter's reference to loving Jesus in today's passage isn't a personal reference to Peter's love. Rather, Peter writes of the readers' love of Jesus. Peter knows that those who have found a new life in Jesus, those who share in the resurrection of Jesus, rightly love him.

Our love for Jesus should be real. Like Peter's readers, we haven't been blessed with physically seeing Jesus, but that shouldn't deter our love or faith. The fundamental reason for the incarnation of God as Jesus was to love and die for humanity. Affirming that in faith rightly prompts us to a response of love and devotion. It is not only suitable for saying (or journaling) each morning, but it is a proper reason to serve and honor the Lord minute by minute each day.

Lord, thank you for your love for me. I love you and seek to serve and honor you with my life. Help me for Jesus' sake and in his name, amen.

OCTOBER 2

Therefore, preparing your minds for action, and being sober-minded, set your hope fully on the grace that will be brought to you at the revelation of Jesus Christ. As obedient children, do not be conformed to the passions of your former ignorance, but as he who called you is holy, you also be holy in all your conduct. (1 Pet. 1:13–15)

"This is audience participation!" our preacher said. Jarrett was teaching on how to live as good citizens of God's kingdom, seeking to bring God's kingdom onto earth as it is in heaven. He wanted each person to do three things daily. Indicating the first, he put both hands up to each side of his head, urging the congregation to do the same as we all said, "Head!" He then formed a heart with his hands and said, "Heart!" His third instruction was holding his hands outstretched saying, "Hands!" He wanted each person daily to live with a conscious effort to use mind, heart, and action for God.

Peter in today's versus does much the same. He instructs his readers to start with "head," telling them to prepare their "minds for action." Peter uses his own graphic metaphor in the Greek that the people are to "gird up the hips" of their minds! With the long tunic worn in Peter's day, people would tuck the tunic up under their belts when they needed to free their legs to run or work strenuously. Without that metaphor readily available in the twenty-first century, the translators instead use the thrust of Peter's message: *prepare* your minds *for action.*

Peter then uses the Greek word for "mind" or "thoughts" and "intentions." We are to live mindfully each day. No default living for the Christian. We must get our heads on straight to live each day intentionally. "Head!" as Pastor Jarrett taught.

Then the heart is set on hoping, or "confidently expecting" (my preferred translation of the Greek *elpizō*—ἐλπίζω) the coming again of Jesus. As Peter has already said, the Christian shares the resurrection of Jesus, and he will come again, an event that moves us in love and expectant trust.

With this "head" and "heart" set, Peter then instructs the "hands." He wants his readers to live holy lives, working for God, not the passions and wasteful ways of those who don't know Jesus. Peter's instructions fit well the threefold admonition of Pastor Jarrett. Each day, let's consciously live "head, heart, and hands" for God!

Lord, aid me as I seek to think about, hope in, and love for you. In Jesus, amen.

OCTOBER 3

Having purified your souls by your obedience to the truth for a sincere brotherly love, love one another earnestly from a pure heart, since you have been born again, not of perishable seed but of imperishable. . . . So put away all malice and all deceit and hypocrisy and envy and all slander. Like newborn infants, long for the pure spiritual milk, that by it you may grow up into salvation—if indeed you have tasted that the Lord is good. (1 Pet. 1:22–23; 2:1–3)

People tend to think in metaphors. A foundational research book on this published in 1980 by George Lakoff and Mark Johnson (*Metaphors We Live By*) explained that peoples' minds naturally use metaphors to process and make sense of ideas and data. That isn't a modern phenomenon. It was just as much a part of thinking in biblical times. Scripture is loaded with metaphors. Peter is a premier example.

Peter seizes on the language of Jesus with Nicodemus in describing the Christian experience as being "born again." He used this concept earlier in his letter as well. In today's passage, he takes the image further, indicating that the born-again Christians grow in their faith and devotion to God, craving spiritual milk to drink. Unlike the writer of Hebrews and Paul, who used milk as a metaphor for immaturity (Heb. 5:12–13; 1 Cor. 3:2), Peter uses it in an affirming way.

Peter sees the worldly traits of malice, deceit, hypocrisy, envy, and speaking ill of others as pollutants or poisons, unfit for one who is born again. Instead, by being reborn in Christ, the Christian is to seek the goodness of Christ, growing just as a baby grows by drinking mother's milk over against the garbage of the world.

This suits a Christian well. The believer who has tasted of God, who has experienced God's loving goodness in salvation, should readily seek out the purity of behavior that accompanies spiritual growth.

How does one do this? Peter has already given that insight in prior verses, writing that the believer should be holy as God is holy. How can one know whether the things she or he does are good or evil? Are right or wrong? Are milk or toxins? By looking to God and his example given in his word. Peter tells his readers that the word of God never fails. It testifies to God, his love, and his moral compass, and it gives those who seek God a basis to know spiritual milk when we taste it!

God, teach me to grow up in you, feeding on your word to be better fit for your purposes in this world. May I live for your glory. In Jesus, amen.

OCTOBER 4

As you come to him, a living stone rejected by men but in the sight of God chosen and precious, you yourselves like living stones are being built up as a spiritual house, to be a holy priesthood, to offer spiritual sacrifices acceptable to God through Jesus Christ. For it stands in Scripture: "Behold, I am laying in Zion a stone, a cornerstone chosen and precious, and whoever believes in him will not be put to shame." (1 Pet. 2:4–6)

Construction today with steel and readily available wood is different from the construction of stone structures built in Peter's day. Therefore, Peter's building metaphor in today's passage needs a bit more thought for the modern reader.

The ancient builders of durable structures would usually find a stone to lay in a corner for the start of construction. This stone would be used to set plumb lines, and it was important for the stone to be substantial enough that it wouldn't readily move once put in place. The stone was also to be cut at proper angles so the building could be made as straight or square as possible. A good builder would go through several options before deciding which stone was best suited to lay as the cornerstone.

Peter seizes on a common early Christian metaphor for Christ. Quoting from Isaiah 28:16, Peter explains that the house of God—God's "temple"—was being built with Christ as the cornerstone. God is the builder, and God chose Christ as the stone substantial enough to hold its position, as true enough to allow for plumb construction of straight and strong walls. In subsequent verses, Peter will quote Psalm 118:22, explaining that while God chose Christ as the cornerstone, others have passed over Christ. Metaphorically, they build their lives on other inadequate stones, thinking Christ a poor building stone. Then in reference to Isaiah 8:14, Peter notes that instead of serving to build a great temple, these people trip over Christ, stumbling instead of serving the true God.

Christians live in the house of God as priests, kingdom citizens, and God's own people. We live in God's house—his temple—constructed on the love and truth of Jesus the Messiah. Peter knows that the only true path through the suffering and difficulties of life is found in the joy of belonging to God through the death and resurrection of Christ. We will never be put to shame—be disappointed—when we trust in Jesus.

Lord, may I live on the truth of Jesus, my redeemer. I rest in your love in him, amen.

OCTOBER 5

But you are a chosen race, a royal priesthood, a holy nation, a people for his own possession, that you may proclaim the excellencies of him who called you out of darkness into his marvelous light. (1 Pet. 2:9)

The southern boy in me understands *y'all* to be not only part of the English language but an important part. Yes, I know that *you* is the plural of *you.* But how do you tell the difference between meaning one person or meaning a group? Ancient Greek distinguished between a plural *you* (y'all) and a singular *you.* Granted, sometimes the Greek plural *you* means the whole group of people individually, but the South takes care of that with "all y'all."

While the individual's relationship with God often draws focused attention in Bible study, the Bible often addresses community needs and relationships for groups of God's people. Today's passage is important for its affirmations about both individuals and also Christians as a group.

Peter uses the Greek plural—in other words, *y'all*—in describing the readers as a "chosen race" or "chosen family," as it can also be translated. This comes in a passage that has just described Christ as a "chosen" stone for the building that is the church (1 Pet. 2:4, 6). It also echoes language of Israel as a nation given throughout the Old Testament. Isaiah 43:20–21 speaks of God having people he "chose" and took as his own to proclaim his glorious deeds.

Peter then alludes to another important Old Testament reference for Israel, found in Exodus 19:5–6, where God says Israel is to be his "own people . . . a royal priesthood and holy nation." Those same words used by Peter to describe the believers in Christ were earlier used of Israel. Paul touches on this concept when he tells the Romans that the church was "grafted" onto the tree that was God's people of Israel (Rom. 11:17–24).

Our role in God's kingdom as a chosen family, a royal priesthood attending to the ministrations of God's presence in this world, is given at the end of the passage. We are to "proclaim the excellencies" of God. This is the role of the church as a whole—y'all. It is also the task of each of us in the church—all y'all. We should live each day proclaiming God's excellencies.

Lord, may I along with your fuller church proclaim your greatness to the world by how I live and what I do to your glory in Jesus, amen.

OCTOBER 6

Beloved, I urge you as sojourners and exiles to abstain from the passions of the flesh, which wage war against your soul. Keep your conduct among the Gentiles honorable, so that when they speak against you as evildoers, they may see your good deeds and glorify God on the day of visitation. (1 Pet. 2:11–12)

Peter was present when the Lord Jesus taught his disciples to pray. As the Lord's Prayer unfolds in Matthew, the request placed before God is "Your kingdom come, your will be done, on earth as it is in heaven" (Mt. 6:10). That Peter took this to heart is not surprising. Indeed, the earliest ancient record shows that the early church was taught to say this prayer three times daily (*Didache* 8:2–3).

Knowing this prayer as a fundamental and routine Christian experience, today's passage comes into sharp focus. Peter hasn't used the term *kingdom*, but he has used kingdom vocabulary in describing the church as a "royal priesthood" and a "holy nation" in the preceding verses. Our life in this world is to be one of "sojourning" or "exile." As the old gospel song says, "This world is not my home; I'm just a-passing through." God will bring a new heaven and new earth to his people, but in the interim, it is the Christian's job to live the promised kingdom lifestyle while in exile. This is the underlying idea behind the prayer of Jesus that the kingdom of God might come on earth as it is in heaven.

How does the believer do this? How do we live so that the kingdom comes around us? When I was young and living in upstate New York, each summer, Mom and Dad would drive us all to Texas to be with our family. Before returning, Mom would pack the car with Wolf Brand chili, a product she couldn't buy in New York but a staple of our diet as Texans living in exile in the North. In this sense, Peter explains that the believer living in this world takes from heaven the ethics and conduct defined by the loving and good God and brings it into the sojourning life in this world.

God's conduct isn't always easy in a world based on satisfying human passions and desires. Ads, music, and shows bombard us with examples and urgings to satisfy base desires. Even the economy is built around the idea of *getting*, in contrast to the teaching of Jesus built around *giving*. If we are to pray, "May God's kingdom come on earth," we are to live it as well. It is who we are as citizens of God.

Lord, give me a heart for your passions over that of this world. Let the world see you in me to your glory. In Jesus, amen.

OCTOBER 7

Be subject for the Lord's sake to every human institution. . . . Servants, be subject to your masters with all respect. . . . Likewise, wives, be subject to your own husbands. . . . Likewise, husbands, live with your wives in an understanding way. . . . Finally, all of you, have unity of mind, sympathy, brotherly love, a tender heart, and a humble mind. Do not repay evil for evil or reviling for reviling, but on the contrary, bless, for to this you were called, that you may obtain a blessing. (1 Pet. 2:13, 18; 3:1, 7–9)

Few English speakers are familiar with the Germanic word *haustafel.* From the German for "house table," the word was likely brought into Christian studies by Martin Luther. *Haustafel* references the family codes contained in the ancient apostolic and early church writings. Today's passage is one of the classic writings of *haustafel.*

The ancient world was built around social structures unlike many of ours today. As early as Aristotle (384–322 BC), one reads of household management. In his *Politics,* Aristotle describes three basic social structures at home: husbands/wives, parents/children, and masters/slaves (see book 1). Peter, like Paul, wrote within these social structures, teaching the Christian how to behave.

These ancient household rules speak into a social world quite different from today. Unlike in Peter's day, slavery is now illegal. Today, children are expected to grow up and leave home and the authority of their parents, something alien in Peter's day. In the twenty-first-century Western world, wives have rights to property, equal rights in society, education, and independence apart from their husbands, unlike in Peter's world. Men no longer hold full legal power over enslaved people, adult children, and wives. Similarly, in the modern West, there is no emperor with power over life and death for all subjects.

The social structures may differ today, but the underlying principles behind Peter's household codes (*haustafeln*) are unchanged. God's people are to live in sympathy, love, respect, tenderness, and humility toward all. Evil is to be repaid with love, not vengeance. How these values are expressed will, of course, differ in today's society. But the drive to express in all relationships the values of God and godliness is no less important. Our goal is to find in our modern households and social world the expressions of God's standards.

Lord, teach me humility, love, tenderness, and sympathy toward others. In Jesus, amen.

OCTOBER 8

For "Whoever desires to love life and see good days, let him keep his tongue from evil and his lips from speaking deceit; let him turn away from evil and do good; let him seek peace and pursue it. For the eyes of the Lord are on the righteous, and his ears are open to their prayer. But the face of the Lord is against those who do evil." (1 Pet. 3:10–12)

This book is the fifth in a series I've written that are kindly published by Baylor University. The first book was on the Psalms. For well over a decade, I had tried to read through the Psalms each month. They had majorly affected my life, and I thought they would affect my children. So I wrote that first book in hopes that my children would make their way through the Psalms, a powerful source of life-enriching material.

The earliest Christians spent a great deal of time in the Psalms. Paul urged the early church to sing them (Eph. 5:19; Col. 3:16). All the ancient apostolic writers quoted from them, including Peter in today's passage. Peter drew his material from Psalm 34:12–16.

I like Peter's usage of this Psalms passage. Peter wasn't the first one to use ideas and language from Psalm 34. James 3 (on the tongue) and Hebrews 12 (on living peacefully with others) also reflect echoes of this passage. Why?

The passage contains core Christian behaviors: watch what you say, do good, seek peace. Peter turns the original Psalm slightly to bring out less of the judgment of the original (Peter stops the last verse prematurely) so that it better applies in the context of suffering, which is Peter's driving concern in the letter. Similarly, Peter alters the arrangement from one that emphasizes long life and prosperity on earth to one that speaks to the eternal prosperity and life found in Christ.

It is good to use Scripture as Peter does. Knowing it and understanding its context allow readers to see in Scripture principles, behavior, and judgment that then apply to the current story one is living. This is why I loved reading the Psalms each month. A psalm might speak to me in one way one time but provide me with a different inspiration on another day. Peter found in the Psalms good, solid teaching, which he utilized to speak into the current lives of his readers. This makes me want to spend more time in the Bible! Written for the ages, it applies to me today.

Lord, thank you for your word. Speak to me through it. In Jesus' name, amen.

OCTOBER 9

In your hearts honor Christ the Lord as holy, always being prepared to make a defense to anyone who asks you for a reason for the hope that is in you; yet do it with gentleness and respect, having a good conscience, so that, when you are slandered, those who revile your good behavior in Christ may be put to shame. (1 Pet. 3:15–16)

A friend was convinced that Jesus was a man—a good man—but that Jesus was not divine God. My friend believed that to be found nowhere in the Bible. He believed the divinity of Jesus was only found in the pages of church history in the centuries following the apostolic age and authorship of the New Testament. Scholars call the study of Jesus' nature Christology.

I gently tried to defend winsomely the divinity of Christ, as Peter calls his readers to do, with a tone and life that reflected trust and faith in Christ and with biblical texts. This very text is a prime example of my friend's misunderstanding of the biblical truths about Jesus.

I began today's passage with 1 Peter 3:15, but Peter's flow started several verses earlier. In the immediate verse preceding my selection, Peter began a quotation from Isaiah 8:12–13, where, in the ancient Greek version of the Old Testament prominent in Peter's day, it read, "Have no fear of them, nor be troubled." This is all well and good, and Peter could have moved on from there. But Peter didn't. Peter continued Isaiah's quote but with one major alteration.

The Isaiah passage continues with "But the LORD of hosts, him you shall honor as holy." The full capitalization of "LORD" is to let the reader know that in Hebrew, Isaiah is using the name of God himself, as revealed to Moses, and not simply the Hebrew word for "lord." Isaiah says to fear the one true God. Peter grabs that command and inserts Christ to be feared *as the* LORD! (Again, Peter is using the Greek Old Testament, so Peter doesn't write the Hebrew name of God.) Peter knew Christ was God and was to be honored and praised as God. Jesus was not simply a good fellow who regretfully met an early death.

Jesus' followers should honor Jesus as Lord not only by the way they live and the praise in their mouths but with persuasive reasoning to lead others to truth. Today's passage is a good reminder for us all.

Lord, may I praise your name by my life. Teach me to teach others Jesus, amen.

OCTOBER 10

For it is better to suffer for doing good, if that should be God's will, than for doing evil. For Christ also suffered once for sins, the righteous for the unrighteous, that he might bring us to God, being put to death in the flesh but made alive in the spirit. (1 Pet. 3:17–18)

Suffering is a deep and often personal topic for many. No one likes to suffer. By definition, suffering is painful. The pain may be physical, emotional, mental, or relational, but the hurt is real. People work assiduously hard to avoid suffering. It comes to everyone but isn't treasured.

People often ask, "Would a good God allow suffering?" Or an ancillary question: "If God is all-powerful, why does he allow suffering?" People today have a different view of suffering from the New Testament writers. They didn't question whether God allowed or willed people to suffer. They knew he did. The clearest example was Jesus. That Jesus would suffer physically, mentally, and spiritually was a purposed and willed decision of the Triune God. Jesus suffered *for a reason*. Jesus was taking on the sins and their consequences of those he had created and loved. The righteous Jesus was suffering because of the unrighteous, including you and me.

This route of suffering was ultimately brought about not by God's behavior but by the sinfulness of Adam, Eve, and their progeny. God didn't create people as machine programs. We aren't computers or puppets. We are real people who have the power and ability to make real choices. God could create a computer program. He could make the perfect robot that executes preprogrammed commands, but that isn't humanity. I can choose to hurt someone with what I say or build them up. Those are my choices. God doesn't put celestial duct tape over my mouth and prevent me from making a bad choice with my words.

So in this real world with real people making real choices, sin runs rampant. Selfishness reigns supreme. People get hurt. Suffering is real. God will fix it all one day, but the new world he will create without suffering isn't here yet. Now consider Peter's admonition. There are times when God will use my suffering to comfort or reach others. This means that sometimes I get called on to suffer for the cause of Christ. Christ did that for me. If I can suffer for his sake, I should not challenge God; I should rejoice that he would use me, let me join his mission, and count me worthy of following Jesus. This is a radically different view of suffering.

Lord, may I serve you on your mission, wherever that takes me. For Jesus' sake, amen.

OCTOBER 11

Since therefore Christ suffered in the flesh, arm yourselves with the same way of thinking, for whoever has suffered in the flesh has ceased from sin, so as to live for the rest of the time in the flesh no longer for human passions but for the will of God. (1 Pet. 4:1–2)

At some point, I decided to learn Korean. The alphabet (*Hangul*) was surprisingly easy, but much of the language came only with great effort. Even after I worked on the basics for nearly a year, a native Korean speaker would speak so rapidly that my ears couldn't decipher what was said. They were speaking a foreign language!

In some ways, today's passage reminds me of learning Korean. Peter speaks of those who suffer in the flesh having "ceased from sin." As of the time I am typing this, I have walked with the Lord for over five decades. I have suffered in that time, albeit not to the point of martyrdom. But despite my suffering, I haven't remotely come close to ceasing from sin! My frustration with my sin is further aggravated when reading the verb tenses in the Greek. Typically, the first verb of one who has "*suffered* in the flesh" refers to something happening in the past, while the second verb, "*ceased* from sin," refers to a past event with an emphasis on the present ongoing consequences. None of my past suffering has left me no longer sinning!

Scholars advance many ways to understand this passage, but I tend to go back to a tighter examination of the second verb, translated "ceased" (*pauō*—παύω). In the passive/middle form in which it is found, it generally means to either take one's rest from sin or cease and be done with sin. I don't think Peter is suggesting that suffering believers will never sin again, for if that was the result of suffering, Peter would not need to instruct his suffering readers to "arm" themselves with an attitude or way of thinking as a safeguard against the old sinful behaviors that are described in the coming verses. Peter is rather indicating that as we suffer for Christ, as we "deny ourselves and pick up our cross and follow" him (Mt. 16:24), our sinful lives of debauchery are over. Following Jesus necessarily and naturally gives us a new purpose and focus.

The key takeaway from this passage is to arm oneself with the attitude of following Jesus. Suffering comes to the believer but isn't a wretched pain to be avoided. Jesus' followers, following a suffering Messiah, should likewise expect to suffer. But Jesus will use that suffering in our lives to make us more like himself.

Lord, give me peace in following Jesus. Work in my suffering for your good. Amen.

OCTOBER 12

The end of all things is at hand; therefore be self-controlled and sober-minded for the sake of your prayers. Above all, keep loving one another earnestly, since love covers a multitude of sins. Show hospitality to one another without grumbling. As each has received a gift, use it to serve one another, as good stewards of God's varied grace . . . in order that in everything God may be glorified through Jesus Christ. (1 Pet. 4:7–11)

I went through a period when I would fast every other day. My fasting wasn't out of piety—or I would have heeded the admonition from Jesus and refrained from talking about it (Mt. 6:16–18)! Mine was a diet and health effort. But I found that on days of fasting, I tended to go to bed earlier. It wasn't because I was out of energy; it was because I was eager for the new day and its breakfast! I knew after going to sleep, breakfast was almost immediate, since time passes differently in sleep.

The New Testament carries a theme resembling that of my experiencing time in alternate-day fasting. For all believers in the resurrected Christ, we can affirm that the "end of all things is at hand." Life itself is fleeting. I believe the saying "The days are long, but the years fly by." With the end of life comes a state Paul equated to sleeping (1 Thess. 4:13). After this sleep comes living in the presence of the Lord for eternity. In a real sense, the end of everything on this earth is near for all.

This rightly motivates the believer. We should live today with a conscious realization of these fundamental truths. Peter calls it living "sober-minded." As we live mindfully, we will pray in deeper communion with God. We will show genuine love to others and not live in bitterness of or dwell on the sins of others. Our efforts will be to help others along their path, showing hospitality and Christian caring with a great attitude. We will understand that each day is a gift from God, and each opportunity to do good is his path set before us. And we will walk through those daily opportunities to his glory and might.

Knowing what is coming and that it is coming soon should affect us all. My constant prayer is that I do not get caught up on life's treadmill where my days fritter away. I pray that I will not miss or ignore the chances to glorify God in my mind, in my life, and with my opportunities. Like my fasting for diet and health, when we are mindful of the limits on life, it modifies how we live.

Lord, give me the mindfulness to not only know you, but to draw close to you, and to live for your glory as a good steward of what you give. In Jesus' name, amen.

OCTOBER 13

Beloved, do not be surprised at the fiery trial when it comes upon you to test you, as though something strange were happening to you. But rejoice insofar as you share Christ's sufferings, that you may also rejoice and be glad when his glory is revealed. (1 Pet. 4:12–13)

Justin Martyr was born around AD 100, a pagan who studied Greek philosophy, especially the Stoics and Plato. He was well educated by the time he came to the Christian faith around the age of thirty-two. Soon after his conversion, he spent his life on the road working to convert the academics of his day. His work included writing defenses of the faith, some of which he wrote to the Roman emperors of his day. Many of his writings survive today and were extremely important in spreading the Christian faith in the middle of the second century. He wrote of the power of seeing Christians willingly suffer martyrdom, and he speaks to the role that played in his coming to faith. Justin himself suffered martyrdom when he was beheaded on order of the Roman emperor.

Suffering for the cause of Christ has a powerful ripple effect. The suffering can produce a sharper focus and more attentive and deliberate walk with God, as Peter has already explained in his letter. But the ripples go out much farther than the life of the one afflicted. Just as Justin and countless others came to faith because of the impact of seeing Christians suffer gladly on behalf of Christ, so others today will notice when they watch you and I suffer without grumbling.

Suffering today becomes martyrdom in a surprising number of countries in the world—fifty by some counts as of this writing. But that doesn't mean that other suffering is easy. Everyone will suffer in life, and Christians often suffer in ways that others don't. Yet how the Christian faces suffering is Peter's focus and should be ours.

Peter knows this world is not God's Eden. This world is a war zone, fallen from purity and driven by sinful and selfish people. Egos and arrogance reign supreme. Passions and desires drive decisions. Into this world of sin, God has claimed a people who he made his own through the suffering death and sacrifice of Jesus. God's people will then suffer. It is part of God's toolbox for bringing more people into faith and for purifying those in the faith. Knowing this, the Christian should count it an honor to share in the suffering of Christ—that is, to join Christ on his mission and be used by God for the good of others. That is a high and important calling!

Lord, give me a godly attitude amid suffering. Let the world see Jesus in me, amen.

OCTOBER 14

So I exhort the elders among you, as a fellow elder and a witness of the sufferings of Christ, as well as a partaker in the glory that is going to be revealed: shepherd the flock of God that is among you, exercising oversight, not under compulsion, but willingly, as God would have you; not for shameful gain, but eagerly; not domineering over those in your charge, but being examples to the flock. (1 Pet. 5:1–3)

Lots of books and seminars center on leadership. What it means to be a leader and how one goes about leading effectively are important to many. Relationships are a core feature of being human, and few interactions don't involve one or more leading while others follow. Even the decision of where a group will go out to eat together requires someone to begin the discussion of "Where should we go?"

In leadership, as well as almost all aspects of life, the Bible speaks. Some might read what I've written so far or even read today's passage and think, "Well, I'm not really in a position of leadership. This doesn't apply to me." Yet almost everyone *does* have times or opportunities to lead. In those times, we can learn from Peter's message in today's verses.

Peter speaks to leaders of the local congregation as a leader himself. So we see in Peter's words not only admonition and instruction to others on how to lead but also Peter modeling leadership. Peter practices what he preaches. Good leaders must do that. Leading is not pointing out to others where to go and what to do. It is getting in front, serving and doing. A good friend of mine took a new job running a yard crew. He began the job not by telling the crew where to dig a ditch. He began by grabbing a shovel and telling them, "Let's get this trench dug here." A good leader leads by example.

Some argue this passage indicates the author isn't Peter the apostle, for surely he would self-identify as such instead of simply writing as "one of many" fellow elders. Yet Peter rightly elevates his fellow leaders by placing himself on the same level as them. Peter will rapidly move in the next verses to the importance of humility, a trait Peter models.

Peter explains leadership is best when leaders don't lord it over others but serve others. Leadership through service—this is a lesson for all of us in life.

Lord, may my life reflect your love for others in humility and service. In him, amen.

OCTOBER 15

Clothe yourselves, all of you, with humility toward one another, for "God opposes the proud but gives grace to the humble." Humble yourselves, therefore, under the mighty hand of God so that at the proper time he may exalt you, casting all your anxieties on him, because he cares for you. (1 Pet. 5:5–7)

I was running late to a semiformal event. I had on nice trousers, a dress shirt, and a sports jacket. I realized that before I left, I needed to start some dinner rolls so they could rise while I was gone. (I love to bake!) I made the mistake of going to the kitchen, removing my jacket, and thinking I could work fast. I didn't tie on an apron. Yes, the flour got all over my clothes. I felt like a fool.

My story begins the study of today's passage because of a unique Greek word Peter uses for "clothe yourselves." It isn't the normal word Paul uses to describe clothing oneself. Peter uses a word for putting on a smock or apron over one's tunic (*egkombōma*—ἐγκόμβωμα). This was worn generally by slaves to keep their tunics clean while working. In modern parlance, Peter tells them to put on the apron of humility to keep their clothes clean!

Scripture speaks often about the importance of humility. A trait modeled by Jesus by dwelling among us as God incarnate (Phil. 2:5–8), genuine humility means recognizing the sovereignty of God over life and living one's place before God as his servant. If anyone had reason to trumpet their virtue, to lord over others their importance, to be an ego-driven commander of praise, it was Jesus. Yet Jesus, while his apostles were arguing over their relative importance in his ministry, took a bowl of water and began the lowly servant's job of washing their feet.

Believers follow Christ most truly when they live in humility. Not a mock or pretend humility. Christians should not seek to take credit for their achievements because they truly see the hand of God over them, and they should live as servants of the King, recognizing God has created all of us in his image.

This attitude of humility, based on a deep understanding of God, arms the believer for life. The apron stops the flour from dusting the suit. Humility stops the filth of sin from marring one's service in life. It leaves believers better able to walk under God's care, not their own efforts.

Lord, I want your care and love to handle this life for me. Let me live in humility to you and others, serving them as you have modeled in Jesus, amen.

OCTOBER 16

Be sober-minded; be watchful. Your adversary the devil prowls around like a roaring lion, seeking someone to devour. Resist him, firm in your faith, knowing that the same kinds of suffering are being experienced by your brotherhood throughout the world. And after you have suffered a little while, the God of all grace, who has called you to his eternal glory in Christ, will himself restore, confirm, strengthen, and establish you. To him be the dominion forever and ever. Amen. (1 Pet. 5:8–11)

In 1977, Keith Green put out his song titled "Satan's Boast." The gist of the song is Satan boasting on his success in the world today. His key to winning? He convinces people that he doesn't exist, a sort of antifaith. Singing from the perspective of Satan, Keith says, "It's getting very easy now 'cause no one believes in me anymore." Satan's boast is that "he used to have to sneak around, but now he just goes through the door!" Deception is easier when no one sees it.

Peter wanted his readers fully aware of the deeds of the demonic. While God wants his children to grow strong, maturing in the faith, Satan also has an interest in the believer; Satan wants to harm the believer. Thus believers must be "sober-minded," or "clearheaded." We mustn't ignore the evil that is going on around us and is at work. We should "be watchful," or "be alert."

What does it mean to be alert to the designs and activities of the enemy? The answer shouldn't be isolated from these verses, for the whole letter, all of Scripture, is written to help God's children better follow him. But in this specific flow of Peter's letter, he instructs the reader to "resist" the devil, staying "firm in your faith." Resisting Satan means standing firm in the face of his onslaught. This standing requires being firm in faith because our own strength isn't sufficient to overcome the wiles of the enemy. But walking and standing in trust of God is the anchor we need to withstand the storms of Satan and life.

Suffering and hardship can be tools of the enemy to move us from living in faith, just as much as ignorance. In whatever way Satan attacks, we can rest assured that our alertness to Satan's work and our trust in God will bring endurance to the glory of God in Christ. This admonition is the last one in Peter's letter because it is important.

Lord, give me faith amid the evil in this world. Open my eyes to evil, and provide the path for victory. In Jesus' name, amen.

OCTOBER 17

Simeon Peter, a servant and apostle of Jesus Christ. To those who have obtained a faith of equal standing with ours by the righteousness of our God and Savior Jesus Christ. (2 Pet. 1:1)

Second Peter begins with several interesting scholastic issues, from the rare spelling of Simon (the Aramaic "Simeon") to the non-Aramaic ancient equivalent to Rocky (the Greek "Peter" rather than the Aramaic "Cephas"). But what interests me most, appealing to the trial lawyer in me, is the phrase "To those who have obtained a faith of equal standing." With this start, Peter sets out one core point that so many of us miss, at least subconsciously. Peter writes as "an apostle" yet sees the faith of his recipients as of "equal standing." God doesn't play favorites on the issue of faith. All believers are rightfully in his full and proper standing, as we all share the righteousness of God, our Savior Jesus Christ.

As I write this devotional this morning, I am reminded of an email I recently received. We were set for a hearing in front of a "Special Master" designated by our trial judge to referee our disagreements. The agenda was set. Then in the pre-dawn hours before the hearing, the lawyers for the defendant filed a massive letter brief, pre-arguing their case. They were seeking to influence the decision-maker *before* all parties got a chance to present their case. They wanted *unequal footing.*

God is not that way. None of us need worry about whether we have "enough" faith, whether our faith is as strong as another's, or whether we have enough righteousness to merit God's attentive care. Our Father sets the footing of all his children on the righteousness of Jesus. Jesus is the great equalizer.

I heard it said once that every person reaches up for God. Some reach higher than others, some seem more righteous than others. But as we all reach up unequally, God still must reach down all the way. No one has a profusion of righteousness that sets them apart in their standing before God. All the righteousness that forms our standing before God is imputed to us by Jesus and comes from his grace. Without the grace of God and the righteousness of Christ, we would all be dust in the wind, of no use to anyone.

Lord, I pray for the righteousness of Jesus. I thank you for it and pray you will transform me into his likeness so I better reflect him. I pray in Jesus' name, amen.

OCTOBER 18

His divine power has granted to us all things that pertain to life and godliness, through the knowledge of him who called us to his own glory and excellence, by which he has granted to us his precious and very great promises, so that through them you may become partakers of the divine nature, having escaped from the corruption that is in the world because of sinful desire. (2 Pet. 1:3–4)

Two for one is usually a great deal. I have one friend who will automatically buy whatever is being sold if he can get two for the price of one. This is true even if he would never buy one in the first place! For my friend, 2 Peter should be his favorite book among the Epistles. Peter is fond of using two terms to describe one idea. Grammarians have an unusual term for this writing trait (*hendiadys*), and it is a bit out of vogue in modern writing, although Shakespeare was quite fond of it!

A classic example of this "two for one" type of writing is found in the work of the ancient poet Virgil (70–19 BC), who wrote, "We drink from cups and gold." Virgil used two words joined by "and" to express one idea. In modern English, we wouldn't write that way. We would say, "We drink from golden cups," making the two words one idea. Today's passage offers this grammatical usage three times!

Peter writes of God's divine power granting believers all things that pertain to "life and godliness." These are expressed as two terms, but what Peter means is best translated in English as "a godly life." Every believer in Christ has God's power available to live a godly life—a good life right before God. Then Peter links this power for a godly life to knowing him who called us to his own "glory and excellence," or his "glorious excellence." This phrase, common in ancient Greece, reflected the rightful honor due to someone who lived an honorable life (here the honor due to Jesus for his life). As we know the excellence of Jesus more and more, we grow in our ability to live godly lives. In knowing Jesus, we walk in his "precious and great promises," another two for one! God's promises are indeed greatly precious. What could be more amazing than escaping from the sin of this world and its tight grip on the sinner?

Peter is making a bold assertion in his own grammatical way. He wants his readers to know that as we grow in knowing Jesus, God is using his divine power to teach us godliness. It is part of his precious promise to his children!

Lord, please give me greater closeness with Jesus. I pray in him, amen.

OCTOBER 19

Make every effort to supplement your faith with virtue, and virtue with knowledge, and knowledge with self-control, and self-control with steadfastness, and steadfastness with godliness, and godliness with brotherly affection, and brotherly affection with love. For if these qualities are yours and are increasing, they keep you from being ineffective or unfruitful in the knowledge of our Lord Jesus Christ. For whoever lacks these qualities is so nearsighted that he is blind, having forgotten that he was cleansed from his former sins. (2 Pet. 1:5–9)

I was twelve years old when my grandfather decided I needed to learn to drive. He would take me out on oil leases where he worked in West Texas and have me drive on the caliche roads, with all their potholes and washed-out areas. It seemed I hit every pothole! He asked me if I was aiming for them, and I told him I didn't see them. When we got back to the house, he told my mom I must be blind as a bat. Mom took me to the eye doctor, who proclaimed, "He *is* blind as a bat!" So began my life with glasses, and it was transformative. School was different, baseball was different, people were different!

In today's passage Peter writes of folks who are blind as bats! These folks have forgotten the cleansing work of Jesus. In very blunt, practical terms, Peter details that they need to grow in faith, knowledge, self-control, steadfastness, godliness, brotherly affection, and caring love. I left out of my recitation of Peter's chain of terms the one that is translated as "virtue" (*aretē*—ἀρετή). It is hard to wrap this Greek word into one English word. For this trait, I might say "excellent character" or the kind of virtue that people appreciate, honor, and desire. This type of virtue is the bedrock that is characteristic of Christ (it is used of him in a preceding verse) and grows out of one's faith.

These traits are not fully achievable in anyone's life, but they are traits in which we grow. Peter adds that these traits should be "increasing." As we grow in these traits, we become more effective and fruitful for God and his kingdom. This is important to how we see the world. These are corrective lenses that change life. We see problems differently, treat others better, live with purpose and direction, deepen our joy and peace, and become kinder and gentler.

Getting glasses changed my life. Growing in the knowledge of Jesus and learning and developing his character in my own life are even more life changing!

Lord, give me greater vision of Jesus as I seek to become godly for you. Amen.

OCTOBER 20

But false prophets also arose among the people, just as there will be false teachers among you, who will secretly bring in destructive heresies, even denying the Master who bought them, bringing upon themselves swift destruction. And many will follow their sensuality, and because of them the way of truth will be blasphemed. And in their greed they will exploit you with false words. Their condemnation from long ago is not idle, and their destruction is not asleep. (2 Pet. 2:1–3)

While taking high school English, I was at the same time taking every speech class our school offered. So while I had English teachers teaching me various forms of writing, I was studying classical rhetoric as well as modern speechmaking, persuasion, and argumentation. All these classes opened my eyes to different ways to use words for different purposes.

Following closely on the heels of these classes on the power of word choice came my training in Latin, ancient Greek, and Hebrew. Included were readings from the Bible as well as other ancient texts. All of this affected my reading of books like 2 Peter, especially the passages in this second chapter. Peter will write of God casting angels into hell in chains until judgment, Noah, Sodom and Gomorrah, Lot, Balaam and his talking donkey, and more in the coming verses. Peter is arguing from a classical rhetorical perspective.

In antiquity, while there was some slight variation, argument and persuasion followed a certain order and approach in presentations. Second Peter closely mirrors a good bit of these ancient rhetorical practices. It began with an introduction to secure the audience's goodwill, including the author's identity and reason for writing. The persuasive purpose is set out in the verses that were covered over the past several days of devotionals. Then chapter 1 ends, and these next chapters continue to give Peter's proofs of his thesis.

Without trying to review the details of all Peter's accounts, although they are chronicled to the greatest extent in the pages of the Old Testament, I want to look at the bigger picture. Peter wants his readers to assiduously follow Jesus and God's truth. True knowledge of Jesus is life changing. Flimsy and destructive teaching, rationalizations that excuse sin, and misdirected attention that draws from the simple truth are all *provably* dangerous! It isn't overly complicated. Follow Jesus!

Lord, I want to know you better and follow you closely through Jesus, amen.

OCTOBER 21

This is now the second letter that I am writing to you, beloved. In both of them I am stirring up your sincere mind by way of reminder, that you should remember the predictions of the holy prophets and the commandment of the Lord and Savior through your apostles. (2 Pet. 3:1–2)

People randomly forget things. I certainly do. At least once a month, I can't find my keys or my wallet. Multiple times I have declared my wallet "stolen," necessitating the cancellation and replacement of all my cards, only to find it in the most unusual places later. I was given those discs to put into my wallet so I could find it, and I lost the discs before I could use them. I need reminders.

Peter writes a "reminder" to his former letter. While scholars debate over what that former letter might have been (1 Peter? Jude? Part of 2 Peter? An unknown letter?), the key to the passage for today's purposes is the reminder. Peter wants his reminder to stir up the reader's "sincere mind." Peter is not using a cooking term in the Greek for "stir up" but rather a word for awakening someone or stirring up a calm sea.

Peter doesn't want his readers to conclude that God has forgotten his promise to return, that God has abandoned his world, or that God is slow to do that which he sets himself to do. God will fulfill his promises in God's good time. Peter will go on to say that God's time is *not* the same as human time. God has purposes beyond our knowledge. His ways often seem mysterious. Peter's example concerns the second coming and the end of days. Peter explains that God hasn't delayed this out of slowness. Rather, God is awaiting the filling of his kingdom. Jesus will return once things are ripe, but that day will be one no one knows.

As one thinks through these assurances of God and the realization of his unique and omniscient timing, it affects us in the here and now. We should live with confidence in God, his goodness, his instructions, and his timing. I need Peter's reminder. Often I seek to wedge God and his plans into my timing and my plans. It's as if I need to help God along. Abraham had this same problem, as he tried to force an heir, lied about Sarah as his wife or sister, and more. I should know better. If instead of pursuing my timing, I wait on God's deliverance, it will make my life much simpler. I can simply seek to live right step by step, day by day.

Lord, I trust you with today and tomorrow. Thank you for your faithfulness. Help me serve you faithfully, remembering what you've promised and trusting in your timing. In Jesus, amen.

OCTOBER 22

Grow in the grace and knowledge of our Lord and Savior Jesus Christ. To him be the glory both now and to the day of eternity. Amen. (2 Pet. 3:18)

Gardens have always fascinated me. The idea that I could stick a seed in the ground, and that seed would become corn, tomatoes, or you name it has a *wow* factor to me. If I watched the plant twenty-four hours a day, seven days a week, I wouldn't notice, as it slowly grows after its first appearance, but seeing it less frequently, its growth is more readily apparent. Without growth, planting a seed is worthless.

Peter closes his letter with a word that applied to gardening as well as people. He tells his readers to "grow" (*auxanō*—αὐξάνω). Peter uses this word in a command form, placing it in the present tense, which his ancient readers would understand as an admonition to do this in each moment of life. Standing still in one's walk with God is never a biblical idea. No one can get where they need to be by staying where they are.

Peter doesn't simply want growth; he wants growth in the right direction. The direction? Jesus! Each of us is admonished to grow daily in the "grace and knowledge" of Jesus. Peter's Greek presents translators with an interesting option. Is Peter writing about growing in the grace Jesus gives or the knowledge about Jesus? Or is something else at play?

Regardless of the translation, the thrust of Peter's command is clear. I am to grow in God's grace or favor. My life should have a daily goal of reaching greater degrees of holiness and maturity in Jesus. This opportunity itself is a gift from Jesus, for without his sacrifice and resurrection, I would be lost growing toward God.

Similarly, I will find growing in God's grace aligned with growing in my knowledge of Jesus. Knowledge in the Greek sense could include an element of intimacy not present in the English idea of knowing. Peter wants his readers to consciously seek to be closer to God and Jesus. This closeness is rooted in pursuing Jesus with our minds as well as our hearts.

My garden plants grow toward the sun. God made them to follow the sun. I am no different. God made me to grow toward his Son. This is to God's glory. Amen.

Lord, grow me, please. I want to be closer to you in Jesus, amen.

OCTOBER 23

Paul, an apostle of Christ Jesus by the will of God according to the promise of the life that is in Christ Jesus, To Timothy, my beloved child: Grace, mercy, and peace from God the Father and Christ Jesus our Lord. I thank God whom I serve, as did my ancestors, with a clear conscience, as I remember you constantly in my prayers night and day. (2 Tim. 1:1–3)

My grandmother Katherine was well into her nineties when she died. In her later years, there were several times she came to my law office, having made an appointment "with her lawyer." She dressed up and came with a serious yet sincere attitude reflecting her purpose. She wanted to get her will just right. It was important to her to not only dispose properly of her possessions but make sure that her descendants understood why she was giving what to whom. She was reflective in thought, long in memory, and deliberate in vocabulary.

Reading Paul's second letter to Timothy evokes memories of my grandmother. Paul knows his end is near. He writes a set of wishes but begins by reminiscing. Paul reflects on Timothy's special place in his life. Describing Timothy as his "beloved child" (not physically but spiritually), Paul strolls down memory lane in the coming verses that follow today's passage. Paul mentions the tears Timothy shed for Paul. Paul recounts the sincere faith that Timothy's mother and grandmother had passed on to him. Remembering Timothy brought the imprisoned Paul joy.

Living with a recognition that all of us will one day pass from this world gives a different focus to life. The psalmist asked God, "Teach us to number our days that we may get a heart of wisdom" (Ps. 90:12). When we live aware of the end, we see others differently, we honor each moment for the eternal opportunity it holds, we treasure what is truly valuable over the ephemeral and temporary, and we shift our priorities.

I want that heart of wisdom. I want to live each moment as it counts. I heard Jarrett Stephens preach once where he had a visual image of jars filled with M&M's or something similar. If each candy was a day of life, he pointed out that no one knows how many any of us have left in our jar. We may assume a lot, but at some point, we will all run out. How do we spend our days? Paul invested in God's kingdom and people like Timothy. It rightly brought Paul joy in the end.

Lord, teach me to number my days, and grant a heart of wisdom in Jesus, amen.

OCTOBER 24

Therefore do not be ashamed of the testimony about our Lord, nor of me his prisoner, but share in suffering for the gospel by the power of God, who saved us and called us to a holy calling, not because of our works but because of his own purpose and grace, which he gave us in Christ Jesus before the ages began, and which now has been manifested through the appearing of our Savior Christ Jesus, who abolished death and brought life and immortality to light through the gospel, for which I was appointed a preacher and apostle and teacher, which is why I suffer as I do. But I am not ashamed, for I know whom I have believed, and I am convinced that he is able to guard until that day what has been entrusted to me. (2 Tim. 1:8–12)

Our son-in-law put a tree swing up in his yard for our grandchildren. This wasn't a normal-sized tree swing. The seat was at the end of a twenty-foot tether. The swing for those children was almost forty feet, taking them nearly twenty feet off the ground at apex. Our two-year-old twin granddaughters were gleeful in that swing. Louise said to me, "Do click, click, click!" I didn't know what she meant until JT told me, "That is the sound roller coasters make at Disney World when they are going up the hill." He then showed me pushing her up, up, up as he said, "Click, click, click." Then the swinging started. Becky asked JT if the girls weren't scared of this, and JT answered, "A little at first, but they are great with us." I know why. JT treasures his daughters, and they know it. They know they are safe in his care.

That story comes to mind as I read today's passage. Paul is encouraging Timothy to endure suffering without shame. Paul's reason is a mature example of our granddaughters'. Paul says, "I know whom I have believed, and am persuaded that he is able to guard" those matters entrusted to Paul. This is important to me. Too often we trust *what* we believe, not *who* we believe. The *who* is the important part.

Our granddaughters were two years old. They weren't trusting in the straps, the chain, the tree limb, or the toddler seat. They were trusting in their daddy. He told them it was safe, and they were having a blast because of that trust.

Paul says God saved us—and not because we deserved it. Our right standing with God comes from his purpose and grace. We can trust him to bring matters to fruition. He is fully trustworthy, and in this, we can live in joy, even amid suffering.

Lord, I commit my life to you. Give me your strength in Jesus, amen.

OCTOBER 25

You then, my child, be strengthened by the grace that is in Christ Jesus. (2 Tim. 2:1)

As a schoolboy, I decided I wanted to be really strong. Body builder strong. Charles Atlas / Arnold Schwarzenegger strong. I got some weights, and I lifted. I spent the good part of the morning getting ready, doing the lifting, and cleaning up for my day. The next morning, I looked in the mirror. It hadn't worked. I was no closer to Arnold than I had been the day before I lifted. What went wrong? Nothing. It's just that the kind of body strength I wanted comes from years of regular lifting, not a day's worth.

Today's passage reminds me of my youth. A good bit of 2 Timothy is written with Greek imperative verbs, meaning verbs that are in the form of an order or command. "Do this . . ." "Do that . . ." type verbs are used. Today's passage is also a command, but something more than an imperative verb is at play. Timothy is told, "Be strengthened." This instruction is in the passive (or middle), so Timothy will get his strength from someone or something beyond himself. What is more, it is in the present tense. This is important. The use of the present tense means this is something that Timothy is to do daily. This is something so important that Timothy should pursue it as a regular activity. Like my weight lifting, this isn't a one and done. It is a day-in, day-out, week-by-week, month-by-month, year-by-year activity.

How is Timothy to be strengthened? By the "grace that is in Christ Jesus." Daily, the believer grows in strength by seeking and relying on Jesus. Paul will go on to detail different aspects of his thought. As believers suffer for the cause of Christ, they are strengthened. Running the race of life in honor of Jesus and by his guidance strengthens our faith and relationship with Jesus. As we serve others for Jesus, we are strengthened. Jesus is the source of empowerment for life. He will transform us through moment-by-moment living for him.

What does this mean practically to me? I need to spend daily time in the word. I need to spend daily time in prayer. I need to rely on Jesus' teachings for my ethics and priorities. I need to share Jesus with others, telling them about who has transformed and strengthened me. I need to give Jesus worship, praise, and adoration for his great mercy, his suffering and sacrifice, and his care and love. This is to be *daily*, and I can be assured of growing strong in him.

Lord, I seek to honor, serve, and tell of you today and every day in Jesus, amen.

OCTOBER 26

The saying is trustworthy, for: If we have died with him, we will also live with him; if we endure, we will also reign with him; if we deny him, he also will deny us; if we are faithless, he remains faithful—for he cannot deny himself. (2 Tim. 2:11–13)

Sociologists identify five generational cohorts that today worship together in churches. The generations are defined by seminal life- and brain-shaping events that have altered how different-aged people learn and experience life. The older group, for example, grew up with only radio and print to teach and entertain them. The most recent generation never knew life without Google to answer their every question. Television isn't as prominent as shows online. Books are written about these generational differences. One area where these differences are most present is in song. Roger Miller sounds quite different from Kaskade.

In worship, music has changed as well. New worship songs are written daily, with powerful lyrics and melodies. The early church was also writing hymns, which spread throughout the ancient world. Paul finds one useful to his message and quotes that hymn in today's passage.

The hymn is built around a handful of stanzas. The first and second stanzas recall the implications of the believer's conversion. As Paul had written in Romans 6, our baptism symbolizes a burial, a sharing in Christ's death, and our coming out of the water symbolizes our new life with Jesus. The believer no longer lives as the world does but lives with and for Christ. Next, the stanzas speak to living with Christ despite what the world throws at us, for as we endure suffering for him, we are assured of sharing in his victory by reigning with him. The hymn's following stanza addresses apostasy—those who deny Jesus and never really give him their lives will be denied by Jesus. The hymn delineates those whose denial of Jesus is only temporary, like Peter with the cock crowing after a triple denial. These people will find repentance, and God will hold them tightly. The reasons for this are given in the final stanza—because God is faithful. God doesn't change and won't act out of character.

I like some modern hymns; they touch me. I like the hymns of my parents and grandparents as well. But this ancient hymn needs a place too. The emphasis on the Christian walk and the faithfulness of God rightly encourage me.

Lord, thank you for your mercy and love. I worship and adore you in Jesus. Amen.

OCTOBER 27

Do your best to present yourself to God as one approved, a worker who has no need to be ashamed, rightly handling the word of truth. But avoid irreverent babble, for it will lead people into more and more ungodliness, and their talk will spread like gangrene. (2 Tim. 2:15–17)

"Do your best!" My dad gave me this advice over and over as a child. When I was about to play baseball, Dad would say, "Do your best." When I was preparing for exams, Dad would encourage, "Do your best." And when I didn't always succeed, Dad would console, "Well, at least you did your best."

I don't think Dad was consciously reciting 2 Timothy, but he could have been! Paul's encouragement to Timothy is to "do your best." Timothy wasn't about to play ball or take an exam. But Timothy was working full time in the church, shepherding, teaching, and leading others in their faith. Paul wanted Timothy to give his best efforts. The purpose of Paul's instruction wasn't so Timothy might satisfy the congregation. Paul wasn't telling Timothy this would win him a popularity contest or get him a raise. Paul wanted Timothy to try his best because the real motivator was God. Timothy was doing God's work. Timothy reflected God.

When we view our lives as missions from God, they demand a different focus. Our service to others is service to God. Our sacrifices for others are sacrifices for God. How we live, what we do, our attitudes, emotions, endurance, joy, and more—these things take on a different light when we think of working for God.

In this sense, Paul wants Timothy to "rightly" handle the word of truth. This means that Timothy is to use Scripture—and likely also all the opportunities God gives Timothy to teach and speak—correctly. The Bible isn't food for idle speculation. Speaking occasions before others aren't opportunities for irreverent babble. Time is precious. No one has a rewind button on life. Time is a zero-sum game. How we spend our moments, how we steward our interactions with others, how we choose our thought paths, the words we express, the ways we while away the day, all of these are moments and chances that can't be repeated.

Paul wanted Timothy to think about the importance of his work and his opportunities. Paul wanted them well spent. After all, Timothy was really working for God, no one else. So Timothy needed to do his best!

Lord, may I carefully serve you through my life today. In Jesus' name, amen.

OCTOBER 28

Now in a great house there are not only vessels of gold and silver but also of wood and clay, some for honorable use, some for dishonorable. Therefore, if anyone cleanses himself from what is dishonorable, he will be a vessel for honorable use, set apart as holy, useful to the master of the house, ready for every good work. (2 Tim. 2:20–21)

As I've mentioned earlier, my sister Kathryn makes amazing pottery. She takes lumps of clay and fashions pieces of her choosing. Some are functional in ordinary ways; some are beautiful works of art. Her platters function well as both. We've displayed some in our kitchen. We've also used them for parties and functions. Kathryn decides what she wants to make and then makes them beautifully.

In biblical times, machine-produced china was unknown. All such items were created by potters. Not surprisingly, then, pottery was a common metaphor seen throughout Scripture. Jeremiah used the image of God as a potter, fashioning Israel's future (Jer. 18:1–11). In Romans 9, Paul effectively uses the pottery metaphor to emphasize God's role in choosing what kind of vessel he would make of his people, whether Jew or Gentile. The pottery metaphor resurfaces here but with yet another different emphasis.

In today's passage, the emphasis is on what kind of vessel we choose to become. Vessels in Timothy's day could be used even more extensively than at my sister's shop. They might be made of clay or wood for daily usage. Or they might be made of precious gold or silver for extraordinary usage and beauty. Some made a meal special; others hauled off scraps and waste.

Timothy is urged to make himself a vessel of honor. In verses 22–26, Paul says Timothy can do so by fleeing youthful passions and chasing down righteousness, faith, love, and peace. These stem from seeking God over the foolishness of the world. An honorable vessel avoids quarreling and treats people kindly. In patience, Timothy should endure, teach, and gently lead others into godliness, and so should we.

Pots can take various shapes. We are remiss if we fail to see that this isn't only a metaphor for God moving among the nations and his people. It is a useful metaphor for how we choose to live. I want to be a useful vessel to my Father.

Lord, may I focus by your wisdom and strength on servicing you in Jesus, amen.

OCTOBER 29

But understand this, that in the last days there will come times of difficulty. For people will be lovers of self, lovers of money, proud, arrogant, abusive, disobedient to their parents, ungrateful, unholy, heartless, unappeasable, slanderous, without self-control, brutal, not loving good, treacherous, reckless, swollen with conceit, lovers of pleasure rather than lovers of God, having the appearance of godliness, but denying its power. Avoid such people. (2 Tim. 3:1–5)

Arghhh. A chain verse! One of those passages that has a list of things but isn't set out as a list. Instead, the items are listed with a bunch of commas. These are the passages that I can too easily skim over the words rather than dwelling on each. There's a reason why when I make a list for the grocery store, I do it one item per line rather than in sentence form with commas separating each word. It takes up more room, but my brain works better with lists. Paul says to avoid being the following:

1. Lovers of self. We should seek to care for others.
2. Lovers of money. Money is God's tool, not mine. Loving it is evil.
3. Proud. God brings down the haughty and lifts the humble.
4. Arrogant. Even Jesus was meek and humble before God.
5. Abusive. Don't hurt others. We are here to help and build them up.
6. Disobedient to our parents. Our Heavenly Father isn't for rebellion to goodness.
7. Ungrateful. An attitude of gratitude isn't just a platitude.
8. Unholy. We are set apart for God's kingdom. We should act like it.
9. Heartless. We are to reflect the great caring of our loving God.
10. Unappeasable. We are to find life's solutions, not problems.
11. Slanderous. If we have nothing good to say of another, we should stay silent.
12. Without self-control. This takes work, but is critical to learn.
13. Brutal. The Christian should be tame, not a savage.
14. Not loving good. God is good. Who shouldn't love good?
15. Treacherous. Judas betrayed Jesus. Let's be genuine and trustworthy.
16. Reckless. This stems from rashness. We should be thoughtful and careful.
17. Swollen with conceit. Ick. Who wants to be that?
18. Lovers of pleasure. We should be loving God.

Keeping this list will require everyone to rely on God's power in their lives.

God, I want to live for you. Help me in Jesus, amen.

OCTOBER 30

Continue in what you have learned and have firmly believed, knowing from whom you learned it and how from childhood you have been acquainted with the sacred writings, which are able to make you wise for salvation through faith in Christ Jesus. All Scripture is breathed out by God and profitable for teaching, for reproof, for correction, and for training in righteousness, that the man of God may be complete, equipped for every good work. (2 Tim. 3:14–17)

Noam Chomsky is the father of modern linguistics. From his position at MIT, he pointed the academic community to the inherent language facility in the human brain. Shown in the earliest cries of an infant, humans are hardwired to communicate. As babies grow, they master the ability to understand and make sounds that are known by others so communication can take place on complicated levels. Because we are made to be people of language, it isn't surprising that the God who made us would choose language to communicate. Rather, it would seem surprising if he didn't.

Paul knew that God had worked by using language to communicate to his people. Paul calls out those writings that had a special imprint of God. He explained that God breathed into those writings, using a compound word for "God" and "breathed" (*theo* + *pneustos*—θεόπνευστος). The *pneustos* part of that word comes from the Greek for "breathe." It is akin to the Greek word for "spirit." God's Spirit has breathed into certain writings, and Paul brings those into focus.

Paul knew that God didn't breathe out Scripture out of boredom. God wasn't whiling away his days making Scripture on a whim. God was bent on communicating special revelation to his people. God was explaining and revealing matters that people would not fully comprehend by just looking at the world God created, although there is a certain revelation and instruction in the created world as well.

Paul says that in God's communication, we will find words that teach us about life. We will find words that help us follow God more closely, correcting us in our errors and training us in ways we should live. Most of all, these are the writings that guide us to faith in Christ. The Scriptures we now call the Old Testament as well as those we group as the New Testament testify to our need for a savior as well as God's saving work in Jesus. The Bible isn't made for a bookshelf; it was given to be read, followed, and shared. We are linguistic people.

Lord, thank you for your words. May I embrace and live them in Jesus, amen.

OCTOBER 31

For I am already being poured out as a drink offering, and the time of my departure has come. I have fought the good fight, I have finished the race, I have kept the faith. Henceforth there is laid up for me the crown of righteousness, which the Lord, the righteous judge, will award to me on that day, and not only to me but also to all who have loved his appearing. (2 Tim. 4:6–8)

While talking with my friend Lisa at a legal convention, she asked me, "What would you put on your own tombstone?" I didn't have to think long. My buddy Pastor Jarrett has a "life verse" that is tombstone worthy. It is in today's passage. I told Lisa, "I would write, 'I have fought the good fight, I have finished the race, I have kept the faith.'" Mercy! Paul sums up life in a powerful way for me. Some scholars call today's passage "Paul's Last Will and Testament." I tend to think of it as his self-written eulogy. Either way, it gives three perspectives of life.

Paul lives in the present as he sees he is being "poured out" in a sacrificial way for God. Paul knows he will soon face martyrdom, and the suffering is daily. Paul next looks to the past as he uses sports metaphors to equate the struggle in life to live rightly on God's behalf. This was a race that he ran for God. Paul also looks forward to the future, when he will receive the crown of laurels that went to one who successfully won the sports competition, envisioning God as giving him that award in God's kingdom.

This passage of antiquity speaks loudly over my life today. I want to understand Paul, but moreover, I want to be ready like Paul. I want my life to count for God. I want to be able to live without complaining during suffering, in conditions that would cause many to wail and complain, and do so with a purpose of serving the eternal King. There is no greater calling.

All of us will reach the end of our days in this life. Death awaits us all. Some will know it is around the corner, while others will meet death as a total surprise. The real question isn't so much how or when will we die but rather, How will we live? What will our eulogy say? We can fight the good fight or ignore it. We can complete the course God gives us or sit down and forget it. We can keep faith with God or live frivolous lives concerned with our own wants, needs, and focus.

I want Paul's affirmation. It would go well on a tombstone!

Lord, may I live to fight the good fight, finish the race, and keep the faith. Amen.

NOVEMBER 1

When you come, bring the cloak that I left with Carpus at Troas, also the books, and above all the parchments. Alexander the coppersmith did me great harm; the Lord will repay him according to his deeds. Beware of him yourself, for he strongly opposed our message. . . . The Lord will rescue me from every evil deed and bring me safely into his heavenly kingdom. To him be the glory forever and ever. Amen. . . . Eubulus sends greetings to you. . . . The Lord be with your spirit. Grace be with you. (2 Tim. 4:13–22)

My buddy Larry sent me a slide entitled "General Pauline Letter Outline":

> Grace.
> I thank God for you.
> Hold fast to the gospel.
> For the love of everything holy, stop being stupid.
> Timothy says hi.

I chuckled. It wasn't far off. But in this letter *to* Timothy, it's Eubulus who says hi.

Second Timothy is a very personal letter, and perhaps that is reflected nowhere as much as in its final verses examined today. Paul needs his cloak for warmth. He needs his books and parchments for reference and his mind. He needs Timothy for support. He has a few more personal comments about folks who helped him and folks who hurt him. Then he signs off.

A side note: we don't know what the books and parchments contained. I suspect some were notes on the sayings of Jesus, for Paul seemed to have a good record of many of those teachings, as he referenced and quoted them in his writings. Matthew could well have been a notetaker for the three years of ministry because his occupation as a tax collector required him to be a writer who kept records and wrote receipts and reports. Early church history records that Matthew wrote gospel accounts in Aramaic/Hebrew that circulated around.

Regardless of what was in the writings, Paul was human. As humans, we need support from friends and Scripture. We have physical, mental, emotional, and spiritual needs. This is part of being human. On a practical level, I ask myself if I am a good Timothy. Do I help encourage and supply these needs to those around me? I should. Do I use Scripture to support those hurting? I should.

Lord, help me show your love to others by helping them in life. In Jesus, amen.

NOVEMBER 2

Jude, a servant of Jesus Christ and brother of James, To those who are called, beloved in God the Father and kept for Jesus Christ: May mercy, peace, and love be multiplied to you. Beloved, although I was very eager to write to you about our common salvation, I found it necessary to write appealing to you to contend for the faith that was once for all delivered to the saints. (Jude 1–3)

The letter called "Jude" is a short one, consisting of twenty-five verses packed into one chapter. To stay on pace in this devotional, the most I can spend on this compact letter is three days. Yet the material begs for more. Even in these opening words, the author, Jude (or "Judas"), is worthy of at least one devotional. After all, he was a younger half brother of Jesus and a full brother to James. He was well educated also. The letter shows Jude had an extensive Greek vocabulary, used the Hebrew Old Testament, and had great dexterity with certain nonbiblical Hebrew writings. I love the way Scripture shows the skeptical brothers of Jesus coming to faith immediately *after* the resurrection.

But instead, we will review the reason Jude wrote this short missive. Jude wanted to "contend for the faith," as it was "once for all delivered to the saints." Jude will go on in the next verses to speak about those who were perverting the grace of God into a license to sin. Jude views this approach to Christianity as one that denies the lordship of Jesus. After all, it was Jesus who asked, "Why do you call me 'Lord, Lord,' and not do what I tell you?" (Lk. 6:46).

Doctrine is important in faith. Who is God? Who is Jesus? What is faith in Jesus? Who is the Holy Spirit, and how does he work? These are all important doctrinal questions—and just a few among many. But no doctrine excuses laxity in the Christian walk. Doctrine gives insight into life. For example, examining the attributes of God takes on practical importance when following a passage like Leviticus 19:2: "You shall be holy, for I the LORD your God am holy."

That Jude should speak of following the words and teachings of Jesus as "contending for the faith" places how I behave today front and center. My words should be carefully chosen to encourage and upbuild others. Modeling God's serving love should be the hallmark of my life. Forgiveness of others should be evident in how I live. I should be holy, as he is holy, and thus contend for the faith.

Lord, I want my faith to be real and mature. Give me insight into you, your character, and your holiness. Help me learn and walk in holiness. In Jesus' name, amen.

NOVEMBER 3

But you, beloved, building yourselves up in your most holy faith and praying in the Holy Spirit, keep yourselves in the love of God, waiting for the mercy of our Lord Jesus Christ that leads to eternal life. And have mercy on those who doubt; save others by snatching them out of the fire; to others show mercy with fear, hating even the garment stained by the flesh. (Jude 20–23)

It's an old child's story with an important lesson. Three little pigs go off together, and each builds a home. The first, in a hurry to finish, builds with straw. The second, a little better (but not much), builds with sticks. The third takes the time and trouble to build with bricks. The big, bad wolf comes pig hunting and, huffing and puffing, blows down the houses of straw and sticks. But the wolf can't get through the brick house. Moral? Take the time to do it right.

The building metaphor didn't start with the three pigs. Jesus spoke of building one's life on a solid foundation (Mt. 7:24–27). Paul often wrote of the church as a building, focusing on the roles of the builder as well as the construction materials (e.g., 1 Cor. 3:9–15). Jude also uses a building metaphor in today's passage.

Today's verses come on the heels of an extended discussion of false teachers who were disrupting the church and tearing it apart. Jude uses Old Testament Scriptures to condemn those false teachers. Jude also uses some more Jewish writings that were more contemporary at the time (1 Enoch and *The Assumption of Moses*) that argued against the impurities propagated by the false teachers. Jude then turns to this building metaphor, urging his readers to "build themselves up." This building isn't built with straw or sticks. Jude wants a solid building that will last. The building is of the "most holy faith." It is a building of "prayer." The readers are to keep in the "love of God."

These building codes for the Christian life aren't simply platitudes. They result in real actions. Not everyone will build so strongly, so the Christian should strive to have mercy for doubters. Our concern should be on the whole building, so we should give our time and attention to anyone needing help and strength.

God doesn't just call individuals; God calls a kingdom, a community, a building! God calls us to be living integrated lives, helping and boosting one another in his love.

Lord, give me concrete ways to show your love to others in faith. In Jesus, amen.

NOVEMBER 4

Now to him who is able to keep you from stumbling and to present you blameless before the presence of his glory with great joy, to the only God, our Savior, through Jesus Christ our Lord, be glory, majesty, dominion, and authority, before all time and now and forever. Amen. (Jude 24–25)

The doxology that concludes the letter of Jude has long been one of my favorites. It cemented into my brain when a fellow West Texan named Billy Sprague recorded the doxology as put to music by Michael W. Smith in 1984. The majestic force of the music with the power and praise of the verses left a mark still ringing in my ears forty years later.

The doxology, or "glory proclamation," begins by noting God as the one who can keep believers from stumbling. This is a biblical truth of God found repeatedly in the Psalms. God keeps feet from "slipping" (Ps. 38:16) or "falling" (Ps. 56:13). God does so by lighting our path (Ps. 119:105). God isn't distant. He cares about each step we take. He shows us the right paths to stand upright and follow his will. This alone is reason to praise the involved God, but there is more.

God also "presents" us as blameless. Jude's Greek has a bit more metaphor than our English readily picks up. The word translated "present" is also a word for "stand" (*histēmi*—ἵστημι). God not only prevents us from stumbling, but he makes us stand *blameless* before the presence of his glory. When the great Old Testament prophet Isaiah found himself before the glory of the enthroned Lord, he not only couldn't stand because he was overwhelmed with a sense of his sinfulness. God had to touch Isaiah with the heavenly sacrifice before Isaiah could go any farther (Isa. 6)! But in the post-resurrection timeline of earth, God keeps us standing because the death and resurrection of Christ make believers blameless in God's sight. We wear the righteousness of Jesus.

So God, our Savior through Jesus, is rightly praised as Jude comes to an end. He is ascribed all glory, majesty, dominion, and authority. It has always been his, and as we recognize it today, we do so affirming that it will always be his. Jude ends his letter in style. The words echo in my mind to the majestic tune of Michael W. Smith and voice of Billy Sprague. But the real source of my joy in this ending is the divine King of kings, who keeps me standing!

Lord, I bless and praise you as the only true God. Your work in my life gives me joy, strength, and confidence. May I always be yours. In Jesus my Lord, amen.

NOVEMBER 5

Long ago, at many times and in many ways, God spoke to our fathers by the prophets, but in these last days he has spoken to us by his Son, whom he appointed the heir of all things, through whom also he created the world. (Heb. 1:1–2)

This book is written to give the reader a daily teaching from the Epistles with a devotional application. This book is decidedly not a commentary. I mine the text for practical use rather than seeking a verse-by-verse parsing. Full commentaries are available to provide insights on authorship, canonicity, date of writing, and more. Those are beyond the scope of a daily devotional. To some degree that is a pity, for the Epistle of Hebrews is ripe for such discussions. Hebrews doesn't take a typical "Epistle" form. It is different. I find affinity with those who reckon it an ancient sermon put in written form (see, e.g., Heb. 13:22).

Its original audience is unknown by location, but the issue it confronts is readily apparent. There were Jews who had confessed Jesus as Messiah and Lord, but as life moved on, they seemed to be faltering and were considering a return to the Judaism of their past. Hebrews confronts this temptation head-on. The Scriptures we call the Old Testament were never intended to set up a religion contrary to Christianity. They were written to lay the groundwork for what climaxes in Christianity. Christianity is the completion of the Jewish story.

So even in the beginning verses, straight out of the gate—without introducing the author, without declaring "Grace and Peace to you," and without any other typical Epistle-type introduction—comes today's meaty passage. God had used prophets to speak to his people in many forms and fashions. Old Testament Scriptures are rife with types of literature—histories, epics, poems, wise sayings, apocalyptic writings, and more. Yet those prophetic voices were all the word of the one God. In the "last days," a common phrase for the time ushered in by the incarnation, death, and resurrection of the Messiah, the same God spoke to his people through Jesus. The God never changed, the message never changed, and the listeners and readers needed to grasp that. Jesus wasn't something new.

God doesn't always move in ways we expect. Like the readers of Hebrews, we find life takes on different forms that don't readily fit our molds. Yet behind all the curveballs in life, a consistent God rings out a consistent message that has never changed. That message is Jesus.

Lord, let Jesus pervade all aspects of my life today. I pray in him, amen.

NOVEMBER 6

He is the radiance of the glory of God and the exact imprint of his nature, and he upholds the universe by the word of his power. After making purification for sins, he sat down at the right hand of the Majesty on high, having become as much superior to angels as the name he has inherited is more excellent than theirs. (Heb. 1:3–4)

In the nascent days of television, the Ken-L Ration dog food company had a series of commercials bolstered by the catchy jingle "My dog's bigger than your dog." The idea was that if you feed your pet their dog food, you would get the biggest, fastest, and best dog. Comparisons come naturally to people, so appeals to "the best" are common.

The writer of Hebrews launches straight into the first point of the message. Jesus truly is the greatest. Period. Jesus' greatness doesn't lie in what he ate, where he grew up and went to school, his socioeconomic background, or if he won the lottery. The greatness of Jesus is inherent in who he is.

When we look at Jesus, we are looking at the brightness of God's glory. Exodus 33:18 records Moses asking God for a chance to see his "glory." God responded that no one could see his glory and live. But in Jesus, we have the radiance of God's glory. Looking at Jesus, we get as close as a human can to seeing God. Jesus is the "exact imprint" of God's nature. To put this idea into bumper-sticker English: see Jesus, see God.

Jesus' death and resurrection are the triumph of God's greatest work. Jesus made true purification for sins. In the old regime of Judaism, blood sacrifices of animals were integral to the forgiveness of sins. The books of Moses set up exacting rules and procedures for such sacrifices. But Jesus truly accomplished a full and just forgiveness and, upon completion, was able to "sit" at God's right hand. Not even angels, God's holy messengers and servants, can hold a candle to the greatness of Jesus. No angel is accorded status as God's "son." Angels are God's tools; they aren't God. Angels serve and *worship* God and his Son. But Jesus holds the entire universe together and is the right inheritor of God's kingdom.

We might want to live in the land of comparison. We can rank teams, determine the popular vote, decide who gets which medal. But Jesus outranks all.

Lord, show me a greater picture of Jesus to pervade my whole life. In him, amen.

NOVEMBER 7

But of the Son he says . . . "You, Lord, laid the foundation of the earth in the beginning, and the heavens are the work of your hands; they will perish, but you remain; they will all wear out like a garment, like a robe you will roll them up, like a garment they will be changed. But you are the same, and your years will have no end." (Heb. 1:8–12)

In the class I teach at church, one Sunday I referred to one of our member's Jewish heritage. This fellow is a friend. He wrote me a kind email telling me that he was by genetics a Jew but that he was no longer Jewish—he was a Christian. I wrote back that the two were not exclusive! Most early Christians were Jews as well. Jesus isn't the end of Jewishness; he is its fulfillment.

Unsurprisingly, then, the writer of Hebrews rightly turns to the Jewish Scriptures, those where "God spoke to our fathers by the prophets" (Heb. 1:1), to read clear passages about Jesus. Even before today's passage, in Hebrews 1:5–9, the writer has already alluded to four Scriptures: Psalm 2:7 (in "You are my Son, today I have begotten you"), 2 Samuel 7:14 (in "I will be to him a father, and he shall be to me a son"), Deuteronomy 32:43 (in "Let all God's angels worship him"), and Psalm 45:6–7 (in "Your throne, O God, is forever and ever, the scepter of uprightness is the scepter of your kingdom. You have loved righteousness and hated wickedness; therefore God, your God, has anointed you with the oil of gladness beyond your companions").

Then in today's passage, the writer quotes Psalm 102:25–27. Jesus created the universe (v. 2), upholds the universe by the word of his power (v. 3), and entered our world through his incarnation and will outlast the universe (v. 8). A time will come when all that is heaven and earth will be rolled up like a garment. But Jesus will remain. Other Scriptures explain Jesus will unroll a new heaven and earth, but the Hebrews writer's point is different. He wants those reading to know that Jesus will never be different. He will remain for eternity. He has no end of days.

The writer wanted to be sure that those who had hitched their wagon to Jesus, those who had given their lives to him in faith, had no reason to seek anyone or anything else. They were tied to the one who outlasts all. Jesus is the one that Scripture had pointed to for ages and ages in the past. I read this and know that I can also trust Jesus. If he is trustworthy for all history and eternity, he is trustworthy for today.

Lord, I give you my today. I lean on you to get me through. In Jesus, amen.

NOVEMBER 8

Therefore we must pay much closer attention to what we have heard, lest we drift away from it. (Heb. 2:1)

My son-in-law JT is a boat guy. He can maneuver a boat better than I can drive a car. I can do OK with a boat in the open water, but trying to dock it in a strong current can be very difficult. You've got to position it with limited maneuverability all while the current wants to take you somewhere else. It makes for a good metaphor and is used by the writer in today's passage.

The author urges the readers to pay attention to God's message in the gospel—the good news about Jesus—lest they "drift away." The word for "drift" can be a nautical term for a boat that isn't at anchor being gradually taken from position (*pararreō*—παραρρέω). Like an untied boat or a piece of wood in a stream, it is an easy visual—the boat or wood slowly drifting away, carried by the current.

This can be quite slow and subtle. Almost unnoticeable. So it is something we should all guard against. The importance of the message of Jesus is not only destiny altering; it is life changing. Staying tied closely to his love, his teaching, his hope-instilling comfort, his community of fellowship, his strength, his joy, and his purpose are all wrapped up in staying close to him. This keeps life anchored where it belongs.

The writer will go on to remind his readers that the old law given to Moses was one with consequences. Israel's history included a large dose of punishment for disobedience to the law. All of life is full of such consequences. Cause and effect are built into the fabric of the world. If you put your finger in the fire, you are going to get burned. It is the way of things.

So unsurprisingly, neglecting the message of Jesus has consequences as well. We will drift. The Christian faith isn't one of no consequences. It offers us the best of life to aid us in this journey to God's eternity. This raises the natural question, How do we stay tied to Christ and his message? We stay tethered to Jesus as we pay attention to him! This is the power of today's verse. Read of Jesus. Think of Jesus. Pray to Jesus. Follow Jesus. Model Jesus. Do this daily. Make it the warp and woof of life. Like JT and a boat, let us navigate the currents each day in God's mercy with Jesus.

Lord, bring me closer to Jesus every day. By your mercy I pray in him, amen.

NOVEMBER 9

For it was not to angels that God subjected the world to come, of which we are speaking. It has been testified somewhere, "What is man, that you are mindful of him, or the son of man, that you care for him? You made him for a little while lower than the angels; you have crowned him with glory and honor, putting everything in subjection under his feet." (Heb. 2:5–8)

The father of my sweet wife, Becky, passed away before I got to know him. Through Becky, I feel I know much about him. She tells me of his home Bible studies and his love for church and the word. His love for his family is evident in all his children. Becky tells me that Psalm 8 was one of his favorite passages of Scripture. It is one of my favorites as well. The writer of Hebrews quotes a section of it in today's passage.

In Psalm 8, the psalmist is stunned over the intricacies of God's creation. The stars are more extensive than human sight. Their presence proclaims the awesomeness of God. Yet in something as small as an infant, God's greatness is also on display. Since the writing of Psalm 8, we've made telescopes that stare back into space and time, recording more galaxies than we can number, and microscopes showing that within an infant are a trillion cells, each a complicated city. God is indeed great. The psalmist then probed the question, "Why would God care about me, one little human?" Yet God clearly did. God made humanity a little lower than the angels, crowning him with glory and honor and giving him dominion over the earth.

Our instructor in Hebrews takes that passage from Psalm 8 and applies it to Jesus. Using the Greek version of the Psalm, he alters the concept slightly to explain God made Jesus just a "little while" lower than the angels during his incarnation here on earth. But now Jesus has resumed his position on the throne and is "crowned with glory and honor because of" his "suffering of death" (v. 9).

This usage of Psalm 8 is brilliant. The Psalm applies to all humanity, yet it also applies to Jesus, who was made human. The purpose of the Psalm is to bring into worshipful obedience all who are rightly stunned over the care, love, and provision of God to his people. Nothing shows God's care better than the incarnate Jesus. Made human, Jesus willingly suffered through life and death to bring humanity into a right and just fellowship with God. We can suffer through life as well, confident in God's loving provision to make us the best we can be, fit for him.

Lord, thank you for your love and care. May I follow my Lord Jesus. Amen.

NOVEMBER 10

For it was fitting that he, for whom and by whom all things exist, in bringing many sons to glory, should make the founder of their salvation perfect through suffering. For he who sanctifies and those who are sanctified all have one source. That is why he is not ashamed to call them brothers, saying, "I will tell of your name to my brothers; in the midst of the congregation I will sing your praise." (Heb. 2:10–12)

In the movie *The Lion King*, Simba, the young lion cub of Mufasa (the lion king), struggles with his identity. Mufasa's evil brother, Uncle Scar, causes Mufasa's death, bringing the land into misery. Late in the movie, Simba confronts Scar. Scar tries blaming Simba for causing a stampede that led to his father's death, but the truth is revealed by two side characters, Timon and Pumba. In a fitting turn of events, Scar is defeated by Simba, who finds his true identity and assumes the throne, restoring prosperity to the land.

Many movies are based on the journey of characters' development. They find who they are in the end, and the plot gives a "fitting" ending. This idea of something "fitting" is built into today's passage. Our teacher in Hebrews isn't speaking of a reluctant lion cub becoming king. But the journey Jesus took to the glory he has today is still rooted in suffering.

Think of it this way. Jesus reigns as God with an ability to erase this world and all its sin. Whether by flood, fire, or simply a snap of his figurative fingers, Jesus could wash everyone and everything away. Some might not even protest, since this world can be quite a mess. Evil is ever-present. Suffering comes to everyone—some of it deserved but much of it simply a fact of life. But instead of snuffing life out, Jesus chose to come into the suffering world, experience suffering himself, and bring rescue to those suffering.

This is why the writer of Hebrews uses a somewhat unusual word for the Bible, rightly translated as "it was fitting." It does fit that Jesus himself would suffer in bringing God's children into God's family. Jesus entered a suffering world to rescue suffering, morally malformed people and bring them into a familial relationship where God nurtures and transforms them. Just as it was fitting for Jesus to suffer on his journey to bring redemption, so it is fitting that his children who join him on that journey trust him in whatever we encounter along the way.

Lord, thank you for your selfless love and the promise I share in Jesus, amen.

NOVEMBER 11

Therefore, holy brothers, you who share in a heavenly calling, consider Jesus. . . . For Jesus has been counted worthy of more glory than Moses—as much more glory as the builder of a house has more honor than the house itself. (For every house is built by someone, but the builder of all things is God.) Now Moses was faithful in all God's house as a servant, to testify to the things that were to be spoken later, but Christ is faithful over God's house as a son. And we are his house, if indeed we hold fast our confidence and our boasting in our hope. (Heb. 3:1–6)

Sometimes life's turmoil instills in people a desire for comfort. When we face difficulties, it isn't uncommon for many to seek out comfort food. When sadness confronts us, we might look for the comfort of a good friend. Some facing loneliness might long for the comforts of home.

Many readers of Hebrews were reared in Judaism. The religious practices of their childhoods include kosher dieting, religious festivals, learning the Law of Moses, attending temple, and even wearing special clothing. All of these were parts of their lives from their earliest memories. Then these folks met Jesus the Messiah and embraced Christianity. They likely experienced a different perspective on life, as their holidays, worship, and even motivation behind daily living changed. But at some point, many were driven to return to earlier sources of comfort. Specifically, they longed for the religious practices of their youth.

For those seeking comfort, a return to normative Judaism seemed in order. They could go back to those things that had meant so much. After all, they may have reasoned, the same God was at play. Jews and Christians knew there was only one God. It was the one true God who had spoken to Moses. To go back to the ways of Moses was comforting and surely fine to do, or so they reasoned.

Yet what they were doing was akin to trading down. In a card hand, they were trading four aces for four jacks. Yes, Moses was great and used by God in mighty ways. But Jesus was so much more. Through Moses, God had constructed a house. Moses was God's servant in the process. But Jesus was God's actual Son. Who would want to trade and follow a servant in a home rather than the esteemed and unique Son? No one who is thinking clearly!

Our true comfort and rest in this life come from Jesus Christ, the Son of God.

Lord, I choose to follow Jesus, in good times and bad. Be with me in him, amen.

NOVEMBER 12

Therefore, as the Holy Spirit says, "Today, if you hear his voice, do not harden your hearts as in the rebellion, on the day of testing in the wilderness, where your fathers put me to the test." (Heb. 3:7–9)

We were faced with a decision about how to handle an issue in court. It seemed our opponents were in the mud and playing dirty. We thought about getting in there with them to whip them. My buddy Richard said to us all, "Team, let's take the high road. There's less traffic on it." He was right.

When God called Israel out of Egypt to deliver them out of slavery into a land flowing with milk and honey, one would think all the Israelites would be rejoicing. Certainly, moving from slavery to life under the care of the delivering God and King should cause each person to be thankful and worshipful. Yet the Scriptures indicate that wasn't so. Over and over, a notable number complained of God's treatment, some even seeking to go back to slavery in Egypt. They complained over the lack of water, lack of food, and difficulties in travel. This on top of their stumbling over the idea of worshiping an invisible God.

These times of complaint were really times of rebellion. God met the rebellion in a direct fashion, not letting it fester and spread in the camp. God hadn't forced the people on the journey; they chose to follow him from Egypt. God had rescued them miraculously, provided for them repeatedly, and promised them the brightest future. So the bellyachers were denied the blessing of entering the promised land.

Over Israel's history, this story replayed itself enough that a psalm was written recounting it. Psalm 95, a well-known psalm that was frequently used during Sabbath services in New Testament times, is quoted by our writer in today's passage. The first half of the Psalm is a call to worship and praise. The second part, from which today's passage comes, was a warning about staying faithful in attitude as well as actions.

As Christians, we should always be cognizant that our journey is one that follows God. We chose this journey, and our lives should reflect not only obedience to him but grateful and worshiping hearts. We will find the true joys in life by holding closely to our Lord, not by complaining or looking for something else.

Lord, may I hold your hand tightly today and every day, following you in joy wherever you lead. In Jesus, amen.

NOVEMBER 13

But exhort one another every day, as long as it is called "today," that none of you may be hardened by the deceitfulness of sin. (Heb. 3:13)

The phone call was convincing. The person in the fraud department of a major bank was calling to ask about possible improper charges on a business Visa card. A fraud alert had been triggered because the card was being used in Miami, while I was in Texas. They needed to know whether to accept the charges or treat it as fraud. I explained the charge couldn't be accurate and should be reported. They explained that they would text me a message and I would need to confirm by texting back. I soon realized the call itself was a scam seeking my banking information. Once I asked the "fraud department" fellow for his name and number so I could call him back, he hung up immediately.

Fraud, trickery, and deceit can be incredibly harmful and destructive. The Greeks had a word for such fraud. It was *apatē* (ἀπάτη). This word circulated in ancient Greek for over one thousand years, so commonplace were fraud and deceit. The writer of Hebrews uses the word in today's passage when speaking of sin. Sin tricks the sinner. It works a fraud as it makes one think their behavior is worthwhile to achieve a certain desired result. In truth, however, the great result is a delusion. The sinner is deceived. The end will not be as expected.

One result of this deceitfulness of sin is given in today's text. Sin makes our hearts "hardened." It sears our consciences, so we don't even notice our sin, excuse it, or justify it. Sin can make us stubborn against what is holy and good. Sin produces the exact opposite of what every Christian should be pursuing. Sin drives a wedge between that which is holy and that which isn't.

I don't want hardness to God and his goodness. I want sensitivity. I want to grow in his grace and strength. I want to be tuned into hearing his will. I want him to find fertile ground in my heart for serving him. I want to hear his Spirit's quiet whispers and nudging. I want to follow him in faith. I want to face life's quandaries with confidence that I am navigating them through his directions. I will not get where I need to be through sin. Any idea that sin is good for me or profitable for my life is a trick. It is a fraud. It is a scam. I should know better.

Lord, I need your touch to avoid this deceitfulness of sin. I don't want my heart hardened to you. Soften my heart. Wash my eyes. Clean my ears. I want to follow you truly. In Jesus, amen.

NOVEMBER 14

So then, there remains a Sabbath rest for the people of God, for whoever has entered God's rest has also rested from his works as God did from his. (Heb. 4:9–10)

Writing on today's passage just happens to coincide with me getting eight hours of sleep, if I add the last two nights together. After two consecutive nights of four hours of sleep, I find this passage that speaks of entering God's rest. My fatigue immediately sends my thoughts into the fundamental truth that weariness is not a twenty-first-century phenomenon. It is something that is ubiquitous through time and culture.

Knowing fatigue and the importance of good rest might influence how someone might approach passages like today's, but we would be giving those passages short shrift if we stopped there. The writer isn't teaching that God gives his people a good night's sleep each night. (Although Proverbs 3:24 teaches that following God's wisdom gives one "sweet" sleep, and Psalm 127:2 says God "gives to his beloved sleep.") The writer has much more in mind.

We see the greater picture as we see the writer speaking of God resting from his work. God wasn't wiped out from six hard days of creation. God's rest was not because he was tired or weary. The rest for God was more akin to the rest in a piece of music. A musical rest references when the instruments (or voices) cease. The rest isn't because folks are tired. It is because the piece calls for nothing more at that moment. In that same sense, God rested on day seven. Instead of meaning God was tired, the rest was an indicator that God's work was completed. Nothing else was needed at that point.

This idea of rest as completed work is aligned with what the writer of Hebrews teaches in the fourth chapter of the book. Even beyond that, however, there is a certain end-times, or "eschatological," aspect to rest. The writer speaks to the end of days and the eternal finality of the rest believers have in God.

I know weariness of the body, especially this morning! But I also know weariness of the soul. I know when I feel too tired to do what I should do or to focus on life rightly. That type of tiredness should awaken me to the importance of focusing on living God's will carefully. Walking with God gives me rest.

Lord, bring peace to my restlessness as I seek to live faithfully in Jesus, amen.

NOVEMBER 15

For the word of God is living and active, sharper than any two-edged sword, piercing to the division of soul and of spirit, of joints and of marrow, and discerning the thoughts and intentions of the heart. And no creature is hidden from his sight, but all are naked and exposed to the eyes of him to whom we must give account. (Heb. 4:12–13)

In my desk drawer are a variety of highlighters. I use them to give emphasis to what I am reading. When typing, I can give emphasis by **bolding** a font, using *italics*, using all CAPITALS, and underlining. The writer of Hebrews had no such tools or conventions. Instead, ancient Greek had different ways of emphasizing words. One of the most common methods was to place a word conspicuously at the front of a sentence or clause. The writer does so in today's passage.

Reading this passage in the Greek, the first word is "living" (a participle from *zaō*—ζάω). The writer is emphasizing this word the way we might by using italics or a bold font. If this were a spoken sermon, the preacher might pound the lectern at this point or say it boldly with a pause afterward: "The word of God is *living*!"

A few verses earlier (3:12), the writer spoke of God as the "living God." As expected, the living God has living words. God's words are reflected in Scripture, as the writer has shown by his previous quotations from and allusions to the Old Testament, which itself frequently affirms that its words were from the Holy Spirit. And God's word warns about God's judgments that came on Israel, who refused to enter God's rest. Scripture, this living word, is, as the writer says here, active.

God's word penetrates deeply. It enters one's psychological makeup ("soul and spirit"), one's physical makeup ("joints and marrow"), and even the deepest recesses of one's thoughts and intentions. No one can hide from God, his word, and his judgments. Everyone decides whether they want to live under wrath or in God's rest.

I not only want God's rest, but I also need God's rest! I want the words of Scripture to reach into my life and affect how I think, feel, desire, and act. For this to happen, of course, I need to spend time in his word. This is my fifth book of daily devotional thoughts from Scripture. Each has grown out of my own personal study. I want the *living* words of God to infuse my life!

Lord, bring me into your rest. Infuse my life with your words in Jesus, amen.

NOVEMBER 16

Since then we have a great high priest who has passed through the heavens, Jesus, the Son of God, let us hold fast our confession. For we do not have a high priest who is unable to sympathize with our weaknesses, but one who in every respect has been tempted as we are, yet without sin. Let us then with confidence draw near to the throne of grace, that we may receive mercy and find grace to help in time of need. (Heb. 4:14–16)

My computer is harsh. It has no mercy. When I hit the wrong key while typing, the effect is instant. The computer will produce my error with precision. Sometimes the error might get fixed, but only if I or someone else has told the computer, "If *X* happens, do *Y*." My computer is cold; it has zero sympathy.

God is not a computer. God isn't cold and harsh in dealing with us and our frailties. We aren't dealing with a God far removed from our reality. God is no old man rocking in a chair, wagging his finger in judgment over each mistake. The real character of God is expressed by the writer in today's passage, and it is quite different from either computer or distant old man.

Humanity stands before God through the work and ministry of Jesus Christ. In a role akin to the ancient high priests of Israel, who would come into the figurative presence of God in the temple and intervene on behalf of the people, Jesus has traversed the heavens into God's throne and there speaks on our behalf as our advocate. He is an advocate who understands life's struggles, for he walked the human life for three-plus decades. Jesus knows firsthand how difficult the temptations of life are. Even though Jesus didn't sin, his direct exposure to humanity gives him an empathy and sympathy that should instill in us confidence.

No Christian should ever return to life before faith. It isn't sensical. In Jesus, we have an entrée into God's presence. We always have access to God. The all-powerful God will honor the high priest Jesus, and we will find his mercy and his grace in each step of our lives. That doesn't mean problems evaporate, but it means we have God's strength to grapple with those problems. Then when we err, our mistakes aren't permanent. God isn't a harsh computer. His mercies and grace will cover our errors with love and give us a bright and eternal future with him. Praise God, and thank you Jesus!

Lord, thank you for your mercies and grace. I need those, and I need you daily. I lean on you for all I face today. In the mighty name of my high priest Jesus, amen.

NOVEMBER 17

In the days of his flesh, Jesus offered up prayers and supplications, with loud cries and tears, to him who was able to save him from death, and he was heard because of his reverence. (Heb. 5:7)

Two great gals had a sick brother. They were worried but overall felt pretty good about it. After all, they were friends with and had access to a great physician, and he made house calls! They reached out to him, and he told them not to panic. Their brother would be fine. However, other things got in the way, and he was late getting there. Too late. The brother died days before his arrival. You likely know this story, for the two women were Mary and Martha, their dying brother was Lazarus, and the great physician was Jesus. The story is in John 11.

Jesus had known from the first moments this drama unfolded that Lazarus' illness would be used for God's glory. The dawdling by Jesus seemed purposeful. He was finally going to see the family, but only *after* Lazarus had already died! Jesus knew he would heal or "wake up" the dead man. Jesus finally arrived on the scene to a bewildered, hurt, and frustrated pair of sisters. Both women knew that if Jesus hadn't delayed, their brother wouldn't be dead. Others were consoling the bereaved family in the absence of Jesus. Tears were pouring down the faces of the sisters, who boldly spoke of their hurt and anguish to Jesus: "If you'd only come when you said you would, we'd have our brother!"

This reality of the depths of their anguish, emotion, and hurt touched Jesus. Jesus headed to the tomb with full knowledge he was going to resurrect Lazarus. Jesus was about to perform a miracle that would turn their mourning into dancing. Jesus was on task to achieve something that would be recorded in Scripture for eternity. Jesus' actions were to confirm his power over the grave, giving hope to his followers that no one in Jesus' family would ever die eternally.

Yet even with this knowledge of what was about to unfold, we read the shortest verse in Scripture: "Jesus wept" (Jn. 11:35). This is the Jesus spoken of in today's passage. Jesus offered prayers to God for Lazarus, crying out with a "loud voice, 'Lazarus, come out'" (Jn. 11:43). God heard Jesus. God saved Lazarus from death. The tears and concern of Jesus came out of his hurt for others, not out of fear or worry. This same Jesus sits on the throne of God, caring for you and me. Knowing this reality rightly makes each day different.

Lord, thank you for your love. I trust my today to you in Jesus, amen.

NOVEMBER 18

About this we have much to say, and it is hard to explain, since you have become dull of hearing. For though by this time you ought to be teachers, you need someone to teach you again the basic principles of the oracles of God. You need milk, not solid food, for everyone who lives on milk is unskilled in the word of righteousness, since he is a child. But solid food is for the mature, for those who have their powers of discernment trained by constant practice to distinguish good from evil. (Heb. 5:11–14)

If Hebrews was indeed the written form of a sermon, a position of many scholars that I share, it is a bit startling in places. One such place is today's passage. Generally, when I preach, I try to build my audience up, not dress them down. While I try to point out areas where improvement is needed, I'm pretty sure I've never told them they are "dull of hearing"! What prompted this accusation?

The audience of this sermon hadn't taken to heart the core of the Christian reality. If they indeed were a group of Jews who were considering returning to their Jewish practices in ways that divorced them from Christian basics, then they never really understood the Jewish Scriptures (the "oracles of God") in the first place! All Scripture, after all, spoke in a united voice to the reality of Christ and his work. This was set out in the opening salvo of this sermon (Heb. 1:1–2).

This passage sets out a challenge to everyone following the Lord. We are called to not only read Scripture prayerfully but also study Scripture and understand why it says what it says. This isn't for only the Gospels, the Epistles, or the Psalms. We should spend time in all of Scripture, seeking to understand why these oracles proceeded from God and what they said when written. Then we should apply them and understand how they rightly speak today.

I have a dear friend that was reading the daily devotional book in this series of five that was published just before this volume. I wrote it on the Minor Prophets. My friend told me it was opening new Scriptures to him. Even though he'd been a Christ follower for over forty years, reading the Bible daily, he spent 99 percent of his time in the New Testament. "The Old Testament just doesn't do it for me," he said. Yet we need to be in all of Scripture. We need the meat. No infant milk for the growing believer. As the preacher of Hebrews says, it will make us more discerning and better able to follow and teach the Lord.

Lord, put a burning in my heart to understand your word better. In Jesus, amen.

NOVEMBER 19

Therefore let us leave the elementary doctrine of Christ and go on to maturity, not laying again a foundation of repentance from dead works and of faith toward God, and of instruction about washings, the laying on of hands, the resurrection of the dead, and eternal judgment. (Heb. 6:1–2)

Randy came to me and several of the leaders in our law firm, and he challenged us on how we should educate our new lawyers. We all knew that law school is great at giving you the framework for being a lawyer, but the skills and knowledge of practicing law develop after law school. Randy urged us to use "competency-based education," where we set a standard of what levels of competency were expected for those who had been practicing one year, two years, three years, and so on. Then we would deliberately seek to get each person where they should be.

Maturity is important in life. We ooh and ahh over babies, but not over a thirty-year-old who acts like a baby. The writer of Hebrews wants Christian believers to grow in faith, which includes growing in understanding. Today's passage sets this out. The writer is ready to set aside the elementary doctrines, examples of which don't seem so elementary to many today. For example, "Repentance from dead works." Yes, most every Christian gets repentance; it is part of the process of becoming a child of God. But many miss the idea of "dead works." The concept that anything we do before being infused with the Spirit of God, even those things that seem good, aren't just diseased or deficient but merit the description "dead" is foreign to some. But when we understand them as "dead," we never want to walk in that way again. Who wants to be doing dead stuff?

The writer isn't going to speak of "mature things" by moving into some esoteric or secret knowledge saved for graduate school. But he will further develop the importance of faith and repentance, which we will turn to shortly.

How does the believer grow? Certainly part of the answer to the equation is self-discipline and effort. Like my lawyers, we can teach believers and give them chances to grow and learn, but they must make that choice. Importantly, however, the writer also uses the passive voice (translated "go on"). The idea in this verb is being *carried* on to maturity. God will teach us and mature us, but we must choose to let him. God will teach us if we are willing.

Lord, teach me. Mature me. Help me grow into my best for you in Jesus, amen.

NOVEMBER 20

For land that has drunk the rain that often falls on it, and produces a crop useful to those for whose sake it is cultivated, receives a blessing from God. But if it bears thorns and thistles, it is worthless and near to being cursed, and its end is to be burned. (Heb. 6:7–8)

As a young boy, I lived in Rochester, New York, where I would occasionally run around outside in bare feet—something fun to do in the lush grasses of upstate New York. However, I made the mistake of doing that after we moved to Lubbock, Texas, in a yard loaded with *Cenchrus longispinus*, commonly known as grass burrs. (Hence the Latin name of "long spine" for the row of spiny prickles that grow on the grass.)

When I first encountered this menace, my feet slammed onto the spines. They penetrated deeply into my feet. I couldn't put any weight on my feet, so I promptly fell to the ground, with the burrs then penetrating my hands and arms. They got all over my clothes, and I was a near tearful mess. "Never again!" I swore to myself.

The writer of Hebrews has put an analogy much like my experience into today's passage. It is a vivid image that I immediately understand. If we as God's people, enjoying the rain of his Spirit, grow bountiful crops, then our life is blessed. But if we take that same rain and instead produce thorns and thistles, it isn't. God will not give us thriving lives if we choose to walk away from him.

This passage follows one of the more difficult passages in Hebrews. The writer has been speaking of the end picture for those who fall away from faith, living in denial of God as heretics. The writer has said that those who know God and understand his grace yet flee God and flee repentance are like the field of thorns and thistles.

As difficult as the preceding verses are, they are clear that God always wants people everywhere to repent and turn to him. Even as a twelve-year-old boy running barefoot in a yard in Lubbock, Texas, I would have understood that we don't want our lives to be filled with thorns and thistles. We want good green grass. We want productive gardens. We want to thrive under God's blessings. This teaching should affect me daily as I make choices on how to live under God's Spirit.

Lord, forgive my sins and sinful ways. Help me better follow you in Jesus' name, amen.

NOVEMBER 21

For God is not unjust so as to overlook your work and the love that you have shown for his name in serving the saints, as you still do. And we desire each one of you to show the same earnestness to have the full assurance of hope until the end, so that you may not be sluggish, but imitators of those who through faith and patience inherit the promises. (Heb. 6:10–12)

Sluggish. Just reading the word in today's passage evokes a visceral reaction in me. It brings back memories of Thanksgiving feasts that left me tired and unable to move. I think about sugar overdoses that have made my brain slow, made my body lethargic, and earned the label "sluggish." Who wants to live like that?

The writer in today's passage urges his readers to live a life that avoids spiritual sluggishness or laziness. The lethargy conveyed in the Greek word chosen (*nōthros*—νωθρός) isn't a trait anyone should want. Instead, we should eagerly pursue being alert, tuned into God and the people around us, and ready for action in whatever tasks he has for us.

The lesson built into today's passage explains that as we follow God, as we love others and serve them in his name, we avoid the sluggishness we dread. Pause and consider this. How can I best show God's love to other followers of Jesus? I have several dear friends who, after almost every encounter, will ask me, "What can I do for you?" They are service minded.

When we serve others in the kingdom, it invigorates us. That doesn't mean we won't have days of physical tiredness or days when we need to replenish our emotional energy. But it means a mind-set of service, so when we have opportunities for God to use us in his kingdom, we seize those chances. We live with an outward focus of what we can do for others, not what others can do for us.

I need this reminder. I need to look for chances to serve others faithfully today. Recently, I was picking up some food to take home for lunch. The fellow who had taken my order, packed my food, and was running my check had a good attitude. I looked at the tip line and asked him, "Do you get this tip if I add it?" He answered, "Yes, sir." I then said, "Do you know Jesus?" He replied, "Well of course! He's why I live my life as I do! He's my Lord." I upped the tip. I told him, "Jesus wants to bless you." Let's make conscious efforts to serve in Jesus' name!

Lord, open my eyes to ways to serve others in Jesus. I pray in him, amen.

NOVEMBER 22

It is impossible for God to lie. (Heb. 6:18)

Why is it that something impossible for God to do comes so easily to people?

I was trying an important case with international and national ramifications. With billions of dollars on the line, the opposing company's lawyers had hired the best experts they could, including a statistician from an Ivy League university. He testified on statistics in a way that I believed clouded the truth and was deceptive. I began my cross-examination with this: "Sir, as a statistician, I am sure you are familiar with the quotation commonly attributed to Mark Twain about three kinds of lies, aren't you?" He was. The gist of the Twain quote is that there are ordinary lies, damnable lies, and statistics. I then proceeded to show how the expert had used statistics to draw a wrong conclusion.

What makes the Twain quote profound enough to include in this day's lesson is that Twain expressed what many believe, albeit not in his terminology. We can easily divide lying into three categories: lies that don't really matter, lies that do matter, and ways of deceiving that might not be outright lies.

Many believe that lies in the first category are fine for telling, at least in a pinch. Does my wife *really* want to know if a dress she just bought for an event "looks good" on her? (Actually, in my case, she really *does* want to know and would get upset if I failed to tell her!) If I am not going to an event because I don't want to, is it OK to make up an excuse? After all, isn't it worse to hurt someone's feelings? Are we dealing with the lesser of two evils?

Similarly, many believe it's fine to purposely leave a false impression. If I mislead someone and they draw the wrong conclusion, isn't that on them?

These ethical questions don't exist with God. God doesn't lie. Period. Full stop. God is fully reliable on his promises. We may not fully understand those promises. We might not see a bigger picture that is there with God. But when God proclaims his promises, we can rely on them. This makes me want to read Scripture with an eye to his promises. It also makes me want to work to be more like him, living in a way where people can say, "He said it, so it must be true."

Lord, may I be like you in my honesty and faithfulness. Show me your promises in Scripture. Help me live in trust and faith. In Jesus' name, amen.

NOVEMBER 23

We have this as a sure and steadfast anchor of the soul, a hope that enters into the inner place behind the curtain, where Jesus has gone as a forerunner on our behalf, having become a high priest forever after the order of Melchizedek. (Heb. 6:19–20)

I have a good buddy who has been a Christian for over four decades. He spends daily time in the Scriptures and has for those four decades plus. He has a graduate degree in ministry. He told me once, "I spend 99 percent of my personal study time in the New Testament. I struggle to get into the Old Testament." Now, this man is incredibly godly, and his faith is the core of who he is. Yet the Old Testament isn't "daily fare" for him, even though it was the "Bible" for Jesus, Paul, and the apostles. It would have been their daily quiet-time study.

A passage like today's (and the successive verses) is so steeped in the Old Testament, it is necessary to understand certain core principles from it to rightly interpret them. Among the doctrines and rules of the Old Testament was the teaching and instruction that God was to be approached in a singular place of worship—first the tabernacle and later the temple. The sacrifices were to be offered there. The priests were in service there. The inner sanctum, the holiest of holy rooms, was there. This holy of holies was a place where only the high priest could enter, and he was to do so only once a year after an elaborate ritual of cleansing for himself and for Israel. The priest did so to intercede for the people he served.

The writer of Hebrews will make the point that Jesus has entered the true presence of God, of which the holy of holies is simply an earthly representation. Jesus did so as the true high priest. Yet the audience of Hebrews, themselves steeped in the Old Testament, would have known that Jesus was not of the right lineage to be a priest that could enter the holiest room. Jesus was not a Levite, and the priesthood was a Levitical priesthood.

So the writer explains that Jesus was another order of high priest, one that preceded the Levitical priesthood, one that was greater than the Levitical priesthood. This will be explained in coming devotionals, but for now it is worth noting. For Jesus is more than adequate to represent you and me in his sacrifice before God. Jesus blazed a true trail into God's presence where you and I find love, forgiveness, and strength to live each day.

Lord, give me your strength today made possible by Jesus in whom I pray, amen.

NOVEMBER 24

For this Melchizedek, king of Salem, priest of the Most High God, met Abraham returning from the slaughter of the kings and blessed him, and to him Abraham apportioned a tenth part of everything. He is first, by translation of his name, king of righteousness, and then he is also king of Salem, that is, king of peace. He is without father or mother or genealogy, having neither beginning of days nor end of life, but resembling the Son of God he continues a priest forever. (Heb. 7:1–3)

If my wife were to walk into the room where I sit, with the proper lighting, I might be able to see her shadow cast into the room before she even arrived. I could likely tell that a person was coming and maybe even be able to discern that it looks a good bit like my wife. Her hairstyle might be discernible, among other things. This would get my attention. Once my wife entered the room, and the reality behind the shadow became obvious, it would be absurd to go hug and address my wife's shadow. I could embrace my wife!

Within this analogy, I find today's passage instructive. Much of the Old Testament so directly gives a shadow of the Jesus who was to come that the audience of Hebrews should never consider returning to their pre-Jesus Judaism. Melchizedek is a great example of this foreshadowing. He was a priest who was in the same "order" of the high priest Jesus. His name alone indicates such. *Melech* is the Hebrew word for "king" (מֶלֶךְ). *Zedek* is Hebrew for "righteousness" (צדק). Of course, Jesus is the true and ultimate King of Righteousness. In Jesus, there is no sin.

Melchizedek was the king of Salem, the old Hebrew word for "peace" (better known in the form *shalom*, as it is said today). In Psalm 76:2, Salem is even translated into the Greek as "peace," the word used by the writer of Hebrews. Melchizedek was worshiped/honored by Abraham, the forefather of all Jews. In a society that honors some as greater than others, the obeisance of Abraham to Melchizedek was seen as an obeisance of all Abraham's future offspring as well. One steeped in the Old Testament would see other foreshadowing also.

All of this was intended to make the reading or listening audience realize that Jesus isn't an afterthought to life or to God's plan. Jesus was God's intention all along. This changes how I live today. Why would I seek answers to life from anyone other than Jesus?

Lord, may I find in Jesus all my answers to the struggles of the day. In him, amen.

NOVEMBER 25

For on the one hand, a former commandment is set aside because of its weakness and uselessness (for the law made nothing perfect); but on the other hand, a better hope is introduced, through which we draw near to God. . . . This makes Jesus the guarantor of a better covenant. (Heb. 7:18–20, 22)

Put five ingredients into a mixer and turn it on, and you can watch the machine do its work, blending the separate ingredients into one. This mash-up process can be rewarding in cooking, but it doesn't work with theology and language in the Bible!

Take, for example, the Old and New Testament. Many people seek to unhook the New Testament from the Old, using passages like today's to justify this. This passage compares the old covenant made between God and Israel on Mount Sinai to the better and new covenant based on Jesus and his death/resurrection.

The labels "Old Testament" and "New Testament" in modern English come from the Latin version of the Bible, largely translated by Jerome in the fourth century. The Latin word for "covenant" is *testamentum*, which comes straight into English as "testament." The New Testament (*Novum Testamentum* in Latin) is a label originally referencing the Christian writings that explain and testify to the death and resurrection of Jesus. The writer in today's passage calls that a "better covenant" (*meliores testamenti* in Latin).

The writer, however, is not talking about the New Testament being better than the Old Testament, for those words weren't even in usage then. In fact, verse 21 (the ellipses in the quotation for today) is a *quote* from the Old Testament to support and prove that Jesus offers a better covenant. These passages are explaining that no one should seek to practice the Jewish laws from Sinai as a basis for relating to God. Those laws were never adequate to make a just relationship between humanity and the Divine One. They were placeholders to set up, foreshadow, and explain a later reality, a covenant based on the sacrificial blood of Jesus, not the blood of bulls and goats.

No one should unhinge one part of Scripture from another. All Scripture testifies to the truth that in Jesus, one finds full and complete forgiveness of all sins and a fully just relationship with God the Father. There is no other way.

Father, I trust Jesus and the covenant of his blood to be your child. In him, amen.

NOVEMBER 26

For it was indeed fitting that we should have such a high priest, holy, innocent, unstained, separated from sinners, and exalted above the heavens. He has no need, like those high priests, to offer sacrifices daily, first for his own sins and then for those of the people, since he did this once for all when he offered up himself. (Heb. 7:26–27)

High school yearbooks are always a fun read, even if they aren't your own. When our yearbooks came out, there was always some event where everyone would be asked to sign the yearbooks of their friends and acquaintances. You can read what is said about one another, often something like "You're sweet!" or "You are nice." One of my favorites is "You asked me to write something. Here it is: something."

The writer in today's passage writes of Jesus, but his words aren't pablum or yearbook fare. His words are profound and important. He describes Jesus as our high priest. Jesus is "holy" (*hosios*—ὅσιος); he perfectly complies with God's standards for pious living. Jesus was faithful in life to God. His moral purity is further explained by similar words used to describe him, translated as "innocent" and "unstained." Jesus is spiritually and morally perfect. He can, therefore, fulfill the role of a perfect high priest who offers sacrifices for us all before God.

The high priests under the Sinai covenant had to offer sacrifices for their own sins before going before God to offer sacrifices for the sins of the people. Not so for Jesus. Jesus committed no sins and therefore had no need to make a sacrifice for himself. So as Jesus approached God, he intervened directly and solely for people. Furthermore, Jesus offered *himself* as the only morally pure, unstained, and innocent sacrifice for you and me, a truly worthy, sufficient sacrifice that would never need repeating. There would never be a need to offer any other sacrifice.

Some might ask, "Why a sacrifice at all? Why can't God simply wave his hand and forgive sin?" This question misses the heart of who God is. God is a just and unchanging God. He can't become unjust. Justice requires punishment for sin. The punishment must be paid, and only Jesus is untainted from sin so that he can pay this debt on our behalf.

Christians aren't perfect. No one has the moral purity to walk with God. Try as we might, God must give purity. He did this in Jesus. We are rightly grateful.

Lord, thank you for forgiveness in Jesus. May I rest in it, as I pray in him. Amen.

NOVEMBER 27

Now the point in what we are saying is this: we have such a high priest, one who is seated at the right hand of the throne of the Majesty in heaven, a minister in the holy places, in the true tent that the Lord set up, not man. (Heb. 8:1–2)

In the 1960s, I had a favorite cartoon on TV. It was *Underdog.* In the introduction to the show, the humble and lovable shoeshine boy/dog would be given a coin for shining shoes, and he would bite it to check whether it was genuine. Jesus does much more than bite a coin to show the genuine truth of his work for sinners.

In the prior chapters, the writer has explained that Jesus has offered himself as a pure and undefiled sacrifice, one truly worthy to substitute for the sins that you and I commit. Jesus' death satisfies the justice required for the sins that bring death. Then to prove the genuineness of Jesus' work, he sat at the right hand of the heavenly throne of God, where he still sits today.

That Jesus sits is an indicator that his work is finished. Jesus has done what needed to be done to forgive your sins and mine. He now sits because his work is completed. I am reminded of one day in class when a fellow student asked my Greek professor, Harvey Floyd, "Dr. Floyd, tell us about the day you got saved!" Dr. Floyd got a big grin on his face as he removed his glasses and said almost wistfully, "That was a grand day, a special day, a day like no other. It was almost two thousand years ago on a hill outside Jerusalem . . ." It wasn't the answer we expected, but it focused us rightly. Jesus saved us and sat at God's right hand.

The Hebrews writer then adds that Jesus sits in the heavenly sanctuary that had been modeled in the earthly tabernacle built under Moses' direction. God had given Moses exacting details on how the tabernacle was to be built because it held symbolic representation of the reality we are to grasp in the work of Jesus. So the tabernacle had a place for sacrifices, and that place had to be passed through on the way to the holy of holies, where God would symbolically sit on his throne, the ark of the covenant. This signified the required sacrifice of Christ before his work could be finished and he joined God on the throne.

In the *Underdog* analogy, the coin is not chocolate wrapped in gold foil. A fake coin would not do as payment for services rendered. So it is with Jesus. Jesus doesn't offer fake forgiveness for you and me. His forgiveness is true and real.

Lord, help me understand the truth of Jesus' work for me. In him I pray, amen.

NOVEMBER 28

Behold, the days are coming, declares the Lord, when I will establish a new covenant with the house of Israel and with the house of Judah. . . . I will put my laws into their minds, and write them on their hearts, and I will be their God, and they shall be my people. . . . For I will be merciful toward their iniquities, and I will remember their sins no more. (Heb. 8:8–12)

Ticking the boxes is a phrase used by my British friends to express the idea of following a list. While I didn't grow up with it, I like the phrase and the concept. I have always been a bit of a list person. Give me a list, and I can get it done—or at least come close. For ancient Israel, the covenant they had with God from Mount Sinai had become a list. They had rites and procedures for each day, week, and season. The law contained lists of things to do and things to avoid doing. Specialists had arisen in Israel who knew the laws in excruciating detail, debating over the finer points in order to tick all the boxes.

The apostle Paul understood the law well. He had trained under the best and used that law to prosecute the church and Christ (Acts 9:4). It wasn't until after meeting the Lord Jesus on the road to Damascus that Paul more accurately and fully began to understand the Sinai covenant. Paul later explained that the Law of Moses was designed to point to Jesus, much like a guardian or teacher gives instruction and protection (Gal. 3:24–25). But in Christ, the believer was no longer "under the law" and therefore no longer had to try to tick all the boxes.

Similarly, the writer of Hebrews discusses the law as the "old covenant" that finds its fulfillment and empowerment in Christ. The center of Sinai worship (the tabernacle at first and later the temple) was built in ways to indicate who Jesus would be and what Jesus would do. The old covenant was important but never intended to be the final and perfect covenant. If we focus on ticking boxes, we aren't focused on Jesus and keeping our hearts and minds set on God.

So in Christ, God fulfilled his words from old. His new covenant through Jesus puts his law into the hearts and minds of the believer as the Holy Spirit indwells within us. Unity with God comes through Christ, the ultimate peacemaker. Part and parcel of this new covenant in Christ is God's full mercy. He remembers sins no more. I'm so thankful for this new covenant. It's far better than ticking boxes.

Lord, I am grateful. May I follow you closer than ever before. In Jesus' name, amen.

NOVEMBER 29

Now even the first covenant had regulations for worship and an earthly place of holiness. . . . But when Christ appeared as a high priest of the good things that have come, then through the greater and more perfect tent (not made with hands, that is, not of this creation) he entered once for all into the holy places, not by means of the blood of goats and calves but by means of his own blood, thus securing an eternal redemption. (Heb. 9:1, 11–12)

Hardly a week goes by when I'm not looking at a résumé or curriculum vitae. Some are people wanting a job; others are witnesses involved in a case. Either way, people list their best and most relevant experiences on paper (or in a computer document). It allows others to see at a glance what the person has accomplished and experienced and gives insight into the person. In the biblical age, résumés didn't exist. There isn't an ancient Greek or Hebrew word for résumé. (Classical Greek had a *biographia*—βῐογρᾰφία—but that was more a written history of life.) The closest the ancients came was the word often translated "name," which stood for a person's reputation, character, and accomplishments. In some places, the word for "name" is even translated as "reputation" (see, e.g., Rev. 3:1).

In this ancient sense of "name," the Scriptures repeatedly speak of the surpassing "name" of Christ. Jesus earned a "name that is above every name" (Phil. 2:9). How the children of God live bears directly on the "name" or reputation of Jesus. So we should live to bring him glory (2 Thess. 1:12). In today's passage, as well as in the extended verses of Hebrews 9 not set out above, the writer gives an extraordinary accounting of the résumé of Jesus. Jesus did what no one else could ever do. Jesus established direct access to all who believe and trust in his work into the very presence of God. I can't get in the door to world leaders and celebrities, but God's door is always open to me as his child.

By his own blood as the sacrifice, Jesus entered the holiest places of God, making a way for those "in Jesus" to be there as well. Understanding the "name" of Jesus as his work, reputation, and actions as Savior gives the true sense behind why the believer prays "in Jesus' name." No one should pray to God out of one's own merit. Anyone approaching God does so because of the merit of Christ. He secured this right to direct access to God for all believers. Because of Jesus, we can boldly "draw near to the throne of grace, that we may receive mercy and find grace to help in time of need" (Heb. 4:16). Jesus has the greatest résumé for all eternity!

Lord, in Jesus' name, by his blood, I bless and pray to you with gratitude, amen.

NOVEMBER 30

Therefore he is the mediator of a new covenant, so that those who are called may receive the promised eternal inheritance, since a death has occurred that redeems them from the transgressions committed under the first covenant. For where a will is involved, the death of the one who made it must be established. For a will takes effect only at death, since it is not in force as long as the one who made it is alive. Therefore not even the first covenant was inaugurated without blood. (Heb. 9:15–18)

Puns. Even reading the word, for some, seems punishing. But puns are punchy. So I choose to punish the reader rather than expunge them.

Some scholars view today's passage as ancient punnery. It is built off the Greek word *diathēkē* (διαθήκη). In the Greco-Roman world, *diathēkē* referred to a will, a document that allotted a person's property. The Jewish Greek Scriptures used the word to refer to a covenant or contract between people. More than half of this word's usages in the New Testament are in the book of Hebrews. In today's passage, the word is translated both ways, as "covenant" and "will." Why?

Some scholars adopt this translation because they believe the writer suddenly shifts into pun mode and shifts from meaning "covenant" in the Jewish sense to meaning "will" in the Greco-Roman sense. Under this interpretation, the writer's point is the necessity of a death for a will to take effect. But this interpretation has one big problem. While a will does not take effect until death under modern law, that was not true under ancient laws of Greece and Rome, which permitted a person to write a will and distribute property under it before any death.

Which leads to another and more commonly accepted explanation. The writer refers generally to the big covenant at Sinai. Before that covenant was ratified, an animal was slain, and the blood was sprinkled on the people (Ex. 24:3–8). Had the slain animals been kept alive, no covenant would have been effective. Once it became effective, God promised Israel they would possess the land and receive his blessings if they stayed obedient. But when they didn't, death was the covenant's agreed consequence. Jesus came, however, and not only was his blood applied to the people, but he inaugurated a new covenant through his death. We are free to be his and freed from the covenant at Sinai. Praise God!

Lord, thank you for forgiveness and freedom bought by the blood of Jesus, in whose name I pray, amen.

DECEMBER 1

But as it is, he has appeared once for all at the end of the ages to put away sin by the sacrifice of himself. And just as it is appointed for man to die once, and after that comes judgment, so Christ, having been offered once to bear the sins of many, will appear a second time, not to deal with sin but to save those who are eagerly waiting for him. (Heb. 9:26–28)

"Lather, rinse, repeat." So much of life is repetitive. We generally sleep each night, eat two to three meals a day, and go to school or work routinely. The Korean language even has multiple words for "go": one (가다) for occasional trips and another (다녀다) for routine journeys. Under the Law of Moses, the "Sinai covenant," sacrifices were a regular thing. People sinned regularly, so sacrifices for sins were regularly performed.

Not so with the sacrifice of Jesus. It doesn't have to be redone each time we sin and need forgiveness. Jesus died once for all sin. When Peter referenced forgiveness of sins at Pentecost, which inaugurated the church or group of people following the resurrected Christ, Peter told them to repent for "the forgiveness of sins"; he didn't assign a time description. It wasn't for the forgiveness of their "past sins." Jesus sacrificed himself for all sins for all time.

The audience of Hebrews were people who grew up in Judaism, met Christ, and became followers of Jesus but then were considering returning to the faith practices of their youth. The writer wants to make unequivocally clear that the old covenant of Sinai was a dead end. It led to death as certainly as holding a finger in fire leads to a burned finger. The old sacrifices were never adequate for true forgiveness of sins. Hence they had to be offered repeatedly.

But with Jesus, once was enough. He gave a pure sacrifice of human life that was more than adequate for the sins of all humanity. Jesus will undoubtedly come again, but not to offer himself again as a sacrifice. He will return to rescue his people from the grave or, for those alive, from this life and bring them into his eternity. Meanwhile, we get in ruts. We perform things over and over. But we should never forget nor fail to embrace the lasting beauty and significance of the eternal price Jesus paid for us.

Lord, I praise you for the sacrifice of Jesus. I need full forgiveness of all my sins, as I seem to pile up a bunch of them! Thank you, Jesus, in whom I pray, amen.

DECEMBER 2

Consequently, when Christ came into the world, he said, "Sacrifices and offerings you have not desired, but a body have you prepared for me; in burnt offerings and sin offerings you have taken no pleasure. Then I said, 'Behold, I have come to do your will, O God, as it is written of me in the scroll of the book.'" (Heb. 10:5–7)

A foundational principle in America is the opportunity for every citizen to choose their lives. My dad worked for the railroad. But that didn't mean I had to be a railroad worker. I am a lawyer, as are three of our children. But they chose to be lawyers; they didn't have to follow Dad in his trade or guild. Choice is a marvelous thing, treasured in the American lifestyle.

But as we celebrate the ability for everyone to choose their course in life, we shouldn't lose sight of the biblical truth that God has set out certain things for us to do. Paul wrote to the Ephesians that God created us for "good works, which God prepared beforehand, that we should walk in them" (Eph. 2:10). God had specific plans for Jesus, a direct calling on his life, and Jesus chose to follow God's design.

Jesus was unique in the purpose God had for him. No other human will be called to sacrifice themselves for the salvation of humanity. Yet Jesus wasn't unique in God having a purpose for him. God has purposes for everyone. And like Jesus, we are to follow God's plan too. A fundamental goal of my life is determining God's purposes for me. On a macro scale, these are big purposes that involve career choices, spouse choices, living-location choices, and more. But also on a micro scale, I should each day be sensitive to who God places in my path for conversation, who he gives me a chance to help, who needs loving encouragement, who needs comfort in grief, as well as who needs light in darkness, hope in despair, truth in a swarm of falsehood, and reliability in a fickle world of unreliable sorts, and so on.

I love the truth that Jesus came and obediently followed God's will in his life. Because of Jesus' life and death, I will spend an eternity with God and his children. Yet I also have Jesus' example to inspire and lead me to follow God today and every day. Walking with Jesus may be difficult or even treacherous at times; as Jesus said, we are to "take up our cross and follow him" (Lk. 9:23). But we can always be assured that the path of God is the right path!

Lord, I want to walk in your path, do the things you have prepared for me, and follow Jesus in obedience. Help me in this, for Jesus' sake and in his name, amen.

DECEMBER 3

And every priest stands daily at his service, offering repeatedly the same sacrifices, which can never take away sins. But when Christ had offered for all time a single sacrifice for sins, he sat down at the right hand of God, waiting from that time until his enemies should be made a footstool for his feet. For by a single offering he has perfected for all time those who are being sanctified. (Heb. 10:11–14)

My buddy Drew sent me a reminder: "One can never learn the gospel too well or understand it too deeply!" Drew was quoting our since passed-on Greek professor Dr. Harvey Floyd. I am reminded of that quote when reading the careful presentation of the gospel in today's text.

The first hearers of the sermon that is the book of Hebrews were Jews who knew well the sacrificial system of temple Judaism. The sacrifices offered for sins were done daily by priests standing before the altar on behalf of the people. But the sacrifice of Jesus was very different: it truly atoned for sins. Christ's payment was one that fully and completely satisfied God's righteous judgment. As such, Christ's sacrifice doesn't need to be repeated or offered daily; he did so only once. Rather than standing to offer sacrifices again, Christ's sacrificial work is finished, and he now sits at God's right hand.

While Christ has finished his sacrificial work, the end is not at hand; he is continuing to work. The author notes, with a nice nod to Psalm 110:1, that Christ awaits God conquering his enemies—that is, Satan and his demonic forces. That psalm, which Jesus also quoted in reference to his ministry (e.g., Mt. 22:41–44), affirms the writer's point: "The Lord says to my Lord: 'Sit at my right hand, until I make your enemies your footstool.'"

The Greek adds another subtle point of emphasis in today's passage. By his single sacrifice, Jesus "perfected for all time those who are being sanctified." "Perfected" is in a Greek verb form that references a historical event completed in the past but with an emphasis on the current effects that resulted from that event. In other words, the work of Christ on the cross was done once, but it alters and perfects everyone for all time (without interruption). This is true, as we in the present are uniquely dedicated and sanctified to God. The great news, the gospel, can never be learned too well or understood too deeply!

Lord, I bow before your salvation, humbly grateful for the work of Jesus, amen.

DECEMBER 4

Therefore, brothers, since we have confidence to enter the holy places by the blood of Jesus, by the new and living way that he opened for us through the curtain, that is, through his flesh, and since we have a great priest over the house of God, let us draw near with a true heart in full assurance of faith. (Heb. 10:19–22)

Morris Albert is likely a nice fellow. I don't know; I've never met him. But he put out what has been termed one of the whiniest songs in the soft rock era—"Feelings." The song lyrics are simple, speaking of the feelings one has prompted by a lost love. The feelings aren't described. They are just announced (some might say whined): "Feelings, whoa, whoa, whoa, feelings . . ."

That song aside, people often speak of feelings as something that can command our attention, invade our thinking, affect our behavior, and ruin our day. Into this potential slavery to feelings comes today's passage. The writer stops any feelings of inadequacy from hindering our prayer life and relationship with God.

Today's passage recognizes that the believer's confidence to come into the presence of God, a presence that we find through prayer, worship, and fellowship, isn't based on feelings. Our approach and relationship to God is secured by an objective reality quite outside how we feel. We are before God with confidence based on the sacrificed blood of Jesus.

Setting forth the Old Testament sacrificial system as a type or shadow of the work of Christ, the writer explains that for those who trust in and follow Jesus, the curtain that separated the presence of God (in a representative way within the holy of holies) from all, save the high priest once a year, is open. Jesus blazed a trail into God's most holy place. He opened this path for all believers to enter.

Other New Testament writers will explore this principle, but it is clearly set out in today's passage. We needn't worry about our ability to call on God based on our own performance, our feelings of love or lack thereof, or any such hindrance. We should readily come to God based on the truth of Jesus and his adequacy, his obedience, his work. How nice to have this confidence! This rightly transforms us all.

Father, with gratitude to Jesus, I come into your presence to discuss my fears, worries, and life. Give me your confidence as you bless me in Jesus, amen.

DECEMBER 5

Let us hold fast the confession of our hope without wavering, for he who promised is faithful. And let us consider how to stir up one another to love and good works, not neglecting to meet together, as is the habit of some, but encouraging one another, and all the more as you see the Day drawing near. (Heb. 10:23–25)

Going to church was easy for us in my teenage years. The church was only a seven-minute drive, and the parking was easy. I'm glad. I developed a load of friends through a very active youth group. The minister, Ken Dye, turned into one of my closest confidants and friends as I grew into adulthood. (We still keep up and enjoy each other almost fifty years later.) My development as a young man was greatly shaped by these church factors.

We often were in church three times a week for services on Sunday morning, Sunday evening, and Wednesday night. On top of that, we would have youth group meetings other weeknights and several times a year on the weekends. Through this time spent together, I learned a great deal of Scripture. Certain sermons and illustrations still echo in my head. I learned songs that crop up often when issues of life arise. One such song occurred to me in reading today's passage.

The old hymn "Standing on the Promises" begins, "Standing on the promises of Christ my king, through eternal ages let his praises ring; glory in the highest, I will shout and sing, standing on the promises of God." This song plays in my head because the passage today teaches the listeners to "go to church!" In the text's terms, it is "Don't neglect meeting together." Church time feeds our lives and transforms us into godliness. We learn and reinforce that the faithful God will keep his promise and be our help and mainstay in life. While life isn't always predictable or easy, the promises of God are steady and reliable. The second verse of the song says, "Standing on the promises that cannot fail, when the howling storms of doubt and fear assail, by the living Word of God I shall prevail, standing on the promises of God."

Going to church, learning songs and Scriptures, hearing sermons and teachings, and fellowshipping with others have formed me. I have learned to stand on God's promises. As the hymn's last verse says, "Standing on the promises I cannot fall, list'ning ev'ry moment to the Spirit's call, resting in my Savior as my all in all, standing on the promises of God." Amen.

Lord, I stand on your promises. Thank you for your love. In Jesus, amen.

DECEMBER 6

But recall the former days when, after you were enlightened, you endured a hard struggle with sufferings. . . . Therefore do not throw away your confidence, which has a great reward. (Heb. 10:32, 35)

My buddy had lived a rough life. His wife lived a rough life. Neither one had made God any kind of priority, and it was obvious. Then while working in a stark and spiritually barren place, my friend found Jesus. The transformation in his life began instantly. I suggested he share his new-found faith with his wife. I explained that the more he grew closer to Jesus, the further he would grow away from his wife, unless she joined him on that journey. She opted not to go to Jesus but to run further away. In those first few years of faith, my friend came under intense personal suffering. As his life changed, his marriage fell apart, his working life altered, his finances were stripped, and his suffering caused him to spend a lot of time in the book of Job.

Moving forward two decades later, my friend's faith has never been stronger. He still faces difficulties and struggles but with a faith that clings tightly to the Lord. He knows from personal experience that God will see him through.

My friend comes to mind reading today's passage. The writer/preacher of Hebrews wants those receiving his message to think back to times of struggle. He wants them to reflect on and learn from their personal story. They had faced insults, disgrace, and reproach, often publicly. Their spouses and children had faced the same. They suffered financially, and some even had their liberty stripped. Yet they endured these events with joy because of their faith and trust that God was supporting them.

As we face difficulties in life, we have different paths through the problems. One option is to do a quick U-turn. But no one who has appreciated the sweetness of God filling their heart should ever choose to turn back. A second option is to try to minimize the experience, cursing God (or at least mumbling and grumbling about him). A number of Israelites did this in the wilderness after leaving Egypt. It didn't turn out well for them. A third option is to tighten one's grip on God, face the wind, and take each step daily knowing that the God who led Shadrach, Meshach, and Abednego through the fire will not abandon us. We all have a story in life—may ours be that third path of faith and trust, to the glory of God.

Lord, be my strength each day. I embrace your love and care. In Jesus, amen.

DECEMBER 7

Now faith is the assurance of things hoped for, the conviction of things not seen. (Heb. 11:1)

My friend Alister McGrath had come into Houston to give a lecture to a group of seminary students planning to give their lives to full-time ministry. Alister is the world's leading expert on C. S. Lewis, and Lewis was the core of his presentation. He shared how Lewis is relevant to the modern preacher and what can be gleaned from Lewis and put into practice. One of Alister's core points was the power of stories in Lewis. Some story lines are obvious—*The Chronicles of Narnia.* Others are more subtle, like the many metaphors and illustrations that pepper Lewis' writings. Lewis worked through stories knowing they fuel our minds. Not only do our imaginations engage with stories, but we find them bypassing the natural defense systems raised as we argue propositions. Instead, we readily relate to stories.

In this sense, beyond the propositional and rational arguments for how to live, the writer of Hebrews turns in chapter 11 to powerful stories. He uses these stories to encourage his readers to endure the hardships of life and trust that God is at work. That is the context of this chapter. Hardships come to all, but believers can trust that God will not only see them through life's struggles but use those tough times to enrich them and make them more suitable for his kingdom's purposes.

In this context, the writer turns to a litany of Old Testament characters, filling in part of each "hero's" story so that the current audience can plug into it. Abel's story included God commending him for his sacrifices of faith. Yes, this story seems to have a poor ending if not viewed with eyes of faith, for Cain killed Abel. But those knowing God know that death was not the end for Abel, and his faith story has spoken throughout the ages. Enoch's story was a compelling one that enchanted the Jewish population in the centuries before Hebrews and even afterward. Enoch's story in Genesis doesn't record his death but simply notes that a time came where "he was not" (Gen. 5:24). God pulled him from his earthly existence. So inspiring was this story that Jews in the New Testament days made fictional stories of Enoch coming back at will into the world, giving secrets of the heavens to certain writers. More of the stories will follow in chapter 11 of Hebrews, but the question begins to form, How is God working in our stories? What do we do with God?

Lord, let me cling tightly to you in life's struggles as my story forms. In him, amen.

DECEMBER 8

These all died in faith, not having received the things promised, but having seen them and greeted them from afar, and having acknowledged that they were strangers and exiles on the earth. (Heb. 11:13)

Faith stories should inspire awe, appreciation, and inspiration. Everyone who hears such stories rightly projects them inwardly, asking questions like, "What would I have done in that situation? What would it be like to be that person?"

The writer of Hebrews uses stories in a powerful way to guide his readers and listeners to a deeper faith walk. The next story is that of Noah. For decades and decades, Noah worked on a boat because he believed God had warned him of a coming cataclysm. The weather patterns weren't noted as irregular during these decades, but Noah was walking by faith, not sight. Through his faith, he saves his family from the flood that washed the world clean.

Next, Abraham left his home for places unknown in a time when travel was difficult and dangerous. He couldn't take an American Express card. He didn't have Google maps. And no realtor was on the internet offering services once he arrived. Yet Abraham trusted God, believing that God had plans in mind for him and his family. Abraham's faith story should continue to inspire us today. God has honored his promises to Abraham that he made millennia ago. He will honor his promises to us too.

The ultimate promise of God—that which assures us of something that follows this earthly existence—is still unseen. Yet even though we can't see it, these episodic stories of faith should instill confidence in us that God will remain faithful to that promise. This rightly changes life today.

I go through the struggles of life, knowing that my job is to trust God and cling to him. That trust may lead to a successful path in the eyes of the world, as it did Abraham and Noah. Or it may lead to a quick exit out of this world, as it did Abel. Yet my concern should never be the immediate consequences. My concern and focus should be humble obedience to and reliance on the all-seeing, all-powerful, all-truthful God. He will not let me go. He will give me strength for today and a promised tomorrow. Praise God!

Lord, I thank you for your love. I trust you with my struggles today. Give me wisdom on how to live and strength for the journey. In Jesus, amen.

DECEMBER 9

And all these, though commended through their faith, did not receive what was promised, since God had provided something better for us, that apart from us they should not be made perfect. (Heb. 11:39–40)

As a young man interested in God and Scripture, I had some glaring holes in the 101s of biblical theology. Today's passage reminds me of one. Scripture and the church affirmed the great price paid by Christ in securing humanity's salvation. But a secret thought I had, which I was too ashamed to discuss with anyone, was the internal question, "Well, if dying for sins was such a big deal, then why didn't God just do something else? He's God, so why didn't he just decide, 'I'll forgive them?' Why did he need to die?"

As I continued to grow in understanding, I began to see the importance of what Jesus taught as noted in Mark 8:31: "The Son of Man must suffer many things . . . and be killed, and after three days rise again." Mark used the Greek word *dei* (δεῖ), which is a word of compulsion. This *had* to happen. There was no other way for God to fix pure forgiveness and give true righteousness to sinful people. God is just, and justice requires the appropriate penalty for human sin. Yet apart from Jesus, there has never been, nor could there ever be, one who could live perfectly and then die as a substitute for others.

Then as I continued to grow, this passage in Hebrews and an ancillary passage in Romans (Rom. 3:25–26) began to expand my understanding. If the world had ended with the resurrection of Christ, if no one had ever come to faith after Jesus rose again, his death was still necessary. The eternal God who exists apart from time had passed over the sins of the faithful found in the Old Testament and the pre-Jesus days. But this same just God could only pass over their sins because the righteousness of Christ could be imparted along with his substituting death on their behalf.

So among the litany of saints the writer records in chapter 11, he detailed many who trusted in God's deliverance, although its ultimate experience didn't happen in their lifetimes. The real deliverance for all of us came in Christ.

Jesus isn't optional for me. He is my only solution to all the crud and junk of sin. He is the purifier. He installs his righteousness in me. The death of Christ cost him dearly and was necessary. I must never lose sight of that.

Lord, "thank you" is not enough. I give my life to you in appreciation of Jesus, amen.

DECEMBER 10

Therefore, since we are surrounded by so great a cloud of witnesses, let us also lay aside every weight, and sin which clings so closely, and let us run with endurance the race that is set before us, looking to Jesus, the founder and perfecter of our faith. (Heb. 12:1–2)

Going to the Super Bowl is a spectacular experience. The stadium is always sold out—standing room only. The fans always include many notables—sports figures, politicians, entertainers, and a who's who of celebrity. The fans all zoom in and watch, play by play, as the two teams fight on the field for the title of world champion. After the game, the winner hoists the Lombardi Trophy high overhead.

We didn't invent the athletic contest, nor the arena. Games and contests were huge in the New Testament world. This gave the writer/preacher of Hebrews a powerful metaphor for the Christian. Having listed a wide array of Old Testament figures who walked faithfully with God, often to their own harm, the writer now places them as the audience in an arena. One can picture an ancient amphitheater filled with these inspiring people of old, watching how we live. We are the runners in this athletic contest, and they are the audience peering down at us.

So the writer tells us to get ourselves ready for the race. We are to strip down to our race gear—no racing with heavy overcoats or high heels! These hindrances to our performance are metaphors for the sins that stick to us and hinder our faithful walk with God. Moreover, in the writer's analogy, this isn't a sprint. We run a distance race that requires endurance, steadfastness, fortitude, patience, and perseverance. Without them, we might quit before the race is over.

We've watched our children compete in various long-distance races, including full and half-marathons. The finish line is always a huge deal. Having an announcer, cheering fans, and a huge banner running over the finish line all serve to increase the contestant's focus on successfully completing the race. In the analogy set forth in Hebrews, we see Jesus at the finish line. He went first and serves as the ultimate motivation and point of focus as we run to him.

This athletic metaphor speaks to me. I won't ever compete in the Super Bowl, but my life before God's watchful eyes is much more important! I want to run my best to Jesus.

Lord, give me eyes for Jesus and strength for the race. I run to you in him. Amen.

DECEMBER 11

For the moment all discipline seems painful rather than pleasant, but later it yields the peaceful fruit of righteousness to those who have been trained by it. (Heb. 12:11)

We disciplined our children as they grew up. We viewed it as one of parenting's least enjoyable tasks—but an important one nonetheless. Our general approach was to use the lowest level of discipline necessary to teach and reinforce good behavior while deterring behavior that would be detrimental to our children. Punishments varied by child as well as by the seriousness of the concern at issue. Some needed little disciplining. When our daughter Rebecca was four or five, for example, we found her sitting in a corner. When we asked her what she was doing, she explained that she had put herself in time-out for some transgression.

Discipline isn't a twentieth- or twenty-first-century invention. Discipline has been known as long as society has been around. Good parents don't let their children grow up without boundaries and lessons of life. If a toddler tends to run out into the street, a good parent will teach them not to. If a child thinks they can find life easier by telling fibs and lies to get out of trouble, a parent will teach them the importance of truth. Sometimes these teachings can be accomplished with something as simple as instruction. Sometimes something greater is required.

Today's passage recounts how the believer should see God's hand on our life. Certainly there are times of festive joy, those proverbial days when the sun is out and the wind's behind us. But we humans have tendencies that aren't always pure. We can find sin creeping in while we blithely go through our day. My buddy Pete tells me the eleventh commandment is "Every day will find at least one good rationalization."

Using the toddler analogy, God won't let us readily run into the street to play. He teaches us obedience through discipline. This isn't harsh; it is reality. In many ways, God's discipline is built into the world. We aren't being mean in teaching our children not to touch a hot stove. God isn't being mean in teaching us not to touch sin. We shouldn't complain about God's discipline. We should more readily accept his hand on our lives, trusting that he is sculpting us into the best we can be for his kingdom purposes. We rest in the assurance that even when times are difficult and we experience pain and hurt, God will bring us into a better place.

Lord, give me trust for you in the difficulties of life. Purify me in Jesus, amen.

DECEMBER 12

Therefore lift your drooping hands and strengthen your weak knees, and make straight paths for your feet, so that what is lame may not be put out of joint but rather be healed. Strive for peace with everyone, and for the holiness without which no one will see the Lord. (Heb. 12:12–14)

We've seen it in the movies. Think *Rocky II* (Stallone loses in *Rocky I*, so I'd rather not use that!), and imagine a depleted boxer, so tired that he can't keep his hands up. His knees get wobbly, and a knockout seems imminent. Then he catches a glimpse of his sweetheart, Adrian, and somehow musters the courage to continue. Finding that next level, he brings his hands back up and his knees find strength to hold him up and finish the fight. And he wins!

In prior verses, the preacher in Hebrews used an athletic event as a metaphor to encourage the believer to continue strong in life. He resumes that metaphor in today's passage, deftly weaving together two Old Testament passages that are a bit obscure. The phrasing about lifting drooping hands and strengthening weak knees was common in antiquity as an expression of athletic endurance. Yet the preacher here uses Isaiah 35:3–4, a passage that spoke to people who seemed abandoned by God. They were assured they would see God and therefore should "strengthen the weak hands, and make firm the feeble knees. Say to those who have an anxious heart, 'Be strong; fear not! Behold, your God will come.'" The writer combines this with the Proverbs 4:26 teaching that believers should "ponder the path" of their feet so that they won't stumble or fall.

Later, the Hebrews writer explains what he means in more practical terms. In verses 14 and 15, he urges his readers to leave at peace with others and deal with any bitterness toward others or God. They should get it out by the roots before it grows into a weed that destroys their lives, as well as the lives of others. They should live for something greater than the moment and the desires and passions of the moment, which will create trouble in areas where life has no reset button.

These ideas translate into great instructions for readers today. Like an athlete, we should push through the difficulties of life with endurance and stamina, trying our best with God's grace and empowerment to do what is right before God. This moves us into a life better than we could ever hope for.

Lord, give me strength to face my day with your holiness in Jesus, amen.

DECEMBER 13

Let brotherly love continue. Do not neglect to show hospitality to strangers, for thereby some have entertained angels unawares. Remember those who are in prison, as though in prison with them, and those who are mistreated, since you also are in the body. Let marriage be held in honor among all, and let the marriage bed be undefiled, for God will judge the sexually immoral and adulterous. Keep your life free from love of money, and be content with what you have, for he has said, "I will never leave you nor forsake you." (Heb. 13:1–5)

When I prepare to teach classes at church, as I reach the end of my preparation, I always try to ask myself, "So what?" I might teach the loftiest ideas, give fresh and deep insights into Scripture, and captivate an audience with engaging stories, but if there is no "So what?" that changes lives, then I have left the realm of a useful teacher and simply become Sunday morning entertainment. So I try to insert into every lesson the answer to "So what?" Generally, this takes the form of a PowerPoint slide entitled "Points for Home." An encounter with God and his word should make a practical difference in life.

The preacher in Hebrews is drawing his sermon to a close. Today's passage begins the final chapter of the book/sermon. The preacher doesn't end with a brilliant passage about how Melchizedek informs our insight into the priesthood of Christ. Nor does he end with a recounting of the tabernacle design given to Moses in the wilderness. Those thoughts were set forth earlier. As the preacher brings his lesson toward its close, he goes into "So what?" mode. He begins to summarize how the lessons of his sermon should affect us daily.

The preacher begins with a simple three-word sentence (in the Greek). Continue to live with a brotherly care and affection for one another. This naturally flows into the exhortation to show hospitality, even to strangers. We don't know God's purposes when he moves someone into our orbit of life. We should be careful to treat all with the love of God. We should live conscious of those who don't enjoy our freedoms and blessings, looking for ways to help and bless them. We should treasure our relationships with those around us, living with them in holiness. Our love should be directed by God (family love to family, neighborly love to neighbors, and brotherly love to others), not steered into an evil love, say, for money or possessions. These practical behaviors stem from lofty Scriptures and deep ideas. We mustn't read the Bible and leave out the Points for Home!

Lord, guide my steps in holiness today for the sake and cause of Jesus, amen.

DECEMBER 14

Now may the God of peace who brought again from the dead our Lord Jesus, the great shepherd of the sheep, by the blood of the eternal covenant, equip you with everything good that you may do his will, working in us that which is pleasing in his sight, through Jesus Christ, to whom be glory forever and ever. Amen. (Heb. 13:20–21)

When I think about all the people who regularly pray for me and my family, I am deeply grateful and inspired. Do you have folks you regularly pray for? Some do this by keeping a list, praying for certain people on certain days. My lists for praying have often had categories, such as praying for salvation for those who haven't yet experienced it. I have a list of people who have wandered away from the daily strength of faith and commitment. Some are on my list for better health, some for endurance in life's struggles, some for protection on a journey, some for provision of life's needs, some for insight into life's difficulties and wisdom into important decisions in the offing. I have lists for those for whom I don't know the current needs, but I set them before God in prayer anyway, knowing God knows their needs.

As the writer of Hebrews draws his sermon/letter to a close, he offers a prayer for his readers. I really like this prayer. It is worth praying for everyone on my list, regardless of where I have them placed. Like the prayer Jesus taught his disciples, this prayer begins by honoring as holy and praising the name of God. The prayer sets out the great things of God. He is the God of peace. He has resurrected Jesus, giving us the great shepherd. He has executed a covenant in his blood, a covenant that sets us aright with God for eternity in ways that are both just and loving. Both this prayer and the Lord's prayer show that praise should normally precede petition.

The prayer then shifts to seeking God's provision for the people. The preacher prays that God will give the people the strength and resources needed to follow God's will. Our need to recognize our dependence on God is fundamental. We can have the best possible path before God, clearly marked and laid out before us, but if God doesn't empower us and provide for us, we will never be able to walk that path. Human strength produces human results. Only the strength and provision of God produce godly results. That is why when we find success in life, we should give all glory and honor to Jesus!

Lord, please strengthen and empower those in my heart to pray for. Give them what they need today to walk in victory for Jesus. To his glory, amen.

DECEMBER 15

That which was from the beginning, which we have heard, which we have seen with our eyes, which we looked upon and have touched with our hands, concerning the word of life—the life was made manifest, and we have seen it, and testify to it and proclaim to you the eternal life, which was with the Father and was made manifest to us—that which we have seen and heard we proclaim also to you, so that you too may have fellowship with us; and indeed our fellowship is with the Father and with his Son Jesus Christ. (1 Jn. 1)

The world when 1 John was written was larger than the world today. For example, this morning, I got up in Boca Raton, Florida, at 4 a.m. Yesterday was an election day, and I was curious about the results of some races in Texas, where I live. I got on the internet to review the full results. Meanwhile, I am also keeping up with an auction that is taking place in London, England—all from my desk in Florida. Walt Disney was right; it's a small world after all!

In the days of 1 John, it took time for news about something in one town to make it to another. Ditto for one region to another. The internet was missing, phones didn't exist, and the postal service existed basically just for the military and government. Travel was more precarious, even though the Pax Romana (Peace of Rome) made travel safer than it had been earlier. The currency varied from region to region, and everyone left home without American Express or any of the charge cards. Motel 6 wasn't yet leaving the light on, and people largely stayed in homes or the great outdoors when traveling.

Not surprisingly, in that world, as heresies grew up around the Christian faith, they could spread like a coronavirus, moving from one person to another, and it was very difficult to stomp out heretical ideas. They could readily spread before someone in another region even knew about them.

Into that world comes the letter of 1 John. To even send a letter to address church concerns was an arduous task. Something important was at stake to take the time and trouble. Reading the letter's beginning sets before our eyes what was so critical. People had lost sight of the simple truth about Jesus. Jesus was really God incarnate. He who existed before time took on flesh. This same truth should be our touchstone in the small world where we live. We should never lose sight of the reality of Jesus. We should never grow past it. He is our rock.

Lord, let me see and lean on Jesus as a first priority today. In him, amen.

DECEMBER 16

This is the message we have heard from him and proclaim to you, that God is light, and in him is no darkness at all. If we say we have fellowship with him while we walk in darkness, we lie and do not practice the truth. But if we walk in the light, as he is in the light, we have fellowship with one another, and the blood of Jesus his Son cleanses us from all sin. (1 Jn. 1:5–7)

Thomas Edison is one of my favorite historical figures, and I never got to thank him! By inventing the lightbulb and making electricity readily useful, he enabled my practice of awakening hours before dawn with no worries and little hassle. I'm not lighting candles, straining my eyes, or tripping over unseen hazards. I flip a switch, and presto! It is light! The darkness is gone. Even at 4 a.m.!

The invasion of light into darkness is guaranteed. I never need to fear that the darkness will somehow defeat the power of a working lightbulb. Wherever light shines, darkness recedes. Light always defeats darkness. It is a good thing too—because lots of problems accompany living and walking in darkness. We fail to see much that is important and much that is beautiful or good to see. I have stubbed many a toe in a dark room. There is a reason most home invasions occur at night. Darkness also hides a lot of sins and transgressions. People live differently before watching eyes than when alone and unseen.

With these basic truths about light and darkness, one isn't surprised to see it readily used as a metaphor for life in Christ. Christ illuminates life. In Christ, we not only see truth about ourselves, but we also see the truth of the world. As C. S. Lewis famously wrote, "I believe in Christianity as I believe that the sun has risen: not only because I see it, but because by it I see everything else."

If the Christian understands that Jesus is light, the Christian shouldn't spend life frolicking in the darkness. If Christ as light is to provide my sight, direction, and strength, why would I frolic in darkness? Dr. Seuss wrote, "You have brains in your head. You have feet in your shoes. You can steer yourself in any direction you choose."

The choice to walk in darkness or light is set before us all. I am thankful for Edison, and I turn on the switch. I want to walk in the lightness of Christ. I want his forgiveness and fellowship. I won't find those in darkness.

Lord, be my light today. May I walk in your warming light in Jesus, amen.

DECEMBER 17

If we say we have no sin, we deceive ourselves, and the truth is not in us. If we confess our sins, he is faithful and just to forgive us our sins and to cleanse us from all unrighteousness. If we say we have not sinned, we make him a liar, and his word is not in us. (1 Jn. 1:8–10)

Some movements in Christianity stun me. I can't understand how some people can teach that they have reached a point of perfection in this life. Over the centuries, movements have formed around the idea that believers can reach a point of perfection where God's special grace comes upon them. This problem was apparently already present when 1 John was written.

Perhaps this idea of perfection stems from Jesus saying, "You therefore must be perfect, as your heavenly Father is perfect" (Mt. 5:48). Yet this clear affirmation of Christ should drive every believer to their knees seeking God's mercy and grace, for as Jesus also said, "If you would be perfect, go, sell what you possess and give to the poor, and you will have treasure in heaven; and come, follow me" (Mt. 19:21). In other words, Jesus' call to perfection is a call to live without even a taint of selfishness, and no one save the Lord himself has or could ever do so.

One of the greatest sins portrayed in Scripture is the sin of pride. Spiritual haughtiness should offend us all. Anyone believing they live sinlessly lives in a house of hubris that itself is sin.

The writer makes this clear in today's passage, especially as shown in the verb tenses. One might say at any point, "I don't sin." But that person is a liar and hence a sinner! The verb for "we have no sin" is in the present tense. It isn't a claim of the past. It means that moment by moment, day by day, I don't sin! This claim is outrageous, as it flies in the face of our constant need and reliance on God and his merciful and forgiving grace.

Sin includes selfishness. And we all sin as even the best human deed is tainted with at least a smidgeon of self-interest. Of course, in my life, as well as that of most of my friends, our sins are so apparent and obvious to us that we are stunned at God's mercy. We desperately seek his forgiveness, and passages like today's are reassuring. For Jesus forgives us of sins without qualification. Thank God!

Lord, I do thank you for the forgiveness of Jesus from all *my sins. In him is amen!*

DECEMBER 18

My little children, I am writing these things to you so that you may not sin. But if anyone does sin, we have an advocate with the Father, Jesus Christ the righteous. He is the propitiation for our sins, and not for ours only but also for the sins of the whole world. (1 Jn. 2:1–2)

Big things can come in small packages. While I've never kept a new car in my pocket, I did hide my wife's engagement ring in there once many years ago. It allowed me to pop the question at a time when she wasn't expecting it.

In today's passage, John puts big things in a small package. Important living instructions are wrapped in key theological truths. Having previously dealt with the false teachers who believed they had achieved moral perfection and explained that everyone is—present tense—a sinner, John then adds that his purpose in writing these truths is to hinder their sinning! In other words, he is saying, "No one is perfect, and I tell you that so you won't sin!" The link between the two ideas is vital. If we believe ourselves better than we are, we sin in pride. If we know our sinfulness, however, we work to avoid sin as much as we can!

Knowing our inability to avoid sinning, John tells the readers about a fundamental truth of life, death, and the hereafter: believers have an advocate with the Father. The Greek word for "advocate" is found in the New Testament only here and in the Gospel of John. The word spoke of a nonlawyer who would come to court to speak on behalf of another (*paraklētos*—παράκλητος). Jesus *the righteous*, one without sin, is our advocate. More than that, he is also our "propitiation," another rare word (*hilasmos*—ἱλασμός).

In John's context, the "propitiation" that is Christ is both a removal of the stain of sin on the believer but also the righteous satisfaction of sin's penalty before God. God's holy character demands the death of sin. Unholiness cannot abide in a holy God. A glass of milk with a drop of ink cannot be pure milk. A grade point average of one hundred cannot include even a ninety-nine without being diminished. So God must deal with sin. Jesus takes care of our sin.

Do we have true moral guilt? Yes! But the price of Jesus' sacrificial death fully satisfies and resolves that guilt both in us and before God. No believer should walk in shame over sin but in joy before the forgiving Father.

Lord, thank you for the forgiveness in Jesus. I can't live without it. In him, amen.

DECEMBER 19

Do not love the world or the things in the world. If anyone loves the world, the love of the Father is not in him. For all that is in the world—the desires of the flesh and the desires of the eyes and pride of life—is not from the Father but is from the world. And the world is passing away along with its desires, but whoever does the will of God abides forever. (1 Jn. 2:15–17)

Several of my children have run marathons. I would have loved to have joined them running, but 26.2 miles isn't in my body, at least as I currently sit. I think it would be such a cool accomplishment, but I doubt I will ever achieve it. Running a marathon in some ways seems as easy as eating a piece of cake compared to the teaching in today's passage. This passage makes me pause, as it gives me great concern. "Don't love the world or things in the world." OK, that instruction is simple enough, but how does one do it? It seems like telling me, "Get up out of your chair, go outside, and run 26.2 miles!" My gut reply is "Not possible!"

So I turn to the Greek to see if it helps me water down this passage to something achievable. It doesn't. It makes it worse. The directive "Don't love the world" is a present imperative in the Greek. That means it refers to *right now and continuing to do so*, a time that is always present. It doesn't mean "When you're at your best, don't love the world's things." Nor does it mean "Get to a point one day where you don't love the things of the world." It says don't do it moment by moment. In the marathon analogy, it means run the marathon now, not after training, not in the past when you were in better shape. Now! No loving of the world or its things.

With Greek grammar being of no help, I tried using the Greek vocabulary to make this more palatable. Could "love" mean something different to John? But alas, no. A word study on the meaning of love doesn't help me either. The verb (*agapaō*—ἀγαπάω) includes the idea of having an interest in or warm affection for. It includes cherishing. A small glimpse is given in the word *world*. Biblically, that often refers not simply to the created cosmos but to the unbelieving world that has yet to come under God's dominion. That is the world I am not to love.

So what am I to do with this passage? First, I confess my struggles with applying this truth in my life to my God and Father. Second, I work to wean myself from loving anything that isn't under God's dominion. Third, I try to find the beauty and peace in God's provisions, thinking of them as like a shovel. I have never loved a shovel, but I have found them useful. Maybe if I can learn that everything is a shovel or tool to be used for God, then this verse won't feel like running a marathon!

Lord, give me a better godly focus on living in the world for Jesus, amen.

DECEMBER 20

And now, little children, abide in him, so that when he appears we may have confidence and not shrink from him in shame at his coming. (1 Jn. 2:28)

Henry Francis Lyte, born in Ednam, Scotland, in 1793, lived a difficult life. Originally intending a life in medicine, Lyte changed careers, becoming a clergyman. When Lyte was nineteen, his brother died unexpectedly, jolting him and driving him deep into Bible study. Lyte became known for his pastoral care, his ability to write poetry, and his preaching.

Life was hard on Lyte. Money was insufficient, and his health was never good. When he was fifty-four, advanced tuberculosis drove him to the southern English coast for family time and a better climate. There he penned the famous hymn "Abide with Me," just months before he died. I can picture him on the coast, his health failing, as the tide ebbs and darkness descends. He writes, "Abide with me, fast falls the eventide. The darkness deepens, Lord with me abide. When other helpers fail and comforts flee, help of the helpless, oh, abide with me."

That song readily comes to mind reading 1 John. Over and over, John instructs his readers that as God and his word abide in us, so we are to abide in him. In chapter 2 alone, John uses the word eleven times. This is a calling to remain and stay in the heart of God, even as God stays and remains in ours. God abides in us through his Spirit, teaching and growing us (1 Jn. 3:9; 4:13). We have the assurance God won't wander and leave us, but we aren't as reliable as he is. We need that constant reminder to stay or abide where our God is.

Lyte's plea for God to abide with him in his last days of failing health should motivate us all to embrace and never leave this comforting God. Lyte's penultimate verse says, "I fear no foe, with Thee at hand to bless. Ills have no weight, and tears no bitterness. Where is death's sting? Where, grave, thy victory? I triumph still, if Thou abide with me." This simple truth applies, but the real thrust isn't a plea for God to still abide with us; it is for us to abide with him. This we do as we "hold" the cross of Jesus before our eyes. Then as Lyte penned in his final verse, God will "shine through the gloom and point [us] to the skies." Then as "heaven's morning breaks, and earth's vain shadows flee," we will find that "in life, in death," the Lord abides with us as we do with him.

Lord, abide with me, for life is empty without you. May I find strength, wisdom, fulfillment, and joy abiding in you. In Jesus, I pray, amen.

DECEMBER 21

See what kind of love the Father has given to us, that we should be called children of God; and so we are. The reason why the world does not know us is that it did not know him. Beloved, we are God's children now, and what we will be has not yet appeared; but we know that when he appears we shall be like him, because we shall see him as he is. And everyone who thus hopes in him purifies himself as he is pure. (1 Jn. 3:1–3)

Some food is so tasty that I eat it rapidly, craving another bite as soon as the first bite is in my mouth. But far better are those meals when delicious food is savored. Each bite is chewed over and over while enjoying each morsel as long as possible. Today's passage reminds me of great food. Part of me wants to read it so fast, as it is so great. Part of me wants to read it slowly, savoring each clause, as I think it through and a great smile breaks out on my face and in my heart.

God's love for us is amazing. It is the kind of love that can make a diamond out of dung. God finds each of us in whatever state we exist—some definitely rougher than others but all rough compared to the glory of God. God takes us and declares we belong to him. We get adopted as children, with all the rights that go into belonging in God's family.

Many consequences flow from being in God's family. It changes the way we are seen by the world. The world doesn't understand God and won't understand us. Those outside the family may not understand our priorities, the things that interest us, the things we seek to avoid, the way we treat others, or even the way we talk. That's to be expected.

Admittedly, as we are adopted into his family, we don't immediately look how we should look. Change occurs slowly. We may have trouble shifting into the mold of God's family, but no worries! God immediately begins to buff, polish, and shine us. He takes us in our rough state and forms his character in us. He begins to change our desires. He molds our character. He gives us a longing for purity and the strength to change old habits. It isn't easy. It doesn't happen overnight. It doesn't come without some pain. But we are assured that as this life comes to an end, we will be the diamonds he saw in us from the beginning.

Lord, deep in my heart, I smile because of your love, even though I am stunned that you love me. May I readily reflect your love and character to the world. In Jesus, amen.

DECEMBER 22

By this it is evident who are the children of God, and who are the children of the devil: whoever does not practice righteousness is not of God, nor is the one who does not love his brother. . . . By this we know love, that he laid down his life for us, and we ought to lay down our lives for the brothers. . . . By this we shall know that we are of the truth and reassure our heart before him; for whenever our heart condemns us, God is greater than our heart, and he knows everything. (1 Jn. 3:10, 16, 19–20)

You've got to love a thermometer. Is it hot or cold? Too hot or too cold? The thermometer doesn't make the temperature; it simply informs you what it is. I read today's passages and think of thermometers. John gives three sentences each that began in the Greek with the words "By this . . ." (*en toutō*—ἐν τούτῳ). This is thermometer language! John says if we want to know the temperature, if we want to know how things really are, we have something by which we can look and see.

The first is how we live without regard to sin. Do we cavalierly live our lives uncaring about the character and commands of our holy God? Do we care about others or care only about ourselves? God cares for the "least of these" (Mt. 25:40). Do we? Regardless of sin, color, nationality, personality, socioeconomic status, or anything else? Are we moved by compassion for those hurting?

The second "By this . . ." is, Do we practice love to the point of sacrifice? Are we willing to take a hit financially to help those in need? Are we willing to donate time to those who need our help? As we are able, do we give comfort to those grieving? Do we pray for people *and* try to give them practical help?

The third "By this . . ." is a bit different from the first two. John knows that sometimes how we feel may not be an accurate reading of the thermometer. At times we might feel isolated from God's love, since each of us stumbles in sin. But John knows that in those days when we feel poorly, we can rely on the objective truth that God loves us. In the same way that we seek to love others who are broken, hurting, and stumbling, God also loves us. He came to us *not because we earned his love* but because he chose to. He loves us despite our sin and is at work to clean us up. I love a good thermometer, and we have one here in 1 John 3!

Lord, help me be what you want me to be, growing in you daily. In Jesus' name, amen.

DECEMBER 23

By this we shall know that we are of the truth and reassure our heart before him; for whenever our heart condemns us, God is greater than our heart, and he knows everything. (1 Jn. 3:19–20)

Before you email or write me, *yes*! I know that today's passage was part of yesterday's devotional, but it needs more attention than I gave it yesterday, so let's keep in it a bit longer.

As a college student, we were in class with our Greek professor Dr. Harvey Floyd. One student asked Dr. Floyd, "How do you feel about your salvation?" Dr. Floyd answered, "That isn't the important question. The important question is, What do I *think* about my salvation? Don't trust your feelings; trust what you know to be true. Feelings change." Dr. Floyd then took us to today's passage.

He told us that even though we were believers in God, even though we'd given God our lives and committed ourselves to him and his kingdom, we would still find days when we would feel isolated from him, days when our prayers would seem unanswered, days when we would feel our sin so intensely that we would doubt whether God would even love us. Feelings aren't reliable.

Dr. Floyd said the Bible is full of folks who have walked that road. He urged us to turn to Psalms 42 and 43 to understand what John was saying. Those two psalms are meant to be read together. In them, the psalmist recounts his intense longing for God, even as he seems abandoned by God. In this time when he felt absolute isolation, he shifted from his feelings to his knowledge and experience. He remembered times of glorying, when he was caught up in the presence of God and the joys of worship. He knew those times would come again, and what he was experiencing was temporary.

We appreciated what Dr. Floyd showed us. But then things took an unexpected turn. Dr. Floyd said even as the psalmist correctly let his head speak to his heart, the result wasn't immediate! The psalmist still felt alone and isolated from God. The psalmist walked through the same head/heart debate time and again. Because, as Dr. Floyd explained, our feelings don't always follow what we know to be true, and in those times, we need to remind ourselves of what we can know with confidence: God loves us, forgives us, and holds us, regardless of how we feel!

Lord, thank you for your love. Let me rest in it with confidence in Jesus, amen.

DECEMBER 24

Beloved, do not believe every spirit, but test the spirits to see whether they are from God, for many false prophets have gone out into the world. (1 Jn. 4:1)

Some friends who formed the Christian community at L'Abri, Switzerland, were telling me about how they raised their children. I asked whether their children watched much TV, and they told me they would let their children watch almost anything except religious programming. I was stunned. I quizzed, "Why?" My buddy explained that their children could tell right and wrong in most shows, but religious shows often had horrific heresy all dressed up in religious clothing, and young children wouldn't know the difference.

Every age has its Christian heresies. Jesus warned of false prophets (Mt. 7:15–20). So did the Old Testament prophets. The heresy du jour varies with cultural trends but must always be identified for what it is. In John's day, it diminished the truth and value of Jesus by denying his fleshly reality. This heresy bloomed fully in the succeeding decades and centuries into what is now termed Gnosticism.

Today's heresies may not so readily deny the physical reality of Jesus, at least within most churches, yet heresies that diminish his work or value are always present, should always be discerned, and should be refuted. For example, no one should allow the idea that Jesus was a white-skinned person whose target audience was other white-skinned people. Any form of racism is a heresy that must be confronted and negated by the church. Ditto for the idea that Jesus loves one nation or another more than others. God did choose the Jewish people as special recipients of his blessings, giving them the honor of receiving and preserving his prophetic words in Scripture, taking on human flesh through a Jewish mother, invading the Jewish nation, choosing Jews for his twelve apostles for beginning his church, and more. Yet even still, Jesus made clear he had come for the nations, not the Jews only (Mt. 28:19).

Our battles may be different, but we are to be on the alert for truth about Jesus. Jesus embodied the truth of God (Jn. 14:6), and to diminish that, distract from that, or misdirect from that will propagate lies and, in a true sense, is blasphemy.

Everyone needs to stay rooted in Scripture, seek the truth of God, and battle that which is contrary to him. This is fighting the spirit of the age.

Lord, give me a discerning spirit to purify my faith in Jesus, amen.

DECEMBER 25

Beloved, let us love one another, for love is from God, and whoever loves has been born of God and knows God. Anyone who does not love does not know God, because God is love. In this the love of God was made manifest among us, that God sent his only Son into the world, so that we might live through him. In this is love, not that we have loved God but that he loved us and sent his Son to be the propitiation for our sins. Beloved, if God so loved us, we also ought to love one another. (1 Jn. 4:7–11)

In high school English, most are taught to write term papers. The writing often begins with an outline, with clear points set forth into an organized flow of thought. John didn't take high school English. While many letters in the New Testament can be readily outlined with a flow of thought from beginning to end, the letter 1 John is more akin to a bouquet of flowers. John has certain themes and ideas (say, a red rose), and he repeats them more in an artistic pattern than in a logical flow of organized thought.

Today's passage is a great example. John is repeating a theme that he has visited several times already in his letter. The theme is the love that should be the hallmark of Christian identity. This theme is worthy of visiting over and over. After all, love was (and is) the defining hallmark of Christ. If God's love is expressed in the ultimate and most obvious form of his incarnation, death, and resurrection, all to save humanity from an eternal death into an eternal life, then those who follow Jesus should also love others intensely (Mk. 12:29–31).

The world has a love, but it isn't the same as God's love. We mustn't think the unbelieving world *can't* show love. It can. The world's love can even show some measure of godly devotion, for everyone is made in God's image and has some pre-wiring for love. The world needs love, can usually understand love on some level, and can also have love. Yet God's love is deeper, much like the ocean depths compared to a pond. It is this deeper love that should be the Christian calling card.

Jesus shows the deeper love. He shows a sacrificial love that seeks the good of others, even at deep personal cost. His is an initiating love that reaches out to folks who aren't readily accepting his love, a forgiving love that goes beyond what people deserve. This is Christ's love and is the love that we are to hold. Let us love one another.

Lord, grow your love in me, so I may better reflect you. In Jesus, amen.

DECEMBER 26

So we have come to know and to believe the love that God has for us. God is love, and whoever abides in love abides in God, and God abides in him. By this is love perfected with us. (1 Jn. 4:16–17)

One of life's greatest joys is finding love. Not some puppy love that has chemicals in one's brain thinking blindly about how great everything is, but a deep, genuine love that is built for good times and bad, seeking others' best even in the worst times, assisting others while they walk difficult roads, and offering mercy that is undeserved. This love might be termed a "1 Corinthians 13 love." It is patient, kind, unboasting, humble, polite, encouraging, selfless, forgiving, enduring, seeing the best, and more.

We can read and write about such love, but a fair question is, "How do we get it?" Most people are really good at giving love to those who deserve it. Like sailing, love is easy when the sun is out and the wind is behind us. But what about when life's storms blow in? How do we love when someone wrongs us atrociously? How do we love when the feelings aren't the same? I have performed many weddings and been to my fair share as well. But I have never been to a wedding where the vows say, "For when times are great, but let's end things when they are rough." The vows are always "For richer and poorer, in sickness and in health." No one goes into marriage expecting love to dissolve. Yet statistics show love isn't easy to keep.

Into these real-life truths comes a profound affirmation by John. We can all experience a growing, maturing love. John uses a word translated "perfected." It is the Greek *teleioō* (τελειόω). It conveys the ideas of getting something to its final state, such as fruit ripening or an animal maturing. We can see our love grow and mature. John gives the key to this maturity: abide in God. The more we grow in the Lord, the more time we spend in prayer, devotion, and worship of him, the more his love will grow in our hearts. God will rewire our brains to better grasp the depths and meaning of his love. He will grow that love within us.

We should all want and seek to love like God. It isn't going to happen on its own. It will come from our abiding in God. As we follow him, he will grow in us, and our love will transform the world!

Lord, I want to love better. Please work in my heart and mind as I live for you. In Jesus' name, amen.

DECEMBER 27

For everyone who has been born of God overcomes the world. And this is the victory that has overcome the world—our faith. Who is it that overcomes the world except the one who believes that Jesus is the Son of God? (1 Jn. 5:4–5)

In ancient Greece, the people worshiped Nike as the goddess who brought victory in war as well as life in general. She was seen as a key divine instrument for success. Her Roman equivalent bore the Latin name *Victoria*, from which derives the modern English word *victory*. This goddess made winners. The goddess Nike is the inspiration for the sports company Nike, with its well-known swoosh logo being one of the two wings typically portrayed extended out from the goddess as she hovered over the winner.

Nike wasn't only the name of the goddess; it was also the Greek word for winning/victory (νίκη). John uses it three times in today's passage, in both its noun and verb forms. The noun is translated as "victory," while the verb is translated as "overcome." But both have the same word root and should be read together.

The goddess Nike isn't how the Christian finds success or victory over the world. Faith in Jesus Christ as the Son of God brings victory in spiritual warfare. In John's immediate context, the battle was against a false theology that was teaching that Jesus was only a human who was at times inhabited by the Spirit of God but was not incarnated God. Trumpeted by a man named Cerinthus, noted by early church writers to be particularly vexatious to John, this heresy was rooted in a belief that God couldn't suffer. Hence the suffering endured by Jesus was experienced not by God but by the man Jesus, whom God would possess at various times.

John is confronting a heresy that is different from most worldly belief systems today, but the source of believers' victory today hasn't changed. Victory is still found in our trust and faith in Christ. The world's challenges are real. Worldly idea systems seek to offer solutions to suffering, difficulty, and trials. Who hasn't thought a lie might help here and there? Or perhaps a bit of selfishness is called for—maybe greed is justified . . . or maybe some gossip to tickle itching ears? No. John makes it clear that trusting in Jesus as God's true Son and then following Jesus' teachings bring true victory. Success isn't found in a pagan goddess or pagan ideology. Success in life comes from God alone.

Lord, may I trust Jesus as I face today's challenges. May he be my victory. In Jesus' name, amen.

DECEMBER 28

Whoever has the Son has life; whoever does not have the Son of God does not have life. (1 Jn. 5:12)

Even a new reader of the Bible would know something is missing in a formulaic, literal understanding of today's passage. Biology dictates that anyone reading or listening to this passage is alive. Dead people don't read books like this.

Yet John is saying something profound. He wrote in a world where ink and paper weren't readily available. It was an expensive chore to write. He wrote words that he deemed important, not throwaways. Far be it from him to write something inane like "Your heart will beat and you will have working brain waves if you have a relationship with Jesus as the Son of God."

John is writing about a different quality of life, something beyond mere existence. This quality can include an eternal aspect, as the Gospel of John profoundly declared that God gave his only Son so that those who believe and trust in him would have eternal life (Jn. 3:16). But John is referencing a different quality of life in the here and now, even before we enter God's eternal kingdom. Also in the Gospel of John, we read that Jesus contrasts what he offers to people versus what the world and its antagonism toward God offer. Jesus explained, "The thief comes only to steal and kill and destroy. I came that they [his sheep—that is, his people] may have life and have it abundantly" (Jn. 10:10). Jesus spoke of life "to the full" or "excessive" life, both viable translations of the word "abundantly" (*perisson*—περισσὸν).

What does this mean practically? In the Christmas season, which celebrates the incarnation of God in the person of Jesus, we have the model for our perspective on life, from joyous celebrations (Jn. 2:1–11) to the preciousness of life and love (Jn. 11). We also have the realization that God understands humanity not only as Creator but also as one who can "sympathize with our weaknesses" and "in every respect has been tempted as we are" (Heb. 4:15) on an existential level as well.

So when we face joys, trials, tribulation, frustrations, suffering, disease, loss, unfilled desires, and more, we can find in Jesus Christ one who loves us and seeks to give us a level of wisdom and understanding that can rightly be described as "life to its fullest." This is the joy of Jesus.

Lord, give me insight in Jesus to live as you intended. In him I ask, amen.

DECEMBER 29

And we know that the Son of God has come and has given us understanding, so that we may know him who is true; and we are in him who is true, in his Son Jesus Christ. He is the true God and eternal life. Little children, keep yourselves from idols. (1 Jn. 5:20–21)

Reality is a pesky thing. We may each have our own version of what is real and what isn't, but regardless of our wishes and thoughts, reality goes right ahead with the truth. I can't alter the truth; I can only choose to believe in it or not.

John finds both faith and understanding linked in the reality of God incarnate as Jesus, the Son of God. Jesus wasn't only a good man. Jesus wasn't merely a physical form in which God's Spirit temporarily set up shop. Through the mystery of the incarnation, God became flesh in Jesus and dwelt with humanity. Hence the name so familiar to the Christmas season, Emmanuel, which means "God with us."

Humanity has no future apart from Christ. Sin is a disease with a death sentence. Sin is a distortion of God's goodness on such a cosmic level that it must be destroyed. It is beyond repair. No one can fix what is irreparably broken. It must be replaced.

We sense this. We try to do better than we have before, and we might succeed to some degree, but we are all still moral failures. And if by some chance we might not think so, we are failing with self-righteous pride, one of the worst sins. We see the destruction that comes from sin. Sin hurts and pulls apart lives and families. It causes pain and depression in spite of pharma's mood-boosting medicines. Despair haunts everyone at some time or another. Yet these periods of sadness, pain, anguish, and loneliness all find answers through Jesus Christ, the Son of God.

Jesus gives unconditional forgiveness. He works to grow his heart and Spirit in our lives. He seeks to rewire our brains. But he also explains why we aren't perfect and why life can be a real stinker. We understand the power of sin, and we see it for what it is. His death was no easy matter, yet it was the only way to conquer sin and its death warrant. Praise God for Jesus, by whom we are set free and through whom we understand freedom.

Lord, forgive me, grow me, make me more like Jesus, as I pray in his name, amen.

DECEMBER 30

And now I ask you, dear lady—not as though I were writing you a new commandment, but the one we have had from the beginning—that we love one another. And this is love, that we walk according to his commandments; this is the commandment, just as you have heard from the beginning, so that you should walk in it. (2 Jn. 5–6)

I love pizza, especially cheesy pizza. I also love my dog Tizzy. She's a cute, old dog. I love my kids, all five of them. I love my grandkids, all ten of them. I love my mom and am glad she is still alive. I love my dad, although he died twenty years ago. I love my sisters and their families. My wife is the love of my life. Each of these statements of love is genuine, yet they differ profoundly in meaning and depth. I love all those things. But what I mean by "love" varies tremendously. I do not feel the same about my wife as I do about pizza or my dog. My love for my wife is quite different from my love for my kids.

"Love" has a host of meanings. This makes it important when reading a passage like today's to understand what John means by "love." We should try to transfix that same meaning into our understanding of the passage.

Ancient Greek had a myriad of different words for "love." John uses the word group with the root *agap-*, *agapē* for the noun and *agapaō* for the verb. This Greek idea of "love" conveys many different ideas in English. It can speak to having a warm regard or affection for another. In this sense, it embodies the English idea of cherishing or having high esteem for another. The word group includes the idea of concern for another. An *agapē* love is one that readily serves another out of cherishing concern.

John is telling his readers to have this genuine concern, this cherishing for one another. This cherishing expresses itself in action. The first level of action is obeying Jesus our Lord, whom we love in the truest sense of the word. Our love for one another doesn't take the same form of obedience that it does to the Lord. But our *agapē* love is still rooted in how we act. Our love for those we cherish is a love that should move us to seek their best good.

When I think of the love of Jesus, I see modeled that cherishing another means taking action for their good. I want to share in his love—not only as a recipient but also to inspire and teach the next generation how to love others.

Lord, help me grow in agapē *love—toward you and others, in Jesus' name, amen.*

DECEMBER 31

Everyone who goes on ahead and does not abide in the teaching of Christ, does not have God. Whoever abides in the teaching has both the Father and the Son. (2 Jn. 9)

We had gone to Disney World with some of our children and grandchildren. At one point in the day, several people wanted to return to the park and ride some adult rides. The problem was that one of our grandchildren was an infant and several were toddlers, so they couldn't ride those rides. These young ones were also wiped out from the theme park experience earlier in the day. Becky and I decided to stay back in the hotel with the little ones while the adults went and rode the adult rides.

This sense of staying behind rather than going ahead is found in today's passage, but with a different result. Some of John's audience, the letter's recipients, were thinking they were running ahead to experience something greater than those who stayed back. These deceived people thought there was something more spiritual and greater than the simple life of obeying and following Jesus Christ, the Son of the Father.

Yet in truth, there was nothing greater than abiding in the teaching of Christ. By leaving the simple obedience of a life faithful to Jesus, they were abandoning their best position. Jesus had said decades earlier, as the Gospel of John recorded, "If anyone loves me, he will keep my word, and my Father will love him, and we will come to him and make our home with him" (Jn. 14:23). God indwells his children, and Jesus indwells his followers. Both do so through the Holy Spirit (Jn. 15:26; 16:13–15). Jesus also had foretold his disciples that on the day the Holy Spirit came to indwell them, they would "know that I am in my Father, and you in me, and I in you" (Jn. 14:20).

I can understand our adult children wanting some time away from immediate parenting responsibilities so they might enjoy the rides at Disney. But it doesn't make sense why anyone would want to leave the peace and joy of staying in the teachings of Jesus Christ and God the Father in order to pursue some fake, superficial, cheap pleasures offered by the world. To settle for these fakes is to be deluded into thinking one is off on a Disney ride when, in truth, one is living in darkness.

I want to follow Jesus. I want to stay in his teaching, obeying his commands.

Lord, give me joy in obedience as I dwell securely in Christ, in whom I pray, amen.

ON TRUTH

I have no greater joy than to hear that my children are walking in the truth. (3 Jn. 4)

My daughter Gracie was teaching her four-year-old to read. Looking for tips, she and I asked an artificial intelligence (AI) program how one should teach a four-year-old to read. The AI answer included reading together books that repeat words over and over. That tip would have made 3 John a great practice book!

John uses the same words over and over in this short one-chapter letter. By the time Gaius, the letter's recipient, reads today's verse, John has already used the word *love* three times: first, he calls Gaius "beloved"; second, John declares that he "loves" Gaius; and third, John then addresses him as "beloved." John has also used the word *truth* four times already: loving Gaius in "truth," hearing testimony that Gaius is "in the truth," confirming Gaius walks "in the truth," and then in today's verse, expressing joy over Gaius walking "in the truth."

John's repetition isn't meant to teach his audience reading skills. John repeats these because they form the foundation for what John has to say. They are also interrelated. John holds a deep and godly love for Gaius, and that love rises to the surface in action. Just as God's love for the world is rooted in action, so the godly love of John finds expression in what he writes and does.

The world doesn't readily understand godly love, although it gets glimpses. Just as a body is made to drink water, all people are made for God's love. Many live in a desert, never getting much love at all. Others live in the desert but occasionally escape to an oasis where some of that refreshing love is found. But John's world is daily satiated by God's love. This love is integral to a life that knows God. Truth and reality go hand in hand with God's love.

John wasn't writing to teach Gaius to read; he was writing in affirmation of the importance of living in real truth, not the world's fiction. And real truth is rooted firmly in God's love. The importance of teaching this to children surpasses even teaching them to read. For while I get joy out of knowing my children and grandchildren can read, like John, I have no greater joy than to hear that my children and grandchildren are walking in the truth!

Lord, I want to live in truth and love, teach truth, and model love in Jesus, as I pray in his name, amen.

ON SELFLESSNESS

Therefore we ought to support people like these, that we may be fellow workers for the truth. I have written something to the church, but Diotrephes, who likes to put himself first, does not acknowledge our authority. (3 Jn. 8–9)

My gardening friends know my hatred of *Cyperus esculentus*. More commonly known by its common name of "nut grass" or "nut sedge," this lawn and garden menace spreads like crazy, ruins your lawn and garden in the process, and is very difficult to kill. Give up on trying to pull it. It will leave a little nut deep underground that spreads tendrils out, producing more and more weeds. Get it early, as soon as you find it, or it will get you. It's detestable.

Meanwhile, I also have some fruit trees I planted. As I planted them, I put long stakes deep into the ground, tying the trees to the stakes for support. I wanted the tree roots to grow deep and wide to allow the trees to stand on their own, even if we got hurricane winds. I knew giving the trees early support was one of the keys.

Today's verses remind me of gardening. John looks to support those being fruitful while dealing with the nut grass that threatens the garden. John wants the church to join in supporting those itinerant missionaries who were traveling to teach and encourage others. These ministers were engaged in important kingdom business, and the more support and encouragement they got, the stronger the kingdom grew and the greater fruit it produced. It also helped the church survive storms of persecution.

Yet in contrast to the fruitful ones were those like Diotrephes, one who should better live up to his name! (*Diotrephes* embodies the Greek idea of supporting or nourishing.) We don't know much about Diotrephes, but he seems to have been a troublemaker in the Christian community. John identifies why: Diotrephes was selfish.

The picture of the Christian community is rooted in the practices of Jesus Christ. Jesus was selfless, putting the needs of others above his own. His followers are called to follow his example. As each strives to build up the other, the entire community is built up. The Christian community should exemplify the metaphor that a rising tide raises all boats. Today's verses should challenge everyone to mindfully live with service in mind, not selfish desires.

Lord, give me a heart for others. Wean me from selfish interests. In Jesus, amen.

ON PEACE

Beloved, do not imitate evil but imitate good. Whoever does good is from God; whoever does evil has not seen God . . . Peace be to you. The friends greet you. Greet the friends, each by name. (3 Jn. 11, 15)

As this year's book of teaching and devotional living draws to a close, the focus from the last verses of this last Epistle is appropriate. Everyone wants peace. We seek peace of mind, peace in relationships, peace in churches, and peace among nations. But John knows that peace isn't accomplished by evil. Evil seeks to destroy peace. So John focuses his final words on encouraging his readers to imitate good, not evil.

John's instructions give rise to a fundamental question for many. How do you know or prove that the things you're doing are good or evil? Do we answer that question by looking at outcomes? Surely not, for no one is truly able to see far enough into the future to know outcomes. As I overheard my daughters affirming to one another, "Yes, I knew it was going to be a difficult conversation, but I couldn't lie. One lie breeds another in support, and it never ends well."

If we wish to know what is good, we can find it rooted in the character of God. The Bible recounts God's encounters with various people and groups over millennia. From these encounters and revelation, we can see God's character and ethos. That becomes the light for our feet. We learn from God what is good and evil. Of course, the clearest revelation of God and his character are found in the life of Jesus, God in the flesh.

John traces good straight back to God. He knew good came from God just as assuredly as two plus two is four. Therefore, John could tell people to find good and do good by urging them to imitate good. See the good from God, see the good from those who follow God, and do likewise.

John's godly counsel on walking in the goodness of God is a key to peace. If we struggle with anxiety over an issue in our personal lives or some problem in the world, our role is to walk in God's goodness and refrain from evil. As we do so, we can have peace that God will be at work. God will accomplish his will as we walk in his truth. That is a faith walk that can last year after year.

Lord, teach me your goodness. Strengthen me to imitate Jesus, as I pray amen.